Andrew's Previews 2016

The year 2016, told through local by-elections

Andrew Teale

A publication of the

Local Elections
Archive Project

Contents

Introduction

Praise indeed from Lewis Baston, who knows a thing or two about how difficult it is to write good electoral profiles. Baston co-wrote a book in advance of the 2005 general election[1], much of which was taken up with in-depth profiles of the marginal seats at that election. I read every word. I learned much.

Baston, of course, wasn't the first to try his hand at the business of writing electoral pen-pics. This has no doubt been done since the advent of multi-party democracy in the UK, but in recent years one of the masters of the practice has been Robert Waller in his *Almanac of British Politics*, an enormous and magisterial tome which went through eight editions from the 1980s up to 2007. Unfortunately since the publication of the eighth edition in 2007 no further editions of the *Almanac* have been forthcoming; but nonetheless Waller is still active on the psephological scene, and an offhand remark by him over the internet directly inspired the title of this book.

What Baston's and Waller's work had in common was a focus on the parliamentary constituency as a unit, and any speculation was understandably focused on the next general election. Where local elections were mentioned (and they often were) it was as a means to an end, not as an end in itself.

This is a shame, for local elections are much more common. They happen every May without fail somewhere in the UK, whereas general elections might only come around twice in a decade. Parliamentary by-elections have become rarer in recent years as the trend is for MPs to become younger and healthier: the year 2016 was a busier than usual year with seven parliamentary by-elections, two due to deaths and five to resignations. But local by-elections, to fill vacancies

---

[1] *Politico's Guide to the General Election 2005*, by Simon Henig and Lewis Baston. Henig is now the leader of Durham council.

among the UK's 25,000 or so principal local councillors from 10,000 or so wards (the numbers change from year to year at the whim of the Local Government Boundary Commissions) happen on a much more frequent basis. This book lists, and discusses, two hundred and forty-six polls, an average of nearly five a week—and that's not counting those by-elections which were timed to coincide with the ordinary May local elections.

The lack of general awareness of local elections increases the scope for what might charitably be called distortion in properly discussing their results. The so-called Lib Dem bar chart is possibly the most well-known (and most widely copied) example of this phenomenon. But even when the results are known, context is so important in discussing what, if anything, this might mean for the future. Saying that Party X has won three seats in Week Y's local by-elections only tells you so much. Combining this with extra information—the majority, the swings involved, the nature of the wards involved, the local issues and personalities—tells you much more.

This subject has always been a bugbear of mine, and back in 2002 I founded what became the Local Elections Archive Project[2] as a freely-accessible online archive of Great Britain's local election results. It may surprise readers to learn that there is no central, official register of local elections, and it is up to the UK's 400-odd local councils to publish their results in whatever manner they see fit. These days every council puts them on their website, but back in 2002 this was not always the case (indeed back in 2002 not every council *had* a website) which made research into the subject of local elections rather difficult. Even now the local election result collector is faced with 400-odd different council websites using 400-odd different formats. Merely keeping track of it all is a nightmare.

The situation with local by-elections is rather better, perhaps because there are fewer of them. The Association of Liberal Democrat Councillors has been publishing their results for over twenty years now, and the various political parties have a good, if not completely infallible, crowdsourcing effort to identify future vacancies.

The amateur psephological community has been blessed with some active web forums over the years, one of which has for some years been running a monthly prediction competition for future local by-elections. I wanted to try and win it, and I also wanted to show off my knowledge–such as it was—and inform other forum users about the contests and their nature. So on 7th September 2010 I put fingers to keyboard and wrote the following on the International Elections board of the *US Election Atlas* forum:

---

[2]`http://www.andrewteale.me.uk/leap/`

A quick heads-up on Thursday's local by-elections, apart from those in Exeter and Norwich (see separate thread).

ASPATRIA AND WHARRELS, Cumbria county council; caused by the death of the Leader of the Council. Very Tory countryside running from the small Cumberland town of Aspatria (between Carlisle and Workington) into the national park as far as the northern edge of Keswick; this division includes Skiddaw, the fourth-highest mountain in England. In 2009 the division voted C 56.8% Lab 24.8% LD 18.4%; unusually the by-election is a straight fight between Conservative and Green Party candidates.

AYRESOME, Middlesbrough; caused by the resignation of a Labour councillor (who had, however, been elected as an Independent). 2007 result here[3]. The name "Ayresome" conjures up images of Middlesbrough FC's old ground at Ayresome Park; put those away, Ayresome Park was in Linthorpe ward. This is a fairly typical working-class Middlesbrough ward on the western edge of the town, hard up against the A 19 and A 66 dual carriageways.

KILNHOUSE, Fylde, Lancs; caused by the death of a Tory councillor. Kilnhouse ward is on the northern edge of St Annes, just off the Blackpool Airport runway. 2007 result here[4]. Lytham St Annes tends to be a fight between the Tories and Fylde Ratepayers, but the Ratepayers aren't standing in the by-election.

LIBERTON/GILMERTON, Edinburgh; caused by one of the Labour councillors winning Edinburgh South at the general election. This is a ward covering peripheral estates on the south-eastern edge of Edinburgh. First preferences in 2007 were Lab 4628 (they ran two candidates) SNP 3471 C 1912 LD 1902 Grn 464 Scottish Socialist Party 208 Solidarity 132 Inds 207 and 123, with Labour winning two seats, the SNP one and the Lib Dem candidate getting enough SNP surplus transfers to overtake the Tory candidate for the other seat. The by-election sees the Pirate Party's first ever local government candidate.

NEWTOWN, Poole; caused by one of the Lib Dem councillors deciding he would rather run a "Buy British" campaign. 2007 result here[5]. Poole is not a town I know at all, but the politics suggest a safe Lib Dem ward.

Two things developed from this beginning. First, it became clear that doing well in the prediction competition was going to take a lot more research than that. Second, it became clear that I enjoyed writing this sort of thing, and I started

---

[3] http://www.andrewteale.me.uk/r79#ward1638
[4] http://www.andrewteale.me.uk/r250#ward3425
[5] http://www.andrewteale.me.uk/r103#ward2448

taking time out every week to do the research required. Eventually the second reason became more important than the first, and I started writing the previews for their own sake rather than as a means to an end.

One compelling personal reason for doing the research was that it linked in nicely with another hobby of mine—quiz. To do well in quiz you have to be able to make and recognise connections between all sorts of apparently disparate things. It's rather like the business of writing this column, which enables me to indulge in research on some of my favourite quiz subjects. In writing these previews I normally take care to include extra facts about a particular ward, partly because it adds colour, light and shade to the profile and partly because it might come up in a quiz. It seems to work: in September 2016 I attended the British Quiz Championships in Coventry and won the Civilisation section ("human geography, cultures, technology, current affairs etc", so the bread-and-butter issues of this column) against a field of many of the greatest quizzers in the country, several of whose names you might recognise from television. The quiz experience also feeds back into the previews because playing quiz enables me to travel the country and write previews drawing from personal experience.

Of course the research involved necessarily draws on all sorts of things other than personal experience. The census and other official statistics are heavily quoted, and I am deeply grateful to Kevin Larkin's website *Boundary Assistant*[6] and the Consumer Data Research Centre[7] for successfully mapping all sorts of census and other statistics which might have a bearing on elections or just be interesting in their own right. The Ordnance Survey continues to draw the best maps in the world, and the Local Government Boundary Commissions for England and Scotland have an extensive online archive from which to draw. (Local Democracy and Boundary Commission for Wales, please copy.) Each of the previews in this book contains a Figure showing previous election results: those from 2002 onwards are taken from my own collection, those earlier than that are based on information published by Colin Rallings and Michael Thrasher in back issues of their long-running series *Local Elections Handbook*, which remains the closest thing to an official election results archive, while by-elections are based on the Association of Liberal Democrat Councillors' archive already referred to. To all the people involved in putting these resources together, I sit at your feet and stand on your shoulders. Thank you.

Despite my best efforts, mistakes do happen sometimes in a project of this size, and the responsibility for any errors is mine alone. Equally, prediction is difficult; prediction involving the future more so; prediction involving the notably crazy

---

[6] http://www.boundaryassistant.org/
[7] http://www.cdrc.ac.uk/

year of 2016 more so again. Not all of what was written in Andrew's Previews in 2016 stood up to the passage of time. I have revised some of the previews to split up some of the longer sentences and paragraphs, correct some mistakes and clarify a few things; but some of the original mistakes and wrong predictions were too good to fix and I have highlighted them with footnotes. Also included with each preview is the result of each by-election—something which of course was not known at the time of writing. See if you can spot the results I failed to see coming.

Andrew's Previews has a complicated publication history, because historically it has mainly been written for other people's blogs. It started out on the *US Election Atlas* forum; was taken up in 2011 by a blog called *Britain Votes*, which became part of the polling company Survation and then became defunct; and from 2012 was then published on various blogs controlled by Kristofer Keane, who at the time was running the major British electoral discussion forum *Vote UK*. In 2016 Andrew's Previews was taken over by Ian Warren, a pollster who blogs and works under the name of "Election Data"; at the time of writing it is published under the aegis of *Britain Elects*, a poll aggregator. I am eternally grateful to Kristofer, Ian and the *Britain Elects* team for their support and encouragement over the years.

I am also grateful to my mum, Heather Teale, for reading the book in draft and pointing out everything I got wrong. This book would have been worse without that effort. Thank you Mum.

This book is a republication of Andrew's Previews for the year 2016. While it might not meet Lewis Baston's original request for a book on every ward in Britain, there are 246 wards dissected here which forms a nice, if not necessarily balanced, sample. As well as that, it can serve as a memoir of 2016, as quiz revision, and as a reference. I hope you find it interesting and useful, and I commend it to the House.

Andrew Teale
Little Lever, Bolton
September 2017

7th January 2016

Welcome to the 2016 psephological year in the United Kingdom. Thanks to the two people who enquired after your columnist's health: he had a hernia operation just before Christmas and recovery has been rather slow. However, there is no problem in putting together a preview for the first council by-election of the year.

Botcherby

Carlisle city council, Cumbria; caused by the death of Labour councillor Terry Scarborough. A former chairman of the Botcherby Community Centre who had played football for Carlisle United, Scarborough had served on Carlisle city council since 2003.

Northern-based readers of this column might have noticed that the weather over the last two-and-a-half months has been filthy. Rain upon rain upon rain upon rain upon rain upon rain continuously since at least the middle of October or so. Your columnist still shudders at the memory of the back half of 2009, when it rained continuously from Wimbledon to Christmas. What happens when you get all this rain? Flooding, that's what. A big problem in a low-lying place like Botcherby ward, an eastern Carlisle suburb incorporated into the city in 1912 and located along the A 69 road towards Newcastle, between the rivers Eden and Petteril. And so it came to pass that when Storm Desmond hit Carlisle on 6th December, Botcherby ward's flood defences—installed at a cost of tens of millions of pounds following a similarly appalling flood in 2005—were overtopped.

It so happened that while all this devastation was going on, nominations were open for a council by-election in Botcherby ward. It remains to be seen how many electors are left to vote here, and it is notable that two of the four polling stations for this by-election are portakabins. The ward itself runs south from the A 69 Warwick Road and includes not just Botcherby but also part of the Harraby area, across the Newcastle–Carlisle and Settle–Carlisle railway lines to the south. It's a very working-class part of Carlisle, with high levels of social renting and

Parliamentary constituency: Carlisle
Cumbria county council division: Botcherby (most), Harraby North (part)
May 2015 result Lab 822 Ind 725 C 516 UKIP 345 Grn 75
May 2014 result Ind 773 Lab 358 UKIP 217 C 131
May 2012 result Lab 693 Ind 311 C 141 UKIP 107 Grn 24
May 2011 result Lab 720 Ind 432 C 287
May 2010 result Ind 1119 Lab 822 C 443 BNP 134
June 2009 county council result Ind 507 Lab 428 C 366 BNP 116 LD 85 Grn 38
May 2008 result Lab 509 C 443 Ind 313 BNP 145
May 2007 result Lab 618 C 400 BNP 217
May 2006 result Lab 602 C 314 Ind 168
May 2005 county council result Lab 1456 C 591
June 2004 result Lab 813 C 602
May 2003 result Lab 698 C 452
May 2002 result Lab 761 C 445
May 2001 county council result Lab 1361 C 581 LD 320
May 2000 result Lab 484 C 456 Socialist Alternative 305
May 1999 result C 611/609/576 Lab 575/557/549

Figure 1: Carlisle, Botcherby

in the top 60 wards in England and Wales for semi-routine occupations and part-time working.

Botcherby ward has existed since 1983 and was traditionally as safe Labour as you'd expect with that demographic profile; at the Labour high point of 1995 they beat the Tories here 82–18. In fact, the only year in which the Tories carried Botcherby was 1999—fortunately for them, that was the year the current ward boundaries came into effect, so Labour had to spend the next four years getting their seats back, Terry Scarborough completing the process in 2003. In recent years Labour have come under pressure in the ward from independents: Robert Betton became the ward's county councillor in 2009 and was elected to the city council in 2010. In his final re-election in May Scarborough was only 97 votes ahead of independent candidate John (Jack) Paton: in terms of votes Labour had 33%, Paton 29%, the Tories 21% and UKIP 14%. Until 2013 the ward had the same boundaries as the Botcherby division of Cumbria county council (the present Botcherby division is rather different), and the relevant county council results are shown in Figure 1.

Defending for Labour is Stephen Sidgwick, who in May contested his home ward, the hopeless (for Labour) Longtown and Rockliffe. Jack Paton stands again as an independent, and the Tories have selected Robert Currie who in May was on the wrong side of a photofinish in the city's Belle Vue ward. UKIP aren't bothering this time, so those are your three candidates.

Result: Ind 381 Lab 250 C 115 [Ind gain from Lab]

14th January 2016

One by-election on 14th January 2016:

Launceston Central

Cornwall council; caused by the resignation of former Liberal Democrat councillor Alex Folkes.

As the name suggests, this is the central of the three divisions wholly or partly covering the town of Launceston. The traditional gateway to Cornwall because of its location on the A 30 road, Launceston is an ancient town with a well-preserved Norman castle, which was a stronghold for the Royalist cause in the Civil War. Today, Launceston (like much of Cornwall) depends on tourism, although there is some industry here including the Natural Fibre Company's woollen mill and a bakery formerly owned by Duchy Originals, and the town is sufficiently important that the ONS recognises it as the centre of its own Travel to Work Area.

Launceston Central division covers the town centre (including the bridge over the River Kemsey and the preserved railway station) together with some rather disconnected residential areas on both sides of the Kemsey. It was created for the first unitary Cornwall council election in 2009; boundary changes in 2013 saw the division expanded slightly at the expense of both Launceston North and Launceston South. Before 2009 the town as a whole had two Lib Dem county councillors and returned two Independents and one Lib Dem to the former North Cornwall district council.

Alex Folkes' first electoral test was in 2002 when he sought election to Lewisham council in London, but he was first elected to Launceston Central at the first Cornwall council election in 2009. It's fair to say that his career on the council was a car crash. During his first term he was repeatedly taken to court by his own council for non-payment of council tax; not that that stopped him becoming the Cornwall cabinet member responsible for finance after the

Parliamentary constituency: North Cornwall
ONS Travel to Work Area: Launceston
May 2013 result LD 551 C 134 Lab 73

Figure 2: Cornwall, Launceston Central

2013 Cornwall council election, in which Folkes increased his majority over the Conservatives to 71–17 and the Lib Dem group took control of the council in coalition with independents.

In November 2014 Folkes suddenly resigned from the cabinet, and shortly afterwards it was revealed that he had been arrested in 2006 on suspicion of possessing child pornography. The council revealed this by writing to every school and youth group in Launceston stating that Folkes was a risk to children, a message reiterated to the press by the council's then chief executive who called on Folkes to resign from the council. Folkes resigned the Lib Dem whip and tried to defend himself, but readmission to the Lib Dem group was not forthcoming. The final straw for Folkes came in October last year, when he was prosecuted by his ex-landlord for leaving his former flat in a squalid state; after that he decided to resign from the council, citing mental health issues.

It remains to be seen whether the many controversies surrounding Folkes have had any effect on the Lib Dem vote in Launceston, but the loss of the North Cornwall parliamentary seat in last year's general election will not have helped the Lib Dem cause here. Readers are warned not to Google the defending Lib Dem candidate Gemma Massey while they are at work, as when I put her name into that search engine I got ten links to a porn star of that name; however, the Gemma Massey standing in this by-election is a 31-year-old businesswoman from Launceston who organises networking and training for local businesses. Massey is up against 60-year-old Conservative candidate Val Bugden-Cawsey, an after-dinner speaker and former cook-housekeeper to Princess Anne who runs a monthly women's lunch club in Launceston. Also on the ballot paper are John Allman of the Christian Peoples Alliance and Roger Creagh-Osborne of the Green Party.

Result: LD 515 C 226 Grn 65 CPA 12

21st January 2016

Six by-elections on 21st January 2016:

Faraday

London Borough of Southwark; caused by the resignation of Labour councillor Dan Garfield, after being fined and sentenced to a 12-month community order for beating his wife. Ironically the Labour group's chief whip, Garfield had served since 2010.

Welcome to inner-city South London. Faraday ward lies on the northern edge of Burgess Park, one of London's more controversial parks having been developed since the Second World War from what was a heavily built-up residential and industrial area. However, the ward is named after one of Southwark's most famous sons: the nineteenth-century scientist Michael Faraday, whose discovery of electromagnetic induction, making practical the use of electricity, has greatly shaped the modern world. A primary school named after Faraday lies at the centre of the ward.

Faraday's discoveries have not led to great riches for the residents of the ward named after him. This has always been a poor area of London. At the same time as the Burgess Park area was being cleared, the area immediately to its north was being redeveloped: the result is that byword for urban decay which is the Aylesbury Estate, now being redeveloped in its turn. The presence of the Aylesbury Estate means that Faraday ward is in the top 10 wards in England and Wales for social housing; the ward also has one of the top 10 black populations in England and Wales. Unsurprisingly in the current climate the ward is very safe Labour, although the Lib Dems did come close in 2002; at the most recent local election in 2014 the Labour slate had 62%, with the Green Party best of the rest on 12%. In the 2012 London Assembly election Ken beat Boris 67–18 in the ward's ballot boxes, while in the London Member ballot Labour led the Green Party 67–9. One of the more unusual features of the previous results for this

Parliamentary constituency: Camberwell and Peckham
May 2014 result Lab 1590/1567/1508 Grn 302/262/251 C 245/216/210 All People's Party
171/163/124 LD 163/139/106 TUSC 113
May 2010 result Lab 2696/2682/2450 LD 869/704/654 C 547/542/444 Grn 293/255 EDP
157
May 2006 result Lab 1809/1728/1641 LD 870/870/839 Respect 359 Ind 219/207 C
210/176/168 Grn 149/145/134
May 2002 result Lab 1301/1220/1198 LD 1128/1114/1079 Ind 349/313 C 96/80/71 Grn
94/92/74
May 2012 GLA results (excludes postal voters)
Mayor: Ken 1503 Boris 414 Grn 112 LD 80 Ind 76 UKIP 30 BNP 25
London Members: Lab 1517 Grn 202 C 193 LD 113 UKIP 78 CPA 45 BNP 42 TUSC 24
EDP 20 House Party 14 NF 9 Hayat 3 Alagaratnam 0

Figure 3: Southwark, Faraday

ward is the presence on the ballot in 2002 of Piers Corbyn, the colourful weather forecaster and brother of a backbench Labour MP called Jeremy: standing as an independent, Corbyn polled 12% and came seventh out of fourteen candidates.

So, probably not too much of a problem for the defending Labour candidate Samantha Jury-Dada, a recent LSE politics graduate who is presently working in Parliament for the Brentford and Isleworth MP Ruth Cadbury. She is up against the Greens' Nick Hooper, who works in the software industry; the Tories' David Furze; Alhaji Kanumansa of the All People's Party (essentially a Labour splinter group of former Southwark councillors), Lauren Pemberton-Nelson of the Lib Dems, independent candidate Dean Porter and UKIP's Toby Prescott.

Result: Lab 1072 LD 255 Grn 138 C 117 UKIP 93 Ind 47 All People's Party 38

Newington

Thanet district council, Kent; caused by the resignation of UKIP councillor Vince Munday, who has emigrated to Thailand. He had served on the council since May last year.

Readers of this column might have noticed that there was a fair bit of attention on Thanet during last year's election campaign, as a result of the UKIP leader Nigel Farage standing for Parliament in the South Thanet constituency, based on Ramsgate and Sandwich. He didn't get in, but UKIP had the consolation prize of winning an overall majority on Thanet council, which had previously been evenly split between Labour and the Tories. The Thanet council term in 2011–15 was very fissiparous, with a long list of defections and by-election changes which eventually cost the ruling Tory group their majority and led to Labour

Parliamentary constituency: South Thanet
Kent county council division: Ramsgate
May 2015 result UKIP 884/845 Lab 728/713 C 390/363
May 2011 result Lab 705/702 C 370/351
May 2007 result Lab 471/438 Ramsgate First 268/196 C 208/197 UKIP 116
May 2003 result Lab 532/498 Ind 235 C 144/140

Figure 4: Thanet, Newington

taking control part-way through. Has anything changed in the brave new UKIP-controlled world since May? On the face of it, no: as well as this vacancy, five UKIP councillors have left the party to form a "Democratic Independent" group and cost UKIP its majority on the council. *Plus ça change, plus c'est la même chose.*

Judging from the seat count, the UKIP surge in Thanet last year came at the expense of Labour who now hold just four seats on the council. In that context it's unsurprising that one of the seats to fall was Newington ward, a working-class inland suburb of Ramsgate off the road to Manston, whose closed airport and the future thereof is one of the political hot potatoes in this part of the world. Previously a safe Labour ward, Newington gave 44% to UKIP last year and just 36% to Labour, the Tories coming in third with 19%. Labour weren't helped by deselecting their long-serving councillor Mike Harrison over homophobic comments he had made about former Labour councillor Ian Driver, who following a dizzying series of defections has ended up in the Green Party. UKIP also hold the ward's county council seats, with the two-member Ramsgate division being safe for them in 2013 but previously Labour-inclined.

Defending for UKIP is Duncan Smithson, who narrowly missed out in Cliftonville East ward last year. Labour have reselected their runner-up from last year, Karen Constantine, who somehow juggles the roles of executive coach, magistrate and mother-of-four while working in London for the Royal College of Midwives. Law teacher Adam Dark stands for the Conservatives. Also standing on a crowded ballot paper are independent candidate Grahame Birchall, the aforementioned Ian Driver for the Green Party, independent candidate Alan Hodder and Jordan Williams of the Lib Dems.

Result: Lab 288 UKIP 229 C 156 Hodder 49 Grn 20 LD 12 Birchall 10 [Lab gain from UKIP]

Crowborough East

Wealden district council, East Sussex; caused by the death of Conservative councillor Peter Cowie at the age of 74. Cowie had only stepped up to the district council in

Parliamentary constituency: Wealden
East Sussex county council division: Crowborough
May 2015 result C 1668/1526 LD 885
May 2011 result C 1026/950 Lab 549
May 2007 result C 581/565 LD 579/510
May 2003 result LD 555/540 C 422/408 Lab 118

Figure 5: Wealden, Crowborough East

May, but was first elected in 2007 to Crowborough town council; he was Mayor of Crowborough in 2013–14 and was instrumental in setting up the town's new community centre. In his working life he had worked for Anglian Water for 21 years and in the Department of the Environment.

Seven miles south-west of Tunbridge Wells, Crowborough is East Sussex' largest inland town, growing in the mid-Victorian period following the completion of the town's rail link to London; at the time it was promoted as a health resort thanks to its relatively high altitude and surrounding forest. Crowborough lies on the eastern edge of Ashdown Forest, the setting for A A Milne's *Winnie-the-Pooh* stories, and also has literary connections as the home of Sir Arthur Conan Doyle, who died here in 1930; Conan Doyle has a statue in the town centre and Crowborough once hosted an annual Sherlock Holmes festival.

Crowborough East is in the top five wards in England and Wales for "other religions", a statistic which appears to be explained by the presence of a large Scientology centre. In the real world, this is a ward which has trended strongly to the Tories over recent years: it elected two Lib Dems in 2003, but the Tories gained one seat in 2007 and picked up the other in 2011 when the remaining Lib Dem councillor (Jane Clark) stood down. Clark was back in the fray last year, losing 65–35 to the Tory slate. The ward is located within the two-seat Crowborough county division, which is safe Conservative.

Defending for the Tories is Philip Lunn. Former Lib Dem councillor Jane Clark again tries to get her seat back, and the ballot paper is completed by Labour's Linda Scotson.

Result: C 517 LD 198 Lab 93

Bushey North

Hertfordshire county council; caused by the death of Conservative councillor Steve O'Brien. Originally elected in 1998 to Watford borough council, he served on Hertsmere borough council from 2008 to 2015 and was first elected to Hertfordshire county council in 2009. O'Brien served for ten years as chairman of the Watford

Parliamentary constituency: Hertsmere
Hertsmere district council wards: Bushey North, Bushey St James (part)
May 2013 result C 995 UKIP 524 Lab 437 LD 321
June 2009 result C 1510 LD 1257 Grn 277 Lab 234
May 2005 result LD 2559 C 1807 Lab 876 Grn 223

Figure 6: Hertfordshire CC, Bushey North

branch of the Conservatives, and in the 2015 Birthday Honours was gazetted MBE for voluntary political service.

For the last of this week's four by-elections in southern England, we travel immediately to the east of Watford. Now essentially a Watford suburb, the growth of Bushey was essentially snuffed out by the creation of the Green Belt, and much of this ward is given over to sport and a large Jewish cemetery. The census figures paint a middle-class commuter profile, with a large Jewish population, and the M 1 motorway (which originally terminated here) links the ward to the outside world.

Bushey was a long-standing Lib Dem hotspot up until the late noughties when long-serving district and county councillor Michael Colne retired, and the Lib Dem vote retired with him. Steve O'Brien gained the county division from the Lib Dems in 2009 and made it safe in 2013, when he had 44% to 23% for UKIP and 19% for Labour. Last year's election results for the one-and-a-half Hertsmere council wards within the division confirm that the area is now safely Conservative.

Defending for the Conservatives is Jane West, a borough councillor within the division. UKIP have selected David Hoy. Watford councillor Seamus Williams stands for Labour, and the ballot paper is completed by the Lib Dems' Shailan Shah.

Result: C 881 LD 333 Lab 286 UKIP 176

Thatto Heath

St Helens metropolitan borough council, Merseyside; caused by the death of Labour councillor Sheila Seddon at the age of 69. Having previously worked at Beecham's pharmaceuticals, Seddon had served on St Helens council since 1999 and was Mayor of St Helens in 2007–08

This is a south-western suburb of St Helens, sandwiched between the recently-electrified Liverpool–Manchester and Liverpool–Wigan railway lines, with Thatto Heath railway station lying on the latter line. It has a very high Christian population—in a Lancashire context that generally means Catholic—and a

Parliamentary constituency: St Helens South and Whiston
May 2015 result Lab 3757 UKIP 871 C 740 Grn 351
May 2014 result Lab 1510 UKIP 483 C 194 Grn 140 LD 85 BNP 51
May 2012 result Lab 1857 Grn 187 C 178 BNP 136 LD 124
May 2011 result Lab 2409 C 395 LD 282
May 2010 result Lab 2995 LD 1071 C 684 BNP 349
May 2008 result Lab 1328 LD 581 C 301 BNP 284
May 2007 result Lab 1274 LD 794 C 201 BNP 187 Community Action 180
May 2006 result Lab 1308 LD 453 Community Action 363 C 217
June 2004 result Lab 1406/1351/1139 LD 713/502/380 UKIP 429 C 326

Figure 7: St Helens, Thatto Heath

working-class profile, as you might expect given that much of the northern corner of the ward is taken up by the enormous Greengate site run by the glass manufacturers Pilkington's. Traditionally the largest employer in St Helens, Pilkington's has been knocked about a bit by the recent recession, but the Greengate site still produces 180,000 tonnes of glass every year. Thatto Heath is also responsible for another St Helens export: Johnny Vegas grew up in the ward.

This is a safe Labour ward whose previous election results show little of interest. In recent years the Labour vote peaked at 75% in 2012, which was Seddon's last re-election. At the most recent election in 2015 Labour beat UKIP 66–15.

Defending for Labour is Nova Charlton; she is opposed by UKIP's Alastair Sutcliffe, the Tories' Lisa Mackarell and the Greens' Damien Clarke who stood here last year. Whoever wins this by-election will be straight back onto the campaign trail to seek re-election in May.

Result: Lab 964 UKIP 182 C 147 Grn 62

Hamilton North and East

South Lanarkshire council; caused by the death of Scottish National Party coun-cillor Lynn Adams at the age of 57. A publican by trade, being landlady of the George in Hamilton, Adams had twice played handball for Scotland and also formerly worked for Motorola. She had served on South Lanarkshire council since 2012.

This is Hamilton's town centre ward, just off the M 74 motorway and also including the Whitehill area to the north and the Ferniegair area to the south-east. Here can be found Hamilton Park racecourse, Hamilton Academicals' football ground and Strathclyde Park, formerly the home of the Dukes of Hamilton and still containing their mausoleum, which claims the record for the world's longest

Parliamentary constituency: Lanark and Hamilton East (most), Rutherglen and Hamilton West (small part)
Holyrood constituency: Hamilton, Larkhall and Stonehouse (most), Uddingston and Bellshill (Whitehill area)
May 2012 first preferences Lab 1831 SNP 1721 C 430 Ind 141 Grn 133
May 2007 first preferences Lab 2556 SNP 1769 C 917 Ind 214 Ind 190

Figure 8: South Lanarkshire, Hamilton North and East

echo. The railway stations at Hamilton Central and Hamilton West (on the Hamilton Circle line) and Chatelherault (on the Larkhall branch) link the ward to Glasgow and Motherwell.

The introduction of PR for Scottish elections in 2007 enabled the SNP to win a seat here, with Labour winning the other two seats comfortably enough ahead of the Tory candidate Andrew Leitch. The gap between Labour and the SNP closed in 2012 to 43–40, and Labour held their second seat just 30 votes ahead of the second SNP candidate—who was the councillor elected in 2007, losing his seat to his running-mate Adams. The general swing from Labour to SNP since 2012 suggests that the Nationalists should have few problems holding this by-election.

Defending for the SNP is Stephanie Callaghan, while Labour have gone for youth in selecting Lyndsay Clelland. Also standing are James Mackay of the Conservatives, Steven Hannigan of the Green Party and Norman Rae of the Lib Dems.

First preferences: SNP 1089 Lab 855 C 469 Grn 83 LD 45
After transfers: SNP 1206 Lab 1052

28th January 2016

Parkfield and Oxbridge

Stockton-on-Tees council; caused by the resignation of Labour councillor David Rose due to work commitments. He had served on Stockton council since 2011.

Welcome to Stockton-on-Tees, the second town within the Teesside conurbation. Although Stockton is an old town which since mediaeval times had had a market and a small port on the Tees estuary, it was the Industrial Revolution that created the town as we know it today. The 1820s saw the opening of the world's first passenger railway, connecting the town with the coalmining district of Shildon and allowing coal to be transported to the town's rapidly-growing ironworking industry. A number of the blast furnaces were in this ward along the north bank of the Tees, although redevelopment means that this area is now industrial estates together with a brand new link road from Stockton to the new town of Ingleby Barwick. However, the ward's population lives in the Oxbridge area to the west of the town centre, Victorian terracing along the Yarm Road and Oxbridge Lane. Also within this ward is the traditional Victorian splendour of Ropner Park, named after the former Conservative MP for the town Sir Robert Ropner, a Prussian immigrant who ran a local shipyard and shipping company.

The sudden and explosive growth of Ingleby Barwick (from almost nothing in 1971 to over 16,000 population in 2001) created problems for the Boundary Commission, as bickering over what to do about the town's representation meant that the 2003 ward boundaries were not ready in time. A special election therefore had to be held in 2005 to bring in the new ward boundaries, with the former Parkfield ward being greatly changed that year: it took the Oxbridge area from Grangefield ward while losing part of the town centre. Since all these areas are safe Labour anyway that boundary change didn't have much partisan effect: although this ward is part of the marginal seat of Stockton South, it's not the area of it that gave the Tories an unexpected hold here in last year's general election. Last year's local elections gave the Labour slate here 46%, to 27% for the Tories and 12% for

Parliamentary constituency: Stockton South
May 2015 Lab 1608/1501 C 950/887 Ind 419 Grn 285 LD 192/179 Libertarian 58
May 2011 result Lab 801/771 Stockton Inds Assoc 451/250 C 444/345 Ind 255 LD 106/93
May 2007 result Lab 820/749 C 410/409 LD 278/276
May 2005 result Lab 1316/1199 C 652/556 LD 482/451

Figure 9: Stockton-on-Tees, Parkfield and Oxbridge

independent candidate Shakeel Noor, with Rose beating the alphabet to come top of the poll.

Defending for Labour is Allan Mitchell, a public sector worker and Ingleby Barwick town councillor. The Tory candidate is Stephen Richardson, who fought the neighbouring Grangefield ward last year. Shakeel Noor is not trying again. Completing the ballot paper are the Lib Dems' Drew Durning and UKIP's Peter Braney.

Result: Lab 598 C 363 UKIP 113 LD 65

4th February 2016

Four interesting by-elections on 4th February 2016, all due to resignations:

Oswestry South

Shropshire council; caused by the resignation of the Leader of the Council, Conservative councillor Keith Barrow, over a scandal. Barrow had failed to declare a personal and business relationship with a director of the accountants and auditors for IP&E, a private company owned by the council. He had served on the unitary Shropshire council since its creation in 2009, and before then on the former Oswestry district council.

Despite its population of only 17,000, Oswestry is one of the major towns in the Marches, that ill-defined and thinly-populated area which tracks the border between England and Wales. Although Oswestry lies on the English side of the border it is economically more entwined with Wales, being the main service centre for much of northern Powys and home of The New Saints, the pre-eminent football team in the Welsh Premier League. As if to prove this point, within Oswestry South division can be found streets with names such as English Walls and Llanforda Rise, an open space called Cae Glas Park, a polling station at the Horeb Welsh Methodist Rooms and a large Victorian building which was once the headquarters of the Cambrian Railways; although Oswestry no longer has a railway service, the station has been preserved and is now a museum. As well as the town centre, as the name suggests this division covers the south and south-west quarter of Oswestry—the Castle and Victoria wards of Oswestry town council.

Barrow had represented Oswestry South since the creation of the unitary Shropshire council in 2009 and was previously a ward councillor for its predecessor, the Castle ward of the former Oswestry district council. These electoral units were normally Conservative but not always safe: the Lib Dems won one of the two seats in Castle ward in 2003, and although Barrow was re-elected in

Parliamentary constituency: North Shropshire
May 2013 result C 488 Grn 337 UKIP 175 LD 62
June 2009 result C 660 Grn 218 LD 301 Lab 79

Figure 10: Shropshire, Oswestry South

2013—the last local elections in Shropshire—comfortably enough, his majority was cut by a strong Green Party performance, with 46% for the Tories, 32% for the Greens and 16% for UKIP. The ward had a minor boundary change in 2013 to reflect changes to the Oswestry parish boundary, gaining a small area from Gobowen, Selattyn and Weston Rhyn division.

This by-election has a rather different line-up from the 2013 poll. Defending for the Tories is Christopher Schofield, an Oswestry town councillor (for Cambrian ward) who runs a B&B. The Green candidate from 2013, Duncan Kerr, is standing again: he is an Oswestry town councillor for Castle ward and children's social worker who fought North Shropshire in last year's general election and came close to saving his deposit. There is no UKIP candidate this time. Completing the ballot paper are the Lib Dems' Amanda Woof, another town councillor for this ward, and Labour's Carl Hopley.

Result: Grn 518 C 367 Lab 95 LD 81 [Grn gain from C]

Bottisham

East Cambridgeshire district council; caused by the resignation of Conservative councillor Vince Campbell, who had served only since May last year, on health grounds. He had previously had a distinguished military career in the Guards.

Sometimes wards look gerrymandered even when they aren't. Such is the case with Bottisham ward, which is based on Bottisham, a village midway between Cambridge and Newmarket noted for its fourteenth-century church. Bottisham isn't quite large enough for two councillors of its own, and the population distribution and strange shape of East Cambridgeshire district combined with some very long and thin parish boundaries in the area means that the village is combined for electoral purposes with three tiny villages eight miles to the south-east on the Icknield Way—Brinkley, Burrough Green and the wonderfully-named Westley Waterless—which have no road connection to Bottisham. The Lords of the Manor here were the Jenyns family, one of whom—Soame Jenyns— was an eighteenth-century MP for Cambridgeshire and commissioner of the Board of Trade, but is best remembered today as a writer and contemporary of Samuel Johnson.

For most of this century Bottisham has been a tightly-fought Tory–Lib Dem

Parliamentary constituency: South East Cambridgeshire
Cambridgeshire county council division: Woodditton
Constituent parishes: Bottisham, Brinkley, Burrough Green, Westley Waterless
May 2015 result C 1100/1002 LD 678/634 Lab 347/339
May 2011 result LD 644/588 C 626/607 Lab 279
May 2007 result LD 769/631 C 570/501 Lab 111
May 2003 result C 583 LD 561/454 Lab 176

Figure 11: East Cambridgeshire, Bottisham

marginal at local level, but the Tories pulled away last year, partly thanks to the general election turnout, to beat the Lib Dems 52–32. The ward forms part of a safe Conservative division (Woodditton) on Cambridgeshire county council.

Defending for the Tories is Alan Sharp, a qualified accountant who has recently retired after twenty years working for a central government department: he has previous experience of local government, being a Huntingdonshire district councillor in the early 1990s. The Lib Dem candidate Steven Aronson, a chiropractor and part-time Hebrew teacher, is having his third tilt at the ward after unsuccessful runs in 2011 and 2015. Also standing are Bottisham parish councillor Steven O'Dell for Labour and Cambridgeshire county councillor (for Littleport) Daniel Divine for UKIP.

Result: C 421 LD 403 Lab 99 UKIP 43

Measham South

North West Leicestershire district council; caused by the resignation of Labour councillor Tom Neilson after he was arrested on suspicion of drug dealing. He had served since 2011 and was a former leader of the Labour group on North West Leicestershire council.

Measham can be found in Leicestershire about ten miles south-east of Burton upon Trent. It may not have become a large town, but it was an early centre of the Industrial Revolution. This was down to Joseph Wilkes, an industrialist and entrepreneur who became the Lord of the Manor of what was then a Derbyshire exclave (thanks to its ancient association with Repton priory). Wilkes essentially founded Measham's coal-mining and brickworking industry, together with promoting the Ashby Canal which once linked the village to the Coventry Canal at Bedworth. Also associated with the area, although not actually produced here, was a type of turn-of-the-century pottery known as Measham Ware, which was particularly popular with canal workers, while the village's famous children include the former Astronomer Royal Sir Frank Dyson, who introduced the

Parliamentary constituency: North West Leicestershire
Leicestershire county council division: Forest and Measham
May 2015 result Lab 654 C 533

Figure 12: North West Leicestershire, Measham South

Greenwich "six pips" time signal. Measham Colliery survived until 1986, while coalmining still goes on here at the controversial Minorca opencast mine.

The Measham South ward has existed only since May when the former two-member Measham ward was divided into two single-member wards. The old Measham ward was Labour-inclined, reflecting the village's history, but it was also a key marginal which voted Conservative in 2007. The only previous result for the present ward was in 2015, when Labour beat the Tories 55–45 in a straight fight. Labour also hold the local county council seat (Forest and Measham), gaining it from the Tories in the 2013 election at which it was a Labour–UKIP marginal.

That Labour county councillor, Sean Sheahan, defends this by-election for Labour; he is hoping for a quick return to the district council, having been Neilson's ward colleague for Measham from 2011 to 2015 and losing his seat in Measham North last year. Another former councillor hoping to make a quick return is the Tory candidate Annette Bridges, who represented Moira ward from 2007 until being a victim of the boundary changes in 2015. Completing the ballot paper is UKIP's Martin Green, who was the runner-up in the 2013 county election and their parliamentary candidate here in 2010.

Result: Lab 257 C 202 UKIP 141

Hexham West

Northumberland council; caused by the resignation of Conservative councillor Colin Cessford for family reasons. Cessford was in his first term on Northumberland county council, having entered politics in 2012 by winning a by-election to Hexham town council after retiring from a 34-year career with the North East Ambulance Service. He had been a county councillor since 2013.

Welcome to Hexham, the major service centre for the upper Tyne Valley. This is an old town which grew up around a monastery which goes all the way back to the seventh century; Hexham Abbey still dominates the town although the current building is largely nineteenth-century. There was a battle here in 1464, a victory for the Yorkists during the Wars of the Roses; while in 1715 the Earl of Derwentwater raised the Old Pretender's standard in the marketplace. The town's traditional industry is leather, while other industries are botanic beer

Parliamentary constituency: Hexham
May 2013 result C 848 LD 540 Lab 261 UKIP 105

Figure 13: Northumberland, Hexham West

(Fentimans is based here) and tourism, the town being the main railhead for the best-preserved parts of Hadrian's Wall. Also here—and part of Hexham West division which covers the western outskirts of the town plus a small rural hinterland—is Hexham racecourse, the most northerly National Hunt course in England.

Hexham racecourse's altitude and exposed position mean that no races are held here in February, so local racewatchers will have to be content with watching the ballot boxes. This one could be interesting, as the large Tory lead in 2013 (when they had 48% to 31% for the Lib Dems and 15% for Labour, whose candidate rejoiced in the name of David Crockit) masks the fact that this was a Lib Dem stronghold before that election.

In a strong field of candidates, Tom Gillanders defends for the Conservatives: he is a retired engineer and Hexham town councillor for Leazes ward (which has the same boundaries as this division) who organises the local Poppy Appeal and recently stepped down from the Territorial Army with the rank of Lieutenant-Colonel after over forty years' service. There is no official Lib Dem candidate, but there is an unofficial one: Derek Kennedy, the former Lib Dem county councillor here (2005–2013) and still a town councillor for Leazes ward, is standing as an independent. Town councillor (for Gilesgate ward) Nuala Rose, a former GP, stands for Labour. Anne Pickering, a former town councillor, ecological consultant and artist who recently organised a 10,000-signature petition against the proposed relocation of Hexham bus station, stands as an independent. Completing the ballot paper is Lee Williscroft-Ferris, a teacher, trade unionist and gay rights blogger standing for the Green Party.

Result: Kennedy 501 C 454 Lab 200 Pickering 125 Grn 89 [Ind gain from C]

11th February 2016

Four by-elections on 11th February, all due to deaths:

Crompton

Bolton metropolitan borough council, Greater Manchester; caused by the death of Labour councillor Sufrana Bashir Ismail at the age of 47, from cancer. The first Muslim woman to be elected to Bolton council, Ismail had served since 2006 and had held a number of senior roles on the council; following treatment for breast cancer, in 2012 she founded a charity, Chemokits, to supply essential items to those undergoing chemotherapy.

Where better to start than in the greatest town in the known universe? Crompton ward is inner north Bolton, running north from Deansgate and Churchgate in the town centre along the Blackburn Road as far as the Astley Bridge junction. Here can be found most of the Halliwell area along Halliwell Road (Halliwell ward is badly misnamed), together with the area around the Iron Church on Blackburn Road, the Theatre Church (RIP) on Seymour Road and the Hall i'th' Wood estate off Crompton Way, named after an early sixteenth century manor house which was once the home of Bolton's most famous son: Samuel Crompton, the inventor of the Spinning Mule which revolutionised the textile industry and led to the rapid industrialisation of Lancashire during the nineteenth century. Crompton is further memorialised in the name of this ward. Hall i'th' Wood itself is now run as a small museum by Bolton council, but the major contributors to the ward's economy now (apart from the town centre) are the Valley, an out-of-town cinema and leisure complex overlooked by Crompton Way; and the Back o'th' Bank Bakery, since 1915 the headquarters and major bakery for Britain's second-largest food and drink brand (after Coca-Cola) and most popular bread, Warburton's. There was formerly an RBS call centre within the ward off St Peter's Way (your columnist once applied for a job there), but that was a casualty of the recession; the building's owner now wants to turn it into a hotel, but the council aren't keen on the idea.

Your columnist made his first steps into quiz league in this ward in around 2004, turning out for the Astley Bridge Conservative Club (which lies less than a hundred yards outside the Crompton ward boundary) in an away match at the Bowling Green on Blackburn Road. The Bowling Green has gone now, and the two pubs next to it along that stretch (the Victoria British Queen and the Old Original British Queen) are derelict. In fact, quiz league venues in this ward don't seem to be doing very well. The Fox and Stork on Halliwell Road closed down around the time of the 2010 general election (during which David Cameron was photographed at Warburton's in front of a large stack of sliced bread) and its team decamped to the Breightmet Conservative Club; since there was already a team playing out of there, the Fox and Stork took account of the new political situation by renaming themselves "Breightmet Coalition". A sadder note was struck last year by the abrupt closure of the grimy but much-loved Dog and Partridge, on Bank Street in the town centre, following an accident in which a Land Rover crashed into the pub and took out the entire bar area; the Dog's quiz team (who bring a bust of Lenin to all their matches) have moved just outside the ward boundary to the thirteenth-century Man and Scythe on Churchgate, but haven't yet plucked up the courage to change their name.

A tale of pubs closing? As well as the fact that pubs haven't been doing too well of late generally, the population of Crompton ward presents particular challenges for the trade. A third of the ward's population are Asian, overwhelmingly from Pakistan, and 33% of the population are Muslim—a figure just outside the top 100 wards in England and Wales. Other highlights of the ward's census figures include a relatively young population (23% of the population are under 15), high unemployment and a lack of qualifications, together with a very high number of economically inactive people (26%, of which 8% are "looking after home or family", 8% are long-term sick or disabled and 6% are students)—all entirely consistent with the general picture. It's not for nothing that Peter Kay's "Max", when he's not running the door at the Phoenix Club, can be found wearing a Pakistan cricket shirt. It's also not for nothing that the main story within the ward over summer 2014 was the proposal for a "super" mosque, soon to be built next door to the present mosque on Blackburn Road; a proposal which attracted noisy protests from all the usual suspects.

Crompton ward was created in 2004 and was the successor to the previous Central ward, which had been safe Labour since its creation in 1980—one of its early councillors was Brian Iddon, who would go on to become the MP for Bolton South East. Roger Hayes, the current Lib Dem group leader on Bolton council, stood as the Liberal/SDP Alliance candidate here in 1982 and

Parliamentary constituency: Bolton North East
May 2015 result Lab 3895 C 1343 LD 641 Grn 306
May 2014 result Lab 2363 UKIP 826 C 456 LD 148 Ind 121
May 2012 result Lab 2375 C 523 LD 273
May 2011 result Lab 2403 C 713 Grn 218 LD 164
May 2010 result Lab 3749 C 1325 LD 938
Oct 2009 by-election Lab 1528 C 935 Ind 377 LD 284 Grn 99
May 2008 result Lab 1985 C 1113 LD 873
May 2007 result Lab 1662 C 1035 LD 482
July 2006 by-election Lab 1793 C 978 LD 224 Grn 96 Soc Lab 35
May 2006 result Lab 1932 LD 1132 C 941 Veritas 190 Soc Lab 129
June 2004 result LD 2258/2225/2043 Lab 1135/929/820 C 954/902/874 Soc Lab 231 Ind 228

Figure 14: Bolton, Crompton

got nowhere. It took until 2000 for the ward to become interesting when the Conservatives selected an Asian candidate and suddenly cut the Labour lead to four points, but there was really no sign that Labour could ever lose here until the Iraq War of 2003: in the local elections of that year Labour lost Central ward for the first and only time to the Liberal Democrat candidate Valibhai Patel, who had come third here as an independent the previous year in a ward with no Lib Dem track record.

The creation of Crompton ward in 2004 and the associated all-out election enabled the Lib Dems to consolidate their position by winning all three of the new ward's seats. However, 2004 was the high-water mark for the Lib Dems in Bolton; Valibhai Patel lost re-election in 2006 to Labour's Sufrana Bashir-Ismail, and after that the ward's Lib Dem vote vanished as quickly as it had appeared. By 2007, thanks to a by-election gain, there was a full slate of Labour councillors again and normal service had resumed. UKIP briefly took over second place in 2014 but didn't stand here in last year's election, at which the 2012–13 mayor Guy Harkin beat the Tories 63–22. This is very much the Labour heart of the very polarised Bolton North East constituency.

In a ward with this social composition, it was perhaps inevitable that somebody would try to play the race card by alleging postal vote fraud, although it's more surprising that the person who originally brought it up was the Tories' election agent. Fraud or no fraud, this election should be very easy for the Labour candidate Bilkis Bashir Ismail, Sufrana's sister. The Tories' Ryan Haslam fights the ward for the third time. Also standing are Gary Veevers for the Lib Dems, Laura Diggle (who stood for Parliament here last year) for the Greens and Paul Eccles of UKIP.

Result: Lab 1961 UKIP 320 C 302 LD 117 Grn 65

Lower Stoke

Coventry city council, West Midlands; caused by the death of Labour councillor Phil Townshend at the age of 57. A solicitor, Townshend had represented Lower Stoke ward since 1999 and at the time of his death was Deputy Leader of the Council; in recent years he did much work behind the scenes to persuade Jaguar to invest in the city, and Coventry City FC to return. His business dealings were less successful: his former solicitors' practice Townshends LLP went into liquidation in 2013 owing a six-figure sum to the taxman, and at the time of his death he was being investigated by police on suspicion of defrauding a vulnerable elderly woman.

To describe this ward in eastern Coventry, your columnist can do little better than quote "greenchristian", a Green Party activist in Coventry who describes it thus:

> "This ward contains Stoke, Stoke Park, Stoke Aldemoor, and most of Lower Stoke, all of which are working class areas. Stoke Aldemoor has a particularly bad reputation. The Lower Stoke area contains a large amount of student housing (all of it Coventry University students), and HMOs have been a major issue in that part of the ward, although the rest of the ward has very few students (at the last census, the ward as a whole had fewer students than the city average). Lower Stoke's demographics are very close to those of the city as a whole. It has, historically, been one of TUSC's better wards in the city—bordering Dave Nellist's former ward St Michaels (and at the end where he does best). At the last by-election here in 2011 (also due to a councillor death), the Socialists managed to turn out almost all of their voters, and given the lack of a TUSC candidate this time I'm wondering how those voters will split (I suspect it will be between some combination of Labour, Green, and UKIP)."

While the Tories did win the ward in 1982 and 1992 and still had enough strength in the early-to-mid Noughties to just about turn it marginal, Lower Stoke ward is safe Labour with not much to comment on, other than the independent candidate here from 2004 to 2008 who was Christine Oddy, the former Labour MEP who fell out with the party after being effectively deselected in 1999. The TUSC candidates in 2014 and 2015 and the Socialist Alternative candidates before 2014 are Nellistites. At the most recent poll in 2015 Labour won with 50% to 21% for the Tories and 18% for UKIP.

Defending for Labour is Rupinder Singh, a Unite activist who defeated former councillor Lynette Kelly for the nomination; Kelly had stood down from the council last year on the mistaken expectation that she would win the Warwick and Leamington parliamentary seat. The Tories have selected school governor

Parliamentary constituency: Coventry North East
May 2015 result Lab 4053 C 1736 UKIP 1493 Grn 499 TUSC 397
May 2014 result Lab 1854 UKIP 938 C 600 Grn 259 TUSC 248 BNP 70
May 2012 result Lab 1748 C 484 Soc Alt 310 UKIP 233 LD 168 Grn 161 BNP 101
Oct 2011 by-election Lab 1366 C 563 Soc Alt 254 BNP 149 Grn 114 LD 79
May 2011 result Lab 2608 C 1018 Grn 353 Soc Alt 291 BNP 261
May 2010 result Lab 3535 C 1647 LD 1264 BNP 503 Soc Alt 273 Grn 256
May 2008 result Lab 1682 C 858 Ind 405 BNP 359 LD 308 Grn 160
May 2007 result Lab 1810 C 1060 Ind 629 BNP 419
May 2006 result Lab 1483 C 1076 Ind 539 LD 457 Soc Alt 292
June 2004 result Lab 1975/1852/1602 C 1396/1334/1163 Ind 1156 LD 765 Soc Alt 561

Figure 15: Coventry, Lower Stoke

and champagne supplier Elaine Yebkal. The UKIP candidate is Harjinder Singh Sehmi, who was a Labour councillor for Cheylesmore ward from 2010 to 2014 before being the Kipper candidate for Cov North West in last year's general election. Also standing are the Greens' Aimee Challenor, who despite being only 18 chairs the party's national LGBT etc group, and the Lib Dems' Christopher Glenn.

Result: Lab 1235 C 344 UKIP 290 Grn 165 LD 124

West End North

Eastleigh borough council, Hampshire; caused by the death of Liberal Democrat councillor Tony Noyce at the age of 72. He had served as an Eastleigh councillor since 2007 and was Mayor of Eastleigh in 2014–15.

There is one London by-election this week, but this isn't it. Instead this is the edge of the Southampton built-up area, although confusingly the north-eastern corner rather than the west end thereof; the M 27 motorway runs through the ward and the area to the north of the motorway is essentially open space. The ward's main public building is the small Moorgreen Hospital, while a street through the ward is named after the forester and environmental activist Richard St Barbe Baker, who was born in West End. Not within the ward—although only accessible from it—is the Rose Bowl cricket ground, a Test venue which since 2001 has been home to Hampshire county cricket club.

Eastleigh council has been Lib Dem-controlled for a long time, and if anything is more popular than the sequence of Lib Dem MPs for Eastleigh from the 1994 by-election to 2015 (Chris Huhne in particular seems to have had a negative personal vote). Like much of Eastleigh, West End North has trended to the Lib Dems over the years: the Tories narrowly won it in 2003, but Noyce recovered the seat in 2007 by which time West End North was already a safe ward. Until

Parliamentary constituency: Eastleigh
Hampshire county council division: West End and Hedge End Grange Park
May 2015 result LD 1156 C 1020 UKIP 446 Lab 280
May 2014 result LD 854 UKIP 408 C 294 Lab 78
May 2011 result LD 853 C 526 Lab 163 UKIP 161
May 2010 result LD 1497 C 969 Lab 231 UKIP 128
May 2007 result LD 904 C 560 Lab 99 UKIP 77
May 2006 result LD 871 C 577 Lab 100 UKIP 64
May 2003 result C 578 LD 547 Lab 108
May 2002 result LD 613/593 C 467/425 Lab 166

Figure 16: Eastleigh, West End North

2015, that is, when the general election led to a revival of the Tory vote: the Lib Dems eventually won that year with 40% to 35% for the Conservatives and 15% for UKIP. The Lib Dems also hold the local county council seat, although the effect of the 2013 by-election can be seen in the county council result where UKIP cut the Lib Dem majority to less than seven points.

Defending for the Lib Dems is Janice Asman, a West End parish councillor. The Tories' Steven Broomfield, who won the 2003 election here but lost his seat in 2007, is seeking to make a return to the council after nine years away. UKIP have selected Hugh McGuinness, a Fair Oak and Horton Heath parish councillor. Also standing are Andy Andrews for Labour and Glynn Fleming for the Green Party.

Result: LD 582 C 315 UKIP 115 Lab 58 Grn 28

Cranford

Hounslow borough council, North London; caused by the death of Labour council-lor Sohan Sangha at the age of 73. Originally from the Punjab in what was then British India, Sangha had served on Hounslow council since 2002; away from the council he was a legal consultant and an active member of the Southall gurdwara.

For our final preview of the week we travel to a small market town not far from the large industrial city of Drumle, as we examine small-town customs and values in Victorian England ... (*consults notes*) Sorry, wrong Cranford. This isn't a Mrs Gaskell novel, it's one of the smallest and prettiest villages in Middlesex, which has since turned into the point on the A 4 (Bath Road) and A 30 (Great South West Road) where the London built-up area ends and Heathrow Airport begins. This ward has a majority Asian population, mostly from India: 21% of the population are Sikh, putting Cranford within the top 20 Sikh wards in England and Wales, and a further 14% are Hindu. Cranford does have an

Parliamentary constituency: Feltham and Heston
May 2014 result Lab 2085/1813/1643 C 987/851/801 UKIP 508 LD 235
May 2010 result Lab 2318/2261/2228 C 1313/1286/1009 Beavers Cranford Party 1030/966/838
BNP 202
May 2006 result Lab 1346/1275/1254 Hounslow Independent Alliance 971/922/815 C 491
LD 431/417 Ind 61
May 2002 result Lab 1122/1036/1035 C 548/541/539 A BEE C 279
May 2012 GLA results (excludes postal voters)
Mayor: Ken 1203 Boris 432 Ind 42 Grn 34 LD 30 UKIP 17 BNP 11
List: Lab 1287 C 292 Grn 55 UKIP 45 LD 31 BNP 19 Hayat 18 CPA 16 EDP 13 TUSC 7
Alagaratnam 4 House Party 3 NF 0

Figure 17: Hounslow, Cranford

important impact on the economy thanks to the Cranford Agreement, which bans eastbound takeoffs from the northern runway at Heathrow; Cranford is directly beyond the end of that runway.

Your columnist has memories of being put up in an airport hotel within this ward courtesy of Sky TV, whose studios are a few miles up the A 4, in early November 2011. I spent that evening drowning my sorrows at a poor TV quiz performance, buying drinks for the show's winner Rob Hannah and persuading him that he would get a prize (he did, I think), marvelling at the fact that Ceefax still existed in London and learning that the local MP Alan Keen had died that day. The resulting by-election, held just before Christmas 2011, was an easy Labour hold; not too surprising given the previous results for Cranford ward which is very safe for Labour. At the most recent London local election in 2014 Labour beat the Tories here 55–26; confusingly, the lead candidate on the Tory slate had headed localist slates in 2010 (Beavers Cranford Party) and 2006 (Hounslow Independent Alliance). The Beavers Cranford Party wasn't the only animal associated with this ward's previous elections thanks to the presence on the ballot in 2002 of A BEE C, a Brentford FC supporters/campaign group. In the 2012 GLA ballot Ken beat Boris here 68–24, while the Labour lead over the Tories was even greater on the list votes (72–16).

Defending for Labour is Sukhbir Dhaliwal, a former bus driver who is seeking to return to Hounslow council having represented Hendon West ward from 2006 to 2010; in 2010 he had contested Feltham North ward, which was then safe Conservative, and lost. The Tory candidate is BA cabin crew member and former Metropolitan Police constable Sukhdev Singh Maras, who fought this ward on the localist slates in 2006 and 2010. Also standing are George Radulski for UKIP, Hina Malik for the Lib Dems and Nico Fekete for the Green Party.

Result: Lab 1264 C 638 LD 265 UKIP 96 Grn 48

18th February 2016

Nine by-elections on 18th February 2016, seven in England, one in Wales and one in Scotland.

Amersham Town

Chiltern district council, Buckinghamshire; caused by the death of Liberal Democrat councillor Davida Allen at the age of 76. A former organic research chemist at the Radiochemical Centre, Allen was a district councillor from 1999 to 2011 and again from May to November 2015.

We start this week in the Chiltern hills at Amersham, the major north-western terminus of the London Underground. The Amersham Town ward runs south from the Underground and railway station to cover the Old Amersham area in the Misbourne valley. Old Amersham's economy was traditionally based on coaching inns, but today has diversified into more high-tech stuff: Thatcher's first privatisation, the Radiochemical Centre, was based here and was briefly called Amersham International (it is now part of GE Healthcare), and the ward is home to the head office of Halma, a FTSE 250 company which has come a long way from its roots as a Ceylon tea trader to become the UK's largest manufacturer of smoke detectors. As might be expected from the town's Metroland and technology profile, this is a solidly middle-class ward: 32% of the workforce are in "lower management" jobs, a figure in the top 100 wards in England and Wales, and 46% of the population hold degree-level qualifications. One major controversy is that the proposed route of High Speed 2 passes through the ward.

Davida Allen's campaigning turned Amersham Town into a Tory–Lib Dem marginal which usually elected Allen and one Conservative (except in 2011 when the Tory slate won both seats); Allen had a clear personal vote and usually ran a long way ahead of her running-mate. Last year the Tory slate had 39%, the Lib Dems 33% and single UKIP and Labour candidates polled 14% each. Without Allen on the ballot that Lib Dem strength doesn't translate to county council

Parliamentary constituency: Chesham and Amersham
Buckinghamshire county council divisions: Penn Wood and Old Amersham (part); Little
Chalfont and Amersham (part)
May 2015 result C 1229/880 LD 1052/545 UKIP 455 Lab 450
May 2011 result C 909/855 LD 772/538 Lab 246/233
May 2007 result LD 713/533 C 644/605 Lab 111
May 2003 result LD 670/509 C 569/536 Lab 95/78

Figure 18: Chiltern, Amersham Town

level, in which the ward is split between two safe Tory divisions; in the 2009 and
2005 elections Allen stood in the former two-member Amersham division and
turned it into a marginal, being on the wrong side of two photo-finishes.

Without Allen's personal vote this will be a difficult defence for the Lib
Dems. They have selected Richard Williams, a furniture designer and former
district councillor. In another twist, the Conservative candidate is Jules Cook
who is Allen's daughter. Also standing are Richard Phoenix for UKIP and Robin
Walters for Labour.

Result: C 489 LD 354 UKIP 67 Lab 64 [C gain from LD]

Sutton

Cambridgeshire county council; caused by the death of long-serving Conservative
councillor Philip Read at the age of 73. A farmer who attended the University of
Leeds, Read's local government career went all the way back to 1973, when he was
elected to East Cambridgeshire district council and Sutton parish council, which
he chaired from 1975 to 1977. Read was first elected to Cambridgeshire county
council in a 1975 by-election; although he lost his seat in 2005, he returned in a
2007 by-election.

Sutton county division covers a large swathe of fenland to the north-west
and west of Ely. It is named after Sutton-in-the-Isle, a large village on an island
in the Fens overlooking the two Bedford Rivers, artificial waterways which were
built in the seventeenth century to contain the overflow of the River Great Ouse
and prevent it from flooding the Fens. Unsurprisingly given its presence in
the Fens, Sutton has an agricultural history; its biggest export today is tractors,
construction and agricultural equipment from Cheffins' monthly auction, which
is described as one of the biggest machinery auctions in Europe. Also within this
county division is the Downham Villages ward, of which the largest, counter-
intuitively, is Little Downham.

As stated, Read had easily won every election for this area since 1975 with the

Parliamentary constituency: North East Cambridgeshire
East Cambridgeshire district wards: Downham Villages, Sutton
May 2013 result C 817 LD 542 Lab 295
June 2009 result C 1131 LD 593 Ind 584 Lab 178
May 2007 by-election C 1077 LD 574 Ind 485 Lab 130
May 2005 result LD 2122 C 1617

Figure 19: Cambridgeshire CC, Sutton

exception of a fluke Lib Dem win in 2005; the new Lib Dem county councillor resigned less than two years later and normal service was resumed in the by-election. At Read's final re-election in 2013 he beat the Lib Dem candidate 49–33; he later resigned from the Conservative party in 2014 in a dispute over the selection for a district council by-election in Sutton, but appears to have returned to the Tory fold since then. That by-election resulted in the Tories losing the district council seat to the Lib Dem candidate Lorna Dupre, who was re-elected in 2015; the Tories hold the other three district council seats in this county division.

Defending for the Conservatives is Mike Bradley, a district councillor representing Downham Villages ward. Lorna Dupre is reselected by the Lib Dems, having been runner-up in the 2013 county election. Also standing are Pete Bigsby for UKIP and independent candidate Owen Winters.

Result: LD 1063 C 651 UKIP 208 Ind 102 [LD gain from C]

Newmarket and Red Lodge

Suffolk county council; caused by the resignation of Conservative councillor Lisa Chambers, apparently after she was removed as the county council's representative on the Newmarket Vision steering group. She had served on the county council since 2005.

This county council division really is appallingly drawn, although that has more to do with the weird shape of the Cambridgeshire–Suffolk boundary around the Newmarket salient. Newmarket is too large to form one county council seat but not large enough for two, which results in this abomination which combines the north-eastern half of the town with five rural parishes, which have very little connection with Newmarket or each other (by road or otherwise) other than that they are in the right place to make up the numbers. The largest of those villages is Red Lodge, a fast-growing twentieth-century village named after its oldest building, the Red Lodge Inn on what was once the main road from London to Norwich. The three district council wards within the division

Parliamentary constituency: West Suffolk
Forest Heath district council wards: Red Lodge, Severals, South
May 2013 result C 968 UKIP 615 Lab 450 LD 136
June 2009 result C 1072 LD 588 UKIP 397 Lab 202
May 2005 result C 1582 LD 932 Lab 883 UKIP 220

Figure 20: Suffolk CC, Newmarket and Red Lodge

are rather different demographically: Red Lodge and Severals (the part of Newmarket within the division) have very high levels of full-time employment; Red Lodge has a young age profile, reflecting its status as a relatively new development; Severals has a relatively high Irish population, reflecting Newmarket's status as a horseracing centre; while the more agricultural South ward (and it shows how badly the boundaries are drawn that the Boundary Commission couldn't come up with a better name) has one of the highest proportions of people living rent-free in England and Wales.

This disparate collection of areas had returned Lisa Chambers to Suffolk county council very comfortably since 2005. At her last re-election in 2013 she had 45% of the vote to 28% for UKIP and 21% for Labour. In the 2015 district council elections the Tories won four of the six district council seats within the division, with two seats in Severals ward going to independent candidates.

Defending for the Conservatives is Robin Millar, the deputy leader of the local district council (Forest Heath), a former Mayor of Newmarket, and parliamentary candidate in 2010 for, er, Arfon in Wales. The UKIP candidate is Roger Dicker, who was Tory councillor for South ward from 2007 to 2011 and for Red Lodge ward from 2011 to 2015; he stood for re-election in Red Lodge in May as a UKIP candidate in what was his first contested election, and lost his seat by just two votes. Labour have selected Newmarket town councillor Michael Jefferys, who from 2011 to 2015 was the only Labour member of Forest Heath district council; last year he lost his district council seat and was also unsuccessful as the Labour candidate for the West Suffolk constituency. Also standing are Tim Huggan for the Lib Dems and Andrew Appleby, a district councillor for Severals ward, for the West Suffolk Independents.

Result: C 644 UKIP 494 Lab 284 West Suffolk Ind 123 LD 76

Chadsmcad

Lichfield district council, Staffordshire; caused by the resignation of Liberal Democrat councillor Marion Bland on health grounds. She was first elected to Lichfield district council in 2007 and had continuous service since a 2014 by-election.

Parliamentary constituency: Lichfield
Staffordshire county council division: Lichfield City North (part formerly in Chadsmead and Curborough wards); Lichfield City South (part formerly in Leomansley ward)
May 2015 result C 747/515 LD 563/357 Lab 547/524 UKIP 382/284

Figure 21: Lichfield, Chadsmead

Not again, I hear you cry. Yes, we are back in the north-western ward of the generally beautiful and well-preserved Midlands cathedral city of Lichfield, a ward which has twice hosted the British leg of the World Quizzing Championships. Note that I said "generally beautiful and well-preserved", for this ward is the exception to the rule: it's a tract of postwar housing, much of it socially rented, which includes Lichfield's most deprived census district. And it votes like it, too.

At district level this ward has voted for all three main parties in the last thirteen years; it returned a Tory and a Labour councillor in 2003 before the Conservatives gained the Labour seat at a by-election just before Christmas 2005. In May 2007 the Lib Dems gained one of the Conservative seats, only to lose it back to the Tories in 2011. One of the Tory councillors was kicked off for non-attendance in late 2013, and the by-election at the end of January 2014 resulted in a Lib Dem gain with the Tories crashing to fourth place behind Labour and UKIP. Boundary changes for the 2015 election saw Chadsmead ward gain an area around Gaiafields Road from Curborough ward and a few streets off Eastern Avenue from Leomansley ward; under these new boundaries the Tories did recover to top the poll, with Marion Bland—who clearly had a personal vote—narrowly holding off Labour for the other seat: the shares of the vote were 33% for the Conservatives, 25% for the Lib Dems, 24% for Labour and 17% for UKIP. Labour do have representation here because they gained the county council seat from the Tories in 2013, and given that the Lichfield City North county division (which covers the whole of the present ward except the part transferred from Leomansley last year) has a safe Tory ward in it Labour must have carried Chadsmead that year.

Paul Ray has the difficult task of defending this three-way marginal ward for the Lib Dems; a solicitor specialising in banking and finance law, he fought Lichfield in last year's general election. The Tory candidate is Brian McMullan, a councillor on the parish-level Lichfield city council and a business studies lecturer at Coventry University. Labour have selected Colin Ball, a credit union volunteer and chairman of the North Lichfield Initiative Board. Jan Higgins, a Kings Bromley parish councillor who fought Tamworth in the general election, stands for UKIP, and the Green Party's Adam Elsdon completes the ballot paper.

Result: LD 300 Lab 195 C 159 UKIP 73 Grn 23

Greasley; and
Toton and Chilwell Meadows

Broxtowe borough council, Nottinghamshire; caused respectively by the death of Stuart Rowland and the resignation of Natalie Harvey. Both were Conservative councillors. Rowland, who was on holiday in Spain at the time of his death, had originally been elected in 2011 for the former Greasley (Giltbrook and Newthorpe) ward, while Harvey, who reportedly didn't enjoy being a councillor, had served only since May.

Not again, I hear you cry. Yes, we are back in the greater Nottingham suburb of Toton, an area with a high councillor attrition rate and a middle-class owner-occupied demographic which belies an industrial past. Toton is a railway town and the site of what was once Europe's largest railway marshalling yard, which took in coal from the Nottinghamshire coalfield and sorted it for distribution all over the UK. The marshalling yard is still there although it's a lot less busy than it used to be, while there is an intriguing possible future development: if High Speed 2 gets off the ground, its East Midlands station could be sited here.

Toton and Chilwell Meadows' third district by-election in four years, and fourth in seven years, is combined with another by-election to Broxtowe borough council from Greasley ward. This ward was brought into being in boundary changes last year but is very similar to the Greasley (Giltbrook and Newthorpe) ward which existed before then. The settlement of Greasley itself was destroyed by the Earl of Rutland, according to Wikipedia, "so he could have a better view"; leaving only a parish of that name which sprawled around the eastern side of the ex-coalmining town of Eastwood. Accordingly the population of the Greasley ward is located in Giltbrook and Newthorpe, modern suburbs of the mining town of Eastwood; the local economy is based on the Giltbrook Retail Park, located just off the A 610 Eastwood Bypass and home to the East Midlands branch of IKEA. Again, this is a middle-class area: owner-occupation is high and there is a significant retired population in the ward. Last year's boundary changes brought in a small (in terms of population) part of the former Eastwood North and Greasley (Beauvale) ward, including the ruins of Beauvale Priory.

Eastwood North and Greasley (Beauvale) was a left-wing ward which was the subject of an election court case in 2011, after its two seats split between Labour and the Lib Dems; the Lib Dem slate was a husband and wife, and the returning officer messed up the count resulting in the wife being declared elected when (it eventually turned out) the husband had more votes. However, the political

Parliamentary constituency: Broxtowe (part: former Greasley (Giltbrook and Newthorpe) ward); Ashfield (part: part of former Eastwood North and Greasley (Beauvale) ward)
Nottinghamshire county council division: Beauvale
May 2015 result C 1933/1726/1605 Lab 1036/993/896 UKIP 795/678 LD 263/220/182

Figure 22: Broxtowe, Greasley

Parliamentary constituency: Broxtowe
Nottinghamshire county council division: Chilwell and Toton
May 2015 result C 2631/2570/1939 Lab 1243/1187/1022 UKIP 773 Ind 632 Grn 585
Dec 2014 by-election C 952 Lab 454 UKIP 340
March 2012 by-election C 831 Lab 385 LD 300 UKIP 228
May 2011 result C 1529/1491/1413 Lab 926/925/837 LD 377/334/304 UKIP 305
Sep 2009 by-election C 1081 LD 474 Lab 296 BNP 58
May 2007 result C 1394/1315/1301 LD 725/719/669 Lab 411/402/387 BNP 205 UKIP 149
May 2003 result C 1183/1126/1118 Lab 504/490/452 LD 446/358

Figure 23: Broxtowe, Toton and Chilwell Meadows

tone of the new Greasley ward was set by the former Greasley (Giltbrook and Newthorpe) ward, which was safely Conservative; and so the new Greasley ward proved to be. In last year's election the Tories won with 48%, with Labour on 26% and UKIP on 20%. This ward provides the Tory majority in the key marginal Beauvale county council division.

Toton and Chilwell Meadows, which escaped the 2015 boundary changes unscathed, is even safer for the Conservatives: last year the Tories had 45% to 21% for Labour, UKIP narrowly taking third place with 13%. Again, this ward provides the Tory majority in a marginal county council division (Chilwell and Toton, this time).

In Greasley Eddie Cubley defends for the Conservatives: he fought the safe Labour Eastwood Hilltop ward last year. Chris Chandler, who was on the Labour slate here last year, tries again as does Tracey Cahill for UKIP. The Lib Dems' Keith Longdon completes the ballot paper.

To hold Toton and Chilwell Meadows the Tories have selected Stephanie Kerry, a deputy manager at a nursery. The Labour candidate is Lisa Clarke, a nurse and one of the activists behind the No More Page Three campaign. There is no UKIP candidate this time. Graham Heal, who contested the ward as an independent last year and polled 11%, now has the Lib Dem nomination, while the Greens (who got 10% here last year) have selected Gordon Stoner.

Greasley result: C 656 Lab 300 UKIP 230 LD 158

Toton and Chilwell Meadows result: C 910 Lab 368 LD 363 Grn 111

Higher Blackley

Manchester city council; caused by the resignation of Labour councillor Anna Trotman for family reasons. She was first elected in 1999 for the former Blackley ward.

All the people, so many people. Welcome to Europe's largest municipal park, the 243-hectare Heaton Park. Once the grounds of the Earl of Wilton, it is home to the scandalously neglected eighteenth-century Heaton Hall, the highest point within the Manchester city boundary from where there are uninterrupted views to the Pennines (when it's not raining, and rain-free days have been in short supply recently). The Earl of Wilton sold the park to Manchester Corporation in 1902; here can now be found a difficult municipal golf course, a preserved tramway, one of England's few reinforced concrete towers (owned by BT and used for telecommunications) and a reservoir where the Haweswater Aqueduct, which supplies a large proportion of Manchester's water, terminates. Since the 1980s Heaton Park has played host to a large number of open-air events, with headliners as diverse as Oasis, Proms in the Park and Pope John Paul II; the park was the venue for the lawn bowls at the 2002 Commonwealth Games (your columnist remembers it well, he was there), while since 2013 it has hosted the annual Parklife music festival. As well as being a large suitable space for this kind of event, most of the housing around Heaton Park is within the borders of Bury council so Manchester don't have to worry too much about the disruption caused to local residents.

Large and interesting though Heaton Park is, this ward is called Higher Blackley and that's where its electorate lives, in generally inter-war housing on the eastern side of the River Irk either side of Victoria Avenue. This is a working-class area, with high levels of social renting and long-term sickness combined with a significant Irish population. This obviously creates a Labour-voting profile although there is a right-wing populist vote: the BNP had a couple of second places here in the late Noughties, and last time the ward polled in 2015 Labour beat UKIP here 57–26. Labour have won every single ward election within the City of Manchester since 2011, and on previous form there is no sign of the redwash ending here.

Defending for Labour is Paula Sadler, who has spent 25 years working for the city council and Northwards Housing. UKIP's candidate is Martin Power who also stood here in 2011 and 2014; a second-generation Irishman, he got into trouble last year as parliamentary candidate for Blackley and Broughton by printing libellous election leaflets and trying to cover this up by scribbling over the contentious bits in biro. Also standing are David Semple for the Tories,

Parliamentary constituency: Blackley and Broughton
May 2015 result Lab 3155 UKIP 1414 C 540 Grn 231 LD 151
May 2014 result Lab 1737 UKIP 1046 C 194 Grn 142 LD 53
May 2012 result Lab 1753 C 226 BNP 221 UKIP 198 LD 100 Grn 98
May 2011 result Lab 1953 C 381 BNP 321 UKIP 235 LD 112 Grn 81
May 2010 result Lab 3037 C 820 BNP 813 LD 581 Respect 111
May 2008 result Lab 1328 BNP 828 C 467 LD 248 Grn 164
May 2007 result Lab 1449 BNP 716 C 372 LD 268 Grn 108 UKIP 82
May 2006 result Lab 1477 C 506 LD 383 Grn 226
June 2004 result Lab 1829/1823/1818 C 601/484/483 LD 597/395/391

Figure 24: Manchester, Higher Blackley

Anne Power for the Green Party, Peter Matthews for the Lib Dems and George Walkden for the Pirate Party.

Result: Lab 1062 UKIP 308 C 130 LD 78 Grn 40 Pirate Party UK 9 (nine)

New Brighton

Flintshire county council; caused by the resignation of Liberal Democrat councillor Amanda Brigg on health grounds. She was in her first term, having served since 2012.

There are a few New Brightons around the UK, but this is probably the most obscure: a small village just outside Mold on the road to Queensferry. The division lies at the eastern end of the Mold bypass, and also extends over it to include part of Mynydd Isa, a post-war Buckley suburb. The ward has a skilled working-class economic profile combined with a high number of retirees.

This is a safe Lib Dem ward, although of the type which tends to vote for the candidate rather than the party. At the most recent Welsh local election in 2012 the Lib Dems had 45% here to 32% for Labour and 22% for the Tories. In what's likely to be the last local by-election in North Wales before the Senedd election in May, all the parties will be looking to make a good impression.

Defending for the Lib Dems is Sara Parker, who back in the 1990s was the founding editor of *Groove*, a Liverpool music magazine; she now runs a community café in Mynydd Isa. The Labour candidate is Linda Pierce, who will be hoping for an improvement on the 21% she polled here in 2004. The Tories have selected Zulya Taylor, a foreign language teacher. Also standing is independent candidate John Yorke.

Result: LD 365 Lab 241 C 141 Ind 60

Parliamentary and Assembly constituency: Delyn
May 2012 result LD 469 Lab 334 C 229
May 2008 result LD 676 Ind 373 Lab 92
June 2004 result LD 913 Lab 240

Figure 25: Flintshire, New Brighton

Oban North and Lorn

Argyll and Bute council; caused by the resignation of independent councillor Duncan MacIntyre on health grounds. He had served on Argyll and Bute council since 1999, originally being elected for the former Ardconnel-Kilmore ward.

Not again, I hear you cry. Yes, we are back in Oban North and Lorn for the third by-election in two years, and the fourth in five years. This geographically vast ward with a high councillor attrition rate essentially contains the whole of the hinterland of Oban but only the northern third of the town itself (the other two-thirds of Oban is in a ward with Mull and various other islands). The ward goes a long way inland along the line of the A 85, past Dalmally and as far as Bridge of Orchy; also here are the Benderloch and Appin areas on the north side of Loch Etive, together with the island of Lismore in Loch Linnhe. As well as tourism, one of the main drivers of the local economy is the hydroelectric power station at Ben Cruachan, knowledge of which once won your columnist a bottle of rare Belgian beer.

The ward was created for the 2007 elections in Scotland which were the first to be held under proportional representation. In 2003 at the last first-past-the-post election, all four of the predecessor wards (Awe, Oban North, Ardconnel-Kilmore and North Lorn) returned independent councillors. Two of the independents were re-elected in 2007, including MacIntyre, while one was defeated; the other two seats went to the Lib Dems and the SNP. The SNP councillor died in 2011 and the SNP held the by-election, polling 44% of the vote; at the decisive stage of the count she had 51% of the vote to 25% for the Tories and 24% for an independent candidate. In the 2012 election the Lib Dem vote collapsed and their seat went to a third independent, who defeated the second SNP candidate by a margin of less than one vote.

In 2014 Oban had three local by-elections. The first was held in May (simultaneously with the European elections) in the other Oban ward, and was unexpectedly won by Labour who had not previously contested the area. For the second, held here in July following the resignation of the SNP councillor, your columnist wrote that "even with Scottish by-elections using the Alternative Vote anything can still happen" and we certainly got an unusual and interesting

Westminster constituency: Argyll and Bute
Holyrood constituency: Argyll and Bute
Oct 2014 by-election SNP 1090 Ind 629 Lab 530 C 415; after transfers SNP 1199 Ind 1080
July 2014 by-election SNP 595 Ind 548 Lab 526 C 445 Ind 301; after transfers Ind 920 Lab 874
May 2012 result SNP 1117 Ind 807 Ind 421 Ind 361 C 332 Ind 222 LD 188 Ind 125 Ind 58
Nov 2011 by-election SNP 1081 C 505 Ind 438 LD 260 Ind 165; after transfers SNP 1179 C 591 Ind 561
May 2007 result SNP 1019 Ind 1005 Ind 779 LD 665 C 387 Ind 200 Ind 188 Ind 176 Ind 140

Figure 26: Argyll and Bute, Oban North and Lorn

result. The SNP topped the poll on first preferences but with less than 25% of the vote, and the nationalist party (whose Oban branch had suffered a damaging split) attracted so few transfers that they failed to make the final round of voting, in which John MacGregor narrowly defeated Labour by 920 votes to 874. MacGregor's election meant that all four of the ward's seats were now in the hands of independents, but that didn't last long. Two weeks later MacGregor was dead, and the SNP got their seat back in the town's third by-election of 2014. In Scotland's first election after the independence referendum, Iain MacLean (who had lost the May by-election in Oban South) beat independent candidate Stephanie Irvine, who picked up the lion's share of the transfers, by 1199 votes to 1080.

For this third Oban North by-election of the current Argyll and Bute council (which is an entertaining mess, with an initial SNP administration falling apart in 2013 and various independent groups keeping themselves busy bickering with each other) the defending independent candidate is an interesting one: Kieron Green, who was the Labour candidate in both 2014 by-elections and runner-up in the July poll that year. The SNP have selected Julie McKenzie, an Oban community councillor. There is no official Labour candidate. Completing the ballot paper are the Tories' Andrew Venner, who stood in both 2014 by-elections and finished fourth both times; and Pat Tyrrell of the Green Party.

First preferences: SNP 1113 C 609 Ind 608 Grn 300
Grn eliminated: SNP 1186 Ind 721 C 640
C eliminated: SNP 1241 Ind 1048 [SNP gain from Ind]

25th February 2016

Four by-elections on Thursday 25th February 2016:

Catterick

Richmondshire district council, North Yorkshire; caused by the death of Conservative councillor Derek Sankey at the age of 67. A former woodcutting machinist, Sankey had moved to Catterick in 1970 to join the RAF Regiment; his local government career began in 2012 when he joined Catterick parish council, and he had served as a Richmondshire councillor since May 2015.

Welcome to what is, if not one of the oldest places in England, certainly one of the oldest names. The second-century geographer Ptolemy drew a famous if rather inaccurate map of the known world, including a latitude system running from the first "clime" at the Equator to the thirty-third clime at the Arctic circle, identifying each clime by a list of places it passes through; Ptolemy's twenty-fourth clime is identified by *Katouraktonion*, a location in Britannia. This was what the Romans were calling at the time *Cataractonium*, a Roman fort at the meeting point of the Great North Road, Dere Street and the River Swale. Four centuries later, at around AD 598, Aneurin's Welsh-language poem *Y Gododdin* describes the Battle of Catraeth, in which the native Britons were routed and massacred by the invading Angles; the location of Catraeth is generally considered to be Catterick. Catterick's location on the Great North Road meant that its economy has traditionally been based on coaching; an A1 bypass for the town was opened in 1959 by Lord Chesham at a cost of £1 million, and is now being rebuilt as a motorway for rather more money than that. However, the main drivers for the town today are tourism, the local racecourse (which is just outside the ward boundary), and the military; Catterick airfield was one of the very first RAF bases, opened in 1914 by the Royal Flying Corps as a training centre (after the Second World War it was the RAF Regiment's training base), and is now run by the Army as Marne Barracks, part of the large Catterick Garrison complex.

Parliamentary constituency: Richmond (Yorks)
North Yorkshire county council division: Catterick Bridge
May 2015 result Ind 570 C 528/392 Grn 208
May 2011 result Ind 512 C 338/263
May 2007 result C 403 Ind 318 LD 247 BNP 123/98
May 2003 result SDP 492 C 326 LD 310

Figure 27: Richmondshire, Catterick

In 2003 Catterick was one of a handful of wards to return a councillor from the continuing SDP: that was Tony Pelton, who stood down in 2007 but returned to the council in 2011 as an independent. Pelton's personal vote means there is only space for one Conservative councillor from Catterick, and Sankey had taken over that role in 2015 from the long-serving Rob Johnson. In 2015 Pelton topped the poll with 44% and the Tory slate had 40%. At county level the ward is part of Catterick Bridge division which is safely Conservative.

This by-election is a straight fight. Defending for the Tories is Simon Young, a Catterick parish councillor. In the independent corner is Jill McMullon, a former Tory district councillor for Middleton Tyas ward who is seeking to return to the council after losing her seat last year.

Result: C 308 Ind 203

Kingswinford North and Wall Heath; and St James's

Caused respectively by the resignation of Conservative councillor Natalie Neale and the death of Labour councillor Mary Roberts. Roberts had served since 2007, Neale since 2014.

Kingswinford is one of those old towns which has been swallowed up by the relentless growth of the Black Country. Historically the town was rather more important than it is now—until 1950 there was a Kingswinford parliamentary constituency whose MPs included Arthur Henderson, Air Secretary in the Attlee administration and son of the Labour Party leader of the same name. Boundary changes and the growth of neighbouring Brierley Hill have lessened Kingswinford's importance, leaving it as a determinedly suburban area with a demographic to match—there are high levels of owner-occupation and a large proportion of the population were born in the UK.

Very different is St James's which is Dudley's town centre ward, a triangular area with the town centre at the eastern corner and Russells Hall Hospital at the southern corner. Dudley's Wikipedia entry makes for grim reading, painting a picture of a decrepit town with a failing town centre—partially the result of competition from the Merry Hell shopping centre in nearby Brierley Hill. The census statistics for St James's ward are stereotypically working-class, with high levels of unemployment and social renting.

So these two wards are chalk and cheese, and their election results now reflect that, although both wards returned a full slate of Lib Dem councillors when they were created in 2004. The winning candidate in St James's ward in 2002 was Lorely Burt, who would go on to serve as MP for Solihull from 2005 to 2015. Labour broke through in St James's in 2006 to make a gain from the Lib Dems with just 26% of the vote in a four-way marginal result, with the BNP polling 21% and UKIP 12%. Since then the ward has generally been a tight Labour/UKIP marginal, although UKIP have won the ward only once (in 2008); Labour were well ahead in the 2015 election where they had 45%, UKIP 28% and the Tories 24%, but a local election turnout and the start of the EU referendum campaign might prompt a closer result.

In fact, Labour are seriously on the defensive in Dudley: they presently hold 37 out of 70 seats on the council plus the St James's vacancy, so a net loss of two Labour seats in this year's elections would see Dudley go to no overall control—and this May they are defending seventeen wards, seven of which voted Tory last year. One of those was Kingswinford North and Wall Heath, another former Lib Dem hotspot where the party has ceased to exist. In this case the ward became a Lib Dem/Tory marginal from 2006: the Conservatives broke through in 2008 and by 2011 had a full slate of ward councillors. Then in 2012 a perfect storm came together: the former Lib Dem councillor Lynn Boleyn (who represented this ward from 2006 to 2010) defected to Labour, the ward's Lib Dem machine collapsed to the extent that they failed to field a candidate, and one of the Tory councillors resigned creating a double vacancy. In one of the most unexpected results of 2012, Labour gobbled up nearly all of the Lib Dem vote to overturn a 23-point Tory lead, and suddenly Labour had two out of three councillors for this affluent ward. Boleyn lost re-election in 2014, narrowly falling to third behind UKIP, and the Tories had to make another gain from Labour in 2015 following a defection; that year the Tories won with 50% to 26% for Labour and 21% for UKIP.

Defending for the Conservatives in Kingswinford North and Wall Heath is Edward Lawrence. Lynn Boleyn, councillor for this ward from 2006 to 2010 (for the Lib Dems) and 2012 to 2014 (for Labour), tries to get back on the council as the Labour candidate. UKIP have selected Mick Forsyth, and the Greens' Andi Mohr completes the ballot paper.

St James's ward is a three-cornered fight. Cathryn Bayton, a life coach (what-

Parliamentary constituency: Dudley South
May 2015 result C 3672 Lab 1944 UKIP 1553 Grn 196
May 2014 result C 1704 UKIP 1090 Lab 1071 Grn 131
May 2012 double vacancy Lab 1574/1482 C 1464/1192 UKIP 560/419 Grn 151/87
May 2011 result C 1895 LD 1599 Lab 814 UKIP 272 Grn 93
May 2010 result C 2972 LD 2873 Lab 887 UKIP 622
May 2008 result C 2003 LD 1610 Lab 429 UKIP 402
May 2007 double vacancy LD 1829/1527 C 1489/1171 UKIP 760/698 Lab 563/285
May 2006 result LD 1874 C 1813 Lab 631
June 2004 result LD 2280/2127/1964 C 1606/1531/1443 Lab 563/562/478

Figure 28: Dudley, Kingswinford North and Wall Heath

Parliamentary constituency: Dudley North
May 2015 result Lab 2641 UKIP 1642 C 1398 Grn 186
May 2014 result Lab 1216 UKIP 1183 C 673 Grn 124
May 2012 result Lab 1321 UKIP 1132 C 396 Grn 109
May 2011 result Lab 1755 C 794 UKIP 554 LD 204
May 2010 result Lab 2030 C 1725 UKIP 1285 LD 853
May 2008 result UKIP 994 Lab 776 LD 631 C 625 BNP 311 Ind 142
May 2007 result Lab 1078 UKIP 814 LD 594 BNP 548 C 533
May 2006 result Lab 895 LD 844 BNP 743 C 586 UKIP 426
June 2004 result LD 1246/1234/1225 Lab 1051/956/838 C 849/796/749 Ind 323

Figure 29: Dudley, St James's

ever that is), defends for Labour. Graeme Lloyd is the UKIP candidate, and the Tories have selected Wayne Sullivan.

Kingswinford North and Wall Heath result: C 1456 Lab 934 UKIP 262 Grn 52

St James's result: Lab 847 UKIP 554 C 427

Studley with Sambourne

Stratford-on-Avon district council, Warwickshire; caused by the resignation of Conservative councillor Nick Moon.

This column often comes across claimants for the title of the largest village in England, so it's rather refreshing that the Wikipedia page for Studley, Warwickshire shoots that claim down by noting that Studley isn't even the largest village in Warwickshire. It's a mere large village on the Roman Ryknield Street, now the A435 road, just to the south-east of Redditch. Although the village traditionally had a needle-making industry, Studley is now very much in the economic orbit

Parliamentary constituency: Stratford-on-Avon
Warwickshire county council division: Studley (part: formerly in Sambourne ward and
Studley ward); Alcester (part: formerly in Alcester ward)
May 2015 result C 655 LD 628 Lab 364 UKIP 207 Ind 111 Grn 44

Figure 30: Stratford-on-Avon, Studley with Sambourne

of Redditch and Birmingham.

Stratford-on-Avon district got new ward boundaries in 2015 which severely screwed the Lib Dems, who had a lock on the former Studley ward, by splitting the village in half and combining each half with adjoining rural areas. This worked rather well for the Conservatives who at the 2015 election won all but one of the Stratford district council seats outside Stratford itself. Studley with Sambourne ward is the western of the two Studley wards, containing most of the rural Sambourne parish; we can see from the 2015 result (C 33% LD 31% Lab 18% UKIP 10%) that this will be a difficult defence for the Tories whose majority is just 27 votes. The Lib Dems do still hold the local county council seat, having gained it from the Tories in 2009.

That defence gets even more difficult when you consider a very interesting candidate list. The outgoing councillor Nick Moon, who had cited a lack of time due to business and voluntary commitments as a reason for his resignation, is nonetheless standing for re-election as an independent. Even more strangely, the official Conservative candidate is Paul Beaman, the Lib Dem councillor for the former Studley ward from 2004 to 2015 and runner-up here in the 2015 election; he is the Studley parish council chairman. The official Liberal Democrat candidate is Hazel Wright, a former long-serving Lib Dem councillor for Studley ward who lost re-election in the other Studley ward last year. Labour have re-selected their candidate from last year, Karen Somner-Brown. Completing the ballot paper is UKIP candidate Nigel Rogers.

Result: LD 632 C 233 Lab 156 Ind 66 UKIP 55 [LD gain from C]

3rd March 2016

Four by-elections on 3rd March 2016:

Bloomfield

Blackpool council, Lancashire; caused by the resignation of Labour councillor John Jones. He had served on Blackpool council since winning a by-election in May 2012; a former hotelier, he was Blackpool's cabinet member for school improvement and children's safeguarding.

It's March, the sea's biting cold, the weather forecast isn't much better, so let's go to the seaside to cheer ourselves up. Yes, here we are on the Golden Mile between the Central Pier and the South Pier, in a ward which includes the old Blackpool tram depot on Rigby Road (which now services only the "heritage" trams following a recent modernisation programme) and the home ground of Blackpool FC. The ward is generally in two halves: behind the Promenade is a warren of terraces most of which are now hotels, while behind that is the former site of Blackpool Central railway station, now demolished with the space occupied by a large car park.

Blackpool FC were in the Premier League only a few years ago but have horribly fallen from grace since then, and the same is true of Blackpool itself which has never recovered from the package holiday revolution of the late twentieth century. In consequence Bloomfield ward's demographics do not make for pleasant reading. The ward is in the top 50 in England and Wales for unemployment (11%), long-term sickness (13%) and private renting (54% of households), the last clearly being an effect of all the hotels in the area.

Despite all this Bloomfield ward was a three-way marginal during the last Labour government, and in 2007 the Lib Dems—who are very weak in Blackpool—gained a seat off Labour. Four years later the Lib Dem vote was down to 4 (four) percent and this ward is now very safe for Labour. Last year the Labour slate had 45% here to 25% for a single UKIP candidate and 20% for the Tories.

Parliamentary constituency: Blackpool South
May 2015 result Lab 1045/902 UKIP 585 C 463/294 Grn 202 Ind 37
May 2012 by-election Lab 731 C 216 Ind 193 LD 73
May 2011 result Lab 849/777 C 322/282 UKIP 159/146 LD 54
May 2007 result LD 555/414 Lab 502/466 C 317/274 Ind 202 UK Fags 193
May 2003 result Lab 822/793 LD 779/662 C 675/657

Figure 31: Blackpool, Bloomfield

Parliamentary constituency: Rutland and Melton
May 2015 result LD 511 C 265
Oct 2014 by-election LD 192 C 179
May 2011 result Ind 335 C 247
Nov 2008 by-election Ind 154 C 148 LD 71
May 2007 result C unopposed
May 2003 result C 285 Lab 186

Figure 32: Rutland, Whissendine

Jim Hobson is Labour's choice to defend the by-election; he has been inspired by his selection to start blogging. The UKIP candidate is the wonderfully-named Spencer Shackleton. Tony Jones stands for the Tories, and the ballot paper is completed by the Greens' Phill Armstrong and the Lib Dems' Neil Close.
Result: Lab 450 C 150 UKIP 118 Grn 32 LD 31

Whissendine

Rutland council; caused by the resignation of Liberal Democrat councillor Sam Asplin on health grounds. Still in his early twenties, Asplin was first elected in a by-election in October 2014 when he was a 21-year-old teaching assistant at Whissendine primary school.

Here we have Rutland's most north-westerly ward, a tiny village in a tiny county. Whissendine lies off the Oakham–Melton road, about 30 miles north-west of Peterborough, and is probably best known for its thirteenth-century church and nineteenth-century windmill. It forms a ward with a relatively old and highly British demographic together with a fairly large retired population.

Whissendine ward has a high councillor attrition rate and this is the ward's third by-election in eight years. It had voted Tory in 2003 and nobody opposed the Conservatives in 2007, but in 2008 Brian Montgomery, the first chairman of the Rutland unitary council, won a by-election as an independent candidate with a majority of just six votes. Montgomery made the ward safe in 2011 but died in 2014, and the pattern then repeated itself: the Tories again narrowly lost the resulting by-election, this time to the Lib Dems' Sam Asplin by 13 votes, and Asplin made the ward safe in the 2015 ordinary election where his majority was 66–34.

Defending for the Liberal Democrats is Kevin Thomas. Christopher Clark is the Conservative candidate, and Marietta King stands for UKIP.

Result: LD 265 C 109 UKIP 33

Bondfields

Havant borough council, Hampshire; caused by the death of Conservative councillor Frida Edwards at the age of 55. Havant's first black councillor, first elected in 2010, Edwards had been the owner of the Hayling Ferry, which connects Hayling Island with Portsmouth, until it went bust last year.

Moving to the south coast and the town of Havant. Havant was greatly expanded in the 1960s by the building of a large council estate in conjunction with Portsmouth Corporation, and Bondfields, covering the West Leigh area, is the eastern of the wards covering that estate; 42.5% of the ward's households are still socially rented and there is a definite working-class profile, although unemployment is reduced by the presence in the ward of a large Pfizer pharmaceutical plant which packages over a million doses of vaccines and other injectable medicines every week. The ward's other main feature is West Leigh Park, the home ground of the non-league football team Havant and Waterlooville.

Despite the demographic profile this is by no means a safe Labour area. Bondfields ward has voted for all three major parties in the last eight years, with the Lib Dems gaining a seat from Labour in 2006 before losing it to the Tories in 2010. Edwards was re-elected in 2014, the last time this ward went to the polls, in a close three-way marginal result with 34% for the Tories, 28% for Labour and a surprising 27% for the Green Party—who had not previously fought the ward. To add to the confusion, the local county division (Bedhampton and Leigh Park) elected one UKIPper and one Tory in the 2013 county elections.

Defending for the Tories is Lance Quantrill, an electricity and gas meter reader and former Richmond upon Thames councillor (West Twickenham ward, 2002–6). Labour, who will be defending this ward in the ordinary elections in two months' time, have selected Tony Berry who has fought unwinnable wards in the last two Havant elections. The Greens are not standing again so it will be interesting to see where their votes go. Completing the ballot paper are the Lib Dems' Catherine Billam and UKIP's Geoff Whiffen.

Result: C 207 LD 187 Lab 148 UKIP 143

Parliamentary constituency: Havant
Hampshire county council division: Bedhampton and Leigh Park
May 2014 result C 401 Lab 340 Grn 318 LD 135
May 2012 result Lab 503 C 335 LD 134
May 2010 result C 882 LD 845 Lab 669 EDP 190
May 2008 result Lab 385 C 318 LD 257 UKIP 121 EDP 71
May 2006 result LD 608 Lab 479 C 228
June 2004 result Lab 555 C 293 LD 285
May 2002 result Lab 803/741 C 226/209 LD 187

Figure 33: Havant, Bondfields

Parliamentary constituency: North Dorset
Dorset county council division: Cranborne Chase
May 2015 result C 1133 UKIP 338 Grn 332
May 2011 result C unopposed
Oct 2008 by-election C 499 LD 442
May 2007 result C 582 LD 242 UKIP 63
May 2003 result C 530 LD 169

Figure 34: East Dorset, Alderholt

Alderholt

East Dorset district council; caused by the resignation of the Leader of the Council, Conservative councillor Ian Monks, who had fallen out with his council group and the Conservative MP for Christchurch over local government reorganistion. Monks had been in favour of subsuming his council into some larger unitary council area. He had been Leader since September 2013 and a councillor since winning a by-election in October 2008.

We finish this week in Alderholt, a large village on the Dorset/Hampshire border around fifteen miles north of Bournemouth. There's not really much to say about Alderholt either from a points of interest or a demographic point of view, although owner-occupation in the village is quite high.

The ward's previous election results aren't very interesting either, with Monks having a very safe seat; in 2011 he was returned unopposed, and last year he beat UKIP 63–19. The local county council seat (Cranborne Chase) is just as safe.

So this by-election is unlikely to be a problem for the Tory candidate Gina Logan, who chairs Alderholt parish council. She is up against Chris Archibold for Labour and David Tooke for the Lib Dems.

Result: C 384 LD 376 Lab 49

10th March 2016

Two by-elections on 10th March 2016:

Kendal Strickland and Fell

Cumbria county council; caused by the death of Liberal Democrat councillor John McCreesh at the age of 61. A former IT engineer with Royal Bank of Scotland and OpenOffice.org, McCreesh had entered politics in 2010 by being elected to Kendal town council, and had served on Cumbria county council since winning a by-election in May 2012. He was a member of the county council's cabinet, holding the Environment portfolio.

One of five county divisions covering all or part of the old county town of Westmorland, Kendal Strickland and Fell covers the north-western quarter of Kendal, running from the town centre along the Windermere Road. Kendal is the economic powerhouse for much of South Lakeland; although the eponymous K Shoes are no longer made here, there are still three competing mint cake companies, while tourism, paper and snuff are all important industries in the town. In this ward can be found the town's main shopping street together with the town hall, the district council offices and the old Westmorland County Hall, while visitors can also see the Quaker Tapestry, a Bayeux-style embroidery illustrating the history of Quakerism. The division's eastern boundary is the River Kent, and this area was badly affected by the Storm Desmond floods in Cumbria last December.

This division has existed in some form or other since the establishment of Cumbria county council in 1973, although the current boundaries date only from 2013. Originally this was a Conservative division, but it was gained by Labour in 1993 and has been Lib Dem only since 2009, when the Lib Dems put together an amazing 37-point swing from Labour to gain the seat with 72% of the vote. The reason for this strange electoral trajectory is one Timothy James Farron, a former county councillor for Milnthorpe who managed to mobilise virtually

Parliamentary constituency: Westmorland and Lonsdale
South Lakeland district council wards: Kendal Fell, Kendal Strickland, Kendal Underley
May 2013 result LD 980 Lab 506 C 191 UKIP 186 TUSC 15

Figure 35: Cumbria CC, Kendal Strickland and Fell

the entire Labour vote in Kendal to vote him into Parliament in 2005; he is now the leader of what remains of the Liberal Democrats, and his party still has a strong grip on his Westmorland powerbase. While Labour had recovered a bit by the most recent county election in 2013 the Lib Dems still had a handy lead of 52–27, and at the 2014 district council elections (the last time Kendal polled) the Lib Dems had 55% across the three wards covered by the division, with the Greens and Labour on 13% each. The division has a rather mixed social profile, with Kendal Fell ward (covering the town centre and points west) being quite middle-class, Kendal Underley ward relatively working-class (with notably high levels of part-time working) and Kendal Strickland somewhere in between.

The Lib Dems are taking no chances with the defence of this by-election by selecting Peter Thornton, the leader of South Lakeland district council (on which he represents his home Whinfell ward, a large rugged area north and east of Kendal). Labour have selected Virginia Branney, who came third in Kendal Fell ward in the 2014 district council elections. Also standing are Harry Taylor for the Tories, David Walker for UKIP and Andy Mason of the Green Party.

Result: LD 1067 Lab 307 C 172 Grn 128 UKIP 106

Maidenhead Riverside

Windsor and Maidenhead council; caused by the resignation of Conservative councillor Andrew Jenner. The Mayor of Windsor and Maidenhead in 2013–14, Jenner's resignation came for personal and family reasons: he has reportedly been in Australia since October. He had served as a councillor since 2011, and before then from 2000 to 2003 for the former St Mary's ward.

We move south from Kendal to another flood-prone ward. Maidenhead Riverside covers the area you might expect from the name: this is north-eastern Maidenhead, running north along the west bank of the Thames from the A 4 bridge. Maidenhead is a prosperous, middle-class town and this ward is typical of it, although there is a sizeable Asian element to the population and 16% of the residents were born outside the EU; ironic given that this is the Home Secretary's constituency.

There are several interesting electoral links between Kendal and Maidenhead. Both seats are represented in Parliament by MPs who fought the North West

Parliamentary constituency: Maidenhead
May 2015 result C 2167/2116/1995 LD 685/653/604 Lab 562/529 Grn 517 UKIP 499
May 2011 result C 1513/1506/1398 LD 864/749/738 Lab 240/231/184 Grn 214
May 2007 result LD 1094/1066/851 C 1048/998/990 Ind 448/270/270 Lab 126/73
May 2003 result LD 1374/1341/1294 C 877/784/723 Lab 117 Grn 86

Figure 36: Windsor and Maidenhead, Maidenhead Riverside

Durham constituency in 1992. Both seats were the subject of a Lib Dem "decapitation" strategy in 2005 in which the party went after senior Tory targets: Tim Collins was knocked out in Westmorland, but Theresa May survived in Maidenhead. The two towns' recent electoral histories have to be understood in the context of that decapitation strategy. Before 2003 this area was covered by St Mary's ward, which was safe Conservative until 1991 when the Lib Dems gained one out of three seats, following up with the other two gains in 1995. Andrew Jenner nicked one seat back for the Tories in 2000, but lost his seat in 2003, and it was those 2003 results which persuaded the local Lib Dems that Theresa May was vulnerable in the 2005 general election. In the end May remained *in situ* and it has been downhill for the Lib Dems in Maidenhead ever since; although the Lib Dems did hold on to two seats in 2007 partly thanks to Jenner falling out with the Tories and standing as an independent that year, the ward has had a full slate of Tory councillors again since 2011, and last year the Tory slate polled 49% to just 15% for the Lib Dems and 13% for Labour.

Defending for the Tories is Judith Diment, a Rotarian who is heavily involved in the campaign to eradicate polio. The Lib Dem candidate is Saghir Ahmed who is fighting the ward for the third time; he is the secretary of the Maidenhead Mosque. Labour have selected Nigel Smith, a former councillor in Ealing in west London (Victoria ward, 1986–90) and chartered surveyor. Also standing are George Chamberlaine of UKIP and independent candidate Jeff Lloyd.

Result: C 916 LD 397 Ind 162 Lab 144 UKIP 95

17th March 2016

Aylsham

Broadland district council, Norfolk; caused by the resignation of Conservative councillor Jo Cottingham who has moved away from the area. Cottingham was first elected for Aylsham ward in 2004 and was deputy leader of Broadland council until 2012; she resigned in 2013 following a complaint about her conduct, but returned to the council in 2015.

We start this week on the River Bure, nine miles north of Norwich. Aylsham was an important town in mediaeval times, a major centre for the linen and worsted industry. Thanks to its location about halfway between Norwich and Cromer, the town became a stop on the coaching route between them, and the coaching Black Boys Inn is one of the town's oldest buildings. Still a local market town and agricultural centre, Aylsham was one of the first British members of the Cittaslow or "Slow City" movement. As well as the town, the Aylsham ward includes the parishes of Burgh and Tuttington to the east, Marsham to the south, and Oulton and Blickling to the north; Blickling is a major tourist attraction thanks to the Jacobean stately home Blickling Hall, a former home of the Boleyn family.

As you might have guessed from the introduction, this by-election is a repeat of one previously fought in 2013. This is a closely-fought Lib Dem *vs* Conservative ward and neither party has held a full slate of councillors at any point since the ward was created in 2004. In 2004 the Lib Dems won two seats to the Tories' one; the Tories gained a second seat in 2007, but lost in the 2013 by-election after Cottingham's first resignation. The May 2015 result marked a return to the *status quo ante*, with Cottingham top of the poll and the Lib Dem by-election winner Steve Riley coming a poor sixth; in terms of votes the Tory slate had 32%, the Lib Dems 31% and a single Labour candidate polled 22%. The Lib Dems hold the local county council seat, increasing their majority over the Tories in 2013 partly thanks to UKIP splitting the Tory vote.

Parliamentary constituency: Broadland
Norfolk county council division: Aylsham
May 2015 result C 1588/1513/1125 LD 1521/1065/926 Lab 1082 UKIP 719/658
July 2013 by-election LD 688 C 501 Lab 181
May 2011 result C 1336/1253/1010 LD 1182/846/752 Lab 542/471 Grn 446
May 2007 result LD 1137/1067/1024 C 1124/1082/1027 Lab 246/230/199
June 2004 result LD 918/907/845 C 854/822/797 Lab 719/461/421

Figure 37: Broadland, Aylsham

This repeat by-election is a fight between the three main parties. Defending for the Tories is their losing candidate from 2015, Hal Turkmen, who is the only candidate to give an address in the ward. The Lib Dem by-election winner from 2013, Steve Riley, wants his seat back; he gives an address at RAF Coltishall. Completing the ballot paper is Labour's candidate Christopher Jenner.

Result: LD 829 C 654 Lab 243 [LD gain from C]

Ashby de la Launde and Cranwell

North Kesteven district council, Lincolnshire; caused by the resignation of Conservative councillor Geoffrey Whittle at the age of 92.

One of the oldest local councillors in England, Whittle may also have been the last local councillor to have served in the Second World War; he spent 19 years in the Royal Air Force followed by 26 years in the NAAFI, and was awarded the Distinguished Flying Medal for navigating his damaged and burning Lancaster back to Britain during a September 1943 operation over Hannover. On Whittle's final retirement from the Forces in 1988 he took up local politics, being elected to East Hampshire district council in 1991 and serving as its chairman in 2000–01. In 2007 Whittle transferred to North Kesteven district council, and one of his final public appearances was at the unveiling of the International Bomber Command Centre just outside Lincoln in October last year, along with 310 other surviving veterans of Bomber Command.

It's particularly appropriate that a person with such a strong association to the RAF as Geoffrey Whittle should have ended up as the local councillor for RAF Cranwell, the home of the Royal Air Force College which trains new RAF officers. Also based here are the Central Flying School, which trains RAF flying instructors, two of the RAF's three military bands and a number of Air Force headquarters and admin divisions. All this adds up to a population of around 3,000 for Cranwell as a whole, dwarfing the village of Ashby de la Launde and the ward's other five parishes, all of them villages off the A 15 Sleaford–Lincoln

Parliamentary constituency: Sleaford and North Hykeham
Lincolnshire county council division: Ruskington and Cranwell
May 2015 result C 1789/1504 Ind 871
May 2011 result 2 C unopposed
May 2007 result C 734/586 LD 570 BNP 297

Figure 38: North Kesteven, Ashby de la Launde and Cranwell

road; however, voter registration and turnout among the military tends to be very poor, so the villages will punch above their weight when it comes to the actual election.

Whittle only had a majority of 16 votes over the Lib Dems when was he first elected to this then new ward in 2007, but the Tory slate here was unopposed in 2011 and in 2015 crushed a single independent candidate 67–33. Things are less safe for the Tories at county council level, where this ward forms two-thirds of the Ruskington and Cranwell division which the Tories held in 2013, three points ahead of UKIP.

Interestingly, that independent candidate crushed by the Tory slate in 2015, Luke Mitchell, is the defending Conservative candidate for this by-election. He is up against Steve Clegg of the Lincolnshire Independents, a well-organised group who hold eight seats on the county council, and Clare Newton of the Lib Dems.

Result: Lincs Ind 457 C 296 LD 69 [Lincs Ind gain from C]

Hutton

Redcar and Cleveland council, North Yorkshire; caused by the death of Conservative councillor Peter Spencer at the age of 80. A qualified accountant, Spencer had been involved in local politics since the 1960s and had represented Hutton ward since 1999; in 2005–6 he was Mayor of Redcar and Cleveland.

The Teesside press reported this month about the recent death of Keith Heaviside of Great Ayton, who had climbed the nearby 1049-foot hill of Roseberry Topping 6,100 times during his life. Anybody who knows Teesside knows why he kept going up there—it's an attractive hill, a miniature Matterhorn, and a fantastic viewpoint. Its summit lies within the Hutton ward of Redcar and Cleveland, which is the western of the three wards covering the town of Guisborough. Traditionally a market town for the local area, Guisborough became prosperous during the Industrial Revolution as a centre of Cleveland ironstone mining; one of the people who became rich from that, ironfounder and Liberal MP Sir Joseph Pease, built the Gothic revival Hutton Hall here as his country seat. Today Guisborough is a commuter town for the Teesside conurbation,

Parliamentary constituency: Middlesbrough South and East Cleveland
May 2015 result C 1997/1963/1792 Lab 1071/950/856 LD 643
May 2011 result C 1562/1532/1367 Lab 940/717/622 LD 672
May 2007 result C 1646/1620/1478 Lab 681
May 2003 result C 1835/1816/1708 LD 847/791/767 Lab 613/605

Figure 39: Redcar and Cleveland, Hutton

with many of its residents working in the chemical industry and attracted by the town's location on the edge of the North York Moors national park.

With that commuter economic profile comes a Tory-voting electoral profile, and this ward is safe Conservative. At the most recent election in 2015 the Tory slate beat Labour here 54–29.

Defending for the Tories is Caroline Jackson, who is up against Labour's Ian Taylor, the Lib Dems' Graeme Kidd, UKIP's Harry Lilleker and independent George Tinsley.

Result: C 879 LD 536 Lab 368 UKIP 116 Ind 56

24th March 2016

Three by-elections on Thursday 24th March 2016:

Dalton;
and Moss Bay

Allerdale council, Cumbria; caused respectively by the resignation of Conservative councillor Colin Sharpe and the death of Labour councillor Bill Bacon. Bacon had served since 2007, Sharpe only since May 2015.

Steel, steel, steel. While Cumbria is probably most associated today with the Lake District and tourism, its coastal towns are surprisingly industrial. Barrow was built on shipbuilding, Whitehaven on mining, Workington on steel. Immediately to the south of Workington lies the Cumbrian iron ore field, which was known for its very-high-quality haematite; when Sir Henry Bessemer invented his new process for mass-producing mild steel, which required very-high-quality haematite, Workington was a natural place to produce it, and Moss Bay became the location of the first large-scale steelworks in the world, securing the town's future. Associated industries included British Steel's engineering arm, production of railway rails (Workington rails were said to hold the world together) and bus and train manufacture—all now gone, and a Google search for Moss Bay steel now results in a scrapyard. The collapse of the steel industry brought all the usual problems, and the location here of the British Cattle Movement Service (a BSE-era government agency) has done little to alleviate the town's depression, although the nuclear site at Sellafield does provide some employment for the area.

The present Moss Bay ward was created in 1999 and lies at the southern end of Workington, containing the Moss Bay and Salterbeck areas along the Solway Road. Its demographics are about as working-class as you can get: Moss Bay is in the top 100 wards in England and Wales for White British population (98.5%), social renting (53% of households), no qualifications (43%), semi-routine employment (24%) and routine employment (27%, this figure being the fifteenth highest in England and Wales). It is as Labour-voting as you might expect from that introduction, and in all five previous elections Labour have been guaranteed at least one of the three seats due to insufficient opposition candidates. The runner-up spot in all elections up to 2011 was held by independent candidate and former Workington town councillor John Bracken, who missed out by just two votes in 2007 but was more easily beaten 61–39 in 2011. Bracken gave up in 2015 and Labour were unopposed here that year. The last contested elections in the area were therefore the 2013 Cumbria county council elections, in which the ward was split between two divisions: Labour held off an independent candidate in Moss Bay and Moorclose division by just 20 votes, while Harrington division (which includes Salterbeck) is independent-held. The losing independent candidate for Moss Bay took the result to the election court, basically because he was unhappy that the returning officer did not offer him a recount, and lost there as well. From 2001 to 2009 the ward had the same boundaries as the former Moss Bay county division, and results for that county division are included in the table below.

Rather different is Dalton ward, which is a rural ward covering the Dean and Greysouthen (pronounced Greysoon) parishes to the south-west of Cockermouth. This was traditionally a coalmining area, but mining ceased in Greysouthen in 1886 and since then the area has become more traditionally rural and commuter, although just as White British as Moss Bay and with a notably large population of 45- to 64-year-olds (37%). Dalton ward was created in 2001 and has been won by the Tories at every election since then with the exception of 2011, when the incumbent Tory councillor stood for re-election as an independent and the Tories did not oppose him. Dalton ward was uncontested in 2003 and 2007, but had an unusually wide (for Allerdale) choice of candidates at the most recent election in 2015, the Tories winning with 48% to 21% for the Lib Dems and 16% for the Green Party. The Tories also hold the local county division (Cockermouth South).

The Dalton by-election has an even wider choice this time of five candidates. The defending Tory candidate is Mike Johnson, who lives in Maryport and fought a Maryport ward last year. Despite their second-place finish here last year the Lib Dems are not standing again; however, the Greens are in the shape of Felicity "Flic" Crowley, a retired schoolteacher from Cockermouth. The UKIP candidate is Eric Atkinson, one of two candidates to live in the ward; the other is Labour candidate Ross Hayman, the husband of the Workington MP Sue Hayman. Completing the ballot paper is independent candidate Marion Fitzgerald, an anti-windfarm campaigner who won a by-election to Allerdale council in June 2013 (from Boltons ward) but lost her seat last year.

Moss Bay has a three-strong field. The defending Labour candidate is Frank

Parliamentary constituency: Copeland
Cumbria county council division: Cockermouth South
May 2015 result C 510 LD 226 Grn 168 UKIP 153
May 2011 result Ind 456 Lab 167 Grn 97
May 2007 result C unopposed
November 2005 by-election C 220 Lab 83
May 2003 result C unopposed
May 1999 result C 305 Lab 122

Figure 40: Allerdale, Dalton

Parliamentary constituency: Workington
Cumbria county council division: Moss Bay and Moorclose (part); Harrington (part)
May 2015 result 3 Lab unopposed
May 2011 result Lab 620/596/572 Ind 395
June 2009 county council result Lab 411 Ind 277 BNP 130 LD 104 C 77
May 2007 result Lab 507/439/432 Ind 430
May 2005 county council result Lab 1172 C 316
May 2003 result Lab 613/531/485 Ind 228 LD 173
June 2001 county council result Lab 1555 LD 389
May 1999 result Lab 629/627/555 Ind 339

Figure 41: Allerdale, Moss Bay

Johnston, who controversially failed to be elected to Workington town council in 2015 due to a messup at the count, but does seem to be a town councillor now so presumably this has been sorted out. He is up against the Tories' Louise Donnelly and UKIP's Bob Hardon, a former Allerdale councillor (Stainburn ward, 2007–11) who fought Moss Bay as the Tory candidate in the 2005 county council elections.

Dalton result: Ind 133 Lab 118 C 93 UKIP 53 Grn 22 [Ind gain from C]
Moss Bay result: Lab 411 UKIP 189 C 33

St Peter's

Kettering council, Northamptonshire; caused by the resignation of Conservative councillor Terry Freer, who had served since 1976, in order to spend more time with his family.

St Peter's ward can be simply described as Kettering town west of the railway line. This is a generally residential ward, although a large amount of its area is taken up by Kettering General Hospital, the main acute hospital for northern Northamptonshire, and the Kettering Business Park whose proximity to the A14

Parliamentary constituency: Kettering
Northamptonshire county council division: Northall
May 2015 result C 1230/1038 Lab 768 UKIP 563 Grn 501
May 2011 result C 922/861 Lab 458/432 EDP 233
May 2007 result C 923/896 Lab 404/365

Figure 42: Kettering, St Peter's

bypass has attracted a number of distribution companies on which Kettering's economy now relies, the traditional boot and shoe industry having gone into decline. Also here is the out-of-town Kettering Conference Centre, the home of the English national volleyball teams. This is a middle-class part of town with notably high employment, the town's thriving distribution industry combining with some commuting to London which is only an hour away by train.

That middle-class profile creates a Tory-voting ward, and Terry Freer with his ward colleague Mary Malin had represented this ward continuously since 1983, rarely being seriously challenged. At the most recent election in 2015 they polled 40% to 25% for a single Labour candidate and 18% for a single UKIP candidate. County-level contests here are more interesting, as St Peter's ward is combined with the safe-Labour William Knibb ward to produce a key marginal which narrowly went Labour in the 2013 county elections.

Defending for the Conservatives is Ian Jelley, whose name regular readers of this column might recognise from the 4th June 2015 election which covered the postponed Kettering council poll in the key marginal Rothwell ward; in that election Jelley lost his seat to his running-mate Karl Sumpter, having served one term as ward councillor for Rothwell. He should have a safer berth here. Labour have selected the wonderfully-named Eugene Dalton-Ruark, a Unite member who works in the distribution industry. The UKIP candidate is Kevin Sills, a Desborough town councillor who was top of the English Democrats' East Midlands list in the 2014 Euro-elections. Also standing are Kirsty Berry of the Greens, the only returning candidate from the 2015 local election here, and Mel Gosliga of the Lib Dems.

Result: C 468 Lab 180 UKIP 149 Grn 93 LD 28

31st March 2016

Fifty years ago today Harold Wilson won his landslide, his biggest majority of 96 coming in the 1966 general election. These days Wilson's Labour successors aren't doing quite so well, and they have few prospects of a gain among this week's by-elections although they should hold a safe seat in the South Wales Valleys. The SNP should have little trouble holding a seat in one of the strongest pro-independence areas of Scotland, while in England the Tories and Lib Dems both have seats to defend in the Yorkshire Dales. But we start this week with an open seat in UKIP's strongest area of the country...

Clacton East

Essex county council; caused by the disqualification of Tendring First councillor Pierre Oxley, after he pleaded guilty to fraud by false representation and was sentenced to two years in prison, suspended for one year.

As the chairman of Clacton Sports Club, Oxley had forged invoices to persuade his own council, Sport England and the Big Lottery Fund to pay out grants of £95,000 for capital work which was never carried out, Oxley instead using the money to meet the club's running costs. The court heard that Oxley, a former cabinet member on Tendring district council, had not personally profited from the fraud.

It's after Easter, the weather's foul, so it must be time for a trip to the seaside. The Clacton East division covers the eastern end of the Clacton seafront, including the suburb of Holland-on-Sea, together with the Great Clacton area to the north of the town centre. This is retirement ghettoland and economically depressed, and as such perfect conditions to elect a UKIP MP, which Clacton as a whole has done twice in the last two years.

But dig down into this corner of Carswell-land and it all starts to get a bit more confusing. Pierre Oxley was first elected to Essex county council from this division in 2005, winning easily as a Conservative candidate. By 2009 he

Parliamentary constituency: Clacton
Tendring district council wards: Haven, St Bartholomews, St Marys, St Pauls
May 2013 result Tendring First 1528 C 1194 UKIP 1106 Lab 477 LD 77 Grn 70
June 2009 result C 2270 Tendring First 1361 BNP 626 Lab 508 Grn 325 LD 238
May 2005 result C 4330 Lab 2427 LD 1206 Grn 263 Community Representatives Party 207

Figure 43: Essex CC, Clacton East

had defected to Tendring First, one of several competing localist groups in this obscure corner of Essex, and stood for re-election under his new colours, losing 43–26 to the new Conservative candidate Linda Mead; a third-place 12% for the BNP that year was an early demonstration that there is a populist right-wing vote here.

In the 2013 county election Oxley improved his vote to 34%, and that was enough to regain his seat as the Conservative vote was split by UKIP, the Tories taking second place 27–25. That was, of course, before the Clacton by-election which resulted in Britain's first UKIP MP elected as such.

A look at the district council results for 2015 only serves to confuse the issue: of the four Tendring wards within the division, two are dominated by the Holland-on-Sea Residents Association, St Marys ward (covering Great Clacton) voted UKIP, and St Pauls ward (the part of the seafront nearest the town centre) split UKIP–Conservative in 2015, but the UKIP councillor for that ward has decided to emigrate and a by-election for that seat is pending.

Overall UKIP came in second to the Conservatives in the 2015 Tendring council elections. In an inspired move, the Tendring Conservatives offered UKIP a coalition deal and Tendring UKIP immediately split over whether to accept it. Those councillors who ended up in the administration were expelled from the UKIP group which has since suffered further defections and problems.

Although Tendring First still exist as an elected force (they have a district councillor) they are not defending this seat which is up for grabs. The Tory candidate Richard Bleach, whose Twitter profile disclaims "All views my own, normally moronic", stood for the district council last year. UKIP's candidate is Ben Smith, who gives an address some distance away in Brightlingsea. Labour have selected Christopher Bird, the Lib Dems Rain Welham-Cobb and the Holland-on-Sea Residents Association have entered the fray, selecting Colin Sargeant.

Result: Holland-on-Sea Residents Association 1781 UKIP 961 C 628 Lab 387 LD 49 [Holland-on-Sea Residents Association gain from Tendring First]

Parliamentary constituency: Skipton and Ripon
North Yorkshire county council division: Mid Craven
May 2015 result C 677 Lab 249 Grn 221
May 2011 result C 496 Lab 217 LD 93
May 2007 result C 409 LD 236
May 2003 result C 404 Ind 199
May 2002 result C unopposed
May 1999 result C 521 LD 158
May 1995 result C unopposed
May 1991 result C unopposed
May 1987 result C unopposed
May 1983 result C 471 All 321
May 1979 result C unopposed
May 1976 result Ind 446 C 362
May 1973 result Ind 468 C 288

Figure 44: Craven, Embsay-with-Eastby

Embsay-with-Eastby

Craven district council, North Yorkshire; caused by the death of Conservative councillor Andy Quinn at the age of 65. He had served as a councillor since 2002 and was chairman of Craven council in 2011–12. Away from the council he had taught carpentry and joinery at the former Keighley College following a career in the military, and right up to his death was working as a lecturer and a health and safety consultant.

England's other two by-elections this week both take place in the Yorkshire Dales. We start with Embsay, a village just to the north-east of Skipton best known for steam; it is the western terminus of the Embsay and Bolton Abbey Steam Railway, a preserved line linking the village with (surprisingly) Bolton Abbey. The ward also includes the village of Eastby and part of the Yorkshire Dales National Park.

Embsay-with-Eastby ward goes all the way back to the founding electoral arrangements of Craven district council in 1973 and only minor changes have been made since then (consequential on changes to the parish boundary). It has been held by the Tories continuously since 1979 and was regularly uncontested in the 1980s and 1990s. Quinn's final re-election came in May last year when he beat Labour 59–22. The Tories also hold the local county council seat (Mid Craven).

Defending for the Tories is Trevor Kent, a retired baker and electrician. He is opposed by an independent candidate, the Embsay-with-Eastby parish council chairman Brian Shuttleworth.

Result: Ind 466 C 117 [Ind gain from C]

Parliamentary constituency: Richmond (Yorkshire)
North Yorkshire county council division: Richmond
May 2015 result LD 673/610 C 411/409 Grn 298
May 2011 result LD 428/421 C 399/269 Ind 215
May 2007 result LD 493/480 C 465
May 2003 result LD 480/381 Richmondshire Independent Group 368 C 323

Figure 45: Richmondshire, Richmond Central

Richmond Central

Richmondshire district council, North Yorkshire; caused by the death of Liberal Democrat councillor John Robinson at the age of 63. A fireman for 32 years, he had served on Richmond town council since 2003 and Richmondshire district council since 2007; he was Mayor of Richmond in 2007–08.

For our second Dales by-election of the week we move from Airedale to Swaledale and the town of Richmond. Just outside the National Park, Richmond is a town whose greatest prosperity came before the Industrial Revolution as it was the marketplace for Swaledale wool and Arkengarthdale lead. Today its economy is based on tourism and the military, and despite its relative isolation the town is still important enough to give its name to a parliamentary constituency. The Richmond Central ward is rather misnamed; while it is the central of the three wards covering the town it only contains the eastern edge of the well-preserved town centre, which is mostly in Richmond West ward.

Richmond Central ward had elected two Liberal Democrats at every election this century but always with small majorities—John Robinson's majority was 15 votes in 2007 and 22 votes in 2011. In that context the Lib Dem performance at the most recent election in 2015—where they had 49% to 30% for the Tories and 22% for the Green Party—was impressive, although it remains to be seen how much of that was due to personalities in this tiny local government district. Going up to county level only serves to confuse the issue, as the town's former Lib Dem county councillor was easily re-elected in 2013 under the label "Save the Friarage Hospital" and was not opposed by the Lib Dems that time.

Defending for the Liberal Democrats is Philip Knowles, a marketing consultant who last year fought his home ward (Newsham with Eppleby) and got nowhere. The Tories have selected Nathalie Carter. Anna Jackson stands for the Green Party, and Richmondshire Independents candidate Lorraine Hodgson completes the ballot paper.

Result: Richmondshire Independent Group 236 LD 205 C 156 Grn 77 [Richmondshire Independent Group gain from LD]

Parliamentary and Assembly constituency: Merthyr Tydfil and Rhymney
May 2012 result Lab 698/543 PC 420 Ind 363
May 2008 result Lab 674/633 Ind 359
Sept 2007 by-election Lab 638 Ind 230
June 2004 result Lab 893/838 PC 273

Figure 46: Caerphilly, Moriah

Moriah

Caerphilly county borough council; caused by the death of Labour councillor Gina Bevan, who had served since 2012.

The last two electoral tests in Wales before the Welsh Assembly elections in May are two local by-elections in the County Borough of Caerphilly. We shall come back next week for the second one in Ynysddu division, but this week we are in Moriah, the south-eastern ward covering the town of Rhymney high up in the Valleys. Moriah ward is on the east side of the valley covering much of Rhymney proper together with Abertysswg to the south, a turn-of-the-century village brought into existence by its pit, as with much of the Valleys. With coalmining extinct in the Rhymney area all the usual problems exist, and Moriah is in the top 25 wards in England and Wales for long-term sickness and disability (14% of the workforce).

The ward is as safe Labour as you might expect for an ex-coalmining area, and at the most recent local elections in 2012 Labour had 47% here to 28% for Plaid and 25% for an independent.

Defending for Labour is David Harse, the leader of Rhymney town council. Despite their second place Plaid are not contesting this by-election; instead the opposition to Labour comes from independent candidates Peter Bailie and Mervyn Diggle, Nigel Godfrey who has somehow found ten people to nominate him as the Conservative candidate, and Ian Gorman of UKIP.

Result: Lab 464 Bailie 196 Diggle 89 UKIP 77 C 7 (seven)

Maryfield

Dundee city council; caused by the resignation of SNP councillor Craig Melville as a result of a row over alleged racist and Islamophobic texts. He had served since winning a by-election in March 2009.

This week's Scottish by-election comes from the centre of Dundee. Maryfield ward contains Dundee city centre, the Abertay University campus, the end of the Tay Road Bridge and the city's docks, running north from the docks to take

Parliamentary constituencies: Dundee East (part formerly in Baxter Park and East Port wards); Dundee West (part formerly in Stobswell and Tay Bridges wards)
Holyrood constituencies: Dundee City East (most of ward); Dundee City West (city centre)
May 2012 first preferences SNP 1746 Lab 1251 C 249 LD 126 TUSC 62
March 2009 by-election SNP 1550 Lab 1013 LD 354 C 224 SSP 52 Ind 35 Ind 28; after transfers SNP 1620 Lab 1052 LD 455
May 2007 first preferences SNP 2188 Lab 1511 LD 644 C 410 SSP 96 Solidarity 83

Figure 47: Dundee, Maryfield

in the area around Baxter and Stobsmuir Parks as far as the Kingsway.

Before PR was introduced most of this area was in just two single-member wards: Baxter Park (which was safe SNP) and East Port (an SNP/Labour marginal). With the introduction of PR in 2007 Maryfield became a three-seat ward with two safe seats for the SNP and one for Labour, the SNP winning the first preferences 51–36 at the most recent election in 2012.

With the general swing to the SNP since 2012 and the good Yes performance in Dundee in the referendum, it's hard to see beyond the SNP's Lynne Short for this by-election. Labour's Alan Cowan, a Unison and GMB activist, will be hoping for a gain which would cut the SNP majority on the city council to one. Also standing are James Clancy for the Tories, Christopher McIntyre for the Lib Dems, Stuart Fairweather for the Trade Unionist and Socialist Coalition, Jacob Ellis for the Greens, independent candidate Brian McLeod and UKIP's Calum Walker.

First preferences: SNP 1383 Lab 634 C 294 TUSC 142 Grn 116 LD 85 Ind 73 UKIP 69

After transfers: SNP 1389 Lab 637 C 304 TUSC 147 Grn 118 LD 87 Ind 81

7th April 2016

Three by-elections on 7th April 2016:

Pocklington Provincial

East Riding council; caused by the death of Conservative councillor Stephen Lane at the age of 67—or 12, given that he was born on 29th February. A farmer for more than 30 years, Lane had been an East Riding councillor since 2007, and had served as vice-chairman of the western area planning, and environment and regeneration scrutiny committees.

The East Riding has some peculiarly large wards for such a generally rural area, and some rather wonderfully-named wards of which Pocklington Provincial is perhaps the most baroque. Pocklington is a market town off the main road from York to Hull, lying at the foot of the Yorkshire Wolds. Its greatest prosperity came in the early Middle Ages; the Domesday survey found it was the largest settlement in Yorkshire after York, and the town thrived as a trading centre for wool. The Industrial Revolution passed the town by and Pocklington's economy is now based on agriculture (notably of rapeseed and sugar beet) and commuting to the major Yorkshire cities. The ward itself contains six other parishes to the west and north-west of the town along the east bank of the Derwent, running as far as Stamford Bridge, a village on the Derwent known for the September 1066 battle in which King Harald Hardrada of Norway was killed and the Viking Age in Britain came to a end.

Since 2003 this sprawling ward has traditionally been a fight between the Tories and an independent slate which won two of the ward's three seats in 2003. The independents lost their seats to the Tories in 2007 and gave up in 2015, when the Tories had 44% to 20% for Labour and 19% for a single UKIP candidate.

Defending for the Conservatives is Paul West, a Pocklington town councillor who was Mayor of Pocklington in 2014–15. Labour have gone for youth in selecting A-level student Lucie Spadone who, unusually for an S, is top of the

Parliamentary constituency: East Yorkshire
May 2015 result C 4542/4426/4118 Lab 2054/2040/1997 UKIP 2001 LD 1684
May 2011 result C 2228/2186/1933 East Yorks Ind 1698/1623/1356 Lab 940/766/678 LD 754
May 2007 result C 2243/2176/1916 Ind 1683/1243 LD 863/614 Lab 730/496
May 2003 result Ind 2261/2052/1171 C 1369/1123/1055 Lab 819 LD 542

Figure 48: East Riding, Pocklington Provincial

ballot paper. The UKIP candidate is Neil Tate who gives an address thirty miles away in Bridlington, and self-employed painter and decorator Andy Strangeway completes the ballot paper as an independent.

Result: Ind 1032 C 980 Lab 490 UKIP 215 [Ind gain from C]

Ynysddu

Caerphilly county borough council; caused by the resignation of Labour councillor Colin Durham, citing work commitments. He had served on Caerphilly council since 2012.

For the last electoral test in Wales before the fifth Welsh Assembly elections in 2016, we are in the lower Sirhowy Valley between Blackwood and Risca. Ynysddu itself is an early-nineteenth-century mining village typical of the Valleys, and probably best known as the home town of the singer Ricky Valance. Also within the division are the villages of Cwmfelinfach, the site of Nine Mile Point colliery which saw South Wales' first sit-in industrial action; the twentieth-century village of Wyllie; and Wattsville which gave its name to a Manic Street Preachers song. Overlooking the valley is the mountain of Mynyddislwyn which once gave its name to a parish covering the whole area as well as to one of the division's famous sons, the Welsh-language poet "Islwyn" (or William Thomas).

In more modern times Islwyn has given its name to a parliamentary con-stituency which sent Neil Kinnock to Parliament for many years. Ynysddu's election results have been more mixed with its two Noughties elections being close fights between Labour and Plaid that saw the parties split the division's two seats. Labour pulled away in the 2012 election to beat Plaid 61–33, both the outgoing councillors polling well ahead of their running-mates.

Defending for Labour is Wattsville resident Philippa Marsden, a member of the Unite national committee, vice-chair of the Islwyn branch of Labour and chair of Newport Harriers athletics club. Marina Pritchard, the second Plaid candidate here in 2012, tries again. Also standing are Matthew Kidner for the Lib Dems and Joe Smyth for UKIP.

Result: Lab 502 UKIP 180 PC 134 LD 36

Parliamentary and Assembly constituency: Islwyn
May 2012 result Lab 719/559 PC 382/224 C 70/57
May 2008 result Lab 572/474 PC 552/411 C 144/99 Ind 112
June 2004 result PC 598/538 Lab 598/576

Figure 49: Caerphilly, Ynysddu

Almond and Earn

Perth and Kinross council; caused by the death of Independent councillor Alan Jack at the age of 76. He had served on Perth and Kinross council since 1999, originally as a Conservative but his final re-election in 2012 was as an independent: that 2012 election was controversial as Jack's campaign went a long way over the election expenses limit, and he was fined £450.

For the last electoral test in Scotland before the fifth Scottish Parliament elections in 2016, we are in southern Perthshire in a large rural ward which sprawls immediately to the west and south of Perth. This is a ward of no towns; the largest settlement is probably Bridge of Earn, a commuter village to the south of Perth, while the Almond part of the ward includes the village of Methven, an away win for the English in 1306 in the days when England and Scotland faced off on the battlefield rather than the rugby field.

Alan Jack's base was in Bridge of Earn which he had represented (as part of the former Earn ward) since 1999. The present Almond and Earn ward was formed in 2007 and was based on the former Earn ward and Strathalmond ward (based on Methven and voting SNP in 2003) together with parts of the former wards of Abernethy and Glenfarg (C), Auchterarder Mid Earn (C), and Strathord and Logiealmond (LD). In the 2007 election to the new ward, the first election held under PR, the Tories tried for two out of three seats and polled 46%, but that was short of two quotas and SNP surplus transfers gave the final seat to the Lib Dems' George Hayton, who had previously been councillor for Kinross Town before being displaced by PR.

In 2012 Alan Jack stood for re-election as an independent, the SNP tried for two seats and the Tories settled for one: the first preferences split 41% to the SNP, 30% for the Tories and just 12% for Jack, but Jack capitalised on some less-than-perfect balancing by the SNP to pick up transfers from everybody else and win the final seat by just 14 votes, defeating the outgoing SNP councillor who lost her seat to her running-mate.

There is no defending independent candidate in this by-election so Alan Jack's seat is up for grabs. In pole position to pick it up, if the first preferences from 2012 are any guide, is the former SNP councillor Wilma Lumsden who

Parliamentary constituency: Ochil and South Perthshire
Holyrood constituency: Perthshire South and Kinross-shire
May 2012 first preferences SNP 1520 C 1112 Ind 444 Lab 369 LD 244
May 2007 first preferences C 2255 SNP 1790 LD 849

Figure 50: Perth and Kinross, Almond and Earn

lost her seat in 2012. The Tory candidate is Kathleen Baird, who previously represented part of this ward as councillor for Abernethy and Glenfarg from 2003; in 2007 she transferred to Kinross-shire ward but lost her seat in 2012. (The Lib Dem candidate whom Baird defeated in 2003 was Danus Skene, whom readers might recall as the losing SNP candidate in Orkney and Shetland last year, although that wasn't even the strangest aspect of his long electoral career.) Also standing are Dave Mackenzie for Labour, former councillor George Hayton for the Lib Dems and Denise Baykal of UKIP.

First preferences: C 1651 SNP 1327 Lab 219 LD 157 UKIP 77
UKIP eliminated: C 1681 SNP 1334 Lab 228 LD 163
LD eliminated: C 1720 SNP 1370 Lab 280 [C gain from Ind]

14th April 2016

Menheniot; and
Wadebridge West

*Cornwall council; caused respectively by the death of Bernie Ellis and the resigna-
tion of Scott Mann, both of whom were Conservative councillors. Ellis, who has
died at the age of 72, travelled the world as a surveyor in the mining industry
before returning to his native Cornwall where he became a farmer; he had been
in local government since 2003, originally on the former Caradon district council.
Mann, a former postman, has gone on to greater things having been elected last
year as the new MP for North Cornwall; his local government career started in
2007 on the former North Cornwall district council.*

We are in the final week of local by-elections before the May elections at which
the entire United Kingdom will go to the polls for the first of three occasions in
this Parliament:[8] whether it's for the Mayor and Assembly in London, the Police
and Crime Commissioners in England and Wales, the Scottish Parliament, the
Assemblies in Wales and Northern Ireland, or one of the 124 local councils which
are holding ordinary elections this year. Cornwall is not among that number,
which perhaps explains why two of its wards are going to the polls just three
weeks before the main event.

Taking the two by-elections in alphabetical order, we start in Menheniot, a
deeply rural division in south-eastern Cornwall which wraps around the town
of Liskeard on three sides. "Menenyut" is the largest parish within the ward,
located south-east of Liskeard and known for its fourteenth-century church; the
village also has its own station on the Cornish main line with occasional request
stops. To the south of Liskeard is St Keyne, home to a museum of fairground
organs and one of the most wonderfully-named railway stations on the network,
"St Keyne Wishing Well Halt" on the Looe Valley line. Also within the ward can

---

[8] Two occasions, as it happened; the Parliament did not last its full term.

be found the villages of St Pinnock, Trewiland and Quethiock.

Menheniot ward was created for the first unitary Cornwall council election in 2009; in the days of Caradon district council most of the area was within Dobwalls and District ward, with parts covered by Menheniot and St Ive, and St Germans wards; and at county level it was split between Liskeard, and Menheniot and St Germans county divisions. Before 2009 Ellis was the only Tory councillor from the area with all the other district and both the county councillors being Lib Dems, so Ellis did well to win the new ward easily in 2009. 2013 was a closer affair, with Ellis eventually winning with 38% of the vote to 31% for UKIP and 24% for the Lib Dems.

Moving north-west we come to Wadebridge, located at the lowest crossing-point of the River Camel. Once a port on the Camel estuary, Wadebridge is now a thriving market town which is a major centre for the local area and was formerly the home of North Cornwall district council. Wadebridge West is an urban ward covering the part of the town to the west of the River Allen.

Wadebridge town as a whole elected three independents in 2003 to North Cornwall council, but two of them lost their seats in 2007 to Scott Mann and the Lib Dem candidate Jeremy Rowe. (The remaining independent, Collin Brewer, had a good personal vote at the time but was later forced to resign from the council over controversial comments about disability.) Mann was easily elected in the new Wadebridge West in 2009 and in 2013 increased his majority over the Lib Dems to 66–24.

Defending for the Tories in Wadebridge West is Sally Dunn, a caseworker for Scott Mann. The Lib Dem candidate is Karen McHugh, an NHS radiographer; also standing are the local Chamber of Commerce chairman Adrian Jones for Labour, town councillor Amanda Pennington for the Green Party and independent candidate Helen Hyland.

In Menheniot the defending Tory candidate is Phil Seeva, a PR man who was Mayor of Liskeard in 2014–15. The UKIP candidate is Duncan Odgers, an electrical engineer who fought the Bristol suburban seat of Kingswood (where he works) in last year's general election but commutes there from his home in Looe. The Lib Dem candidate Charles Boney also has a Bristol connection, having been a Bristol city councillor in the 1980s and 1990s (originally elected as Labour) and fought Bristol West twice in general elections for the Lib Dems; he now runs a vineyard in St Keyne and chairs the South East Cornwall branch of the Lib Dems. Labour's Martin Menear and the Greens' Richard Sedgley complete the ballot paper.

Menheniot result: C 532 LD 472 UKIP 177 Lab 67 Grn 65

Wadebridge West result: LD 604 C 356 Lab 222 Ind 111 Grn 95 [LD gain from C]

Parliamentary constituency: South East Cornwall
May 2013 result C 549 UKIP 450 LD 352 Grn 93
June 2009 result C 746 LD 433 UKIP 389

Figure 51: Cornwall, Menheniot

Parliamentary constituency: North Cornwall
May 2013 result C 830 LD 308 Lab 129
June 2009 result C 761 LD 322 UKIP 188

Figure 52: Cornwall, Wadebridge West

Taunton Halcon

Taunton Deane district council; caused by the resignation of Liberal Democrat councillor Christopher Appleby in order to join the police. He had served only since May last year.

For a town some distance from the sea, it's curious that Taunton Halcon ward's largest employer is the UK Hydrographic Office, a government-owned organisation which produces Admiralty charts, tide tables and other nautical and astronomical publications for the benefit of the Royal Navy and sailors all over the world. The Hydrographic Office is in the most unfashionable part of Somerset's county town; Halcon ward lies in eastern Taunton running to the M 5 motorway at junction 25, and is a deprived working-class area. The ward has one of the highest rates of part-time working in England and Wales (19.3%) and its census figures also stick out for high levels of semi-routine work, low qualifications, social renting and children.

Most areas with this sort of demographic profile vote strongly Labour, but Labour are not organised here (their stronghold on Taunton Deane council is in the small but politically radical town of Wellington). Instead the Lib Dems perform strongly in Halcon and held all the district and county council seats until 2015 when the Tories nicked one of the three district council seats with a majority of just two votes; the votes last year were 40% for the Lib Dems, 36% for the Tories and 24% for the Green Party, although the Green share may be affected by the Tories not running a full slate and there being no Labour or UKIP candidates. The local Lib Dems seem to have trouble holding on to their district councillors: this is the third local by-election here caused by the resignation of a Lib Dem councillor in as many years.

Defending for the Lib Dems is twenty-something Chris Booth, the organiser for the Taunton Deane branch of the Lib Dems. The Tories have also gone for youth in reselecting Livvi Grant, their unsuccessful candidate here last year, who

Parliamentary constituency: Taunton Deane
Somerset county council division: Taunton East (most), Taunton South (part)
May 2015 result LD 1012/1001/889 C 891/851 Grn 605
Oct 2013 by-election LD 282 UKIP 172 C 165 Lab 146
May 2013 by-election LD 457 UKIP 295 C 179 Lab 159 Grn 78
May 2011 result LD 694/539/529 C 475 Lab 420
May 2007 result LD 804/709/679 C 372/354/326 Lab 154

Figure 53: Taunton Deane, Taunton Halcon

is a researcher for Taunton Deane's Tory MP Rebecca Pow. Continuing the young-candidate theme is Craig Rossiter, the youth officer for the local branch of the Green Party. Completing the ballot paper are Robert Bainbridge for UKIP and Kieran Canham for Labour.

Result: LD 389 C 222 Lab 133 UKIP 118 Grn 42

19th May 2016

St Helier

Merton council, South London; caused by the death of Labour councillor Maxi Martin. A councillor for St Helier ward since 1998, Martin had been Mayor of Merton in 2003–04 and had served since 2010 as Merton's cabinet member for children's services.

With the May elections now safely out of the way for another year, the local by-election calendar resumes this week with a single contest in South London. We're in the St Helier estate here, one of several 1930s "cottage" housing estates built on garden-city principles by the London County Council; in this case 40,000 people were homed by 1936 on what had previously been lavender fields between the village of Morden and the town of Carshalton. The estate straddles what is now the border between Merton and Sutton boroughs, and confusingly both boroughs have a St Helier ward; this is the Merton one. At the centre of this ward lies St Helier railway station, opened in 1930 to serve the estate on what is now the Sutton Loop line, while the northern end of the ward is better served by the London Underground's southernmost station, Morden on the Northern Line. The name of the estate, incidentally, is in honour of the former London County Council alderman Baroness St Helier.

The demographics of St Helier ward bear all the usual London hallmarks of a diverse population, and also show high levels of social renting and long-term unemployment. This is, as you might expect from those statistics, a working-class area and a safe Labour ward. In the 2014 local elections the Labour slate polled 59% of the vote here, with UKIP's 20% best of the rest despite their candidate, Andre Lampitt, having been disowned by the party during the campaign for racist tweets. Two weeks ago London was at the polls for the Mayor and Assembly elections; Sadiq Khan beat Zac Goldsmith in the ward's ballot boxes 45–33, while the list votes split 48% for Labour, 23% for the Tories and 10% for UKIP (the ward breakdowns for the Mayor and Assembly elections don't include postal

Parliamentary constituency: Mitcham and Morden
May 2014 result Lab 2010/1916/1673 UKIP 663 C 505/435/421 LD 203
May 2010 result Lab 2385/2206/2185 C 1373/1189/1161 LD 762 BNP 426/358
May 2006 result Lab 1347/1246/1196 C 974/931/778 BNP 599 Ind 583 LD 430
May 2002 result Lab 958/947/840 C 532/519/509 LD 324 BNP 302 Grn 192/178 UKIP 164
May 2016 GLA results (excludes postal voters)
Mayor: Lab 1222 C 907 UKIP 188 Grn 112 LD 94 Britain First 50 Respect 47 Women's Equality 35 CISTA 32 Ind 26 BNP 23 One Love 7
List: Lab 1335 C 638 UKIP 286 Grn 134 LD 114 Women's Equality 67 Britain First 63 Respect 45 CPA 33 BNP 26 Animal Welfare 23 House Party 10

Figure 54: Merton, St Helier

votes, so these figures aren't directly comparable with 2014).

Defending for Labour is Jerome Neil, a co-founder of a multimedia company and the only candidate to give a Morden address. Continuing the theme of UKIP candidates here with distinctly dubious tweets is Richard Hilton, a former Tory councillor (Lower Morden ward, 2010–14) who fought the local parliamentary seat in last year's general election and got into trouble then for a tweet saying that "Jihadi John" should have killed himself; he gives an address over 70 miles away in Newbury, Berkshire. Also standing are Susan Edwards for the Conservatives, Asif Ashraf for the Lib Dems and John Barraball for the Green Party.

Result: Lab 1436 C 282 UKIP 191 LD 59 Grn 55

26th May 2016

Northallerton (North Yorkshire County Council); and Northallerton South (Hambleton Council)

Both caused by the death of Conservative councillor Tony Hall at the age of 66. A structural engineer by trade, Hall had dedicated many years of his life to public service: four times Mayor of Northallerton, he joined Hambleton council in 1999 and served in its cabinet from 2006 to 2010; at the time of his death he was vice-chairman of Hambleton council. Hall had been a North Yorkshire county councillor since 2005, and was the county council's executive member for children's services from 2012 to 2015.

Northallerton has been in the news this week, as North Yorkshire county council—based in the town and its largest employer—approved a proposal to carry out fracking in the Ryedale district. It might seem strange that this small town—population around 16,000—is the county town of North Yorkshire rather than such larger and more important towns as Scarborough, Harrogate and York itself, but Northallerton became a major town in mediaeval times under the auspices of the Bishops of Durham. Later the town became a stopping point on the Great North Road from Edinburgh to London, and for the East Coast Main Line, and its location in the centre of the Vale of Mowbray—the wide valley between the Pennines and the North York Moors—meant it became a major agricultural and market centre. Agriculture and light industry still underpin Northallerton's economy today.

The population figure above is slightly misleading, as the Northallerton urban area has outgrown the parish boundary and much of the built-up area to the south of the railway station   including County Hall   is part of Romanby parish rather than Northallerton proper. Just to make things even more confusing, there have been recent ward boundary changes in Hambleton which means that the ward and county division boundaries don't match up. The Northallerton county division covers all of Northallerton parish except for the part of

Parliamentary constituency: Richmond (Yorkshire)
May 2013 result C 825 UKIP 489 Lab 259
June 2009 result C 1191 Lab 431
May 2005 result C 1311 Lab 983 Ind 925

Figure 55: North Yorkshire CC, Northallerton

May 2015 result C 1414/758 UKIP 762 Lab 739/654

Figure 56: Hambleton, Northallerton South

the town centre which was within Northallerton Broomfield ward before 2015; Northallerton South ward covers the town centre and east of the town but not the south of the built-up area so might better have been called Northallerton Central (as the predecessor ward was before 2015).

Tony Hall had a safe county council seat; at his the most recent re-election in 2013 he beat UKIP 52–31. On the district council, from 2003 to 2015 Hall shared representation of Northallerton Central ward with independent councillor John Coulson. In 2015 Coulson retired and Hall easily topped the poll in the new Northallerton South ward with an enormous personal vote, polling nearly twice as many votes as his running-mate Huw Jones who finished just four votes behind UKIP for the second seat; shares of the vote were 49% for the Conservatives, 26% for UKIP and 25% for Labour who weren't far off winning a seat themselves.

There's a large degree of crossover between the candidates in these two by-elections. Defending both seats for the Conservatives is Caroline Dickinson. UKIP have selected Stephen Place to contest the county by-election, while their candidate in the district poll is Northallerton town councillor Dave Robertson. The Labour candidate in by-elections is David Tickle. Completing the ballot papers are Chris Pearson of Yorkshire First, standing in both polls, and the Greens' Michael Chaloner who stands only in the county by-election.

Northallerton result: C 654 UKIP 278 Lab 233 Yorkshire First 131 Grn 58
Northallerton South result: C 541 Lab 232 UKIP 222 Yorkshire First 133

Stapenhill

East Staffordshire council; caused by the resignation of East Staffordshire's only UKIP councillor Steven Dyche after less than a year on the council. A former BNP candidate, Dyche was elected in 2015 and served on the council's audit and health scrutiny committees.

Stapenhill is essentially a suburb of Burton upon Trent located on the far

Parliamentary constituency: Burton
Staffordshire county council division: Burton Trent
May 2015 result Lab 1251/1235/865 UKIP 1228 C 963/819/714 Grn 488
May 2011 result Lab 913/891/825 C 584/487/474 BNP 342 Ind 269
May 2007 result Lab 962/707/685 BNP 592 C 473/468/400
Sept 2005 by-election Lab 624 C 268 UKIP 45
May 2003 result Lab 1436/1180/1139 C 585/569/518

Figure 57: East Staffordshire, Stapenhill

side of the river. Traditionally a brickmaking settlement, Stapenhill's character was greatly changed from the interwar period by the construction of large council estates by Burton Corporation, and this can still be seen in the ward's demography. Burton's economy being based on brewing and manufacturing, the ward has very high levels of routine and semi-routine working; however, unemployment is not particularly high.

This demographic mix creates a Labour ward with UKIP potential in the current political climate. The BNP had come second in Stapenhill in the 2007 election with 30% of the vote, demonstrating the potential for a radical right-wing party to break through here; and so it came to pass that UKIP did indeed break through in 2015, polling 31% with their single candidate Dyche; the Labour slate topped the poll with 32%, but their third candidate lagged a long way behind the two councillors seeking re-election. The Tories were third, not far behind on 25%. Labour have a lock on the local county division, the badly-drawn Burton Trent which was one of only three seats the party won in the 2009 Staffordshire county elections; in 2013 Labour had 47% to 29% for UKIP and 19% for the Tories.

Hoping that UKIP's toehold on East Staffordshire council won't go for a Burton is Sally Green, who was runner-up here in the 2013 county elections. Labour want their seat back, and have selected their Burton party secretary Craig Jones who is still in his twenties. The Tory candidate is Michael Teasel, secretary of the Staffordshire Regimental Association. Also standing are Thomas Hadley of the Green Party, Stapenhill parish councillor Susan Paxton—the only candidate to give an address in the ward—standing as an independent, and former district councillor Hugh Warner for the Liberal Democrats.

Result: Lab 536 UKIP 348 C 208 Ind 75 Grn 24 LD 18 [Lab gain from UKIP]

2nd June 2016

Seven by-elections on 2nd June 2016, one of which is unfinished business from May:

Oban North and Lorn

Argyll and Bute council; caused by the resignation of councillor Iain Macdonald due to pressure of business.

If once is happenstance, twice is coincidence and thrice is conspiracy, what's four times? Yes, this column has once again ended up in that beautiful corner of the Scottish Highlands which is served by the town of Oban, for the second by-election of the year, the fourth in two years, and the fifth in five years. This really is getting beyond a joke, people; as well as all this the electors of Oban North and Lorn have had to be dragged out for the independence referendum in September 2014, the Westminster election in 2015 and the Holyrood election last May, and will be back at the polls later this month for the EU membership referendum. Consequently, your columnist has described this ward several times before and this time will confine himself to saying that it covers the whole of Oban's hinterland together with the northern third of the town itself.

Iain Macdonald was first elected for this ward in 2012 as an independent candidate, gaining his seat from the Liberal Democrats and beating the second SNP candidate in the final round of counting by less than one vote; the other three seats for the ward went to two other independents and the leading SNP candidate.

The ward's high councillor attrition rate began to assert itself in the summer of 2014 with the resignation of the SNP councillor; with the party's Oban branch having suffered a damaging split (they had unexpectedly lost a by-election in the other Oban ward earlier in 2014) the defending SNP candidate was top in the first round of the resulting by-election but with less than 25% of the vote, and attracted so few transfers that they failed to make the final round of voting, in

Westminster constituency: Argyll and Bute
Holyrood constituency: Argyll and Bute
Feb 2016 by-election SNP 1113 C 609 Ind 608 Grn 300; after transfers SNP 1241 Ind 1048
Oct 2014 by-election SNP 1090 Ind 629 Lab 530 C 415; after transfers SNP 1199 Ind 1080
July 2014 by-election SNP 595 Ind 548 Lab 526 C 445 Ind 301; after transfers Ind 920 Lab 874
May 2012 result SNP 1117 Ind 807 Ind 421 Ind 361 C 332 Ind 222 LD 188 Ind 125 Ind 58
Nov 2011 by-election SNP 1081 C 505 Ind 438 LD 260 Ind 165; after transfers SNP 1179 C 591 Ind 561
May 2007 result SNP 1019 Ind 1005 Ind 779 LD 665 C 387 Ind 200 Ind 188 Ind 176 Ind 140

Figure 58: Argyll and Bute, Oban North and Lorn

which Labour candidate Kieron Green narrowly lost to independent candidate John MacGregor.

MacGregor died just two weeks later, and the SNP got their seat back in the ensuing by-election which was the first to be held after the independence referendum, narrowly beating independent candidate Stephanie Venner in the final round.

As stated, this is the second council by-election here of 2016, with long-serving independent Duncan MacIntyre having retired on health grounds at the start of the year; that by-election, held in February, saw a second SNP gain, beating Kieron Green (this time standing as an independent) 54–46 in the final round. With Iain Macdonald having defected to the SNP during his term, the Nationalists now had three seats out of four in the ward having had none following the July 2014 by-election. I hope you're keeping up at the back there, this is interesting stuff.

Macdonald's defection makes it rather difficult to identify a defending candidate for this by-election, particularly given the entertaining mess which is Argyll and Bute council which is nominally ruled by a galaxy of independent groups who appear to keep themselves busy by bickering with each other. Two veterans of all three by-elections return for a fourth tilt: independent candidate Kieron Green (who had the Labour nomination in both 2014 polls and was runner-up in February) and Conservative candidate Andrew Venner. The SNP candidate is Breege Smyth, who appears to be a radio producer from North Connel, and the Lib Dems are having a go this time by selecting Isle of Mull resident David Pollard.

First preferences: SNP 1055 Ind 711 C 591 LD 294
LD eliminated: SNP 1097 Ind 821 C 668
C eliminated: Ind 1160 SNP 1138

Denbigh Lower; and
Dyserth

Denbighshire council; caused respectively by the deaths of Independent councillor Richard Davies and Conservative councillor Peter Owen. Davies, a retired PE teacher, was in his first term having originally been elected in 2012. Owen's political career started on the former Rhuddlan district council although his service on the modern county council only goes back to 2004 (when he was elected as an independent).

Denbigh is an old town: it was a Marcher Lordship in the days when those were important things, and was largely destroyed twice in the fifteenth century (once in the Glyndwr revolt, once in the Wars of the Roses). It's basically for those historical reasons that we now have a county called Denbighshire, whose boundaries have never been particularly fit for purpose even in the current incarnation (the pre-1974 Denbighshire was an enormous sprawl which included Wrexham, and the current Denbighshire council is based in Ruthin). Today Denbigh is a sleepy market town overlooking the Vale of Clwyd midway between St Asaph and Ruthin, with its main industries (glove-making and the North Wales psychiatric hospital) having died a death in recent years. The Denbigh Lower ward (in Welsh, *Dinbych Isaf*) is one of three covering the town, being the eastern part of Denbigh running down to the River Clwyd.

Further down the Vale of Clwyd is Dyserth (*Diserth*), a village just south of Prestatyn tucked under the Clwydian Hills and whose economy was traditionally based on quarrying.

Both of these divisions lie within the marginal constituency of Vale of Clwyd, which is Tory at Westminster but was held by Labour in the Senedd election last month. However, Denbigh Lower's local politics, as in much of rural Wales, is dominated by independents, with independent councillor John Bartley having a large personal vote. Davies won his seat in 2012 gaining his seat from Plaid Cymru; he had a 74-vote majority over a third independent candidate. Previous results for Dyserth suggest that it may be a better indicator of the national picture, with Labour having cut Peter Owen's majority to 51–38 in the 2012 election; Owen had a larger majority in 2008 and was unopposed (as an independent candidate) in 2004.

Both by-elections have attracted a large field. In Denbigh Lower the defending independent candidate is Mark Young, a chocolatier, who was runner-up in 2012. Plaid have selected Rhys Thomas. Also standing are Gwyn Williams for the Lib Dems, Lara Pritchard for the Tories and John McGuire for Labour. Dyserth will be defended for the Tories by community councillor Andy Hughes,

Parliamentary and Assembly constituency: Vale of Clwyd
May 2012 result Ind 977/579/505/204 PC 386 LD 138 C 1118
May 2008 result Ind 993 PC 664 C 471 Lab 261
June 2004 result PC 678 Ind 664/587/477

Figure 59: Denbighshire, Denbigh Lower

Parliamentary and Assembly constituency: Vale of Clwyd
May 2012 result C 369 Lab 275 LD 84
May 2008 result C 327 Ind 181 Lab 87 LD 58 PC 56
June 2004 result Ind unopposed

Figure 60: Denbighshire, Dyserth

who was the independent runner-up here in 2008; Labour have selected welfare rights manager Richard Jones-Abbas, and also standing are Heather Prydderch for the Lib Dems, independent community councillor Dave Parry, independent David Williams and Plaid's Janice Williams.

Denbigh Lower result: Ind 389 PC 315 C 159 Lab 108 LD 101

Dyserth result: David Williams 177 Parry 159 C 140 LD 107 Lab 87 PC 21 [Ind gain from C]

Aldershot Park

Rushmoor borough council, Hampshire; postponed from 5th May due to the death of the Conservative candidate Ron Hughes. Hughes was an outgoing councillor with ten years' service in Manor Park ward, and had served as the council's cabinet minister for housing; he had been deselected in Manor Park and had found a new berth in this ward.

The large May elections usually generate various pieces of unfinished business; with tens of thousands of candidates standing, there are usually a few candidates who sadly die between their nomination being submitted and polling day. That causes the election in the ward to be postponed to a later date with nominations reopened. Aldershot Park is the only ward to suffer this fate this year, which is an unusually low figure for even-numbered May elections (odd-numbered years are on different scales and not really comparable).

Aldershot Park is a working class ward covering the south eastern corner of the army town of Aldershot. I say "working-class", but the town's Army presence makes interpreting the census statistics fairly difficult; there are high rates of social renting and "lower supervisory, technical" work, but employment rates are unusually high for such an area. There is also a fast-growing Buddhist

Parliamentary constituency: Aldershot
Hampshire county council division: Aldershot East (most)
May 2015 result C 1153 Lab 1065 UKIP 840
May 2014 result Lab 877 C 693
May 2012 result Lab 811/754/677 C 451/406/401 LD 202

Figure 61: Rushmoor, Aldershot Park

population in the ward, an effect of Gurkha immigration in recent years which has been concentrated in the Aldershot area.

Rushmoor's wards were redrawn in 2012 but this ward had only minor changes from the Heron Wood ward which existed from 1979 to 2012. For much of this period Heron Wood was a three-way marginal, but Labour only lost the ward twice: to the Lib Dems in 2004 and 2008 (in both cases Labour won the seats back in by-elections). The Lib Dem challenge disappeared in the Coalition years, but the Tory vote has remained strong and they gained a seat from Labour in Aldershot Park in 2015; the shares of the vote last year were 38% for the Tories, 35% for Labour and 27% for UKIP who fought the ward for the first time. At county level almost all of the ward is within the Aldershot East division, a marginal which Labour gained from the Tories in 2013.

The outgoing Labour councillor Mike Roberts, a veteran councillor who has represented this ward and Heron Wood since 1979, is standing for re-election to what would be his eleventh term of office. The replacement Tory candidate, following Ron Hughes' death, is Matthew Collins. Jeffery Boxall is the UKIP candidate, and the Green Party—who weren't on the original candidate list— have entered the fray with Lucy Perrin.

Result: Lab 525 UKIP 314 C 264 Grn 41

Barking and Somersham

Mid Suffolk district council; caused by the resignation of Conservative councillor David Card, who had served since 2015.

This is a rural ward covering seven parishes in central Suffolk, a few miles north-west of Ipswich. Despite the order of names, the largest of these (with 597 electors) is Somersham, although Barking is perhaps more accessible with Somersham being in the middle of nowhere and reachable only by country lanes. Also within the ward is a small corner of the town of Needham Market. The ward has a old age profile and a large retired population.

If you thought that this bucolic description meant a sleepy Tory ward, you'd be wrong: 2015 was the first time there had been a Tory councillor for this area.

Parliamentary constituency: Central Suffolk and North Ipswich
Suffolk county council division: Bosmere
May 2015 result C 542 Suffolk Together 411 UKIP 194 LD 154
May 2011 result Suffolk Together 493 C 310 LD 121
May 2007 result Suffolk Together 362 C 286 LD 266
Oct 2004 by-election LD 281 C 183 UKIP 86
May 2003 result LD unopposed

Figure 62: Mid Suffolk, Barking and Somersham

The old Barking ward was independent-held up to 1995, and then Lib Dem from 1995 to 2007 (several elections before 2007 were uncontested). In 2007 the ward was gained by a localist party which is in contention for the title of "most risible party name on the register", being called "Suffolk Together". It took the general election turnout in 2015 for the Tories to knock out the Suffolk Together councillor; the result last year was 42% for the Conservatives, 32% for Suffolk Together and 15% for UKIP. The Tories do not hold the local county division (Bosmere), which has been Lib Dem for some years.

Defending for the Tories is a young candidate, Jemma Lynch of Needham Market. Neither Suffolk Together nor UKIP have returned to the fray, so completing the ballot paper are Lib Dem Mark Valladares, Anne Killett of the Green Party and Labour's William Marsburg.

Result: Grn 212 C 210 Lab 154 LD 38 [Grn gain from C]

Lewes Bridge

Lewes district council; caused by the resignation of Liberal Democrat councillor Daisy Cooper who had served only since 2015.

Here we have an old and rather beautiful town, located within the South Downs National Park at the point where the River Ouse cuts through the South Downs. Tourism, together with administration (East Sussex county council and Sussex Police Authority are based here) and manufacturing are major employers, with tourists drawn not just by the town's old buildings and beautiful location but also by the Lewes Bonfire, a celebration of Guy Fawkes Night in which well-known figures are burned in effigy. Fawkes himself and Pope Paul V are always on the bill, but there are also more up-to-date characters—recent Lewes Bonfires have burned Osama bin Laden, Sepp Blatter, Jeremy Clarkson and David Cameron (complete with a pig). Despite or perhaps because of this, Lewes Bridge ward has a high proportion of people claiming no religious affiliation. The Bridge ward, one of three covering the town, covers part of the town centre

Parliamentary constituency: Lewes
East Sussex county council division: Ringmer and Lewes Bridge
May 2015 result LD 905/641 Grn 677/410 Ind 540 Lab 529/447 C 395/359 UKIP 240
May 2011 result LD 735/620 Grn 576/424 Lab 324/318 C 280/255
May 2007 result LD 687/532 Ind 402 Seagulls Party 262 Grn 249/246 C 203/201 Lab 113
May 2003 result LD 585/583 C 239/212 Grn 196/192 Lab 160/159

Figure 63: Lewes, Lewes Bridge

and railway station together with the suburbs of Cliffe and South Malling on the east bank of the Ouse.

The local Lib Dems are no doubt still smarting from the 2015 election in which they lost not only the Lewes parliamentary constituency but also one of the two seats in Lewes Bridge ward, which was gained by the Green Party. In a fractured 2015 result, the Lib Dem slate had 28% of the vote in Lewes Bridge, the Greens 21%, an independent 16%, Labour 16% and the Tories 12%. The Lib Dems do still hold the local county division (Ringmer and Lewes Bridge).

Defending for the Lib Dems is Will Elliott, who represents the ward on Lewes town council. The Greens have selected Johnny Denis, a business management consultant. The Labour candidate is acupuncturist Richard Hurn. Completing the ballot paper is Roy Burman for the Conservatives.

Result: LD 543 Grn 345 Lab 212 C 117

Sherborne Rural

Dorset county council; caused by the resignation of Conservative councillor Michael Bevan who had served since 2009.

Large rural division time: Sherborne Rural county division covers no fewer than forty parishes completely surrounding the town of Sherborne. The largest centre of population is Yetminster, a stop on the Heart of Wessex railway line about four miles south of Sherborne, whose population just creeps above 1,000.

Sherborne Rural has been a tight Tory–Lib Dem battle at county level for many years: Bevan gained it from the Lib Dems in 2009 and held it in 2013 with 37% of the vote, to 35% for the Lib Dems and 22% for UKIP. Recent boundary changes in West Dorset mean that the wards and county divisions no longer match up, but in the wards wholly or partly in the division the Tories hold five council seats and the Lib Dems one (in Yetminster and Cam Vale ward).

Defending for the Tories is Mary Penfold (oh crumbs!), district councillor for Frome Valley ward which covers part of the division. The Lib Dems have selected Matthew Hall, a district and town councillor in Sherborne. UKIP have

Parliamentary constituency: West Dorset
West Dorset district council wards: Beaminster (part), Frome Valley (part), Queen Thorne,
Yetminster and Cam Vale
May 2013 result C 1258 LD 1168 UKIP 746 Grn 129 Lab 85
June 2009 result C 2080 LD 1871 Lab 112
May 2005 result LD 2993 C 2809

Figure 64: Dorset CC, Sherborne Rural

not returned to the fray, so the Labour candidate Geoff Freeman completes the
ballot paper.

Result: LD 1287 C 1212 Lab 95 [LD gain from C]

9th June 2016

The four local by-elections on 9th June 2016 are all in urban wards and fall into two pairs. Two, appropriately given the pre-eminent political topic of the moment, are in towns in the East of England where UKIP have done well in recent years. The other pair are two wards in south London, one of which had an unusual distinction in last month's Mayor and Assembly elections. Read on...

Basildon Laindon Park and Fryerns

Essex county council; caused by the death of Labour councillor William Archibald at the age of 84. Archibald was a veteran of local government who started his career in 1963 on the former Basildon Urban District Council, and was leader of the UDC from 1971 to 1973 and its last chairman in 1973–74; in 1973 he was elected to Essex county council, serving as its chairman in 1986–87, and had served since then with the exception of the 2009–13 term. He returned to Basildon district council in 2002 and served two further terms of office (2002–4 and 2010–14). Away from local government he was an electrician and a passionate supporter of vocational education.

For the first of this week's four local by-elections, all of which are in England, we travel to Basildon, an Essex new town which will forever be etched in psephologsts' hearts thanks to its early declaration in the 1992 general election, indicating that the Major government was on course for re-election. Like many New Towns, Basildon has shown some instability in its voting patterns over the years, and a series of swingy elections in recent years (UKIP did well in 2014, the Tories in 2015 and Labour in 2016) have left Labour as the largest party on Basildon council but the Tories, with half as many seats and being the third largest group, running a minority administration with the support of UKIP and two UKIP splinter groups.

This two-seat county division, which covers the northern third of Basildon between the A 127 road and the railway line, takes in some of Labour's best wards

Parliamentary constituency: Basildon and Billericay
Basildon district council wards: Fryerns, Laindon Park, Lee Chapel North
May 2013 result Lab 2277/1980 UKIP 2175/1684 C 958/784 LD 215/187 NF 171 Grn
138/116 Ind 119 TUSC 73
June 2009 result C 2349/2282 Lab 2094/1686 BNP 1612/1608 LD 1240/1215
May 2005 result Lab 6707/5349 C 4107/3904 LD 1903/1539 Grn 1177

Figure 65: Essex CC, Basildon Laindon Park and Fryerns

in the town—Fryerns and Lee Chapel North voted Labour even during the nadir years of the last government while the Tories do best in Laindon Park ward—but that didn't stop Labour losing both seats in the county division in the calamitous county elections of 2009, the Tories gaining the division with just 32% of the vote to 29% for Labour, 22% for the BNP (remember them?) and 17% for the Lib Dems. Labour staged a recovery over the 2009–13 term, gaining Laindon Park ward on the district council in 2012, but then UKIP got organised in Basildon: in the 2013 county elections Labour gained one of the Tory seats, but UKIP gained the other; shares of the vote were 37% for the Labour slate, 36% for UKIP and 16% for the Conservatives. Since 2013 we've had a full cycle of elections to Basildon district council; UKIP carried all three wards in 2014, 2015 was back to the *status quo ante*, while in May this year UKIP gained Laindon Park from Labour, who held Fryerns and recovered a by-election loss from UKIP in Lee Chapel North; shares of the vote across the division in May were 39% for Labour, 36% for UKIP and 22% for the Conservatives.

Defending for Labour is Gavin Callaghan, the leader of the Labour group on the district council and re-elected for another four years in Pitsea North West ward in May. The UKIP candidate is Frank Ferguson, UKIP's district councillor for Lee Chapel North ward since 2014. The Conservatives have selected Gary Maylin, a mature student studying sociology at the LSE who came second in Laindon Park ward in May's district elections. Completing the ballot paper is Philip Rackley of the Green Party.

Result: UKIP 2034 Lab 1600 C 878 Grn 264 [UKIP gain from Lab]

South

North East Lincolnshire council; caused by the resignation of Labour councillor
Chris Stanland, who had served since 2015.

We travel north to what is still called, for historical reasons, the South ward of Grimsby although that name is no longer geographically accurate. Grimsby has been dealt a rough hand by geography, history and culture: although the

Grimsby–Cleethorpes conurbation is one of the largest urban centres in Lincolnshire, it's a long way from anywhere else of importance; the major local industry (fishing) was destroyed by the Cod Wars with Iceland; and the town has recently suffered the indignity of having Sacha Baron Cohen satirise it in a film (which was filmed not here but in Tilbury, Essex). Recent media which *was* filmed here included the 2006 film *This Is England*, a story of young skinheads set in 1983, and the second series of *Skint*, a Channel 4 reality TV series following the long-term unemployed.

As you might have guessed from those last two items, this is not a rich town. South ward in particular, a tract of housing off the A 46 Laceby Road, has all the demographic hallmarks of a sink council estate: unemployment is extremely high (nearly 11% at the time of the 2011 census, putting the ward in the top 40 in England and Wales), those jobs that exist are all at the bottom end of the social scale, 41% of the workforce have no qualifications, 40% of the households are socially rented, and 25% of the population are under 16.

Awful though those indicators are, this isn't even the worst ward in Grimsby for multiple deprivation.

Put all this together with the current political climate, and you can see why UKIP made the Great Grimsby constituency a top target for the 2015 general election; they had a track record in the town's local elections, the long-serving Austin Mitchell, who had succeeded Tony Crosland in a 1977 by-election, was retiring, and UKIP had recruited as their parliamentary candidate the former Tory who had lost to Mitchell by just 714 votes in the 2010 election. In fact UKIP finished third and Labour increased both their majority and their share of the vote. That good 2015 result was reflected in South ward, which Labour comfortably held after having lost the ward to UKIP by 30 votes in 2014; the UKIP councillor elected that year was a Labour defector, re-elected under her new colours. Created on its current boundaries in 2003, South ward was a Labour/Lib Dem marginal in the Blair and Brown years, the Lib Dems being helped in the Blair years by an electoral pact with the Tories who didn't stand in the ward. The ordinary election results in May suggest that UKIP have peaked in Grimsby, Labour beating them in South ward 54–28.

Defending for Labour is Janet Goodwin, who finished a close second in May in the normally-Tory Scartho ward, immediately to the south of South ward. The UKIP candidate is Stephen Whittingham, chairman of the party's Great Grimsby branch. Also standing are Paul Batson for the Tories, Val O'Flynn for the Trade Unionist and Socialist Coalition and Loyd Emmerson for the Green Party.

Result: Lab 758 UKIP 462 C 312 Grn 40 TUC 26

Parliamentary constituency: Great Grimsby
May 2016 result Lab 913 UKIP 483 C 251 TUSC 54
May 2015 result Lab 1681 UKIP 1278 C 742 Lab 172 TUSC 83
May 2014 result UKIP 690 Lab 660 Ind 238 C 200 LD 97 Grn 52
May 2012 result Lab 968 UKIP 421 LD 264 Ind 198
May 2011 result Lab 1411 LD 496 UKIP 456
May 2008 result LD 689 Lab 563 C 338 Ind 175 Ind 135 Ind 68
May 2007 result Lab 763 LD 735 C 314
May 2006 result LD 770 Lab 675 Ind 529
June 2004 result LD 929 Lab 824 Ind 507 Ind 249
May 2003 result Lab 719/562/516 LD 714 Ind 656/613/574

Figure 66: North East Lincolnshire, South

Parliamentary constituency: Dulwich and West Norwood
May 2014 result Lab 2242/2202/2183 C 436/434/423 Grn 364/317/257 LD 164/161/133
UKIP 142
May 2010 result Lab 2670/2597/2588 C 1654/1611/1585 LD 1055/1016/852 Grn 462/347/332
May 2006 result C 1402/1352/1283 Lab 915/838/790 Grn 631 LD 521/408/368
May 2002 result C 1579/1571//1509 Lab 1034/1001/899 Grn 251/182/178 LD 237/180/165
May 2016 GLA results (excludes postal voters)
Mayor: Lab 2102 C 622 Grn 376 LD 153 Women's Equality 118 UKIP 62 Cannabis is
Safer than Alcohol 36 Britain First 28 Respect 24 BNP 11 One Love 9 Ind 6
List: Lab 1795 Grn 581 C 522 LD 209 Women's Equality 206 UKIP 107 CPA 39 Animal
Welfare 29 Britain First 29 Respect 26 House Party 17 BNP 13

Figure 67: Lambeth, Gipsy Hill

Gipsy Hill

Lambeth borough council, South London; caused by the death of Labour councillor Niranjan Francis at the age of 59. A former Merchant Navy captain who ran the Gipsy Hill post office and a Kent care home, Francis had served on Lambeth council since 2010.

We move into London for the second half of this week's previews. Gipsy Hill is the south-eastern corner of the London Borough of Lambeth, covering most of the West Norwood area and served by Gipsy Hill and West Norwood stations on the Crystal Palace line. West Norwood was traditionally rather middle-class, and Gipsy Hill was a safe Conservative ward as recently as 2006, but rapid demographic change in recent years has turned the ward into a Labour fortress: in the 2011 census 29% of the population was black and 9.3% (the fifth-highest figure in England and Wales) were mixed-race, and social renting and unemployment are fairly high.

In the 2014 local elections the Labour slate beat the Tories 67–13, which is an amazing swing of 34% since the 2006 elections; at the GLA elections in May Sadiq Khan beat Zac Goldsmith 59–18 in the ward's ballot boxes, while the list ballot gave Labour 50% with the Greens second on 16% and the Tories third on 15%.

Defending for Labour is Luke Murphy, an "irregular hiker" according to his Twitter who gives an address in Brixton. The Tory candidate is Leslie Maruziva, a black Zimbabwean working in regeneration. Also standing are Pete Elliott for the Green Party, Rose Jesse for the Lib Dems, Elizabeth Jones for UKIP, independent candidate Robin Lambert and Steve Nally of the Trade Unionist and Socialist Coalition.

Result: Lab 1220 Grn 1184 C 210 LD 84 UKIP 73 Ind 24 TUSC 19

Surrey Docks

Southwark borough council, South London; caused by the resignation of Liberal Democrat councillor Lisa Rajan, who is moving to Manchester where her husband has a new job. She had served since 2002.

Low-lying, marshy and close to the river, unsuitable for farming but close to the City and downstream of London Bridge, the Rotherhithe peninsula was a natural location for dockbuilding. In 1696 the Howland family, the local landowners, had built here the largest dock of its kind in the world, able to accommodate 120 sailing ships. The dock became successful as a base for Arctic whalers, eventually being renamed Greenland Dock in their honour, and expansion over the years led to the peninsula being covered by nine docks at the time of the Second World War. Damage caused by wartime bombing and the advent of containerisation, which the Surrey Docks couldn't handle, led to the docks closing in 1969 and most of the docks themselves were filled in.

From the Thatcher years the derelict Surrey Docks area was extensively redeveloped under the auspices of the London Docklands Development Corporation, with a huge number of yuppie flats for young professionals springing up together with some new industry (including the printworks for the *Daily Mail* and *Evening Standard*), while the remaining docks were turned into London's largest marina. And so it came to pass that there is now enough population in the Surrey Docks to form an electoral ward, although the ward name is now an anachronism, "Surrey Quays" (as in the East London Line station which serves the ward) being more generally applied to the area nowadays.

The yuppie flats have left their mark on the ward's demographics: Surrey Docks ward is in the top 100 in England and Wales for population aged 30–44 (33%), White non-British (23%), Buddhism (1.75%), degree-level qualifications

Parliamentary constituency: Bermondsey and Old Southwark
May 2014 result LD 1039/837/780 Lab 712/697/632 C 655/562/548 UKIP 502/468 Grn 486/360
May 2010 result LD 2385/2310/1986 C 1463/1331/1259 Lab 942/902/788 Grn 445 Ind 185
May 2006 result LD 1100/1037/1009 C 735/702/665 Lab 441/384/340 Grn 334/244
May 2002 result LD 1034/1012/966 C 351/339/311 Lab 268/210/189 Grn 124/84/76
May 2016 GLA results (excludes postal voters)
Mayor: Lab 1140 C 901 LD 538 Grn 267 UKIP 108 Women's Equality 65 Respect 27 Cannabis is Safer than Alcohol 17 Britain First 16 BNP 11 Ind 10 One Love 6
List: Lab 857 LD 752 C 668 Grn 398 UKIP 204 Women's Equality 122 CPA 36 Animal Welfare 31 Britain First 29 Respect 20 BNP 15 House Party 12

Figure 68: Southwark, Surrey Docks

(56%) and full-time employment (55%), just outside the top 100 for population born in other EU-15 countries (7%) and over half the workforce are at management or professional level. Politically this adds up to a Lib Dem ward, particularly given that Simon Hughes was the local MP until last year. At the most recent local elections in 2014 the Lib Dem slate topped the poll with 31% of the vote, Labour were second on 21%, the Tories (who were the main challengers in the ward through the Noughties) fell to 19% and UKIP had one of their better figures in inner London with 15%.

In the GLA elections in May this was the strongest Lib Dem ward in London on all three ballots, and the Lib Dems actually carried the ward (by 9 votes over Labour) on the constituency ballot—not something you see very often in a GLA election. Sadiq Khan led here in the mayoral ballot with 37% to 29% for Zac Goldsmith and 17% for the Lib Dems' Caroline Pidgeon, while the list vote had 27% for Labour to 24% for the Lib Dems, 21% for the Tories and 13% for the Greens.

So the Lib Dems still appear to be in relatively good shape in this corner of London. Their defending candidate is Dan Whitehead, a solicitor whose manifesto includes more buses for Surrey Quays and a footbridge over the river to connect the ward with the Isle of Dogs. The Labour candidate is Will Holmes, a trade union official and charity trustee. The Tories have selected Craig Cox, a strategy consultant advising government departments who has local government experience as a councillor in Broxtowe, Nottinghamshire in 2011–12 (for the by-election-prone Toton and Chilwell Meadows ward, for which see this column *passim*). Toby Prescott is the UKIP candidate, fighting his third Southwark by-election of the year. Completing an all-male ballot paper are Colin Boyle of the Green Party and John Hellings, an independent candidate who was on the UKIP slate in 2014, an independent candidate in 2010 and on the Labour slate in 2006.

Result: LD 1523 Lab 619 C 380 Grn 218 UKIP 187 Ind 10

16th June 2016

Valley Hill

King's Lynn and West Norfolk council; caused by the death of long-serving independent councillor Mike Tilbury at the age of 80. One of the original King's Lynn and West Norfolk councillors from 1973, Tilbury had served as both Leader and Mayor of the council, and it was largely his efforts which saved the Dabbling Duck pub in Great Massingham, which was bought by the council to prevent its conversion into housing. For some of his time on the council Tilbury had been a Labour figure, and he was the Labour candidate for North West Norfolk in the 1983 general election, coming third with 19% of the vote.

In a week in which Britain has celebrated the (official) ninetieth birthday of its monarch, it's appropriate that the only local by-election to take place on 16th July 2016 is in a ward with royal connections. The Valley Hill ward—answers on a postcard as to what this name represents—is a collection of seven parishes a few miles to the north-east of King's Lynn. Furthest inland lie Great Massingham, home to an RAF airfield during the Second World War, and its sister village of Little Massingham; in the centre of the ward are Congham, Hillington, Flitcham with Appleton and Anmer, while the ward meets the Wash coastline at Peter Black Sand near the village of Wolferton.

Until 1969 Wolferton had a railway station, a grand structure with Tudor-style waiting rooms completely out of kilter with the rural surroundings and sparsely-populated catchment area; the reason for this becomes clear when you consider that Wolferton was the railhead for Sandringham House, bought in 1862 by Queen Victoria as a residence for the Prince of Wales and Princess Alexandra of Denmark, and now traditionally the winter home for the Queen and the Royal Family. Also within the ward is Anmer Hall, where the Duke and Duchess of Cambridge and their family live when not in London.

The Royal Family might not vote, but one notable resident who will vote in this by-election is the local MP and Congham resident Sir Henry Bellingham,

Parliamentary constituency: North West Norfolk
Norfolk county council division: Dersingham
May 2015 result Ind 899 C 466
May 2011 result Ind 766 C 238
May 2007 result Ind 597 C 299
May 2003 result Ind 701 C 344 Lab 97

Figure 69: King's Lynn and West Norfolk, Valley Hill

who has represented this area (with broken service) since 1983 when he defeated Tilbury and the outgoing MP Christopher Brocklebank-Fowler, who had been the only Conservative to defect to the SDP. Sir Henry's home ward hasn't seen much change in its last three elections, with Mike Tilbury cruising to re-election against only Tory opposition: at his last re-election in 2015 Tilbury won by the margin of 66–34. For a clue as to the ward's political leanings without Tilbury's personal vote, we can look up to county level: Valley Hill is in the Dersingham county division, where the Tories increased their majority in 2013 in what was generally a poor election for them in Norfolk. In that year Dersingham gave 47% to the Conservatives, 28% to UKIP and 21% to Labour.

There is no independent candidate to succeed Mike Tilbury, so this seat is up for grabs. Probably best placed is the Conservative candidate Tim Tilbrook, a financial advisor. Taking the other candidates alphabetically, UKIP's Andrew Carr runs a dental company, the Green Party's Michael de Whalley is a computer software professional who stood here in the 2015 general election, Labour's Edward Robb gives an address in Great Massingham and the Lib Dems' Kate Sayer is a former Hillington parish councillor.

Result: C 266 Lab 157 LD 102 UKIP 96 Grn 27

23rd June 2016

Sunninghill and South Ascot

Windsor and Maidenhead council, Berkshire; caused by the resignation of Conservative councillor George Bathurst, who had served since 2011. He is concentrating his time on promoting the Windsor Link railway project, which aims to link together Windsor's two railway stations and connect them to Heathrow Airport.

As many disappointed bondholders in Lloyds Bank found out last week, it's always important to read the small print. Electoral law has a lot of small print in it, and it's in a rather sorry state at the moment: the law governing elections in the UK was last consolidated in 1983, and the many electoral changes and constitutional innovations that have happened since then (the devolved institutions in Scotland, Wales and London, postal voting on demand, elected mayors, police and crime commissioners, the short-lived Inner London Education Authority) have resulted in bits and pieces being bolted on to the 1983 law until it's started to sag under its own weight. One of the most impenetrable parts of electoral law relates to combination of polls, with the point of this being to streamline two elections which take place simultaneously: for example, allowing both ballot papers to be issued by the same polling staff. Not all possible poll combinations are allowable, and the Government had to rush out new rules earlier this year to allow Welsh Assembly elections to be combined with Police and Crime Commissioner elections.

You might have noticed that this week there is a referendum on Britain's membership of the EU. Perhaps in order that there aren't any distractions from the referendum, the Government didn't make any provision for this referendum to be combined with any other poll, and the Electoral Commission tried to persuade returning officers and local parties not to schedule any local by-elections for this week. Unfortunately, either the message didn't reach Ascot or the local parties didn't bother to read the small print; whatever the reason, the electors of Sunninghill and South Ascot are going to have to queue up at two separate

Parliamentary constituency: Windsor
May 2015 result C 2012/1852/1635 LD 621/499 Ind 604 Grn 542 Lab 504 UKIP 492
May 2011 result C 1334/1326/1318 LD 430/268/235 Lab 420 Grn 339
May 2007 result C 1076/1072/1058 LD 542/455/441 Lab 163
May 2003 result C 914/904/896 LD 698/686/678 Grn 145 Lab 136

Figure 70: Windsor and Maidenhead, Sunninghill and South Ascot

polling stations in order to cast their votes and the returning officer is going to have to incur the hassle of accommodating and the expense of staffing two separate polling stations. Not good.

Anyway, this ward is fairly well described by its name, and is generally built-up and residential although it does include the Georgian country house of Tittenhurst Park, home at various times to the philanthropist Thomas Holloway, the prison reformer and London county councillor Xenia Field, the entrepreneur and failed Liberal Party candidate Peter Cadbury, John Lennon (who built a recording studio in the grounds), fellow Beatle Ringo Starr and Abu Dhabi ruler Sheikh Zayed. South Ascot is the less fashionable part of Ascot (if such a thing can be said to exist) although it was once home to the exiled King Zog of Albania; its census statistics are skewed by the presence of St Mary's boarding school, which propels the ward into the top 100 in the UK for population aged 16 or 17. Ascot railway station (which lies on the Waterloo–Reading line and is a junction for trains to Guildford) can be found on the ward's northern boundary.

The ward is as Tory as you might expect and has got more so over the course of this century. At the most recent election in 2015 the Tories had 42% of the vote here, with the Lib Dems (13%), an independent candidate (13%) and the Green Party (11%) leading a five-way fight to be runner-up.

Defending for the Conservatives is Julian Sharpe, who lives in Sunninghill and is an organiser for the local carnival. The Lib Dem candidate is Tamasin Barnbrook, who fought Ascot and Cheapside ward last year. The Independent candidate from last time is not trying again and neither are the Greens, so the ballot paper is completed by Spike Humphrey for Labour and Nicole Fowler for UKIP.

Result: C 1443 Lab 601 LD 264 UKIP 214

30th June 2016

Four by-elections on Thursday 30th June:

St Michael's

Bexley council, South London; caused by the resignation of Conservative councillor Joe Pollard, who is now working abroad. Pollard had served since 2006.

Your columnist is writing this on Friday afternoon last week, as the UK dissolves into political and financial meltdown. In this immediate wake of Brexit, it's not immediately clear what the impact of the Leave vote on the UK party system will be (if this is even an important consideration right now). It's ironic that the first electors to get the chance to react to Brexit are those of St Michael's ward, covering the north-eastern corner of Welling. This is a ward populated by London's aspirant working class: St Michael's is in the top 100 wards in England and Wales for intermediate-level jobs and Level 1 qualifications (*ie* fewer than five GCSEs), but also has high owner-occupation rates. Not surprisingly given this demographic, Bexley as a whole was 63% Leave last week—a rebuke to the political legacy of Sir Edward Heath, who was MP for this area (then part of the Bexley constituency) at the time he was leading Britain into the Common Market in 1973.

St Michael's election results are now almost unrecognisable from those in 2002, when Labour won all three seats in a three-way marginal result. The Conservatives decisively gained the ward in 2006 and held all three seats until 2014 when they lost a seat to UKIP who only stood one candidate in the ward; shares of the vote were 35% for the Tories, 33% for UKIP and 22% for Labour. This is the third time the ward has been to the polls in two months following the referendum and the London elections in May, in which the Tories' Zac Goldsmith carried the ward's ballot boxes with 51% to 25% for Labour's Sadiq Khan and 11% for UKIP's Peter Whittle; the GLA list vote was closer with 39% for the Conservatives, 23% for Labour and 20% for UKIP, while further down

Parliamentary constituency: Bexleyheath and Crayford
May 2014 result C 1352/1314/1140 UKIP 1280 Lab 857/769/720 BNP 407
May 2010 result C 2692/2623/2298 Lab 1554/1392/1269 LD 884/724/615 BNP 813 EDP 562
May 2006 result C 2062/1907/1890 Lab 1101/1090/1023 LD 457/450/413
May 2002 result Lab 1023/981/972 C 887/775/766 LD 831/760/752 UKIP 134
May 2016 GLA results (excludes postal voters)
Mayor: C 1402 Lab 701 UKIP 302 LD 119 Grn 80 Britain First 74 BNP 35 Women's Equality 23 Respect 12 Cannabis is Safer than Alcohol 12 One Love 5 Zylinski 1
List: C 1099 Lab 657 UKIP 546 LD 124 Grn 99 Britain First 91 Women's Equality 49 BNP 46 Animal Welfare 32 CPA 31 Respect 18 House Party 5

Figure 71: Bexley, St Michael's

the results Britain First had 3% and finished sixth (out of twelve) on both ballots.

Defending for the Tories is Ray Sams, a councillor for this ward from 2006 until he lost his seat to UKIP in 2014; he was Mayor of Bexley in 2011–12. The UKIP candidate is Keith Forster, the treasurer of the party's Bexley branch. Labour have gone for youth in selecting Sam Marchant, a social media analyst. Also on the ballot paper are Michael Jones of the BNP (whose head office used to be in Welling), Derek Moran for the Green Party and the Lib Dems' Simone Reynolds.

Result: C 939 Lab 840 UKIP 456 LD 117 BNP 105 Grn 54

Leatherhead North

Mole Valley council, Surrey; caused by the resignation of Conservative councillor Santiago Mondejar Flores, an IT professional, who has served since 2015.

Moving out of London, we come to the market town of Leatherhead, beloved of radio traffic reporters thanks to its location just off the congested M 25 motorway. The motorway's junction 9 lies within this ward, prompting several multinational companies to locate their UK offices here including CGI, Halliburton and Unilever; also here is the headquarters of the Police Federation. That's not the only police connection to this ward as it was the former location of Surrey Sound Studios, where The Police recorded many of their early songs. The ward also includes the town's railway station (a junction for the Victoria–Dorking and Waterloo–Epsom–Guildford lines) and its town centre; Leatherhead High Street came in the top five of a 2002 BBC poll for the UK's worst shopping street, but Wikipedia suggests it has improved a bit since then. The ward's census statistics show that employment is high, with 48% of the workforce being employed full-time.

Former councillor Mondejar's Twitter feed is filled with Remain retweets,

Parliamentary constituency: Mole Valley
Surrey county council division: Leatherhead and Fetcham East
May 2016 result LD 528 C 453 UKIP 279 Lab 255 Grn 66
May 2015 result C 1064 LD 915 UKIP 571 Lab 455 Grn 122
May 2014 result C 525 LD 519 UKIP 512 Lab 248
May 2012 result LD 535 C 495 Lab 270 UKIP 213
May 2011 result LD 820 C 669 Lab 278 UKIP 209
May 2010 result LD 1125 C 1113 Lab 353 Ind 275 UKIP 187
May 2008 result LD 866 C 621 UKIP 170
May 2007 result LD 829 C 577 Lab 190 UKIP 105 Grn 43
May 2006 result C 757 LD 754 Lab 221
June 2004 result C 511 LD 492 Lab 489
May 2003 result LD 517 C 364 Lab 343
May 2002 result LD 721 Lab 438 C 317

Figure 72: Mole Valley, Leatherhead North

and Mole Valley—perhaps thanks to all those multinationals and the importance of research to its economy—voted 53% Remain last week. At council level this ward and the council as a whole tends to be a close fight between the Lib Dems and Conservatives: the Lib Dems have won Leatherhead North eight times since 2002 to four times for the Conservatives, with some close majorities (including a couple of close three-way fights). Since 2014 the score is 2–1 in the Tories' favour, but the Lib Dems won the most recent contest in May's ordinary election on a low share of the vote: 33% to 29% for the Tories, 18% for UKIP and 16% for Labour. The ward is part of the Conservative-held county division of Leatherhead and Fetcham East, although the Tory majority comes from elsewhere in the division.

Defending for the Conservatives is Tracy Keeley, who stood in Fetcham West ward in May and had a very bad result in what previously had been a Tory-held ward; a violin teacher, she has previous local government experience as a town councillor in Yorkshire. The Lib Dem candidate is Joe Crome, general manager of the Leatherhead Youth Project. UKIP's Simon Chambers and Labour's Marc Green try again after their third- and fourth-place finishes here in May, and the Green Party's Vicki Elcoate completes the ballot paper.

Result: LD 862 C 340 UKIP 157 Lab 135 Grn 28 [LD gain from C]

High Town

Luton council, Bedfordshire; caused by the resignation of Labour councillor Aysegul Gurbuz. Just 20 years old and having served since 2015, Gurbuz resigned after a series of anti-Semitic tweets by her were revealed.

Parliamentary constituency: Luton South
May 2015 result Lab 1442/1039 C 791/748 Grn 479/329
May 2011 result Lab 1008/899 C 491/437 Grn 191 LD 176/126
May 2007 result Lab 672/617 C 592/563 Grn 248 LD 195/191
May 2003 result Lab 647/497 C 462/461 LD 205/149 Grn 175 Ind 114

Figure 73: Luton, High Town

The High Town area of Luton lies immediately to the north of the town centre, a hilly area dominated by Victorian terraces. The local economy was originally based on hat-making, and there are still a number of hatters here. Wardown Park, the home of the minor cricket county of Bedfordshire, lies within the ward, and High Town's Wikipedia entry paints a Bohemian picture with a large number of small shops and businesses. Luton railway station, a major stop on the Midland main line from St Pancras to Bedford and Leicester, lies on the ward's southern boundary. Students at Bedfordshire University form a large part of the population, and High Town is a highly multiracial area (41% White British, 21% White Other, 18% Asian, 12% Black); the ward is in the top 100 in England and Wales for population from the new EU states (13%) and private renting (46% of households).

A ward like this is of course safe Labour, although the Tories came close to gaining High Town in the 2007 election. At the most recent poll in 2015 Labour beat the Tories here 53–29, although on the Labour slate Gurbuz was a long way behind her running-mate Andy Malcolm who was standing for re-election. In last week's referendum Luton voted 56.5% Remain.

To replace Gurbuz Labour have selected another young Asian woman, but this time one whose equality credentials are impeccable: Maahwish Mirza graduated last year from the University of Warwick, in which she was Education Officer and Deputy President of the Students' Union in 2014–15. (Declaration of interest: your columnist has honorary life membership of Warwick Students' Union.) The Tory candidate is Sue Garrett, who runs the party's Luton branch office. Also standing are Lyn Bliss for the Green Party, independent candidate John French, UKIP's Grace Froggatt and Clive Mead for the Lib Dems.

Result: Lab 505 Grn 273 LD 181 C 141 Ind 102 UKIP 69

Rhoose

Vale of Glamorgan council; caused by the death of independent councillor Philip Clarke in a motorcycle accident. A former commercial pilot, he had served since 2012.

Parliamentary and Assembly constituency: Vale of Glamorgan
May 2012 result Ind 882 C 810/727 Lab 713
May 2008 result C 1169/1143 PC 556 LD 552 Lab 520
June 2004 result C 1240/1085 Lab 729

Figure 74: Vale of Glamorgan, Rhoose

Wales' southernmost mainland division, Rhoose (in Welsh, *y Rhŵs*) is a large rural electoral unit in the centre of the Vale of Glamorgan. Rhoose itself, just to the west of Barry, is a fast-growing commuter village for Cardiff with excellent transport links: it is the location for Cardiff Airport which takes up a lot of the division's acreage, and its railway station on the Vale of Glamorgan line reopened in 2005 with the longest name on the National Rail network: the 33-letter "Rhoose Cardiff International Airport". Also within the ward is the rural community of Llancarfan, which in the sixth century was a *clas* (ecclesiastical community) associated with St Cadoc.

Philip Clarke had topped the poll in this two-seat division in the 2012 election with 37% of the vote, gaining his seat from the Conservatives whose slate had 34% (the other 30% went to Labour); the Tory loss was an embarrassing one as the councillor who lost his seat was the Leader of the Council, Gordon Kemp. Clarke had previously fought the division in 2008 as the Plaid Cymru candidate, finishing as a distant runner-up four votes ahead of the Lib Dems' Eluned Parrott; Parrott would go on to be elected to the Welsh Assembly in bizarre circumstances in 2011, being promoted to first on the Lib Dem list for South Wales Central after the original lead candidate turned out to hold an office which disqualified him from membership of the Senedd.

Two independent candidates have come forward to succeed Clarke: Rachel Banner is a long-standing anti-devolution campaigner and was the main spokesperson for the "no" side in the 2011 referendum on giving law-making powers to the Senedd, while Adam Riley is campaigning to stop Vale of Glamorgan council closing Rhoose Library. Former Vale of Glamorgan council leader Gordon Kemp, having lost his seat in 2012, wants it back and is the Conservative candidate. The Labour candidate is Graham Loveluck-Edwards, a digital marketing manager, scrapyard director and chairman of Rhoose Runners. Completing a crowded ballot paper are James Fyfe of the Pirate Party, the Lib Dems' Robin Lynn and the Plaid candidate Ian Perry.

Result: Riley 598 C 520 Lab 401 Banner 399 PC 104 LD 24 Pirate Party 4 (four)

Friday 1st July 2016

Newington

Thanet council, Kent; caused by the resignation of UKIP councillor Mo Leys, who said in a resignation statement that he could no longer stand under the UKIP banner. A former soldier, he had served since 2015.

For the second time in six months we return to the Isle of Thanet, but in a rather different political context to our last visit. We're in the South Thanet constituency from which Nigel Farage sought election to Parliament last year; although he didn't get in, UKIP had the consolation prize of winning an overall majority on Thanet council, which had previously been evenly split between Labour and the Tories. The Thanet council term in 2011–15 was very fissiparous, with a long list of defections and by-election changes which eventually cost the ruling Tory group their majority and led to Labour taking control part-way through. The Kipper takeover appears to have made not a jot of difference to this political culture, with four or five UKIP councillors wandering off to form a splinter group and wiping out the Kipper majority; on top of that, a further UKIP councillor emigrated to Thailand shortly after his election last year, and the resulting by-election was lost to Labour. *Plus ça change, plus c'est la même chose.*

Judging from the seat count, the UKIP surge in Thanet last year came at the expense of Labour who now hold just five seats on the council, following that by-election win. In that context it's unsurprising that one of the seats to fall was Newington ward, a working-class inland suburb of Ramsgate off the road to Manston, whose closed airport and the future thereof is one of the political hot potatoes in this part of the world. Previously a safe Labour ward, Newington gave 44% to UKIP last year and just 36% to Labour, the Tories coming in third with 19%. Labour weren't helped by deselecting their long-serving councillor Mike Harrison over homophobic comments he had made about former Labour councillor Ian Driver, who following a dizzying series of defections ended up

Parliamentary constituency: South Thanet
Kent county council division: Ramsgate
Jan 2016 by-election Lab 288 UKIP 229 C 156 Ind 49 Grn 20 LD 12 Ind 10
May 2015 result UKIP 884/845 Lab 728/713 C 390/363
May 2011 result Lab 705/702 C 370/351
May 2007 result Lab 471/438 Ramsgate First 268/196 C 208/197 UKIP 116
May 2003 result Lab 532/498 Ind 235 C 144/140

Figure 75: Thanet, Newington

in the Green Party. This was the ward where the by-election was held after a UKIP councillor emigrated; the by-election took place in January and resulted in a Labour gain with 38% of the vote, to 30% for UKIP and 20% for the Tories. UKIP hold the ward's county council seats, with the two-member Ramsgate division being safe for them in 2013 but previously Labour-inclined.

Faced with the prospect of losing their last seat in the ward, UKIP have selected Roy Potts to defend this by-election. Having got one of their 2015 slate elected in January, Labour are hoping to do the double by selecting their other candidate from 2015, former Mayor of Ramsgate David Green, who has sixteen years' service on Thanet council as a member for Eastcliff ward (1999–2015). The Conservatives have reselected their January candidate Adam Dark, a law teacher, while the Lib Dems' Matthew Brown completes the ballot paper, hoping to improve on the 12 votes his party got in January.

Result: UKIP 295 Lab 281 C 125 LD 33

7th July 2016

By-elections on 7th July 2016:

Appleby (Appleby)

Eden council, Cumbria; caused by the death of Independent councillor Keith Morgan at the age of 73. Morgan was a veteran of local government, having been first elected to Eden district council in 1991 as a leader of the campaign to save the Settle–Carlisle railway; he had represented this ward since 1999. Also an Appleby town councillor since 1983, Morgan served twice as chairman of Eden council in 2007–08 and 2012–13.

For the first of this week's three by-elections we take a trip up to the old county town of Westmorland. Appleby-in-Westmorland (as the town was renamed following local government reform in 1974) can be found in the shadow of the High Pennines within a bend of the River Eden; this curiously-named ward is the half of the town lying to the south-west of the river, with the other half forming Appleby (Bongate) ward. With the demise of the town as a county town (although Westmorland county council was never based here, instead being run from Kendal) Appleby has been left with tourism as the driver for its economy, together with the Appleby Horse Fair, dating back to at least the twelfth century, which brings to the town each June gypsies and travellers from all over the UK and Ireland. The census statistics show an old and almost uniformly British population: 32% of the population are aged over 64 and 98% were born in the UK, 25% of the workforce are retired, and those jobs which exist are generally routine work; the ward also has high levels of Christianity (73%). The general area is still recovering from the effects of Storm Desmond last December; a major landslip caused by the storm means that Appleby has been the effective northern terminus of the Settle–Carlisle line so far this year, and trains to Carlisle are not expected to resume before 2017.

Appleby was once a pocket borough controlled by the Lowther family (the

Parliamentary constituency: Penrith and the Border
Cumbria county council division: Appleby
May 2015 result Ind unopposed
May 2011 result Ind unopposed
May 2007 result Ind unopposed
May 2003 result Ind 192 Ind 191

Figure 76: Eden, Appleby (Appleby)

Earls of Lonsdale) whose MPs included Pitt the Younger and Viscount Howick (later Earl Grey), although that didn't stop Appleby from becoming the only county town disenfranchised by Grey's Great Reform Act. As a remote area of England, Eden is one of the last strongholds of the rural independent councillor and has a very large number of unopposed elections: this appears to be only the third contested election to Appleby (Appleby) ward since it was created in 1973, and the first since 2003 when Morgan was re-elected by a majority of just one vote, 192 to 191. Looking up to county level, the Appleby county division was safe Tory in 2013 but covers a large rural area outside the town itself.

Defending for the independents is Karen Greenwood, who works in Appleby's tourist information centre. In the first contested election in this ward for thirteen years, she is opposed by the Tories' Philip Guest, an IT marketer.

Result: Ind 187 C 67

Carlford

Suffolk county council; caused by the death of Conservative councillor Peter Bellfield. A Suffolk county councillor since winning a by-election in 2003, Bellfield had formerly worked in the financial services industry and was chairman of the council's pensions committee.

This is a large rural division which essentially covers the countryside between Ipswich, Woodbridge and Framlingham. It contains twenty-six parishes, none of which are called Carlford; the name instead commemorates the former Carlford Hundred, which took in much of this area. The largest centre of population in the division is probably Grundisburgh, a village of around 1600 souls notable for its fourteenth-century church which contains a mediaeval mural of St Christopher.

Bellfield had a safe seat; at his last re-election in 2013 he polled 59%, with UKIP's 19% being best of the rest. Unfortunately recent ward boundary changes in the local district (Suffolk Coastal) completely fail to match up with the county division boundaries and as a result it is not possible to draw conclusions from

Parliamentary constituency: Central Suffolk and North Ipswich
Suffolk Coastal district council wards: Framlingham (part), Fynn Valley (part), Grundis-
burgh, Hacheston (part), Wickham Market (part), Woodbridge (part)
May 2013 result C 1565 UKIP 504 Lab 374 LD 208
June 2009 result C 2172 LD 865 Lab 236
May 2005 result C 2828 LD 1324 Lab 916

Figure 77: Suffolk CC, Carlford

them. The Suffolk Tories are having a horrible run at the moment, having lost five by-elections and control of the county council in the last two months, but this should be more fruitful territory for them.

Defending for the Tories is Robin Vickery, an Ipswich borough councillor. UKIP have not followed up their second-place finish in 2013, so Vickery is opposed by Revd Canon Graham Hedger, priest-in-charge for much of the division, who is the Labour candidate; Jon Neal for the Liberal Democrats; and Jacqueline Barrow for the Green Party.

Result: C 1142 Lab 344 LD 228 Grn 176

Mostyn

Conwy county borough council; caused by the resignation of Labour councillor Jobi Hold. Hold has been unable to attend meetings of the council due to his job captaining a boat in the oil and gas industry; when on dry land he is now living in Cornwall.

It's July, the weather's nice, so let's go to the seaside. Specifically, we're in Llandudno, a town on the North Wales coast which has a long history (there are Bronze Age copper mines on the Great Orme above the town) but whose development really began in earnest in the mid-nineteenth century under the auspices of the landowner, Lord Mostyn. A major storm in 1859 which damaged the town's pier put paid to early ideas of turning Llandudno into a major Irish Sea port; instead the town developed as a seaside resort and its connection to the railway network in 1858 ensured the town has been filled with holidaymakers ever since. Many people (including your columnist) come for the Victorian weekend each May, in which Mostyn Street—the town's main shopping street, just behind the North Promenade—is turned into a funfair. The Mostyn family have left their mark on the town in other ways: Oriel Mostyn, endowed by one of the family, is one of the UK's leading galleries of contemporary art; and the present Lord Mostyn, who still owns much of the town, was reported in 2013 to be the 13th-richest person in the UK under the age of 30 (he's over 30 now).

Parliamentary and Assembly constituency: Aberconwy
May 2012 result Lab 436 Ind 250 C 243/199 Ind 235 LD 131 Ind 72 Ind 38 Ind 33
May 2008 result Lab 331/277 C 304/275 Ind 182 Ind 173 PC 147
June 2004 result Lab 505/504 Ind 224 LD 187/155 Ind 170 C 157/130

Figure 78: Conwy, Mostyn

Mostyn's demographics aren't particularly notable, although the workforce tends towards the lower end of the class scale. This makes it the strongest of Llandudno's five divisions for Labour, although Labour only ran one candidate here in the 2012 election: Jobi Hold topped the poll with around 45%, a long way ahead of a tight three-way race for the other seat which was won by independent candidate Dewi Miles on 26%, seven votes ahead of the leading Conservative candidate and fifteen votes ahead of independent Janet Jones. Miles gained a Tory seat previously held by Janet Howarth, who had moved to another Conwy division and later briefly served on the Welsh Assembly, losing her seat to UKIP in May's election.

Defending for Labour is Emily Owen, a Bangor University student who works for a local estate agent and spent part of last week completing the Three Peaks challenge, climbing Snowdon, Scafell Pike and Ben Nevis for the benefit of a dog rescue charity. There are two competing independent candidates, Richard "The Lion" Enston and John Thomas. The Tory candidate is Greg Robbins, a Llandudno town councillor (and Mayor of Llandudno in 2011–12) who has recently defected to the party from Plaid Cymru. Also standing are Penelope Appleton for the Lib Dems and John Humberstone, who stood here as an independent in 2012 and came eighth out of nine candidates, for UKIP.

Result: Lab 248 C 200 LD 126 Thomas 88 UKIP 75 Enston 27

14th July 2016

Ten by-elections on 14th July 2016:

Forest Gate North

Newham council, North London; caused by the resignation of Labour councillor Ellie Robinson, who has taken up a new post with the London Assembly as an advisor to Mayor Sadiq Khan. She was first elected to Newham council in 2010.

It's worth saying a few things here to start this week's column. June is normally a busy month for local by-elections, as vacancies from April and May are cleared before the summer holidays and we start to deal with what might be termed "collateral damage" from the May elections as councillors move on to bigger and better things which they have been newly elected to.

The Labour takeover of City Hall in May has led to quite a lot of such collateral damage, with two by-elections this week arising from councillors leaving to take up posts in Mayor Khan's administration and several more in the pipeline, including a by-election for the elected mayoralty of Hackney which will see an entire London borough go to the polls. However, this year the EU referendum—with which no other poll could be combined, although the returning officer for Windsor and Maidenhead didn't get that message—has had the effect of pushing most of June's vacancies back into July where they are being compressed into a much shorter period before the summer holidays. This means that your columnist has twenty wards to write about over this week and the next, so apologies to my readers (hello Sid, hello Doris) if there is less detail here and next week than you might have come to expect. Having said that, in the case of Forest Gate North your columnist is very grateful for help received this week from Tim Roll-Pickering, who is the election agent for the Conservative candidate.

So it is that we start the week in West Ham. Forest Gate North is the part of Forest Gate lying to the north of the Great Eastern railway line, with Forest Gate station on the ward's southern boundary and Maryland station just off the south-western corner; wholly within the ward is Wanstead Park station on the Gospel Oak–Barking line, although that's currently closed for electrification works. This is a long and thin ward running from west to east which has been left relatively untouched by the redevelopment seen in Stratford and the Royal Docks area; much of the housing is still Victorian, with the effect of wartime bombing still visible in many streets where replacement houses are in a different style to the original. The "village" area at the eastern end of the ward, close to the heathland of Wanstead Flats, is gentrifying quickly, although that effect hasn't yet reached the centre of the ward or the Maryland area at the western end. Nearly all of the ward is built up, although it does contain Forest Lane Park and West Ham Cemetery.

While the census statistics perhaps might not catch the full effect of the recent gentrification, they are very typical of Newham as a whole. The White British population is just 21%, with consequent very high scores for pretty much every other ethnic group. The ward is in the top 100 in England and Wales for black population (25%), people born in the new EU states (11%) and those with non-UK qualifications (15%); the over-45 population is very low, 60% of households are rented in some way or another and there is also a significant student population.

The political complexion of the ward should be obvious from the word "Newham", where it's now ten years since anyone other than Labour won an election. There's not much indication this is going to change in Forest Gate North, whose predecessor wards last failed to return a full Labour slate in the Tory landslide of 1968. One of the past candidates who tried and failed to break the Labour monopoly was local resident Gerard Batten of UKIP, who finished last here in 2002 but has since gone on to greater things as an MEP for London (for how long, who knows?). At the most recent borough elections in 2014 Labour had 58% of the vote, with the Greens best of the rest on 14% only just ahead of the Tories. Sadiq Khan beat Zac Goldsmith here 65–15 in May, while in the London Members ballot the Greens ran second in the ward's ballot boxes with Labour winning 61–11.

So, not much for the Labour candidate Anamul Islam, who is described as a long-standing trade union and community activist, to worry about here. The Greens, who will be looking to put down a marker in one of their best Newham wards, have selected conservation campaigner Elisabeth Whitebread. Also standing are Conservative candidate John Oxley, a barrister working in family law, and the Lib Dems' James Rumsby who has withdrawn from the campaign for personal reasons but will still appear on the ballot paper.

Result: Lab 1150 Grn 681 C 301 LD 57

Parliamentary constituency: West Ham
May 2014 result Lab 2324/2126/2120 Grn 562/559 C 548/490/480 TUSC 222 LD 206
CPA 174/146
May 2010 result Lab 3652/3631/3335 Grn 905 C 836/730/710 CPA 411/347 Ind 267
May 2006 result Lab 1678/1552/1443 Respect 757/720/673 Grn 603 C 517/454/418 CPA
409
May 2002 result Lab 1333/1265/1253 Grn 628 C 344 Socialist Alliance 272 UKIP 233
May 2016 GLA results (excludes postal voters)
Mayor: Lab 2238 C 507 Grn 272 LD 95 Respect 79 UKIP 79 Women's Equality 65
Cannabis is Safer than Alcohol 36 Britain First 35 BNP 16 Zylinski 15 One Love 5
London Member: Lab 2138 Grn 369 C 312 UKIP 144 Women's Equality 133 LD 129
Respect 91 CPA 55 Britain First 36 Animal Welfare 34 BNP 25 House Party 19

Figure 79: Newham, Forest Gate North

Barnsbury

Islington council, North London; caused by the resignation of Labour councillor James Murray, who has taken up a new post with the London Assembly as Deputy Mayor for Housing. He was first elected in 2006.

Moving further into London, Barnsbury ward is stereotypical Islington running from the Angel at the southeast corner to the Caledonian Road and Barnsbury North London Line station at the northwest corner. Barnsbury developed from the nineteenth century onwards as an escape from the overcrowded City and industrial Clerkenwell, and as the first staging post out of London on the Great North Road. Wikipedia's list of famous Barnsbury residents reads like a rollcall of the great and good: Tony Blair, Benjamin Britten, Ian Holm, Walter Sickert, Simon Rattle, Grayson Perry. Although Barnsbury's census statistics are overall similar to Forest Gate North, there are two major differences: the White British population here is still (just) over 50%, and 51% of the workforce have degrees with another 11% being full-time students—very much middle-class. The ward is in the top 100 in England and Wales for population born in the pre-2004 EU states (7.6%) and, interestingly, for those who did not answer the census question on religion (16.2%).

The first Barnsbury ward election on the current boundaries in 2002 was safe Lib Dem, with Labour a long way behind in second; in a tie for the runner-up spot that year was human rights barrister and Labour candidate Emily Thornberry, who has since gone on to greater things as MP for the local Islington South and Finsbury constituency and (at the time of writing, this may have changed since) Shadow Foreign Secretary. Labour did very well to gain all three seats in 2006 on a 14% swing, 22-year-old James Murray beating the alphabet to top the poll, and

Parliamentary constituency: Islington South and Finsbury
May 2014 result Lab 2110/1948/1910 C 710/604/594 Grn 467/447/327 LD 400/309/286
TUSC 100
May 2010 result Lab 2399/2165/2064 LD 1460/1358/1221 C 1204/1198/1111 Grn 557/528/490
Ind 87
May 2006 result Lab 1072/986/973 LD 888/789/744 C 445/437/426 Grn 432/394/391
June 2003 by-election LD 940 Lab 311 C 182 Grn 136
May 2002 result LD 1127/1046/1036 Lab 600/600/561 Grn 238/227 Ind 199 C 183/174/153
May 2016 GLA results (excludes postal voters)
Mayor: Lab 1798 C 722 Grn 240 LD 172 Women's Equality 119 UKIP 105 Britain First
34 Respect 27 Cannabis is Safer than Alcohol 21 BNP 14 One Love 8 Zylinski 2
London Member: Lab 1548 C 590 Grn 341 LD 240 Women's Equality 213 UKIP 185
Britain First 53 Animal Welfare 31 Respect 31 House Party 20 CPA 16 BNP 14

Figure 80: Islington, Barnsbury

with the implosion of the Islington Lib Dems this has become a safe ward for
Labour. The Tories took over second place at the most recent borough elections
in 2014, Labour winning 56–19; in May Sadiq Khan beat Zac Goldsmith here
55–22 while in the London Members ballot Labour had 47% to 18% for the Tories
and 10% for the Greens.

Defending for Labour is Rowena Champion, a family law barrister. Another
barrister, Edward Waldegrave, is the Conservative candidate; also standing are
physics teacher and former asylum-seeker Ernestas Jegorovas for the Green Party,
Lib Dem candidate Bradley Hillier-Smith and independent Robert Capper.

Result: Lab 1192 LD 409 C 367 Grn 302 Ind 40

Trowbridge Grove

Wiltshire council; caused by the death of independent councillor Jeff Osborn at the
age of 73. Osborn started his career at fifteen by joining the Merchant Navy; in
1962 he enlisted in the Royal Engineers with whom he served in Germany, Cyprus
and Aden, and with the SAS in Hereford. He started his political career in the
1980s as a Labour figure and was their candidate in Somerton and Frome in the
1983 general election; after that he ended up in the Liberal Democrats, representing
Trowbridge for twenty years initially on the former West Wiltshire district council.
Twice Mayor of Trowbridge and a long-serving member of Wiltshire council's
health committee, Osborn left the Liberal Democrats over the coalition's health
policy, and his final re-election was as an independent. He leaves behind his wife
Helen, also a Wiltshire councillor, and two daughters.

Moving out of London, we come to Trowbridge, the county town of Wilt-

Parliamentary constituency: South West Wiltshire
May 2013 result Ind 842 C 142
June 2009 result LD 816 C 311 Lab 70

Figure 81: Wiltshire, Trowbridge Grove

shire and headquarters of Wiltshire county council. Although Trowbridge is an old market town, its economy was traditionally based on textiles; in 1820 Trowbridge had over twenty factories producing woollen cloth, a similar level to several northern industrial towns. Today the town's largest employers are the council and Apetito, a frozen food company.

The Grove ward covers south-western Trowbridge and has been the Osborns' personal fief for many years, both under its original guise (as the Trowbridge South West ward of West Wiltshire council) and now. At the inaugural Wiltshire council election in 2009 Osborn (then a Lib Dem) beat the Tories 68–26; in 2013 as an independent he was not opposed by the Lib Dems and polled 86% in a straight fight with the Tories. Wiltshire's district councils were abolished in 2009, so there's not much else to go on to give clues as to what might happen here without an Osborn on the ballot.

Defending for the independents is Robert Wall. The Tories have selected David Halik, a town councillor and former Mayor of Trowbridge. The Lib Dems have returned to the fray by selecting Chris Auckland, who works in social housing. Also standing on a crowded ballot paper are Shaun Henley for Labour, Philip Randle for the Greens and UKIP's Simon Selby.

Result: LD 421 C 196 UKIP 123 Lab 77 Ind 74 Grn 27 [LD gain from Ind]

Astley

North Norfolk council; caused by the resignation of Conservative councillor Steven Ward due to pressure of work. He had served since May last year.

For the first of today's rural by-elections we're in Norfolk. The Astley ward contains seven parishes, none of which are called Astley; instead the name commemorates the Astley family of Melton Constable Hall, an at-risk stately home regarded as the finest example of the Christopher Wren style. Melton Constable itself was the most important settlement in the ward, being a junction of four railway lines and home to the main workshops for the Midland and Great Northern Joint Railway; but the works closed in 1934 and thirty years later the railway was gone as well, and the loss of that work means that Melton Constable's population has halved since 1911. Today Astley ward as a whole has a relatively old age profile and high levels of self-employment (17% of the workforce were

Parliamentary constituency: Broadland
Norfolk county council division: Melton Constable
May 2015 result C 734 Grn 344 Lab 233
May 2011 result C 359 LD 257 Lab 156 Grn 134
May 2007 result LD 475 C 331 Grn 75
July 2003 by-election LD 441 C 346 Ind 38 Lab 32
May 2003 result Ind 349 C 267 LD 144 Grn 54

Figure 82: North Norfolk, Astley

self-employed in the 2011 census).

The ward has had a volatile recent political history, with the four ordinary elections since 2003 electing four different councillors. Astley elected an independent in May 2003, but went Lib Dem in a by-election just two months later; the Lib Dems lost the ward to the Conservatives in 2011 and didn't stand in the 2015 election, in which the Tories beat the Green Party 56–26. The ward is part of the Melton Constable county council division, which is just as volatile: Lib Dem in 2005, Tory gain in 2009, UKIP gain in 2013; the predecessor county division of Erpingham and Melton Constable was Labour-held from 1993 to 2001 in what was perhaps the last hurrah of Labour strength in agricultural Norfolk.

Defending for the Tories is Jo Copplestone, an artist. The Greens have selected Mandy Huntridge who is the only candidate to give an address in the ward. Callum Ringer is the Labour candidate, the Lib Dems return to the fray with Pierre Butifoker, and the UKIP county councillor David Ramsbotham completes the ballot paper.

Result: LD 319 C 198 UKIP 133 Grn 81 Lab 51 [LD gain from C]

Byram and Brotherton

Selby council, North Yorkshire; caused by the death of Labour councillor Jack Crawford at the age of 69. First elected in 1995 for the former Byram cum Sutton ward (although with broken service), Crawford had been chairman of Selby council in 2012–13.

Anybody who has travelled up the old A1 through Yorkshire has passed through this ward. Generations of travellers will be familiar with Ferrybridge, the crossing point of the A1 and the M62 motorway, and its large power station. On the other side of the power station, the River Aire and the county boundary are Brotherton, bypassed by the old A1, and its twin village of Byram cum Sutton. Further up the Great North Road is Fairburn, once sliced in two by a busy dual carriageway but now enjoying some relief thanks to the completion of

Parliamentary constituency: Selby
North Yorkshire county council division: Mid Selby
May 2015 result Lab 648 C 480 UKIP 345

Figure 83: Selby, Byram and Brotherton

a motorway bypass for the area. Just outside the ward boundary is Kellingley, home to the UK's last deep coal mine until its closure last Christmas; the presence of the now former coalfield gives this area a working-class economic profile.

Selby council got new ward boundaries in 2015 which makes comparison rather difficult; this new ward is a cut-down version of the former two-seat Fairburn with Brotherton ward, with Birkin and Burton Salmon parishes having moved out in the boundary changes. Fairburn with Brotherton was a key Labour/Tory marginal, but the new ward appears to be better for Labour: in 2015 Crawford had 44% of the vote to 33% for the Conservatives and 23% for UKIP. At county council level this ward is combined with better Tory territory to form the reliably Conservative Mid Selby division.

Defending for Labour is Steven Shaw-Wright, a former coalminer, Selby town councillor and present Mayor of Selby. He is opposed by Bryn Sage, the Tory candidate, who runs a digital health company. UKIP have not nominated a candidate, so the ballot paper is completed by Chris Whitwood of the regionalist movement Yorkshire First.

Result: C 251 Lab 224 Yorkshire First 91 [C gain from Lab]

Wibsey

Bradford council, West Yorkshire; caused by the death of Labour councillor Lynne Smith. Smith had spent twenty years working in the voluntary sector with disabled people and also taught at university before being elected to Bradford council in 2006; in her council role she was chairman of the council's governance and audit committee.

Wibsey ward is the first part of Bradford that drivers see when they come off the M 606 motorway. A relatively late part of the West Yorkshire conurbation to develop, Wibsey was not incorporated into Bradford until 1899 and much of its housing stock is inter-war. As well as Wibsey village, the ward also includes much of the Odsal area including the Richard Dunn sports centre, named after a local boxer who fought Muhammad Ali.

The red corner have held the upper hand in recent fights for the Wibsey ward title, with opposition to Labour in recent years coming from the populist right: the BNP took one of the three seats in 2004 but lost it back to Labour in

Parliamentary constituency: Bradford South
May 2016 result Lab 1651 UKIP 739 C 547 Ind 310 LD 156 Grn 121
May 2015 result Lab 2683 UKIP 1795 C 1228 LD 247 Grn 216 TUSC 55
May 2014 result Lab 1467 UKIP 1355 C 499 LD 191
May 2012 result Lab 1753 UKIP 781 C 399 LD 384
May 2011 result Lab 1814 C 809 UKIP 373 LD 243 EDP 226
May 2010 result Lab 2454 C 1422 LD 1158 BNP 765 UKIP 291
May 2008 result Lab 1397 C 921 BNP 595 LD 410 EDP 183 UKIP 100 Democratic Nationalists 26
May 2007 result Lab 1546 BNP 1128 C 821 LD 558
May 2006 result Lab 1427 BNP 1251 C 928 LD 513
June 2004 result Lab 1460/1426/1331 BNP 1355 C 1341/1279/1234 LD 581/380

Figure 84: Bradford, Wibsey

2006. In 2012 UKIP took over as runners-up here; they were close in 2014 but Labour were well ahead in May's ordinary election, polling 47% to 21% for UKIP and 16% for the Conservatives.

Defending for Labour is Joanne Sharp, chair of the party's Wibsey branch. UKIP's candidate is Jason Smith, chair of the party's Bradford branch who fought the ward in 2015. The Tories have reselected their regular candidate for the ward Richard Sheard, who works for a software company. Lib Dem candidate Angharad Griffiths completes the ballot paper.

Result: Lab 1207 UKIP 655 C 451 LD 70

Newquay Treviglas; and
St Teath and St Breward

Cornwall council; caused respectively by the resignations of UKIP councillor Mark Hicks and independent councillor John Lugg. Hicks, who had served since 2013, has resigned for personal reasons. Lugg, who started his local government career over forty years ago and was first elected to the former North Corwall district council in 1979, is suffering from poor health.

There are two Cornish by-elections this week. One comes in the village of St Columb Minor, once the major settlement in its area but now an eastern suburb of the seaside resort of Newquay; it is the major part of Newquay Treviglas division, whose name refers to Treviglas College, a secondary school and sixth-form college located just outside the village.

Further up the north coast is St Teath and St Breward division, which runs from the summit of Cornwall's highest point, Brown Willy, down to the sea, surrounding the town of Camelford on three sides. The Brown Willy moorland is known for prehistoric remains and also for granite and china clay quarrying, while the division's largest centre of population is the slate-quarrying village of Delabole, once the location of the world's deepest man-made pit and since 1991 home to the UK's first commercial onshore windfarm; Delabole's proximity to the Atlantic Ocean and high altitude (around 800 feet) made it a perfect site for a windfarm.

Newquay Treviglas was created for the inaugural 2009 Cornwall council election and was won in its first contest by independent candidate Harry Heywood, who had previously been Restormel district councillor for the Rialton ward which covered the area before 2009. Heywood stood down in 2013 and his seat went to UKIP on a low share of the vote, 30% to 27% for the Conservatives, 25% for the Lib Dems and 18% for Labour.

St Teath and St Breward is another 2009 creation, surviving unchanged in the 2013 boundary review except for its name—the 2009 division with the same boundaries was simply called St Teath. Before 2009 most of this area was in the Camelot ward of North Cornwall council, which Lugg represented as an independent with large vote shares; St Breward was in a ward with Blisland to the south which was Tory unopposed in 2003 but a Lib Dem gain in 2007. Lugg's popularity has carried over to the unitary Cornwall council, and at his last re-election in 2013 he beat the Tories 65–35 in a straight fight.

So the previous form in both divisions doesn't really tell us all that much, although it says something of the disarray that Cornwall UKIP find themselves in that they have not found a candidate to defend Newquay Treviglas. From winning six seats in 2013, this will be UKIP's fourth by-election loss in Cornwall since then and they have another seat to defend later this year. With Newquay Treviglas up for grabs, the Tories have selected a strong candidate in Carl Leadbetter, the Mayor of Newquay who represents the ward on Newquay town council; he is a former hotelier and had served in the RAF. The Lib Dem candidate is Paul Summers, a former town councillor who has recently retired after 36 years as a teacher. Julian Grover is the Labour candidate. Completing the ballot paper is George Edwards, a former Mayor of Newquay and former Restormel councillor for the town, who lost his seat on Cornwall council in 2013—in those previous elections he was a Lib Dem, but he is now standing as an independent.

In St Teath no fewer than three independents have come forward to succeed Lugg. Taking them alphabetically, Eddie Jones is a former chairman of St Teath parish council; William Kitto gives an address in St Teath; and Susan Theobald is a former clerk to St Teath parish council. On the party political side of a crowded ballot paper, the Conservative candidate is Jeremy Stanford-Davis of St Teath;

Parliamentary constituency: St Austell and Newquay
May 2013 result UKIP 266 C 237 LD 218 Lab 156

Figure 85: Cornwall, Newquay Treviglas

Parliamentary constituency: North Cornwall
May 2013 result Ind 628 LD 388 C 204
June 2009 result (St Teath) Ind 957 C 512

Figure 86: Cornwall, St Teath and St Breward

the Lib Dems' Dominic Fairman is a farmer who has diversified into camping and yurts; and the Labour candidate David Garrigan has resorted to crowdfunding websites to finance his campaign.

Newquay Treviglas result: LD 486 C 210 Lab 87 Ind 58 [LD gain from UKIP]

St Teath and St Breward result: LD 620 Kitto 242 C 202 Theobald 181 Jones 73 Lab 66 [LD gain from Ind]

Marchog; and
Y Felinheli

Gwynedd council; caused respectively by the resignations of independent councillor Chris O'Neal and Plaid Cymru councillor Siân Gwenllian. O'Neal, who has served since 2012, resigned after pleading guilty to assaulting an employee of the taxi firm he formerly ran; he also spent part of last year in court being cleared of a blackmail charge. Gwenllian was first elected in 2008, and is moving on to bigger things after being elected as Plaid Cymru AM for Arfon in this year's Senedd election.

North Wales is having a bumper crop of by-elections this month, with a poll in Llandudno last week and a third Gwynedd poll coming up next week. Marchog division consists entirely of Maesgeirchen, a huge isolated 1930s-era council estate cut off from the city of Bangor by Bangor Mountain. 57% of the households are still socially rented—one of the top 40 figures in England and Wales—and the demographic indicators are as bad as you'd expect from an isolated council estate, with only 28% of the workforce in full-time employment and high scores in every other category for economic activity except "self-employed" and "retired".

Doing better is Y Felinheli, a village on the south bank of the Menai and historically a port; in 1825 a narrow-gauge railway opened connecting the village with the Dinorwic slate quarry in Llanberis, and readers of a certain age might

Parliamentary and Assembly constituency: Arfon
May 2012 result Ind 365/248/76 Lab 218/143
May 2008 result Lab 247/184 Ind 202
June 2004 result Lab 324/172 Ind 303

Figure 87: Gwynedd, Marchog

Parliamentary and Assembly constituency: Arfon
May 2012 result PC unopposed
May 2008 result PC unopposed
June 2004 result Lab 384 Ind 354

Figure 88: Gwynedd, Y Felinheli

know the village better under the name of Port Dinorwic. During the Second World War Y Felinheli was a centre for building landing craft, and its harbour is still in use today for pleasure boating and sailing. The village's location midway between Bangor and Caernarfon means there is commuting to both towns, and a number of Bangor University students live here.

Gwenllian never faced a contested election in her eight years on Gwynedd council, having been unopposed in 2008 and 2012. The last contested election in Y Felinheli was in 2004 with Labour narrowly beating an independent candidate. Marchog's representation had a clearout in 2012, with the previous Labour and Independent councillors losing their seats to two new independent councillors.

Both by-elections are straight fights. In Marchog the defending independent candidate Dylan Fernley is challenged by Labour's Luke Tugwell; both candidates give addresses on the estate. In Y Felinheli the new Plaid candidate is Gareth Griffith, who is opposed by Bangor-based Conservative candidate Andrew Kinsman.

Marchog result: Ind 211 Lab 112
Y Felinheli result: PC 614 C 49

21st July 2016

There are again ten by-elections on 21st July 2016, nine in England and one in Wales.[9] The Lib Dems were the clear winners of last week's by-elections with four seat gains, but that's unlikely to be repeated this week as they are not in contention in any of the wards polling this week. The Conservatives are defending six seats, two in Devon and one each in Lancashire, Northampton, Nottinghamshire and Surrey; Labour are defending two seats in London and one in Reading; and Plaid Cymru have a defence in Gwynedd. We shouldn't expect much change this week: the three Labour defences and five of the six Tory seats are in safe wards and the Plaid defence shouldn't be too difficult unless local factors come into play, which leaves one standout marginal by-election...

Chorley Rural North

Lancashire county council; caused by the death of Conservative councillor Mike Devaney at the age of 78. A former senior manager at British Gas, Devaney had served on Lancashire county council since 2009 and was chairman of the council in 2013–14. He was also a former Chorley councillor, representing Clayton-le-Woods North ward from 2007 to 2011.

Last week this column went from south to north, so this week it's time to reverse the direction and go back south; the north is a particularly good place to start this week as possibly the most interesting by-election of the week is to Lancashire county council.

The Chorley Rural North county division is based on Clayton-le-Woods, a large affluent commuter village which occupies much of the space between Chorley and Bamber Bridge. Smaller settlements in the division include Cuerden, Brindle and Hoghton. The division is also known for the fortified Elizabethan manor house of Hoghton Tower (pronunciation guide: HORton), still owned

---

[9]In fact there were ten English by-elections and eleven in total this week: the Great Wyrley Town poll had not come to my notice at the time this was written.

Parliamentary constituency: Chorley
Chorley council wards: Brindle and Hoghton, Clayton-le-Woods North, Clayton-le-Woods West and Cuerden
May 2013 result C 1525 Lab 1402 UKIP 642 LD 140
June 2009 result C 1849 Lab 950 UKIP 931
May 2005 result C 2442 Lab 2160 LD 1380

Figure 89: Lancashire CC, Chorley Rural North

by the de Hoghton family, and the eighteenth-century Cuerden Hall, now a care home.

The three Chorley council wards in the division are an interesting bunch. The rural Brindle and Hoghton is in the top 50 wards in England and Wales for Christianity (in a Lancashire context that usually means a large Catholic population), and has high levels of owner-occupation and a commuter economic profile. Clayton-le-Woods North ward, which accounts for half the electorate, is more working-class, with high levels of social renting and long-term sickness. Clayton-le-Woods West and Cuerden ward falls somewhere in between, with a high level of apprenticeships in its workforce.

The political preferences of the three wards reflect their social composition. Clayton-le-Woods North, despite returning a full slate of Lib Dems in 2002 in a three-way marginal result, is a Labour-inclined marginal which the Conservatives did well to win at every election from 2004 to 2010. However, since the Conservatives got into government Clayton-le-Woods North has trended to Labour and in May Labour beat the Conservatives here 62–38 in a straight fight. Clayton-le-Woods West and Cuerden is a key marginal which the Conservatives held 51–49 in 2014 and gained from Labour 52–48 at its most recent election in 2015. Brindle and Hoghton ward is safe Conservative, although the Tories were run close by an independent in May's election. The presence of Brindle and Hoghton makes the county division as a whole a Tory-inclined marginal, in which Labour are competitive but can't quite get over the line: at the last county election in 2013 the Conservatives had 41% to 38% for Labour and 17% for UKIP.

Defending for the Conservatives is Alan Cullens, Chorley councillor for Clayton-le-Woods West and Cuerden since 2015 and previously for Clayton-le-Woods North from 2008 to 2012; he fought Chorley in the 2010 general election. Labour have reselected their 2013 candidate Yvonne Hargreaves, who fought Brindle and Hoghton in May. The UKIP candidate is Christopher Suart, and the Lib Dems' Stephen Fenn completes the ballot paper.

Result: C 1144 Lab 1042 UKIP 303 LD 125

Parliamentary constituency: Newark
Nottinghamshire county council division: Balderton
May 2015 result C 1265/1207 Lab 956

Figure 90: Newark and Sherwood, Balderton

Balderton South

Newark and Sherwood council, Nottinghamshire; caused by the death of Conservative councillor Gordon Brooks at the age of 72. A former apprentice engineer at the Worthington Simpson pump works in Balderton, Brooks rose by the time of his retirement in 2006 to be chief inspector of Ministry of Defence contracts. His local government career started in 1987 on Balderton parish council; he was first elected to Newark and Sherwood council in a 1990 by-election, had continuous service from 2003 and was chairman of the council in 2008–09. He leaves behind his wife Betty, also a Newark and Sherwood councillor, two children and four grandchildren.

One of the largest villages in Nottinghamshire, Balderton is a Newark suburb, just outside the town on the Great North Road towards London. The major employer is Flowserve (originally Worthington Simpson), a company which manufactures pumps for the chemical, water and pharmaceutical industries, and that gives the area a slightly more working-class profile than might be expected from a suburb.

Not that that stops the Conservatives, who have a lock on all Balderton's council seats. It helps that the opposition are disorganised here: since 2007 the Tories have been guaranteed one of the two seats in Balderton South (and its predecessor ward, Balderton West) because only one opposition candidate stood. In 2015 (the only previous result on the current boundaries) that was a Labour candidate, whom the Tory slate beat 57–43. The Conservatives also hold the wider Balderton seat on Nottinghamshire county council.

This by-election is also a straight fight. In the blue corner is Lydia Hurst, a Balderton parish councillor for the ward. In the yellow corner is Marylyn Rayner, chair of the Lib Dems' Newark branch.

Result: C 483 LD 103

Westone

Northampton council; caused by the resignation of Matthew Lynch, a Conservative councillor who has moved away from the town. He had served on Northampton council since 2011, and before then on Kettering council from 2003 to 2011.

Parliamentary constituency: Northampton North
Northamptonshire county council division: Headlands (southern part), Boothville and
Parklands (northern part)
May 2015 result C 1318 Lab 722 LD 315
May 2011 result C 669 LD 520 Lab 339 BNP 105

Figure 91: Northampton, Westone

For the first proper urban preview of the week, we move south to Northampton. An old town with a manufacturing base (particularly boots and shoes), Northampton has greatly expanded since the Second World War as a result of being designated a New Town, and its population is still growing strongly. The Westone area is mostly New Town development in the east of the town around Northampton College, one of the largest FE colleges in the Midlands; it's generally one of the better-off parts of town and scores well on the deprivation indices.

Westone ward was created for the 2011 election from part of the old Headlands ward, which was safe Lib Dem; however, the disastrous Lib Dem administration in Northampton in 2007–11 helped the Tories to win Westone in 2011, and they increased their majority in 2015 to 56–31 over Labour. The remaining Headlands ward (now safe Labour) anchors a county division which covers much of Westone ward and was a three-way Labour/UKIP/Conservative marginal in the 2013 county elections; the rest of Westone is covered by the safe Tory county division of Boothville and Parklands.

Defending for the Conservatives is Greg Lunn, a fitness instructor who fought the town-centre Castle ward in 2015. The Labour candidate is Toby Birch, chairman of the local charity Community Space Northampton. Hoping to make a comeback is Brian Markham, former district councillor for the area and the Lib Dem candidate here in 2011 and 2015; he completes the ballot paper.

Result: LD 583 C 319 Lab 270 [LD gain from C]

Exmouth Littleham; and
Honiton St Michael's

East Devon council; caused respectively by the death of Alison Greenhalgh and the resignation of David Foster, both of whom were Conservative councillors. Greenhalgh, a former headteacher and OFSTED inspector, had served since 2011. Foster, who in 2012 became the youngest ever mayor of Honiton at 35, had also served since 2011; he cites work and family commitments for his resignation.

For the week's two West Country by-elections we are in small towns in eastern Devon. Exmouth, Devon's fifth-largest town, is a tourist centre at this time of year and a commuter town for Exeter, but its major function out of season is as a retirement centre: Exmouth Littleham ward is in the top 100 in England and Wales for population aged 65 and over (37%) and 27% of the workforce are retired. Littleham, named after one of the former parishes covering the town, is Exmouth's southern ward covering the town's coastline, most of the beach and the beauty spot of Orcombe Point, which marks the western end of the Jurassic Coast.

Further inland is Honiton St Michael's, the western of the two wards covering Honiton. Honiton is an old market town on the Fosse Way and the A 30 London–Exeter road, known for its Georgian architecture (largely a product of the town having been mostly destroyed by fire in the mid-eighteenth century) and its traditional lace-making industry; one strange custom which took place this week is the annual Hot Pennies ceremony, dating from the Anarchy, in which warm pennies are thrown from balconies in the High Street to crowds of local people. The ward also includes a small part of the town which has spilled over the town boundary into Gittisham parish. No doubt some electors will be delighted to know that their polling station is a pub—the Heathfield Inn.

East Devon is a very strong Tory district and much of the opposition to them comes from independents: an independent slate, the Independent East Devon Alliance, came from nowhere to become the official opposition on the council after the 2015 council election, and on the same day in the general election independent county councillor Claire Wright finished second in the East Devon constituency with 24% of the vote. Exmouth Littleham returned two Lib Dems and one Conservative in the 2003 election but has had a full slate of Tories since 2007. In 2015 the Tory slate polled 43% and were opposed by single candidates from four parties who were all closely bunched together: the Independent East Devon Alliance were runners-up on 31%, with the Greens last on 28% and the Lib Dems and UKIP in between. Honiton St Michael's has been Tory at every ordinary election this century but a by-election in February 2009 narrowly elected a Lib Dem; last year the Tory slate led with 43% to 23% for the UKIP slate, 22% for the Independent East Devon Alliance candidate and 21% for independent candidate John Taylor.

At county council level Exmouth Littleham is combined with the Lib Dem ward of Exmouth Town to create a very marginal Lib Dem county division—the Lib Dem majority was cut to 10 votes in 2009 before increasing to 75 votes in the 2013 election. The Honiton St Michael's county division takes in the rural Coly Valley ward, and is a Tory-held marginal: in 2009 the Tory lead was 6 points over the Lib Dems, in 2013 they were eight points ahead of UKIP.

The Exmouth Littleham by-election is a three-way fight with the Independent East Devon Alliance, UKIP and the Greens withdrawing from the fray.

Parliamentary constituency: East Devon
Devon county council division: Exmouth Littleham and Town
May 2015 result C 1667/1636/1489 Independent East Devon Alliance 1224 LD 1170 UKIP 1164 Grn 1102
May 2011 result C 1577/1548/1474 Lab 764 Ind 679 UKIP 493
May 2007 result C 1276/1203/1154 LD 930/833/802 Lab 246 UKIP 216
May 2003 result LD 1056/903/857 C 947/885/858 Lab 270

Figure 92: East Devon, Exmouth Littleham

Parliamentary constituency: Tiverton and Honiton
Devon county council division: Honiton St Michael's
May 2015 result C 1400/1390/1304 UKIP 734/636/599 Independent East Devon Alliance 723 Ind 690
May 2011 result C 998/963/813 Grn 676 Ind 543/294 Lab 375 LD 307/215/167
Feb 2009 by-election LD 636 C 609
May 2007 result C 1101/1072/929 Lab 476
May 2003 result C 956/836/769 LD 553/504 Lab 312/234 Grn 256

Figure 93: East Devon, Honiton St Michael's

The defending Tory candidate Bruce de Saram is fighting his second by-election campaign in three months after being elected to Exmouth town council from this ward in April. The Lib Dems have selected Alex Sadiq; she is secretary of a vehicle repair company with the puntastic name of Exepress Autos. Completing the ballot paper is Labour's Keith Edwards.

To hold Honiton St Michael's the Tories have turned to Jenny Brown, a hotelier who fought Seaton ward last year. UKIP have reselected Ashley Alder who was top of their slate here last year; she is the Deputy Mayor of Honiton for 2016–17 and represents this ward on the town council. Another town councillor for this ward is Jeff Taylor, the independent candidate from 2015 who now has the Independent East Devon Alliance nomination. Completing the ballot paper is town councillor Henry Brown, standing for Labour.

Exmouth Littleham result: C 547 LD 467 Lab 193
Honiton St Michael's result: C 362 Ind East Devon Alliance 211 Lab 197 UKIP 140

Southcote

Reading council, Berkshire; caused by the resignation of Labour councillor Matt Lawrence due to pressure of work. He had served since a July 2014 by-election and was elected to a full term in 2015.

Parliamentary constituency: Reading West
May 2016 result Lab 1325 C 515 LD 129 Grn 106
May 2015 result Lab 1802 C 1476 UKIP 576 Grn 187 LD 179
July 2014 by-election Lab 1019 C 340 UKIP 226 Grn 69 LD 49
May 2014 result Lab 1286 C 626 Grn 213 LD 110
May 2012 result Lab 1364 C 478 LD 142 Grn 112
May 2011 result Lab 1543 C 858 LD 193 Grn 157
May 2010 result Lab 1836 C 1466 LD 638 Grn 108
May 2008 result Lab 1333 C 1067 LD 139 Grn 85
May 2007 result Lab 1028 C 898 LD 168 Grn 103
May 2006 result Lab 1108 C 748 LD 203 Grn 122
simultaneous with May 2006 by-election Lab 1252 C 837
June 2004 result Lab 1266/1254/1212 C 788/701/654 LD 330/322

Figure 94: Reading, Southcote

The Southcote ward of Reading can be found on the south-western edge of the town along the A4 Bath Road. It is named after the former Southcote Manor, much of whose land was developed into the ward's housing during the twentieth century. The lords of Southcote Manor supplied several MPs for Reading over the centuries, including the regicide MP Daniel Blagrave who inherited the manor from the Tudor mathematician John Blagrave. The ward includes another mansion, whose land has been preserved as Prospect Park.

Southcote has returned Labour councillors consistently since the current ward boundaries were drawn up, and under current political conditions is a safe ward. The Tories run a rather distant second here; in May Labour's lead over the Conservatives was 64–25.

Defending for Labour is Dr Jason Brock, who is a teaching fellow in Modern British and Intellectual History at Royal Holloway, University of London, and chairman of the party's Reading branch. The Conservatives have reselected their regular candidate for the ward Russell Martin; also standing are Mark Cole for the Liberal Democrats (who also stood here in May) and Green Party candidate Alan Lockey.

Result: Lab 934 C 381 LD 77 Grn 66

Warlingham West

Tandridge council, Surrey; caused by the death of Conservative councillor Glynis Whittle, who had served since 2000; she was chairman of the council in 2008–09 and chairman of the Conservatives' East Surrey branch.

Parliamentary constituency: East Surrey
Surrey county council division: Warlingham
May 2016 result C 593 LD 218 UKIP 144 Lab 82
May 2014 result C 593 UKIP 319 LD 238
May 2012 result C 591 LD 218 UKIP 135
May 2010 result C 1226 LD 583 UKIP 172
May 2008 result C 814 LD 312
May 2006 result C 843 LD 374
June 2004 result C 824 LD 358
May 2002 result C 727 LD 285 Lab 55
May 2000 result C 786/750 LD 312/298 Lab 64

Figure 95: Tandridge, Warlingham West

Welcome to commuterland. This is not just commuterland, this is Southern Railway commuterland, although somehow the lines serving Warlingham (the Caterham and Oxted branches) have escaped unscathed in the mayhem caused by Southern's current emergency timetable. Warlingham itself, on the escarpment of the North Downs, has all the demographic indicators you'd expect for a commuter area: owner-occupation rates are high (89%) and 46% of the workforce are in some sort of management or professional occupation.

The ward is as Conservative as you might expect and the party is not seriously challenged. In May's ordinary election the Lib Dems regained second place after losing it to UKIP in 2014, but still trailed the Tories 57–21.

Defending for the Conservatives is Keith Prew, who represents the ward on Warlingham parish council. The Lib Dems have reselected their May candidate Celia Caulcott, an academic and vice-provost at UCL, and UKIP's Martin Haley completes the ballot paper.

Result: C 367 LD 218 UKIP 64

Bellingham

Lewisham council, South London; caused by the resignation of Labour councillor Ami Ibitson who is taking up a new role in Sadiq Khan's administration at City Hall as, according to her Twitter, an "aspiring professional transport geek". She had served on Lewisham council since 2006.

Moving over the Greater London boundary, we are now in South London in Bellingham, one of the "cottage estates" built by the London County Council in the immediate aftermath of the First World War. While the Bellingham estate dominates the ward named after it, also within the ward are Lower Sydenham and Bell Green; the Bell Green area is being regenerated, with a high-end retail

Parliamentary constituency: Lewisham West and Penge
May 2014 result Lab 1819/1690/1505 People Before Profit 451 C 432/403/366 Grn 329/273/241
LD 194/151/142 TUSC 144
March 2011 by-election Lab 1100 C 340 LD 334 People Before Profit 264 Grn 100
May 2010 result Lab 2380/2269/1925 LD 1472/1220/1170 C 1048/911/761 People Before
Profit 318 Grn 300/258/217
May 2006 result Lab 878/849/780 C 498/461/438 LD 455/448/383 Grn 350
May 2002 result Lab 1182/1065/1056 C 510/484/472 LD 389 Grn 277
May 2016 GLA results (excludes postal votes)
Mayor: Lab 1563 C 542 Grn 173 UKIP 169 LD 106 Britain First 67 Respect 52 Women's
Equality 40 Cannabis is Safer than Alcohol 22 BNP 21 Zylinski 20 One Love 6
List: Lab 1520 C 389 UKIP 253 Grn 217 LD 106 Britain First 73 Women's Equality 66
CPA 51 Respect 43 Animal Welfare 37 BNP 16 House Party 15

Figure 96: Lewisham, Bellingham

park opening recently on the site of a former gasworks.

The Bellingham and Beckenham Hill railway stations, on Thameslink's Blackfriars–Sevenoaks line, are on the eastern boundary of the ward, while the non-estate parts of the ward are served by Lower Sydenham, a Southeastern station on the Hayes (Kent) branch.

Bellingham's census indicators bear the hallmarks of a former council estate, with 44% of the households still being socially rented. The estate has seen significant immigration from Nigeria, and the ward is in the top 50 in England and Wales for black population (34%) and mixed-race population (7.5%). Unemployment and associated indicators are high.

The result of this is a Labour ward which is not under serious threat from anybody else. In the 2014 election the Labour slate had 54%, with second place taken by a local left-wing group called Lewisham People Before Profit who had 13%, just ahead of the Conservative slate which had the same score.

In May's mayoral election Sadiq Khan beat Zac Goldsmith here 56–19, while in the London Members ballot Labour led with 55% to 14% for the Conservatives and 9% for UKIP.

Defending for Labour is Sue Hordijenko, a former Director of Programmes at the British Science Association. The Lewisham People Before Profit candidate is David Hamilton, a piano teacher and lecturer. The Conservatives have selected Ross Archer, who works for a not-for-profit organisation helping companies and consumers from falling victim to financial crime. Also standing are Ed Veasey for the Liberal Democrats and Edwin Smith for UKIP.

Result: Lab 940 C 302 LD 180 Lewisham People Before Profit 129 UKIP 104

Parliamentary constituency: Hackney South and Shoreditch (except for Cecilia Road which is in Hackney North and Stoke Newington)
May 2014 result Lab 2094/2082/1916 Grn 751/738/717 LD 240/202 C 190/184/167
May 2016 GLA results (excludes postal votes)
Mayor: Lab 2388 Grn 379 C 260 LD 106 Women's Equality 86 Respect 46 UKIP 40 Cannabis is Safer than Alcohol 28 Britain First 18 One Love 7 BNP 6 Zylinski 5
List: Lab 2188 Grn 547 Women's Equality 179 C 172 LD 105 UKIP 54 Respect 43 Britain First 33 Animal Welfare 26 CPA 20 House Party 17 BNP 8

Figure 97: Hackney, Hackney Central

Hackney Central

Hackney council, North London; caused by the resignation of Labour councillor Sophie Linden who is taking up a new role in Sadiq Khan's administration at City Hall as Deputy Mayor for policing and crime. She had served on Hackney council since 2006, initially for Dalston ward before moving to Hackney Central ward in 2014.

This is, as stated, Hackney's central ward. Hackney was an important village in Tudor times, and St Augustine's Tower survives from that period as the only vestige of mediaeval Hackney. The growth of London caught up with Hackney in Victorian times and much of the ward's housing stock is still from that era, although Hackney Town Hall is a good example of 1930s municipal architecture; on the same square as the Town Hall is the Hackney Empire, a theatre on whose stage Charlie Chaplin and Marie Lloyd (who lived around the corner in Graham Road) performed. The ward is served by two railway stations, Hackney Central on the North London line and Hackney Downs on the West Anglia main line.

Hackney is deprived, inner-city London with high levels of unemployment and a fair number of students; the ward is in the top 100 in England and Wales for black population (30%), mixed-race population (7.1%), social renting (51% of households) and Buddhism (1.8%). The present ward boundaries only date from 2014 when the Labour slate beat the Greens 64–23, although the Hackney Central ward which existed from 2002 to 2014 was very similar both in boundary and political profile. In May Sadiq Khan beat the Green Party mayoral candidate Siân Berry 71–11; the Labour/Green margin was closer in the London Members ballot at 65–16, with third place in that vote going to the Women's Equality Party who polled 5%.

Defending for Labour is another Sophie, Sophie Conway, who is a youth advocate for a children's charity. The Green candidate is Siobhan MacMahon, a former co-chair of the Green Party's youth wing. Also standing are Russell

Parliamentary and Assembly constituency: Arfon
May 2012 result PC 388 Ind 290
May 2008 result Ind unopposed
June 2004 result Ind unopposed

Figure 98: Gwynedd, Waunfawr

French for the Lib Dems, former Hackney councillor Christopher Sills for the Conservatives, and independent Mustafa Korel.

    Result: Lab 1354 Grn 178 LD 113 C 101 Ind 55

Waunfawr

Gwynedd council; caused by the resignation of Plaid Cymru councillor Eurig Wyn. One of Plaid's most prominent politicians, Wyn started his political career on the old Gwynedd county council in 1989, and was one of the two Plaid Cymru members of the European Parliament from 1999 to 2004. He returned to Gwynedd council in 2012, and has resigned for personal reasons.

For the fourth and final North Wales by-election of the month, we move away from the coast and inland. One of the two highest electoral units in England and Wales, the Waunfawr division is a large mountainous area, most of which (including Waunfawr village itself) is within the Snowdonia National Park. Waunfawr and Caeathro, a village just outside Caernarfon, are the main centres of population; the Caernarfon–Beddgelert road and the recently reopened Welsh Highland Railway link the division together, and there are no fewer than four narrow-gauge railway stations within the division boundary, three on the Welsh Highland and one—the summit station—on the Snowdon Mountain Railway. The summit of Snowdon itself lies on the division boundary.

It took until 2012 for there to be a contested election in Waunfawr this century, with Wyn challenging the sitting independent councillor Gwilym Williams and winning 57–43. So, not much previous form to go on. This by-election is again a straight fight, between Plaid's Edgar Wyn Owen, who runs a social enterprise for people with learning difficulties, and Labour's Paul Scott, a journalist and NUJ executive member.

    Result: PC 358 Lab 114

Great Wyrley Town

South Staffordshire council; caused by the resignation of Conservative councillor Brian Bates. He had served since winning a by-election in November 2005.

Parliamentary constituency: South Staffordshire
Staffordshire county council division: Cheslyn Hay, Essington and Great Wyrley
May 2015 result C 1787/1602/1584 Lab 979/826/743 UKIP 825
May 2011 result C 1182/1101/1048 Lab 537 UKIP 361
May 2007 result C 1117/1052/1016 Lab 405/387
Nov 2005 by-election C 395 Lab 320
May 2003 result C 778/739/679 Lab 503/443/409

Figure 99: South Staffordshire, Great Wyrley Town

There's no central register of local by-elections; while the political parties' crowdsourcing efforts are usually good sometimes one slips through the net. Such was the case with this poll in Great Wyrley Town, which only reached your columnist's notice on the weekend before polling day.

Great Wyrley itself is a post-industrial village lying just outside the West Midlands metropolitan boundary; it runs immediately south from the M 6 Toll junction T7 along the Walsall–Cannock road. Historically the village was known for coalmining—the collieries being connected to the outside world by the now-derelict Wyrley and Essington Canal—and for the Great Wyrley Outrages, a series of livestock killings in the early 20th century. George Edalji, the son of the local vicar (who was originally a Parsee from Bombay, and may have been the first south Asian to be an English vicar) was convicted of one of the killings, but later exonerated thanks to detective work by Arthur Conan Doyle. Served by Landywood station on the Cannock Chase line, the ward is in the top 50 in England and Wales for population born in the UK (98.5%); economically it's mixed but mostly in the better half of the deprivation indices.

That gives the Tories the edge in what has become a safe ward for them. In last year's ordinary election the Tory slate polled 67%, to 37% for the Labour slate and 31% for a single UKIP candidate. The Tories also hold the the two Staffordshire county council seats for the local division (Cheslyn Hay, Essington and Great Wyrley) which was a Tory–UKIP marginal in 2013.

Defending for the Tories is one of those county councillors, Mike Lawrence. He is opposed by two reselected candidates from 2015, Ken Bullock for Labour and Malcolm McKenzie for UKIP.

Result: C 357 Lab 230 UKIP 114

Tuesday 26th July 2016

One by-election on Tuesday 26th July 2016:

The Hangers and Forest

East Hampshire council; caused by the death of Conservative councillor Judy Onslow at the age of 70. First elected in 1999 for the former Hangers ward, Onslow was chairman of the council in 2010–11 and had also served as cabinet member for the environment.

It's a long-standing practice for elections in the UK to be held on Thursdays. By law, ordinary local elections are on Thursdays unless otherwise provided for; the devolved institutions have electoral timetables based around Thursdays; and the recent Fixed Term Parliaments Act set the dates for ordinary general elections as Thursdays. In fact, the only ordinary electoral event not tied to a Thursday is the European Parliament elections, although that might not be much of a problem for the UK in the near future. By-elections, on the other hand, are not subject to the normal rules; any ordinary working day will do. So it is that two of this week's seven by-elections are not on a Thursday, starting with this Tuesday poll in Hampshire.

The Hangers and Forest is one of the more rural wards of one of Hampshire's more rural districts. The Hangers themselves are a range of low but steep hills which mark the eastern end of the Hampshire Downs, while the Forest is Liss Forest, a hamlet surrounded by forest land used as a military training site. Apart from Liss Forest, the main centres of population are Greatham (pronounced Grettm) on the old Farnham–Petersfield road, and Hawkley. The entire ward lies within the South Downs national park, and its location on the A 3 London–Portsmouth road gives it a commuter economic profile.

Onslow held a safe Conservative seat; she was unopposed in 2003 and at her last re-election in 2015 had 69% of the vote, with an independent candidate coming second on 18%. The Tories also have little trouble in the local county

Parliamentary constituency: East Hampshire
Hampshire county council division: Petersfield Hangers
May 2015 result C 983 Ind 257 Lab 184
May 2011 result C 726 Justice and Anti-Corruption Party 275
May 2007 result C 671 Ind 175
May 2003 result C unopposed

Figure 100: East Hampshire, The Hangers and Forest

division (Petersfield Hangers).

The defending Tory candidate is Keith Budden, chairman of Liss parish council which covers Liss Forest. The independent candidate from 2015 is not standing again, but the Labour candidate from 2015 (Neil Owsnett) is. Don Jerrard, who was Onslow's only opposition in 2007 and 2011, stands for his own Justice and Anti-Corruption Party, and the Lib Dems' Roger Mullenger completes the ballot paper.

Result: C 236 LD 227 Justice and Anti-Corruption 41 Lab 17

Wednesday 27th July 2016

One by-election on Wednesday 27th July 2016:

Totnes

South Hams council, Devon; caused by the resignation of David Horsburgh who was the only Labour member of the council. A Totnes town councillor for 24 years, and twice Mayor of Totnes, but a district councillor only since May last year, Horsburgh's resignation came due to work and family commitments.

The town of Totnes has a large amount of myth and legend around it—going back to Brutus of Troy and Uther Pendragon—but its attested history begins in 907 when King Edward the Elder fortified it. The town quickly became an important market town thanks to its location at the lowest bridging point of the navigable River Dart, and being on one of the major ancient roads through the West Country. By 1523 Totnes was assessed by the Exchequer as the sixteenth richest town in England—ahead of major cities such as Worcester, Gloucester and Lincoln. Although Totnes is no longer on the main road through the South West, it is a stop on the Great Western main line from London to Plymouth. Today Totnes is probably better known for its bohemian lifestyle, being declared by *Time* magazine in 2007 to be the capital of New Age chic; a large number of artists and musicians live here.

South Hams was re-warded last year, and the current Totnes ward is a straight merger of the former Totnes Bridgetown and Totnes Town wards; Bridgetown returned an independent and a Lib Dem councillor from 2003 to 2011, while Town split Lib Dem/Labour in 2003, returned two Lib Dems in 2007 and two Green councillors narrowly in 2011; one of the Green councillors had been elected as a Lib Dem in 2007. At the last ordinary election in 2015 the ward was safe Green with the Green Party slate polling 34%; however, they stood only two candidates for the three available seats, and Labour (19%) narrowly beat the Lib Dems (17%) and Tories (14%) for the final seat. One of the two Green councillors

Parliamentary constituency: Totnes
Devon county council division: Totnes Rural
Oct 2015 by-election Grn 570 LD 558 Lab 432 C 268 Ind 63
May 2015 result Grn 2215/1839 Lab 1265/1137/1111 LD 1150 C 928/815/754 UKIP 693
TUSC 349

Figure 101: South Hams, Totnes

resigned shortly after his election on health grounds, and the Greens held the by-election last October but by just 12 votes over the Lib Dems; shares of the vote in a fragmented election were 30% each for the Greens and Lib Dems, 23% for Labour and 14% for the Conservatives.

Two things have happened during this by-election campaign to suggest a very different result this time. Firstly, Labour are not defending this by-election and the seat is up for grabs. Secondly, the town's Green Party county councillor Robert Vint (the Greens have held the county seat here since 2009), who is also a district councillor for the ward, defected to the Lib Dems during the by-election campaign. With local MP Sarah Wollaston having prominently defected from Leave to Remain during the referendum campaign, and this poll being combined with no fewer than four by-elections to Totnes town council following a rash of resignations, clearly political instability is the order of the day here. Perhaps a series of poor omens for the new Green candidate Alan White, a potter working at Dartington Pottery. The Lib Dems' John Birch, a solicitor and travel blogger, hopes to make it third time lucky after being runner-up in both 2015 elections. The Tories have selected party staffer and Vote Leave campaigner Andrew Barrand, who gives an address in Paignton; he will be hoping that nobody remembers the 2013 Surrey County Council election in which he was the election agent responsible for losing the Tories a safe seat by missing the nomination deadline. Completing the ballot paper is 18-year-old Alex Mockridge; she is standing as an independent.

Result: LD 812 Grn 499 Ind 391 C 137 [LD gain from Lab]

28th July 2016

There are five by-elections on Thursday 28th July 2016, four in England (two of which are in London) and one in Wales. In contrast to last week's procession of mostly safe seats (although there was an unexpected Lib Dem gain in Northampton), today's crop has something for everyone. There is a Labour defence in London where the party will be looking to see off the Lib Dem threat, and Labour also have clear opportunities to make gains in Newport, where the Lib Dems are defending their last seat on the council and a majority of one vote, and in Worcestershire where the Tories are defending a key marginal ward. The Conservatives are also in some trouble in their other defence in Cornwall, where they are under pressure from the Cornish nationalists. But first up today is a Lib Dem defence in South London which might not be as safe as it looks on paper...

Carshalton Central

Sutton council, South London; caused by the resignation of Liberal Democrat councillor Alan Salter, who had served since 2010. An accountant, his resignation came amid allegations of financial irregularities; Salter has since been arrested on suspicion of fraud by false representation, and police investigations are ongoing.

Now here's a rare sight—a by-election in a Liberal Democrat-held parliamentary seat. We're in Carshalton, a picturesque Surrey village built around two ponds which has been swallowed up by the growth of London. Carshalton's economy was traditionally based on lavender, but with no land left for lavender fields the area now has a commuter profile, with Carshalton station (on the Victoria–Mitcham–Sutton and Wimbledon Loop lines) and Carshalton Beeches station (on the Victoria–West Croydon–Sutton line) linking the ward to central London; since Southern Railway run most of the constituency's trains transport is probably a major political issue at the moment.

The Lib Dems have had a lock on Sutton council since 1990, with the biggest recent Tory challenge coming in the 2006 election when they gained two of the

Parliamentary constituency: Carshalton and Wallington
May 2014 result LD 1634/1469/1460 C 1077/989/974 UKIP 671 Lab 393/384/351 Grn
324/309/205 CPA 90 TUSC 74
May 2010 result LD 2676/2488/2377 C 2062/2033/1724 Lab 528/419/397 Grn 388/305/208
May 2006 result LD 1578/1365/1336 C 1473/1387/1375 Grn 356/238 Lab 216/207/203 CPA
116
Nov 2002 by-election LD 996 C 837 Lab 268 Grn 103
May 2002 result LD 1502/1446/1391 C 903/868/861 Lab 262/246/213 Grn 244/209/180
2016 GLA elections (excludes postal voters)
Mayor: C 1302 Lab 871 LD 424 Grn 167 UKIP 153 Women's Equality 42 Britain First
34 Respect 16 Cannabis is Safer than Alcohol 16 BNP 12 Zylinski 12 One Love 3
List: C 980 LD 675 Lab 620 UKIP 328 Grn 232 Women's Equality 83 Britain First 51
Animal Welfare 34 CPA 24 Respect 21 BNP 17 House Party 5

Figure 102: Sutton, Carshalton Central

three seats in Carshalton Central, but the Lib Dems recovered those gains in
2010. At the most recent London borough elections in 2014 the Lib Dem slate
won with 38%, to 25% for the Tories, 16% for a single UKIP candidate and 9% for
the Labour slate; in the London mayoral election in May Zac Goldsmith had
43% to 29% for Sadiq Khan and 14% for the Lib Dems' Caroline Pidgeon, while
the Lib Dems were a rare second in the London Members ballot with 22%, to
32% for the Tories, 20% for Labour and 11% for UKIP.

By-elections where the previous councillor resigned under a cloud are often tricky defences. Chris Williams, a recently-retired teacher, has the task of
defending this seat for the Lib Dems. His main opposition will probably come
from the Tory candidate Melissa Pearce, a civil engineering manager. The UKIP
candidate is Bill Main-Ian, a former royal protection police officer and wheelchair
user who chairs the party's Sutton branch and stood here in last year's general
election. Labour have selected Sarah Gwynn, who gives an address in Croydon
but is described as an active campaigner. Also standing are Ross Hemingway for
the Green Party and Ashley Dickenson for the Christian Peoples Alliance.

Result: LD 1250 C 1061 Grn 211 Lab 176 UKIP 150 CPA 29

Harringay

*Haringey council, North London; caused by the resignation of Labour councillor
James Ryan who is taking up a new job in Sadiq Khan's administration at City
Hall. He had served only since 2014.*

Our other London by-election of the week is a very different area to Carshalton. Harringay ward is a long, thin ward bounded on the west side by the East

Coast Main Line and on the east side by the high street of Green Lanes; since every other road within the ward runs west–east between the two the ward's street layout is known as the Harringay Ladder, a series of uniformly Victorian terraces. The ward also includes Finsbury Park, one of London's great Victorian parks and home to the London Mets baseball team.

A quick look at the cosmopolitan Green Lanes will tell you that this area has been a major focus for immigration. Harringay ward is in the top 100 in England and Wales both for population born in the old EU states (8%) *and* in the new EU states (13%); not surprisingly therefore it is also in the top 100 for the White Other ethnic group (32%), for population aged between 30 and 44 (32%) and for private renting (46% of households); there is a large student population, employment is high and the employment profile is mixed. When London-based politicians talk about immigration being positive for the economy, perhaps this is the sort of area they are thinking of. The Ladder is served by no fewer than four stations, Harringay and Hornsey on the East Coast Main Line, Harringay Green Lanes on the Gospel Oak–Barking line (closed for electrification) and Turnpike Lane on the Piccadilly line of the Underground, while the park is served by Manor House station on the Piccadilly line and by the major transport interchange of Finsbury Park itself.

A safe Labour ward in 2002 with evenly-split opposition, Harringay was aggressively targeted by the Lib Dems in their 2006 assault on Haringey council which saw them top the poll across the borough but win fewer seats than Labour, who continued in office on the council. The Lib Dems did gain two of the three seats in Harringay ward that year, held on to them in 2010 and weren't all that far off keeping hold of a seat in the 2014 election where Labour got their full slate back; shares of the vote that year were 43% for the Labour slate, 30% for the Lib Dems and 17% for the Greens. However, the London Assembly poll in May provides Labour with grounds for optimism, with Sadiq Khan polling 61% here to 13% for the second-placed Green candidate Siân Berry, and Labour winning the London Members ballot with 50% to 19% for the Greens and 10% for the Conservatives, the Lib Dems actually finishing fifth behind the Women's Equality Party.

Defending for Labour is Zena Brabazon, a former Haringey councillor (for St Ann's ward in Tottenham) who was deselected for the 2014 election. The Lib Dems have also selected a former Haringey councillor, Karen Alexander who represented this ward from 2006 to 2014. The Green candidate is Jarelle Francis, a businessman in the fashion industry. Also standing are Cansoy Elmaz for the Conservatives and Neville Watson for UKIP.

Result: Lab 1054 LD 765 Grn 325 C 99 UKIP 36

Parliamentary constituency: Tottenham
May 2014 result Lab 1683/1395/1372 LD 1182/1139/878 Grn 657/572/558 TUSC 219/165/132 C 219/212/200
May 2010 result LD 2244/1987/1800 Lab 2159/1974/1601 Grn 602/555/368 C 447/435/407 Ind 292
May 2006 result LD 1308/1159/1075 Lab 1254/1068/1024 Grn 345/343/339 C 187/163/152
May 2002 result Lab 1014/869/844 Grn 413/359/306 C 401/376/306 LD 383/267/235
2016 GLA elections (excludes postal voters)
Mayor: Lab 2220 Grn 468 C 435 LD 209 Women's Equality 139 Respect 32 Cannabis is Safer than Alcohol 31 UKIP 30 Zylinski 19 Britain First 18 BNP 9 One Love 8
List: Lab 1835 Grn 676 C 348 Women's Equality 305 LD 289 UKIP 51 Respect 44 Animal Welfare 43 Britain First 24 House Party 17 CPA 12 BNP 8

Figure 103: Haringey, Harringay

Parliamentary constituency: Mid Worcestershire
Worcestershire county council division: Droitwich West
May 2015 result C 983/897 Lab 829/604 Grn 381
May 2011 result C 679/587 Lab 622/461
May 2007 result C 585/553 Lab 538/492
May 2003 result Lab 473/442 C 314/306

Figure 104: Wychavon, Droitwich West

Droitwich West

Wychavon council, Worcestershire; caused by the resignation of Conservative councillor Catherine Powell, who had served since 2015. Her resignation was due to work commitments.

Out of London, and we come to Worcestershire. The Droitwich West ward consists of a series of entirely post-war council estates along the A 38 Droitwich bypass, close to a large industrial estate at Berry Hill which provides employment for the area. As a result the local employment base is working-class and geared towards manufacturing, and much of the housing is still socially rented. However, the ward's good road connections to Worcester and Birmingham means there is a commuting element to the ward. The ward has a relatively high population from the new EU states (just under 4% at the time of the last census).

This social profile makes the ward a key Labour–Conservative marginal. Labour did well here in the 2003 election, but the Conservatives narrowly gained both seats in 2007 (by majorities of 47 and 15 votes). Labour got one seat back in 2011, but the 2015 result was another Tory sweep; shares of the vote were 45% for the Conservatives, 38% for Labour and 17% for a single Green Party candidate. If Labour can get their act together under Corbyn, surely this should be a gain?

The Tories have gone for youth in defending this by-election; their candidate George Duffy is a 19-year-old farmworker. The Labour candidate is Droitwich Spa town councillor Alan Humphries. The Greens have not nominated a candidate, so the ballot paper is completed by Adrian Key of the Lib Dems and Andy Morgan of UKIP.

Result: C 281 Lab 161 UKIP 132 LD 97

Newlyn and Goonhavern

Cornwall council; caused by the resignation of Conservative councillor Lisa Gorman, who had served since 2013.

It's worth saying a word about the number of Cornish by-elections. This is the sixth so far this year with a seventh to come in September, which seems like a lot; but it must be remembered that Cornwall council is the fourth-largest elected body in the UK with 123 members—only Durham council, the Scottish Parliament and the House of Commons have a larger membership. Cornwall council is twice the size of a small metropolitan borough council and perhaps three times the size of the average English district council, so in that context seven by-elections in a year, while still quite a lot, is not excessive.

It's also worth saying a word about the name of Newlyn and Goonhavern division. This is not the Newlyn which is a small fishing village outside Penzance known for its Ordnance Datum, from which all altitudes in the UK are measured. Rather, this Newlyn refers to St Newlyn East, an inland village which forms the centre of a rural ward covering the countryside immediately to the south of Newquay, and the hills to the south of it on the A 30 road called the Newlyn Downs. This was traditionally a mining district, and in Victorian times the major employer was the East Wheal Rose lead mine—despite a disaster in 1846 when the mine was flooded by a thunderstorm. St Newlyn East vies for the title of the ward's largest village with Cubert; also within the ward are Goonhavern and Crantock. In summer the ward is filled with tourists, with attractions including the Lappa Valley steam railway and the Elizabethan manor Trerice House. The electors of Mitchell, a small village on the A 30, will no doubt be pleased to see that their polling station is a pub—the Plume of Feathers.

Before local government in Cornwall was reorganised in 2009 the Lib Dems had most of the county and district councillors for this area, so the Conservatives did well in 2009 to win here with a big majority over the Lib Dems. There was a change of Conservative candidate for the 2013 election, and Lisa Shuttleworth (as

Parliamentary constituency: Truro and Falmouth (part: Cubert and St Newlyn East parish and part of Perranzabuloe parish); St Austell and Newquay (part: Crantock parish)
May 2013 result C 555 MK 529 Lab 118
June 2009 result C 621 LD 394 Ind 368 Lib 94 Lab 64

Figure 105: Cornwall, Newlyn and Goonhavern

she was then) held the seat only narrowly, beating the Cornish nationalist party Mebyon Kernow 46–44.

This by-election has a large field. Defending for the Conservatives is Paul Charlesworth, finance officer and fundraiser for the charity Hearing Loss Cornwall. Mebyon Kernow's Rod Toms stands again; he is a retired scientist and St Newlyn East parish councillor. Also standing are Vicky Crowther for Labour, former Lib Dem councillor for much of the area Kenneth Yeo as an independent, two other independent candidates—Rob Thomas and James Tucker—and official Lib Dem candidate Maggie Vale.

Result: LD 247 C 234 Yeo 163 Mebyon Kernow 161 Lab 77 Tucker 75 Thomas 54 [LD gain from C]

St Julians

Newport council, South Wales; caused by the death of councillor Ed Townsend, who was the only Liberal Democrat member of the council, at the age of 64. A former journalist with the Birkenhead Post *and the* Daily Mail, *Townsend came to Wales as head of corporate relations for BT. He was first elected to Newport council in 2004, and was the council's cabinet member for economic regeneration from 2008 to 2012 and deputy leader of the council from 2008 to 2011. He is survived by his wife Carmel, six children and two grandchildren.*

You're not from Newport. You've probably never been there either. I'll bet you a fiver. Well, if you'd made that wager with your columnist you'd now be five pounds lighter; although I haven't been to Liswerry I have heard of Pillgwenlly (it was the subject of a column three years ago) and I have passed through St Julians (in Welsh, *Sain Silian*) division. Running north-east along the Caerleon Road from the end of the Newport Bridge over the Usk, St Julians is centred on junction 25 of the congested M 4 motorway; the name commemorates St Julius of Caerleon, a local Christian who was martyred during the reign of the Roman emperor Diocletian. In modern times the major local controversy was the construction of a new primary school on a former landfill site next to the Usk containing hazardous materials. The major demographic feature of the

Parliamentary and Assembly constituency: Newport East
May 2012 result Lab 1020/981/957 LD 958/873/863 C 299/266/243
June 2008 postponed poll LD 1148/1029/985 C 581/552/542 Lab 492/467/432 PC 111
June 2004 result LD 1718/1560/1548 Lab 774/632/469 C 312/277/257 Ind 306/170 PC 147

Figure 106: Newport, St Julians

division is a large student population. Gun crime doesn't appear to be a major local concern, with a total of two weapons offences recorded in the division so far this year; on the other hand, gun-crime statistics are sometimes misleading. Ask any politician and they'll tell you it's true.

Ed Townsend had been possibly the most important Lib Dem campaigner in Newport: he fought Newport East in every Westminster and Senedd election from 2003 to 2011, his best result coming in the 2010 Westminster poll when he had 32% of the vote, although he was actually closer to Labour in the 2007 Senedd election. In the 2011 Senedd poll Townsend fell to 19% and third place as the Coalition in London burst the Lib Dem bubble; a year later eight of the party's nine city councillors went straight outta Newport, with Townsend as the last man standing. In what had previously been a Lib Dem ward safe as, er, houses, the Labour slate in St Julians surged from third place to beat the Lib Dems 45–42, with Townsend saving his own seat by a single vote over the third Labour candidate. To add insult to injury, one of the two victorious Labour candidates was Rhys Hutchings, variously also known as Rhys, Dwain Xain Zedong, P Xain and Zardoz of the hiphop group Goldie Lookin Chain—probably best known for the No 3 hit *Guns Don't Kill People, Rappers Do* and with a back catalogue which is far too filthy to enumerate before the 9 o'clock watershed.

There will still be a Townsend on the ballot paper as the Lib Dems attempt to keep their toehold on Newport council—Ed's widow Carmel Townsend, herself a former councillor for the ward from 2008 to 2012. Labour have made the slightly more conventional choice (compared to Hutchings) of Phil Hourahine, a governor at St Julians primary school. Also on the ballot paper (perhaps "standing" isn't the best choice of phrase given the rest of this sentence) are Carol Bader for the Conservatives, Andrew Byers for UKIP, Plaid Cymru's Chris Priest and Mirka Virtanen of the Green Party.

Result: LD 948 Lab 432 UKIP 156 C 135 PC 71 Grn 25

4th August 2016

There are seven by-elections on 4th August 2016. Let me take you on a trip from north to south, starting and finishing on the coast—for where better is there to be in August? There are four Tory defences this week, two in marginal wards in the North of England (in one of which the outgoing councillor is rather under a cloud) and two safe seats in Nottinghamshire; Labour defend two urban seats, a three-way marginal in Ashford (Kent) and a safe seat in Brighton; and the final seat up this week is an open seat in Staffordshire which in recent years has been a Labour vs UKIP marginal. Confused? Let me explain...

South East Holderness

East Riding council, East Yorkshire; caused by the resignation of Conservative councillor Arthur Hodgson, who had served since 2007.

(Important news events over the last few weeks make googling for "Hodgson resignation" and expecting to be enlightened as to this by-election rather a fruitless exercise.)

Mention the name John Smeaton and you might think of a former Glasgow Airport baggage handler. But there was another famous John Smeaton, an eighteenth-century civil engineer best known for the penultimate Eddystone lighthouse. One of that Smeaton's lighthouses can be found at Spurn Point, that narrow strip of sand-dunes which stretches halfway across the end of the Humber estuary. Although the dunes have been knocked about a bit by recent weather events which have taken out the road, there is still a population at Spurn Point which is the base for one of the UK's very few paid full-time lifeboat crews.

Spurn may appear to be the end of land for those travelling on the North Sea ferries out of Hull, but of course it is the start of land for those arriving here from the continent: one of those was Henry of Bolingbroke, who landed at Ravenspurn to start his deposition of Richard II in 1399. Ravenspurn was a port

Parliamentary constituency: Beverley and Holderness
May 2015 result C 2406/2400/2313 UKIP 2043 Lab 1783/1591/1531 Ind 660
May 2012 by-election C 1187 Lab 1011 Ind 971
May 2011 result C 1791/1534/1482 Ind 1281 Lab 951/920/892 LD 569 Ind 560/543/465/255
May 2007 result C 2086/1869/1612 Ind 1313 LD 975/703/622 Lab 627/591/537
May 2003 result C 1591/1452/1272 Lab 938/745/689 LD 914/834/668 Ind 778

Figure 107: East Riding, South East Holderness

here, long lost on this rapidly-eroding coast.

Not that there are many people arriving in this ward from the continent today. The 2011 census found only 72 people here from the new EU states with South East Holderness' population being almost homogeneously British and to a large extent retired; perhaps one explanation for the large Leave vote across the East Riding in the recent referendum.

With the demise beneath the waves of Ravenspurn, Ravenser Odd (once a more important port than Hull, sending a representative to the Model Parliament of 1295 but destroyed by the Grote Mandrenke storm in 1362) and around 30 other coastal settlements in Holderness, the ward's main centre of population is now Withernsea, a seaside resort at the northern landfall of the Greenwich meridian, known for the fact that its lighthouse lies inland in the middle of the town centre. The East Riding's wards tend to be on the large side in both geographic and population terms, and Withernsea is one of thirteen parishes making up the South East Holderness ward.

The Conservatives have monopolised South East Holderness' three councillors at every election this century, but the ward is trending away from them. Labour and an independent both came close at a 2012 by-election, and UKIP performed well here in 2015 when the shares of the vote were 35% for the Conservatives, 30% for UKIP and 26% for the Labour slate.

Defending this three-way marginal for the Conservatives, and in the unusual position for a T of the top half of the ballot paper, is David Tucker, an electrical projects director from Easington, the nearest village to Spurn. UKIP have selected Andrew Weaver, a logistics manager and former coalminer who fought his home ward (Mid Holderness) last year. Labour's Patrick Wilkinson, despite not having yet reached his 19th birthday, already has a track record as an election winner having been returned to Withernsea town council in a by-election last November at the age of 18 years 43 days. Also standing are Withernsea-based independent Dave Edwards, who hasn't been put off by his last-place finish here last year, and Lib Dem candidate Helen Wright.

Result: C 917 Lab 806 UKIP 390 Ind 173 LD 98

Parliamentary constituency: Penrith and the Border
Cumbria county council division: Alston and East Fellside
May 2015 result Ind 710/446 C 487
May 2011 result Ind 436/177/161 C 390 Lab 242
May 2007 result Ind 533 Ind 498 Ind 235
May 2003 result 2 Ind unopposed

Figure 108: Eden, Alston Moor

Alston Moor

Eden council, Cumbria; caused by the resignation of Conservative councillor David Hymers. Hymers had served only since 2015; he held the economic development portfolio on Eden council but resigned after his business affairs were featured in Private Eye*'s Rotten Boroughs column; one of his businesses had gone into liquidation owing a seven-figure sum.*

From the Holderness coast to the High Pennines east of Eden; the River Eden, that is. Alston vies with Buxton for the title of England's highest market town, lying in the valley of the South Tyne over 1,000 feet above sea level. The town's economy was traditionally based on mining, with large deposits of lead, silver and coal in the area.

The nearby village of Nenthead, at over 1,500 feet, dates only from the mid-eighteenth century, built by the London Lead Company to serve the Nenthead mines and the UK's first village to have electric street lighting; we retain the connection with John Smeaton, who worked on the drainage in the Nenthead mines. Tynehead, once another thriving mining village but now reduced to a single house, was once the location of England's highest primary school, while Garrigill lies on the Pennine Way at the end of the descent from its highest point, Cross Fell.

With the end of mining in the area (although there are thought to be significant zinc deposits below Nenthead) the population of Alston Moor parish, which includes the town, all those villages and a large amount of moorland, has crashed from over 6,800 in 1831 to around 2,100 today, and Alston's Wikipedia page paints a picture of a town in serious decline. The town's last bank closed in 2015 and Channel 4 were in town in 2006 with a documentary examining a serious male–female imbalance in the local population. Tourism, farming and metalworking are now the main local employers; self-employment rates in the ward are high and there is a relatively old age profile.

The male–female imbalance doesn't extend to Alston Moor's two district councillors, who are gender-balanced. Independent councillor Patricia Godwin was re-elected last year for a second term at the top of the poll, with new Conservative candidate Hymers narrowly beating an independent candidate for the other seat. Alston is represented by an independent on Cumbria county council (in Alston and East Fellside division).

Defending for the Tories is Stephen Harrison, a farmer who has diversified into holiday accommodation. In a straight fight, he is opposed by the Liberal Democrat candidate Thomas Sheriff.

Result: LD 302 C 251 [LD gain from C]

Silverdale and Parksite

Newcastle-under-Lyme council, Staffordshire; caused by the death of councillor Eileen Braithwaite who had been elected as UKIP but had left the party.

More mining up in the hills as we come to the first of this week's three repeats—wards which readers with long memories (hello Sid, hello Doris) will have seen in this column before. Silverdale Colliery, in the range of hills that runs west from Stoke-on-Trent, was greatly expanded in the 1970s and closed as late as 1998; it was Staffordshire's last deep coal mine. Its legacy can still be seen in the ward's working-class demographic, with 35% of the workforce having no qualifications (although a further 7% are studying for one, being students at the nearby Keele University).

Newcastle-under-Lyme is rather unusual in that it was electing UKIP councillors long before electing UKIP councillors became fashionable. Braithwaite herself was first elected in 2003 under the label of the "Caring Party", gaining what had previously been a safe Labour seat by 12 votes; the Caring Party then folded into UKIP and Braithwaite was re-elected in the 2007 election which also saw the Kippers gain Silverdale's other council ward (Knutton and Silverdale). Braithwaite lost her seat in 2011 but got back on the council in 2014, only for the UKIP group to suffer a damaging split (now where have we heard that before?) in which she and two other Kipper councillors walked off to become independents. The split happened before the most recent election in this ward in 2015 which thus had no UKIP candidate; Labour won with 47% to 23% for Eileen's husband Richard, standing as an independent, and 22% for the Conservatives. UKIP held the local county council seat by two votes over Labour in 2013, although the county councillor is also one of the splitters; the county division includes Keele University, demonstrating once again that students don't vote in local elections.

Defending for the independents is Gary White, vice-chairman of Madeley parish council (a couple of miles to the west) and partner of independent councillor for Madeley Simon White. UKIP want their seat back, and have selected Lynn Dean. Labour also want their seat back, and have selected Gareth Snell, a former

Parliamentary constituency: Newcastle-under-Lyme
Staffordshire county council division: Keele, Knutton and Silverdale
May 2015 result Lab 888 Ind 435 C 416 Grn 100 TUSC 62
May 2014 result UKIP 477 Lab 385 C 122 Grn 36 TUSC 21
July 2013 by-election Lab 387 UKIP 254 C 58 TUSC 14
May 2011 result Lab 471 UKIP 431 C 112
May 2010 result Lab 612 UKIP 457 C 320 LD 254
May 2007 result UKIP 537 Lab 282 C 107 LD 76
May 2006 result Lab 389 UKIP 296 C 125 LD 119
May 2003 result Caring Party 323 Lab 311 LD 83 C 75
May 2002 result Lab 480/369 Caring Party 110/100 LD 105/101 C 100/82

Figure 109: Newcastle-under-Lyme, Silverdale and Parksite

leader of the council who lost his seat in 2014. Completing the ballot paper is the Tories' James Vernon, who stood here in a 2013 by-election and in 2014.

Result: Lab 399 UKIP 174 C 80 Ind 54 [Lab gain from UKIP]

Bingham (Nottinghamshire county council); and Cranmer (Rushcliffe council)

Both caused by the death of Conservative councillor Martin Suthers. A contemporary of Ken Clarke, Norman Fowler and John Gummer in the Cambridge University Conservative association, Suthers had a long career in local government, being first elected in 1967 to the pre-reform Nottingham city council: he fought Nottingham West in the 1970 general election and was Lord Mayor of Nottingham in 1988–89. During his mayoral year he was appointed OBE for political and public services. He was first elected to Nottinghamshire county council in a 2000 by-election, serving as deputy leader of the council from 2009 to 2013 and as deputy leader of the Conservative group since 2013. He was in his first term on Rushcliffe council, having been elected for Cranmer ward in 2015.

From the West to the East Midlands for the safest Tory defences of the week. Bingham is an old Roman town at the junction of the Fosse Way and the Nottingham–Grantham road, which has grown rapidly in recent years thanks to Nottingham overspill and commuting. Despite this growth, Bingham isn't large enough to have a county division all to itself, and to make the numbers up the Bingham county division includes a series of villages in the Vale of Belvoir along the Nottingham–Grantham railway line, of which the largest is Aslockton. Aslockton forms the focus of a district ward named in honour of its most famous son Thomas Cranmer, the Archbishop of Canterbury during the reign

Parliamentary constituency: Newark
Rushcliffe district council wards: Bingham East, Bingham West, Cranmer (part: Aslockton and Whatton-in-the-Vale parishes), Thoroton (part: Elton-on-the-Hill, Flawborough, Granby, Hawksworth, Orston, Sibthorpe and Shelton parishes)
May 2013 result C 1522 Lab 738 LD 725 UKIP 656
June 2009 result C 2020 LD 1207 Ind 510 Lab 410
May 2005 result C 2709 LD 1915 Lab 1478 Ind 146

Figure 110: Nottinghamshire CC, Bingham

Parliamentary constituency: Newark
Nottinghamshire county council division: Bingham (part: Aslockton and Whatton-in-the-Vale parishes), Radcliffe on Trent (part: Car Colston, Scarrington and Screveton parishes)
May 2015 result C 995 Lab 410

Figure 111: Rushcliffe, Cranmer

of Edward VI, compiler of the first two editions of the Book of Common Prayer and a martyr to the cause of the English Reformation. Further east in the county division is the village of Thoroton, where the former Lord Chancellor, Lord Falconer of Thoroton, owns property.

Suthers held safe county and district seats; in the 2013 county election he had 42% in Bingham to 20% each for Labour and the Lib Dems and 18% for UKIP, while in Cranmer ward in 2015 (the first contest on the ward's current boundaries) he beat Labour 71–29 in a straight fight.

It's a family affair for the two defending Tory candidates: defending the Bingham county division for the Tories is Bingham West district councillor Francis Purdue-Horan, whom the Tories have forgiven for a widely-reported gaffe during his year as Mayor of Rushcliffe in 2015–16 in which he dedicated the Queen song *Fat Bottomed Girls* to "all the girls of Bingham"; while Purdue-Horan's wife Maureen Stockwood, a former Mayor of both Bingham and Rushcliffe, is defending the Cranmer district ward after losing her seat in the 2015 district elections. Labour once put up a candidate in Cranmer ward called Rupert Bear (since you asked, a retired divorce lawyer who once worked for the same Nottingham law firm as Suthers) but for that by-election they have reselected their 2015 district candidate Chris Grocock, while the county by-election will be fought for Labour by Alan Walker. Completing both ballot papers is the 2015–16 Mayor of Bingham Tracey Kerry, standing as an independent.

Bingham result: C 1270 Ind 1232 Lab 382
Cranmer result: C 318 Ind 138 Lab 130

Beaver

Ashford council, Kent; caused by the resignation of Labour councillor Jill Britcher, who is moving away from the borough. She had served since winning a by-election in February 2013.

From one Belvoir to another: the Beaver ward of Ashford, the second of this week's three repeats. One of the boom towns of modern Britain thanks to its location and good transport links, Ashford is an old market town which became a major railway junction in the nineteenth century. It is now linked to London and (subject to French security checks) the Channel Ports by the M 20 motorway and the Channel Tunnel Rail Link, with high-speed trains taking just 37 minutes to reach St Pancras. The growth of Ashford has meant the town has spilled outside its old boundaries to swallow up several surrounding villages, and Beaver ward (named after Beaver Lane), which was originally the south-west corner of the town, is now just part of the urban sprawl.

Beaver ward is a fairly working-class area and was safe Labour in 2003. Unusually it swung towards the Conservatives at the next two ordinary elections. In May 2011 the two Labour candidates were just 29 and 27 votes ahead of the Conservatives; the Ashford Independents, a well-organised localist group with five Ashford councillors, finished in a strong third place. One of the Labour councillors died shortly afterwards; the resulting by-election, in November 2011, saw Labour increase their majority over the Conservatives in a much more crowded field, and there was more bad news to come for the local Tories as their candidate in that by-election, landlord Cengizhan Cerit, was subsequently sent to prison for forging nine of the ten signatures on his nomination papers. A further by-election in February 2013, caused by the resignation of the first by-election winner, saw the Labour majority greatly improve. However, in 2015 Labour finally did lose a seat in the ward: not to the Tories, but to UKIP in a close three-way result: shares of the vote that year were 31% for the Labour slate, 30% for the single UKIP candidate and 27% for the Tory slate. The ward's working-class UKIP credentials are borne out by Beaver being in the top 100 wards in England and Wales for lower supervisory or technical jobs (12% of the workforce) while unemployment and social renting are high.

So, this is a difficult defence for Labour who are under pressure on two fronts. Their candidate is Caroline Harris, who represents South Ashford on various NHS local health groups. The UKIP candidate is Ryan Macpherson, a security consultant and former special constable. The Tory candidate Jo Gideon has a lot of local government experience: she was a Thanet councillor from 2003 to 2015 and fought Scunthorpe in the 2015 general election. Completing the ballot

Parliamentary constituency: Ashford
Kent county council division: Ashford South
May 2015 result Lab 817/645 UKIP 812 C 715/423 Grn 195/135 Ind 126
Feb 2013 by-election Lab 296 C 158 UKIP 155 Ashford Ind 85 LD 79 Ind 34 Grn 19
Nov 2011 by-election Lab 336 C 249 LD 173 Ashford Ind 111 Grn 26
May 2011 result Lab 481/479 C 452/335 Ashford Ind 308/261
May 2007 result Lab 554/545 C 377/369 LD 184/175
May 2003 result Lab 636/619 C 261/259

Figure 112: Ashford, Beaver

paper is Green Party candidate Elizabeth Wright.

Result: UKIP 373 Lab 243 C 240 Grn 31 [UKIP gain from Lab]

East Brighton

Brighton and Hove council, East Sussex; caused by the resignation of Labour councillor Maggie Barradell, who had served since 2015.

We finish this week's previews as we started: by the seaside. The seafront of East Brighton ward consists of part of the Kemptown area around the Royal Sussex County Hospital, a traditionally bohemian area of Regency-style architecture. Above it is the redeveloped and rather isolated council estate of Whitehawk, in a dry chalk valley with Brighton racecourse looping around it. Much of the eastern half of the ward is open countryside, part of which is within the South Downs National Park.

Brighton and Hove was famously run by the Green Party from 2011 to 2015, but the Green administration quickly became unpopular and crashed and burned in the 2015 election, putting Labour back in minority control. The Green surge never got anywhere near taking East Brighton ward, with Whitehawk making this one of the strongest Labour wards in the city: in May last year the Labour slate polled 46% to 22% for the Conservatives (whose vote presumably comes from the Kemptown waterfront) and 20% for the Greens in third place. Going back a few years, the Tory slate here in 2007 included a celebrity candidate, the former Dollar singer David Van Day, to little discernible effect.

So the Labour candidate Lloyd Russell-Moyle should have little trouble defending this seat: he fought Lewes at the last general election and is a consultant for the United Nations on children and young people. The Tory candidate is David Plant, the commercial director of a building services company and former captain of the non-league side Whitehawk FC. The Greens have selected Mitch Alexander; she is setting up an organisation running drama workshops on the

Parliamentary constituency: Brighton Kemptown
May 2015 result Lab 3229/3225/2918 C 1563/1510/1416 Grn 1357/1021/855 LD 546 TUSC 255
Oct 2012 by-election Lab 1596 C 531 Grn 436 UKIP 148 LD 59 TUSC 55
May 2011 result Lab 2059/1862/1616 Grn 955/815/627 C 940/826/803 LD 323/218 TUSC 142
May 2007 result Lab 1539/1401/1262 C 1000/997/931 Grn 621/467/445 LD 401/400/377 Brighton and Hove Inds 257 Soc Lab 109
May 2003 result Lab 1545/1451/1223 C 1062/1017/976 LD 770/682/553 Grn 623/553/396 Soc Lab 176

Figure 113: Brighton and Hove, East Brighton

Whitehawk estate. Also standing are Leigh Farrow (a former Tory city councillor) for UKIP, Andrew England (head of chemistry at Roedean School) for the Lib Dems and independent candidate Ramon Sammut.

Result: Lab 1488 C 514 Grn 286 UKIP 152 LD 116 Ind 31

11th August 2016

After a manic few weeks on the local by-election front, it's time to quieten down for the summer holidays. There are three polls this week, one in England and two in Scotland, with the three big parties at Westminster defending one seat each.

Irvine West

North Ayrshire council; caused by the resignation of SNP councillor Ruth Maguire, who was elected to Holyrood in May as the MSP for Cunninghame South. She had served since 2012.

For the first of the week's two Scottish by-elections we are in Ayrshire in a town both old and New. Irvine was one of Scotland's most important towns in the Middle Ages as one of the major ports on the west coast; although the port declined during the nineteenth and twentieth centuries it remained strategically important as a base for the ICI-Nobel explosives factory in nearby Stevenston. Famous people associated with the old town include Edgar Allen Poe, who attended the local grammar school for a short time, and Robert Burns who worked for some months at a local heckling shop—not the council chamber but a location for preparing flax for spinning.

Irvine was changed out of all recognition in the 1960s by being designated as a New Town, and now has a population of around 34,000, with construction and retail being the major sectors of the local economy. In its New Town guise Irvine has given Scotland not one but two First Ministers—Jack McConnell, who was brought up on Arran but born here, and a then 21-year-old law student who appeared on the ballot paper in 1992 for Irvine North ward in the last elections to Cunninghame district council, shortly after being the SNP candidate in Glasgow Shettleston in the previous month's general election—Nicola Sturgeon, the present First Minister of Scotland.

Sturgeon's old stomping ground has voted Nationalist at every level since

Westminster constituency: Central Ayrshire
Holyrood constituency: Cunninghame South
May 2012 result Lab 2065 SNP 1889 C 614 LD 246 Ind 187 Soc Lab 81 TUSC 51
May 2007 result Lab 2994 SNP 2247 C 799 Solidarity 517 LD 453 Soc Lab 103

Figure 114: North Ayrshire, Irvine West

2012, even in the independence referendum in which the ward was 50.6% Yes. However, Scotland's local councils were last elected in 2012 which was before Labour fell apart in the country, and in the 2012 elections to Irvine West ward Labour topped the poll with 40% to 37% for the SNP and 12% for the Conservatives. In the previous 2007 election Labour had won two seats to one each for the SNP and Tories, but the Tory seat was only won because the SNP only stood one candidate that year; in 2012 the SNP made no such mistake and Ruth Maguire narrowly beat the Tories to gain the final seat by 67 votes.

Defending for the SNP is a semi-celebrity candidate: Robin Sturgeon, father of Nicola. Labour have selected Louise McPhater, a mother of four children and Glasgow University student who works at a local community centre. The Tory candidate is Angela Stephen; also standing are Nick Smith for the Lib Dems, regular Socialist Labour Party candidate Bobby Cochrane and the ward's first Green candidate Joan McCormick. As with all Scottish local by-elections since the introduction of PR in 2007, the Alternative Vote will be used. No doubt all the candidates will be hoping to emulate the old motto of the Royal Burgh of Irvine: *Tandem bona causa triumphat* (the good cause triumphs in the end).

First preferences: SNP 1164 Lab 1029 C 629 Soc Lab 131 Grn 94 LD 48
After transfers: Lab 1301 SNP 1277 [Lab gain from SNP]

Renfrew South and Gallowhill

Renfrewshire council; caused by the death of Labour councillor Eddie Grady at the age of 66. He had served since 2007.

Take the train from Irvine towards Glasgow and the last stop before Glasgow for most trains is Paisley Gilmour Street, which lies at the south-west corner of this ward. Running roughly between the railway line and the M 8 motorway is the troubled housing estate of Gallowhill, one of three parts of this ward; to the south-east is the large Hillington industrial estate, while to the north of the motorway lies a large amount of new housing on the site of the former Renfrew Airport, in operation from 1933 (the first regular destination was Campbeltown) to 1966 when its services transferred to the present Glasgow Airport nearby. The ward's good transport links to Glasgow make this an economically mixed area

Westminster constituency: Paisley and Renfrewshire North
Holyrood constituency: Renfrewshire North and West
May 2012 result Lab 2098 SNP 1887 C 197 SSP 90 LD 86
May 2007 result Lab 2348 SNP 2087 Ind 294 C 291 LD 246 Solidarity 127 SSP 90

Figure 115: Renfrewshire, Renfrew South and Gallowhill

with something for everyone.

In the two previous elections on these boundaries Renfrew South and Gallowhill has been a close Labour–SNP fight with Labour having the edge: Labour led 43–38 in the 2007 election and 48–43 in 2012, and in both elections comfortably won two seats to the SNP's one. However, that was before Labour's vote in Scotland imploded, and Labour have a real fight on their hands to hold this seat.

Defending for Labour is Edward Grady, Eddie's son, who holds the rank of Captain in the Army (he is the commander of a local company of cadets) and works in education as a support worker. The SNP candidate is Jim Paterson, a community campaigner, former trade union activist and caseworker for the local SNP MP Gavin Newlands. Also standing are Mark Dougan for the Tories and Ross Stalker for the Lib Dems.

First preferences: SNP 1309 Lab 1012 C 366 LD 53
After transfers: SNP 1356 Lab 1180 [SNP gain from Lab]

Ombersley

Worcestershire county council; caused by the death of Conservative councillor Maurice Broomfield at the age of 87. A fruit farmer from Bromsgrove, Broomfield was one of the members of the original Bromsgrove district council elected in 1973, and was chairman of that council in 1977–78; after losing his district council seat to Labour in the Tory nadir of 1995 he was returned to Worcestershire county council, where he had served since its divorce from Herefordshire in 1997.

Altogether now: dum-de-dum-de-dum-de-dum, dum-de-dum-de-daa-d (*switches radio off*). The music just quoted may be named after the Yorkshire village of Barwick in Elmet, but for many years now it has been used to introduce *The Archers*, that simple saga of farming folk which is generally accepted to be inspired by the Worcestershire villages of Inkberrow and Hanbury. Hanbury forms part of the Ombersley division of Worcestershire county council, a sprawling rural area which wraps around the north side of Droitwich and is clearly the bit which was left over after the rest of Wychavon district had had its county divisions drawn.

The largest centres of population are Hartlebury and Ombersley on the

Parliamentary constituency: Mid Worcestershire (part: Dodderhill, Hartlebury and Ombersley wards and part of Lovett and North Claines ward), Redditch (part: part of Inkberrow ward)
Wychavon district council wards: Dodderhill, Hartlebury, Inkberrow (part: Hanbury, and Stock and Bradley parishes), Lovett and North Claines (part: Elmbridge, Elmley Lovett, Hampton Lovett and Westwood parishes), Ombersley
May 2013 result C 1292 UKIP 894 Lab 231 LD 139 Grn 137
June 2009 result C 2296 LD 561 Grn 327 Lab 201
May 2005 result C 3344 Lab 945 LD 916

Figure 116: Worcestershire CC, Ombersley

Worcester–Kidderminster road. Ombersley has for centuries been the seat of the Lords Sandys, a family which has participated in government for centuries. Edwin Sandys was Archbishop of York under Elizabeth I; Samuel, 1st Lord Sandys was Chancellor of the Exchequer under the Earl of Wilmington; most recently Richard Hill, 7th Lord Sandys was a Lords Whip under Heath and Thatcher. At Hartlebury can be found Hartlebury Castle, former residence of the Bishops of Worcester and home to the Worcestershire County Museum. The division's only railway station is also at Hartlebury, on the Birmingham–Kidderminster–Worcester line.

Broomfield had a safe seat, although he was run relatively close by UKIP at his final re-election in 2013, winning 48–33. It's difficult to compare last year's Wychavon district council results with this, partly because the ward boundaries don't match up and partly because of a lack of UKIP candidates for the district council, but the Tories hold all the district council seats within the division.

Defending for the Conservatives is Peter Tomlinson, district councillor for Ombersley and hoping to make the step up to county level. The official UKIP candidate is Richard Keel, who fought most of this area last year as parliamentary candidate for Mid Worcestershire. Doug Ingram, a Hartlebury parish councillor who was the UKIP candidate here in the 2013 county elections, stands as an independent. Completing the ballot paper is the Lib Dem candidate Peter Evans.

Result: C 956 LD 224 UKIP 212 Ind 120

18th August 2016

This is August, this is supposed to be quiet. Well, the local parties don't seem to have listened and 18th August sees nine council by-elections in England for a total of ten seats. Two of these are or were in northern Yorkshire, with a Lib Dem defence in Teesside and an independent representing a ward which has been covered in this column very recently. All the other by-elections are south of the Thames, with a crucial double by-election in Ramsgate for a ward which UKIP carried in their 2015 surge, and Labour defending two seats in Gravesend and one in South London. But we start this week in Surrey with three Tory defences all in the town of Farnham. You thought Surrey politics was boring? Think again...

Farnham South (Surrey county council);
Farnham Castle (Waverley council); and
Farnham Shortheath and Boundstone (Waverley council)

Caused by the resignations of two Conservative councillors. The first and third vacancies are caused by the resignation of David Munro, who was elected in May as Police and Crime Commissioner for Surrey; a former Royal Engineers officer who served in Northern Ireland and the Falklands, he had served on Surrey county council since 1996 and Waverley council since 2003. The Castle ward vacancy is caused by the retirement of Paddy Blagden at the age of 86. Blagden, the father-in-law of the Canterbury MP Julian Brazier, was one of the few councillors notable enough to have his own Wikipedia page thanks to his work on demining, being head of the UN Mine Action Service from 1992 to 1995 and then in 1998 becoming a founder member of the Geneva International Centre for Humanitarian Demining. Before his demining career Blagden spent 35 years as an officer in the Royal Engineers, retiring in 1988 with the rank of Brigadier; during his time in local government he served as Mayor of Farnham in 2013–14.

You wait years for the chance to write about a Farnham by-election and then, like buses, three come along at once. Farnham is possibly the archetypal Surrey commuter town, located close to the North Downs on the western border of Hampshire; the railway (now the Alton branch of South West Trains) came here in 1848, and the development of nearby Aldershot as an Army town secured Farnham's prosperity. It is the largest town within Waverley district, although the council is in fact based in Godalming.

Much of Farnham South county division's housing stock is from a later, post-war, era, and its economic profile is middle-class with very high qualification rates. The county division includes the ruins of Waverley Abbey, established in 1128 as Britain's first Cistercian abbey, which gives its name to one of England's more obscure local government districts. Another ruin here is Farnham Castle, which saw action in the Civil War; for centuries the castle was home to the Bishops of Winchester—one of its famous residents was the fifteenth-century Cardinal Henry Beaufort who presided at the trial of Joan of Arc—and more recently it was the venue for the wedding of a South African exile called Thabo Mbeki, who would later go on to succeed Nelson Mandela as the country's president. Farnham Castle gives its name to a ward which covers the town centre of Farnham together with the village of Dippenhall to the west.

On paper Farnham Castle looks the most interesting of these three by-elections. It was a safe Lib Dem ward in 2003, in which year the Lib Dems gained majority control of Waverley council despite polling fewer votes than the Conservatives. Since 2003 the Lib Dem organisation in Waverley has completely fallen apart (they were wiped out on the council in 2011 and haven't got back yet) and one of their two councillors sought re-election as an independent in 2007; the resultant vote split helped the Tories to win both seats in the ward. The Conservatives increased their majority in 2011, but lost one seat in Farnham Castle in 2015 to a new party called Farnham Residents and Blagden only had a majority of 61 over the resurgent Liberal Democrats, although they only ran one candidate. Shares of the vote in 2015 were 35% for Farnham Residents, 26% for the Tories and 24% for the Lib Dems.

Farnham Shortheath and Boundstone, a ward in the south of the town running along the A287 road towards Haslemere, has a slightly more straightforward history; it was narrowly Lib Dem in 2003 but a decisive Tory gain in 2007. However, the Farnham Residents did well here in 2015 as well and gained one of the two Conservative seats, the Tories topping the poll 45–41.

The Farnham South county division, which survived Surrey's redistricting in 2013 unchanged, was a safe seat for Munro; at the most recent county election in 2013 he had 50% of the vote with UKIP and an independent tying for second

Parliamentary constituency: South West Surrey
Waverley council wards: Farnham Bourne, Farnham Shortheath and Boundstone, Farnham Wrecclesham and Rowledge
May 2013 result C 1677 UKIP 542 Ind 542 Ind 344 Lab 233
June 2009 result C 2823 LD 1118 Lab 222
May 2005 result C 4053 LD 2326 Lab 574

Figure 117: Surrey CC, Farnham South

place on 16%.

Defending the county seat for the Conservatives is Wyatt Ramsdale, a Waverley councillor representing the Farnham Wrecclesham and Rowledge ward. The UKIP candidate is Paul Chapman, an engineering consultant in the oil and gas industry and chairman of the party's Surrey Heath branch—he gives an address in Frimley Green. Mark Westcott, the independent candidate who tied for second in 2013, is standing again; he is an architect and landscape architect. Also on the county ballot paper are Fabian Wood for Labour, Joanne Aylwin for the Lib Dems and Jerry Hyman, the leader of the Farnham Residents.

In Castle ward the defending Tory candidate is Nicholas le Gal, a student at Oxford Brookes University who works in the hospitality industry; he is the son of Denise le Gal, one of the two remaining Tory county councillors for Farnham. Jerry Hyman is the Farnham Residents candidate, hoping to double up at both district and county level. The Lib Dems have reselected Stewart Edge, the chairman of the party's Waverley branch and treasurer of the William Cobbett Society (Cobbett was from Farnham); Edge is hoping to return to Waverley council after serving for two terms in 1999–2007. Completing the Castle ward ballot paper is UKIP's George Hesse.

Finally, Shortheath and Boundstone ward looks set to be a battle between two former Tory Waverley councillors who lost their seats to the Farnham Residents in 2015—Donal O'Neill, formerly of Farnham Upper Hale ward, defends for the Conservatives, while the Farnham Residents have secured something of a coup by recruiting John Ward, Tory councillor for this ward from 2007 to 2015. Also standing are Jim Burroughs for UKIP, Sylvia Jacobs (another former councillor for the ward) for the Lib Dems and independent candidate Andrew Jones.

Farnham South (county council) result: C 932 Farnham Residents 754 LD 269 Ind 139 UKIP 89 Lab 77

Farnham Castle (district council) result: Farnham Residents 386 LD 292 C 229 UKIP 43 [Farnham Residents gain from C]

Farnham Shortheath and Boundstone (district council) result: Farnham Residents 356 C 233 LD 90 Ind 43 UKIP 26 [Farnham Residents gain from C]

Parliamentary constituency: South West Surrey
Surrey county council division: Farnham Central
May 2015 result Farnham Residents 1043 C 797/641 LD 736 Lab 438
May 2011 result C 669/600 Ind 218/201 LD 204 Lab 152
May 2007 result C 489/466 Ind 417/387 LD 303/258 UKIP 101 Lab 84
May 2003 result LD 631/630 C 424/402 Lab 78

Figure 118: Waverley, Farnham Castle

Parliamentary constituency: South West Surrey
Surrey county council division: Farnham South
May 2015 result C 1064/806 Farnham Residents 958/781 Lab 337
May 2011 result C 1027/988 Lab 415
May 2007 result C 779/761 LD 375/359 Ind 360/314 Lab 42
May 2003 result LD 715/706 C 646/573 Lab 89

Figure 119: Waverley, Farnham Shortheath and Boundstone

Northwood

Thanet council, Kent; a double by-election caused by the resignations of councillors Konnor Collins and Helen Smith, who were elected as UKIP but had left the party. Collins and Smith have been charged with theft of gardening equipment from a local garden centre, while Smith also faces charges of assault and dangerous driving and Collins has faced questions over his claimed military service. They had served since 2015.

Since it's August, it must be time for the seaside. And so it is for the third time this year that this column finds itself in Thanet dealing with a UKIP defence. Northwood ward lies in the north of the town, running from the railway station northward along the A 254 Margate Road; like much of Ramsgate as a whole it has a working-class economic profile.

Thanet council was taken over by UKIP in the 2015 election, rather as a consolation prize following the failure of Nigel Farage to get into Parliament from the South Thanet constituency, which is based on Ramsgate. UKIP did particularly well in Ramsgate that year mostly at the expense of Labour, for whom Northwood was previously a safe ward. The 2011–15 Thanet council was both finely balanced and fissiparous: one of the Labour councillors for this ward in that term had a particularly dizzying series of defections, eventually ending up in the Green Party, but despite that Labour actually took control of the council partway through the term following a series of by-election losses by the ruling Tory group. UKIP did very well in Northwood ward in the 2015 election, gaining all three seats with 46% to 29% for the Labour slate and 25% for the Tories, but

Parliamentary constituency: South Thanet
Kent county council division: Ramsgate
May 2015 result UKIP 1351/1344/1214 Lab 830/800/784 C 726/645/622
May 2011 result Lab 971/951/877 C 726/658/616
May 2007 result Lab 812/781/675 UKIP 525 C 525/488/393
May 2003 result Lab 801/789/780 C 499/459

Figure 120: Thanet, Northwood

the party have since lost their majority on Thanet council thanks to a five-strong splinter group walking off. In addition, the Kippers have had to defend two by-elections in the neighouring Newington ward, after both their councillors for that ward resigned within a year, and one of the seats was lost back to Labour.

With the UKIP splinter group not defending these seats we have two open seats in a by-election with high stakes: two UKIP regains will put the Kippers back in majority control of Thanet council. Their candidates are Lynda Piper and cafe-owner George Rusiecki. Labour have selected Helen Crittenden, who recently returned from a four-year round-the-world trip in a Land Rover, and Kaz Peet, a DJ. On the Tory slate are Charlie Leys, a University of Kent student, Broadstairs and St Peters town councillor and recent defector from UKIP, and Prince William lookalike Marc Rattigan. Also standing are Grahame Birchall for his own Party for a United Thanet, John Finnegan and Jordan Williams on the Lib Dem slate, and independent candidate Colin Grostaste. Some of the electors in this by-election will be thrilled to know that their polling station is a pub: the Windmill on Newington Road.

Result: UKIP 488 (Piper)/394 (Rusiecki) Lab 356 (Crittenden)/325 (Peet) C 282 (Leys)/246 (Rattigan) Ind 136 LD 64 (Williams)/48 (Finnegan) Party for a United Thanet 44

Gravesham East (Kent county council); and
Pelham (Gravesham council)

Both caused by the death of Labour councillor Jane Cribbon at the age of 66. Originally from Dublin, Cribbon had served on Gravesham council since 1999 and was chair of the planning committee; she was first elected to Kent county council in 2005, lost her seat in 2009 and returned in 2013.

For our second and third Kent by-elections of the week we catch the train along the north coast of Kent from Ramsgate to Gravesend. An old maritime town on the Thames estuary, Gravesend is still important to navigation thanks to being the base of the Port of London's pilots, who are much in demand as

Parliamentary constituency: Gravesham
Gravesham district council wards: Central, Chalk, Riverside, Riverview, Singlewell,
Westcourt, Whitehill
May 2013 result Lab 3659/3581 C 2786/2250 UKIP 2342 EDP 663 LD 380 TUSC 265
June 2009 result C 3713/3343 Lab 2321/2296 EDP 1425 Grn 1236 LD 1010/873 Ind 899
May 2005 result Lab 7060/6726 C 6304/5671 LD 1990/1909 Grn 1102

Figure 121: Kent CC, Gravesham East

Parliamentary constituency: Gravesham
Kent county council division: Northfleet and Gravesend West
May 2015 result Lab 1792/1708/1625 C 1246/1131/1038 Grn 525
May 2011 result Lab 1327/1300/1270 C 766/739/706 UKIP 235
May 2007 result Lab 967/956/943 C 759/694/658 LD 203/148
May 2003 result Lab 844/826/805 C 562/512/506

Figure 122: Gravesham, Pelham

ships manoeuvre into Tilbury docks on the opposite side of the river. Those with long memories who remember the 1952 film *The Long Memory*, in which John Mills lived in a fishing boat here, may be relieved to know that the town has been substantially redeveloped since then; the Christianfields council estate has been completely rebuilt since 2007 and the town's railway station has recently followed suit, with a third platform appearing over Christmas 2013.

The railway station and waterfront lie at the heart of the district council's Pelham ward, which is not part of the Gravesham East county division which covers the eastern two-thirds of the town.

The Gravesham parliamentary constituency has a reputation as a bellwether, having voted for the winning party at every election since World War One with the exceptions of 1929, 1951 and 2005. The Gravesham East division, which returns two members to Kent county council, is similarly marginal: it was Labour by 4.5 points in 2005 when Cribbon had one of the largest mandates in UK local government history, topping the poll with over 7,000 votes, before becoming fairly safe Tory in the Labour nadir of 2009.

It became obvious leading up to the 2013 county elections that Labour would regain the division, and one of the Tory county councillors actually did the chicken run *before* the 2013 county elections, winning a by-election for the neighbouring safe division of Gravesham Rural just before Christmas 2012. Labour did indeed regain in 2013 with 36%, to 28% for the Tories and 23% for UKIP. Pelham ward, by contrast, is safe Labour; in 2015 Labour, the Tories and the Greens took the Pelham 1-2-3 with 50%, 35% and 15% respectively.

Defending Gravesham East for Labour is Lyn Milner, a veteran district councillor representing Riverside ward. As if there weren't enough Kentish marshes in the division already, the ballot paper provides us with two more, Diane Marsh (a former district councillor and defector from UKIP) for the Tories and Mark Marsh for the Lib Dems. The official UKIP candidate is Tina Brooker, a legal secretary and pro-streetlight campaigner. Completing the ballot paper is Martin Wilson for the Green Party.

In Pelham the defending Labour candidate is Jenny Wallace, a letting agent from Higham. The Tories' Conrad Broadley is hoping to return to the district council after losing his seat in Singlewell ward in 2011. Also standing are Marna Gilligan for the Greens, Emma Foreman for the English Democrats, Gary Harding for UKIP and Sharan Virk for the Lib Dems.

Gravesham East result: C 1758 Lab 1538 UKIP 1272 Grn 209 LD 110 [C gain from Lab]

Pelham result: Lab 494 C 325 LD 101 UKIP 91 Grn 35 EDP 24

Tooting

Wandsworth council, South London; caused by the resignation of Labour councillor Ben Johnson who is taking up a new post in City Hall as a senior adviser to the Mayor of London Sadiq Khan. He had served since 2010.

The electors of Tooting must be getting a bit sick of this, as this is the fourth time in four months they have been called out to the polls following the GLA election in May and the parliamentary by-election and EU referendum in June. The Tooting ward lies generally west of the A24 Stane Street/Tooting High Road taking in Streatham Cemetery and St George's Hospital; St George's is a teaching hospital, part of the University of London, and as a result the ward's demographics are skewed by a large number of students living in the area, most of whom will not be around in August. Famous students and staff to have come out of St George's include the vaccination pioneer Edward Jenner, the mathematician and Egyptologist Thomas Young, the new Tooting MP Rosina Allin-Khan, the ill-fitting-white-shirt-wearer Harry Hill and the ill-fitting-white-suit-wearer and Olympics obsessive Paul Sinha. Tooting Broadway underground station, on the Northern Line, links the ward to central London.

If Tooting's demographics are skewed by the presence in the ward of St George's Hospital, Tooting's local election results are skewed by the presence in the ward of both Wandsworth council, with its unbelievably-low-council-tax policies boosting the Tory vote, and Sadiq Khan whose personal vote boosts the Labour total. Khan represented this ward on the Labour slate from 1994 to

Parliamentary constituency: Tooting
May 2014 result Lab 2499/2495/2371 C 1583/1525/1427 Grn 622 LD 361/327/286 UKIP 292 TUSC 115 Communist 112
May 2010 result Lab 3416/3291/3154 C 2399/2129/2125 LD 1075/1022/933 Grn 540/494 Communist 138
May 2006 result C 1707/1682/1596 Lab 1643/1616/1560 Grn 507 LD 399/393/368 Communist 136
May 2002 result Lab 1534/1407/1358 C 936/924/877 LD 360/354/239 Grn 339
May 2016 GLA results (excludes postal voters)
Mayor: Lab 3286 C 975 Grn 240 LD 129 Women's Equality 83 UKIP 54 Respect 51 Cannabis is Safer than Alcohol 23 Britain First 18 Zylinski 16 BNP 12 One Love 8
London Member: Lab 2757 C 946 Grn 408 Women's Equality 219 LD 210 UKIP 122 Respect 70 Animal Welfare 43 CPA 33 Britain First 24 House Party 21 BNP 18

Figure 123: Wandsworth, Tooting

2006, when he stood down from Wandsworth council having made the step up to Parliament the previous year; that year the Tories gained two of the three seats in Tooting ward, but Labour recovered them in 2010. The differences I'm talking about can be seen in the most recent Wandsworth council and GLA results: in the 2014 council elections Labour won with 45% to 28% for the Conservatives and 11% for the Green Party, while in the GLA elections last May Khan had a whopping 67–20 lead over Zac Goldsmith, greatly outperforming the London Members ballot where Labour led the Tories 57–19. The true strength for the Tories and Labour probably lies somewhere in between these two sets of elections.

Defending for Labour is Paul White, who works in IT. The Tories have selected Thom Norman, a PR man. The Green Party candidate is Roy Vickery, a botanist and former Natural History Museum curator. Also standing are Eileen Arms for the Lib Dems and Alexander Balkan for the SDP—not the last time this week that this column will be discussing that particular blast from the past. Sadly, there is no Tooting Popular Front candidate.

Result: Lab 1467 C 644 LD 267 Grn 116 SDP 15

Ormesby

Redcar and Cleveland council, North Yorkshire; caused by the resignation of Liberal Democrat councillor Ann Wilson on health grounds. She had served since winning a by-election in December 2009.

We move north for the first of this week's two North Yorkshire by-elections, although it might be a little controversial these days to describe Ormesby as North Yorkshire. The Ormesby ward covers affluent suburbia on the edge of Middles-

Parliamentary constituency: Redcar
May 2015 result LD 1358/1298/1083 Lab 681/616/590 UKIP 621 C 413 Ind 180/163/151
May 2011 result LD 1090/1031/947 Lab 657/601/579 C 249
Dec 2009 by-election LD 1084 Lab 210 UKIP 103 C 77
May 2007 result LD 1140/1082/1038 C 366 Lab 360
May 2003 result LD 1959/1847/1784 Lab 577 C 459

Figure 124: Redcar and Cleveland, Ormesby

brough; its most notable building is Ormesby Hall, a Palladian mansion house which was formerly the home of the Pennyman family and is now a National Trust property. Also within the ward is part of Nunthorpe, a planned suburb built around Nunthorpe railway station by Sir Arthur Dorman for workers at his Dorman Long steelworks.

Ormesby is the only Lib Dem defence this week and on the basis of past form they are unlikely to face a serious challenge. In 2015 the Lib Dem slate had 42% to 21% for Labour and 19% for a single UKIP candidate.

Defending for the Lib Dems is Carole Morgan, who gives an address in Nunthorpe. Labour have selected Alison Suthers, their second letting agent candidate of the week, from Newton under Roseberry. UKIP have reselected their 2015 candidate Ian Neil, who also stood for the Middlesbrough parliamentary seat that year. Completing the ballot paper are Cameron Brown for the Conservatives and Philip Lockey for the North East Party.

Result: LD 980 UKIP 137 Lab 126 C 41 North East Party 15

Catterick

Richmondshire council, North Yorkshire; caused by the death of Independent councillor Tony Pelton at the age of 77. Pelton was one of Richmondshire's longest-serving councillors, having been first elected in 1995 under the SDP label; he stood down from the council in 2007 but returned in 2011 as an independent. Away from politics he ran a bookshop in Richmond.

Catterick might not be the oldest village in England, but it bears one of the oldest names: *Katouraktonion,* a location in Britannia, appears on Ptolemy's map of the world identifying the twenty-fourth clime in the latitude system he was using. At the time the Romans had a fort at the meeting point of the Great North Road, Dere Street and the River Swale which they called *Cataractonium.* Around AD 598, as described in Aneurin's Welsh-language poem *Y Gododdin,* the native Britons were routed and massacred by the invading Angles in the Battle of Catraeth, a location which is generally considered to be Catterick. In

Parliamentary constituency: Richmond (Yorks)
North Yorkshire county council division: Catterick Bridge
February 2016 by-election C 308 Ind 203
May 2015 result Ind 570 C 528/392 Grn 208
May 2011 result Ind 512 C 338/263
May 2007 result C 403 Ind 318 LD 247 BNP 123/98
May 2003 result SDP 492 C 326 LD 310

Figure 125: Richmondshire, Catterick

more modern times Catterick's location on the Great North Road meant that its economy has traditionally been based on coaching; an A 1 bypass for the town was opened in 1959 by Lord Chesham at a cost of £1 million, and is now being rebuilt as a motorway for rather more money than that. However, the main drivers for the town today are tourism, the local racecourse (which is just outside the ward boundary), and the military; Catterick airfield was one of the very first RAF bases, opened in 1914 by the Royal Flying Corps as a training centre (after the Second World War it was the RAF Regiment's training base), and is now run by the Army as Marne Barracks, part of the large Catterick Garrison complex.

Pelton's large personal vote in Catterick meant that he topped the poll in every election this century where he stood; in 2015 he had 44% of the vote to 40% for the Tory slate. The Tory councillor elected for Catterick in 2015 died a few months afterwards, and the Tories held the by-election in February this year, beating an independent candidate 60–40. The Tories safely hold the local county council division (Catterick Bridge).

The losing independent candidate in the February by-election, Jill McMullon, is now the defending candidate in this by-election rather than the challenger; she is a former Tory district councillor for Middleton Tyas ward (perhaps better known as Scotch Corner) who lost her seat last year. Hoping to give Catterick a full Tory slate for the first time is Stephen Wyrill, a dairy farmer and national chairman of the Tenant Farmers Association. Also standing are David Coates for the Lib Dems and Robbie Kelly (who gives an address some distance away in Arkengarthdale) for the Green Party.

Result: C 228 LD 203 Ind 112 Grn 3 (three)

25th August 2016

The Lochs

Fife council; caused by the retirement at the age of 80 of independent councillor Willie Clark. A veteran of Scottish local government, Clark was first elected in 1973 to the pre-reform Lochgelly district council; with local government reform in 1975 he stepped up to Fife regional council, transferring to the present Fife council on its establishment in 1995. Although since the advent of party registration he had appeared on ballot papers as an independent, he was in fact a Communist, and was the last Communist to hold elected office in Great Britain.

Old parties never really die, they just fade away slowly. Last week's by-election column made not one but two references to that Eighties throwback called the SDP, and it may surprise readers to learn that Britain was still electing an avowed Communist to office as recently as 2012. Well, if anywhere was going to do that The Lochs ward was a good candidate: named after the Lochs Ore, Glow and Filty, this was the heartland of the Fife coalfield, a series of villages to the north of Dunfermline and Cowdenbeath. The end of mining has led to depopulation in the area: Kelty, the ward's largest settlement, has seen its population fall from 9,000 to 6,000 over the last four decades despite its proximity to the M 90 motorway making it attractive for Edinburgh commuters. That's not an advantage enjoyed by the Benarty area to the east (covering the villages of Ballingry, Lochore and associated settlements) which is classed as a "regeneration area" and suffers from high unemployment.

Willie Clarke's personal vote was massive: at the last first-past-the-post election to Fife council in 2003 he had 95% of the vote in Ballingry and Lochore ward, although that score was boosted because he was not opposed by Labour that year. At the first PR Fife council election in 2007 Clarke was elected at the top of poll with 28%, with Labour (39% between two candidates) and the SNP (21%) winning the other two seats. The 2007 election resulted in the SNP taking over Fife council in coalition with the Lib Dems, and in consequence the SNP vote

Westminster constituency: Kirkcaldy and Cowdenbeath (part), Dunfermline and West Fife (part)
Holyrood constituency: Cowdenbeath (part), Dunfermline (part)
May 2014 by-election Lab 2039 SNP 834 UKIP 277 C 164
May 2012 first preferences Lab 1729 Ind 1025 SNP 708 Ind 165 C 99
May 2007 first preferences Lab 1779 Ind 1291 SNP 957 LD 259 C 170 Solidarity 81 Ind 72

Figure 126: Fife, The Lochs

fell back to 19% in the 2012 election with 46% for Labour and 28% for Clarke; that might have put the SNP seat in danger, but Labour failed to balance their candidates and the SNP held the final seat fairly comfortably. One reason for the lack of Labour balance is that their ticket was headed by Alex Rowley, leader of the council from 1995 to 2007 who had remained leader of the Labour group in opposition. Rowley returned to the council leadership in 2012 as Labour formed a minority administration on Fife council, but made the step up to Holyrood in 2014 by winning a by-election for the Cowdenbeath constituency (he was re-elected to the Parliament this year, but from the regional list after losing his constituency to the SNP). After his election to Holyrood Rowley resigned from Fife council, and Labour held the resulting by-election on Euro-election day in 2014 in the first round, beating the SNP 62–25. That was, of course, before the independence referendum and the political situation is rather different now.

Defending for the Communists—not a phrase your columnist has cause to write very often—is Thomas Kirby, the only candidate not to give an address in the ward (he lives in Methil, although he was Ballingry born and bred); he was the election agent for the Communists' North East Scotland candidate in this year's Holyrood election. The Labour candidate is Mary Lockhart, a Yes campaigner in the Indyref and the candidate in last place on the Labour Mid Scotland and Fife list in May. Lea McLelland of the SNP is described as a community activist; she has been prominent in a local campaign against cuts to bus services for the ward. Completing the ballot paper are Malcolm McDonald for the Conservatives and Bradford Oliver for the Lib Dems. Whoever wins this by-election will have to work fast to secure themselves a berth in next year's Fife council election, in which boundary changes are expected to result in this ward being abolished.

First preferences: Lab 1318 SNP 1079 C 270 Communist 86 LD 45
After transfers: Lab 1459 SNP 1124 [Lab gain from Ind]

1st September 2016

Five by-elections this week, three in Dorset, one in Cornwall and one in Teesside.

Kinson North

Bournemouth council, Dorset; caused by the resignation of Conservative councillor David Turtle who is moving out of the UK. He had served only since 2015.

For our first poll this week we are in Kinson, a former Dorset village which was annexed by Bournemouth in 1931, resulting in a change to what was then the county boundary between Dorset and Hampshire. Kinson's North ward lies on the northern edge of the Bournemouth–Poole conurbation, with a large part of its acreage being the River Stour's floodplain. Although the names of the remaining two Conservative councillors (Battistini and Angiolini) might suggest this is the Italian quarter of town, in fact only around 1.2% of its population is from the EU-14; the ward's census statistics are generally unremarkable although qualification rates are low and the population skews more towards the working-class end of the workforce.

Despite this, Kinson North was safe Lib Dem in the 2003 election, in which the Lib Dems performed well across Bournemouth generally. From there it developed into a three-way marginal: the Lib Dems did well to hold all three seats in 2007 but narrowly lost out in 2011 to two Tories and a Labour candidate. After that the Lib Dems gave up here, but the rise of UKIP meant this ward was still close in 2015 when the Tory slate had 33% and gained the Labour seat, the single UKIP candidate polled 27%, Labour 21% and a two-person Green slate 10%. However, that's not the whole story of the 2015 election in this ward, because Bournemouth council messed up the poll by delivering Kinson North's ballot papers to Kinson South ward's polling stations and vice versa; that led to a court case which resulted in Kinson South's two Conservative councillors being unseated and having to stand again in a re-run last December. No such court case was launched in respect of Kinson North (the election court being

Parliamentary constituency: Bournemouth West
May 2015 result C 1638/1579/1439 UKIP 1362 Lab 1060/918/814 Grn 526/484 LD 453
May 2011 result C 914/891/803 Lab 827/730/693 LD 804/788/732 Ind 427
May 2007 result LD 838/786/784 Lab 725/630/616 C 706/673/665 UKIP 406/363
May 2003 result LD 1154/1076/1030 Lab 728/669/663 C 420/411/401 Ind 272

Figure 127: Bournemouth, Kinson North

Parliamentary constituency: Christchurch
East Dorset council wards: Ameysford, Ferndown Central (part), Hampreston and Longham (part), Parley
May 2013 result UKIP 2222/2027 C 2187/2025 Lab 567/466
June 2009 result C 3575/3460 UKIP 1780/1691 LD 913/873 Lab 368
May 2005 result C 5390/5306 LD 2422/2316 Ind 1497 Lab 1480 UKIP 1083

Figure 128: Dorset CC, Ferndown

rather expensive) but the 2015 results here should nonetheless be treated with some caution.

Defending for the Tories is John Perkins, who was the losing Tory candidate in Kinson South in last year's void election; he works in the insurance sector. The UKIP runner-up here in 2015 Duane Farr tries again; he was the UKIP candidate in the Kinson South rerun last December at which point his Twitter described him as an "NHS pain management volunteer". The mind boggles. Dennis Gritt, regular Labour candidate for the ward and councillor here from 2011 to 2015, shows, er, determination by trying again. The Green Party candidate is Carla Gregory-May who is involved in her local school's Parents, Teachers and Friends Association. Completing the ballot paper is Stephen Plant of the Lib Dems.

Result: C 556 Lab 517 UKIP 313 LD 116 Grn 102

Ferndown (Dorset county council); and Parley (East Dorset council)

Both caused by the death of Conservative councillor John Wilson at the age of 74. A retired engineer originally from Leeds, he had moved to Ferndown in the 1970s to join his family's motor business. Wilson was first elected to Dorset county council in 2001 and was chairman from 2009 to 2016; he had served on East Dorset council since 2011.

Cross the River Stour from Kinson North along the A347 and you leave Bournemouth, entering the Parley ward of East Dorset council. This is the village of West Parley, a Bournemouth commuter village on the road to, and now for

Parliamentary constituency: Christchurch
Dorset county council division: Ferndown
May 2015 result C 1899/1740 UKIP 859/790 Ind 309 Grn 288/246

Figure 129: East Dorset, Parley

all intents and purposes part of, Ferndown. West Parley has grown dramatically since the Second World War; its Wikipedia page, at the time of writing, attributes this to "the Baby Boom from 1921 to 1951, this was when everyone was procreating tenfold due to welfare benefits and due to lower income jobs." Steady on, there! Many of those baby boomers have now retired to Parley, which is now in the top 100 wards in England and Wales for population over the age of 64 (35%) and in the top 20 wards in England and Wales for owner-occupation (94% of households). Those among the ward's population who are still young enough to work give the workforce a middle-class profile. Although this ward is only over the river from Kinson North, it's a world away socially. These statistics are for the 2011 version of Parley ward; East Dorset was re-warded last year but Parley ward only had minor changes to its boundaries.

Parley is part of the wider Ferndown county division, a two-seat division covering Dorset's second-largest inland town (after Dorchester). Ferndown is a mostly twentieth-century development—until 1972 its parish council was still known by its former name of Hampreston—and essentially functions as a dormitory town for the Bournemouth–Poole conurbation.

Parley ward is very safe Conservative with little of interest in its previous results; in 2015 (the only previous contest on these boundaries) the Tory slate beat UKIP 57–26. Ferndown county division is a different matter, with UKIP gaining a seat off the Tories in the 2013 election; the UKIP slate topped the poll that year 45–44. That result came as a surprise to UKIP's councillor Ian Smith, who didn't turn up for the count because he didn't think he would win. That UKIP surge didn't follow through into the 2015 East Dorset elections; although boundary changes confuse the issue, the Tories hold all the district seats wholly or partly within the division.

The future of local government in Dorset is up in the air at the moment, with a consultation under way on a number of proposed council mergers. This makes the Ferndown county council by-election important not just for its marginality but as an indicator of what might happen in the future. The Tory campaign is led by Steven Lugg, a former soldier, management accountant, live music fan, district councillor for Ferndown Central ward and Ferndown town councillor for Central North ward. He is opposed by Peter Lucas, a Ferndown town councillor for Longham ward who was the losing UKIP candidate in the 2013 county election.

Also standing are Peter Stokes (who gives an address in Christchurch) for Labour and Jason Jones (from Corfe Mullen) for the Lib Dems.

Four candidates have come to Parley, but only one can win. On previous form the Tories' Andrew Parry should be in pole position; he is opposed by Lawrence Wilson for UKIP, Brian Cropper for Labour and Jason Jones (again) for the Lib Dems.

Ferndown result: C 2046 UKIP 1092 LD 260 Lab 190

Parley result: C 631 UKIP 369 LD 84 Lab 52

Four Lanes

Cornwall council; caused by the resignation of UKIP councillor Derek Elliott, who has become disillusioned by how the council is run. He had served since 2013.

Moving to Cornwall for our fourth by-election of the week. The Four Lanes division lies in the hills immediately to the south-west of Redruth: Four Lanes itself is a village on the Redruth–Helston road, over 700 feet above sea level. While Four Lanes is relatively modern, the ward also includes Carn Brea, a Neolithic settlement on a hilltop west of Redruth: to the north of that is the village of Illogan Highway on the old A 30 road.

The present Cornwall council has been through a dizzying series of boundary changes in its seven-year lifespan. At its inaugural election in 2009 most of this area was in Carn Brea South ward, which returned a Lib Dem in a freak vote split with just 28% of the vote. The Lib Dems didn't defend the successor division of Four Lanes in 2013, and a similar freak vote split elected UKIP's Derek Elliott, who also had 28% to 21% for the Tories, 20% for Labour and 17% for the continuing Liberal Party. Going back before Cornwall's local government reorganisation in 2009 confuses the picture even more: this area was then a Labour stronghold, covered by the Carn Brea division of Cornwall county council and the Illogan South ward of Kerrier district council; despite the different names those units had the same boundaries.

Whatever you call this area—Illogan South, Carn Brea, Carn Brea South, Four Lanes—it's likely to produce another fractured result in this by-election. Defending for UKIP, who have already lost four seats in Cornish by-elections since 2013 and will have just one seat left on the council if this one goes down the Swanee as well, is Dan Hall   and the fact that Hall gives an address fifteen miles away in St Ives doesn't give much indication that UKIP think they can hold here. The Tory candidate is Peter Sheppard, a Carn Brea parish councillor. The Labour candidate is Peter Williams, who gives an address in Falmouth; since there is already a Tory Peter Williams on Cornwall council a Labour gain here would

Parliamentary constituency: Camborne and Redruth
May 2013 result UKIP 239 C 173 Lab 169 Lib 143 MK 115

Figure 130: Cornwall, Four Lanes

give endless scope for confusion. The continuing Liberals are not standing this time, so the ballot paper is completed by two more Carn Brea parish councillors— Christopher Lawrence for Mebyon Kernow and independent Bernard Webb— and Nathan Billings for the Lib Dems, who are on a hot streak in Cornwall at the moment with three by-election gains since April.

Result: LD 300 Ind 144 C 128 Lab 125 MK 111 UKIP 57 [LD gain from UKIP]

Grangefield

Stockton-on-Tees council, County Durham; caused by the death of Labour councillor Mike Clark at the age of 61. A former journalist and NUJ father of the chapel at the Middlesbrough Evening Gazette, *Clark had also been head of communications for Middlesbrough council before entering local government. He had served since 2011.*

To finish off this week we're in Teesside with a classic Tory/Labour marginal. Grangefield ward is a socially mixed area in western Stockton-on-Tees; although the Grangefield area itself is slightly run down the ward also takes large bites into the more affluent suburbs of Fairfield and Hartburn. At the centre of ward is the Grangefield Academy, a large new secondary school which is the successor to Stockton secondary school (whose former pupils included the first Labour speaker Lord Maybray-King) and Grangefield grammar school (which educated Ridley Scott).

Grangefield's two seats split equally between the Tories and Labour at the first election on the current boundaries in 2005, and the next two elections were also close (the Tories winning in 2007, Labour in 2011). In the 2015 election Labour consolidated their lead over the Tories to 49–35. Paradoxically the ward voted Tory in 2005 on the same day that Labour won the Stockton South constituency by 14 points, but Labour in 2015 on the same day that the Tories won the Stockton South constituency by 10 points.

With any path for Labour back to power (assuming they are interested in wielding power at the moment) running through Stockton South, this a by-election to watch. Mike Clark's widow Helen still sits on the council for Grangefield ward, and Labour are seeking to keep the ward's representation in the family by selecting his daughter Eleanor Clark, who runs an environmental project in the ward. The Tories have reselected Stephen Richardson, who was

Parliamentary constituency: Stockton South
May 2015 result Lab 1795/1663 C 1297/1221 UKIP 459/416 LD 143/115
May 2011 result Lab 1303/1297 C 1180/1110 LD 128
May 2007 result C 1054/999 Lab 992/984 LD 321/301
May 2005 result C 1415/1252 Lab 1326/1316 LD 491/461

Figure 131: Stockon-on-Tees, Grangefield

runner-up here in the 2015 election and is fighting his second Stockton by-election of the year after contesting the neighbouring Parkfield and Oxbridge ward in January. Completing the ballot paper are Daniel Dalton for UKIP and Nick Webb for the Lib Dems.

Result: C 807 Lab 689 UKIP 58 LD 44 [C gain from Lab]

8th September 2016

For the four by-elections on 8th September 2016 we travel to four areas which look, at first sight, like they should be safe Labour. In reality they are anything but, and in many cases the threat to them comes not from the Conservatives but from the new forces which are assailing Labour in their strongholds: UKIP and independents. Up this week are a council estate in Kent which UKIP have already taken over; part of Mansfield, a depressed East Midlands town which voted 71% Leave less than three months ago; and a Labour *vs* UKIP fight on the edge of Sheffield. But we start in one of the towns which epitomised the reason why we have a Conservative government today, where Labour will be desperate to improve their position against a backdrop of their national policies threatening the town's future...

Parkside

Barrow-in-Furness council, Cumbria; caused by the death of Labour councillor Susan Opie at the age of 64. She had served since 2011 and previously from 2004 to 2008 for the former Parkside ward.

This is Barrow-in-Furness, a manufacturing town at the far end of the Furness peninsula, which is a very long way from anywhere thanks to the presence of the deeply-indented Morecambe Bay around which those who journey to Barrow (and there are few of them) must travel. The only game in town here is defence: Barrow's economy is entirely based on the renewal of Britain's nuclear deterrent, and BAE Systems is gearing up to start building the Navy's new Successor-class submarines in Barrow later this year following a Commons vote last July to renew Trident.

One of those who voted against renewal was Jeremy Corbyn, and here lies Labour's long-term problem in the town. While Barrow should be a safe Labour town in normal circumstances, Barrovians do not like voting for a party which opposes the nuclear deterrent: the town voted Conservative in the Thatcher

Parliamentary constituency: Barrow and Furness
Cumbria county council division: Newbarns and Parkside (most), Hindpool (part),
Risedale (part), Ormsgill (part)
May 2015 result Lab 1259/1106/1073 C 1026/708
May 2011 result Lab 863/857/787 C 503/444/414 Ind 235
May 2010 result Lab 1411 C 746 LD 472 BNP 113
May 2008 result Ind 495/476 LD 420 Lab 403/390/375 C 371/300/299

Figure 132: Barrow-in-Furness, Parkside

landslides and the Tories cut the Labour majority in the constituency to under a thousand votes in last year's general election, when it looked likely that a Labour government would need support from the anti-Trident SNP.

Labour's position looks even worse in the light of the forthcoming parliamentary boundary changes, in which Cumbria loses a seat. In that process the Barrow and Furness constituency is likely to take in some Tory-voting rural areas in the Lake District; that would turn it into a notional Tory seat once again.

The Parkside ward was once on the northern edge of town but is now in the centre of Barrow's urban sprawl. It is named after the Edwardian Barrow Park, laid out around a hill which once housed a Bronze Age hillfort and now is home to the town's cenotaph; but most of the population lives in terraces of the same era on the western side of Abbey Road, once the main road out of town. The ward also includes the town's main secondary school, the troubled Furness Academy, and Barrow's railway station, once run (as Barrow Central) by the Rev Awdry's Fat Controller but now operated by Northern Rail and the southern terminus for the Cumbrian Coast line. The ward is in the top 10 in England and Wales for Apprenticeship qualifications (8.8% of the workforce)—an effect of all the shipbuilding—and is generally a fairly desirable part of town.

On slightly different boundaries, Parkside ward returned Tory councillors in 2006 and 2007, and in the first contest on the current boundaries in 2008 the winning candidates were two Independents and a Lib Dem. Since then it has been Labour all the way: the opposition to Labour in Barrow is now poorly organised, and Labour were guaranteed a seat in Parkside at the 2015 election thanks to the Tories, the only opposition candidates, not fielding a full slate. Despite this, Parkside turned in a close result, with Labour winning 55–45 and the third Labour candidate coming in just 47 votes ahead of the Tory slate. At county level the ward is divided between no fewer than four Cumbria county council divisions, but most of it lies in the Newbarns and Parkside division which is better territory for Labour.

Defending for Labour is Lee Roberts, who works for Rolls-Royce at the shipyard and gives an address on Walney Island. The Tories have reselected their second candidate from last year Roy Worthington, a taxi driver and president of the Furness Rotary Club. Completing the ballot paper is the ward's first UKIP candidate Colin Rudd, chairman of the party's Barrow branch.

Result: Lab 317 C 257 UKIP 34

Mosborough

Sheffield council, South Yorkshire; caused by the death of Labour councillor Isobel Bowler at the age of 52. Sheffield's cabinet member for neighbourhoods, Bowler had also chaired the Police and Crime Panel for South Yorkshire. She had served since 2010.

For our first proper Labour *vs* UKIP contest of the week we travel south-east from Barrow to south-east Sheffield. Incorporated into Sheffield only in 1967, before which it was part of Derbyshire, Mosborough ward covers a series of housing estates on the edge of Sheffield most of which have been developed from the 1970s onwards. The largest of these is the Halfway estate, built in 1975 and laid out in such a way that no two houses look directly onto each other; the curious name comes from the Halfway House pub in what was originally a mining village called Holbrook, that name being dropped because there was already another Holbrook in Derbyshire. Mosborough itself has also been greatly expanded by housing development, while in the north of the ward is the Waterthorpe council estate and the large Crystal Peaks shopping centre, opened in 1988 to serve the city but suffering in competition with the larger and better-connected Meadowhall which opened two years later. A bus station at Crystal Peaks, together with the Halfway branch of Sheffield's tram network, links the ward to Sheffield city centre.

The building of the estates led to the old Mosborough ward becoming grossly oversized, and it was divided in two in the 2004 boundary changes with the present Mosborough being only the southern half of the pre-2004 one (the northern half became the new Beighton ward). Since then the population has stabilised and the ward was unchanged in Sheffield's rewarding this year.

Like much of Sheffield in that period, Mosborough was a Labour *versus* Lib Dem contest in the Noughties but the Lib Dems won it only once, in the Labour nadir of 2008. UKIP took over second place in 2014, and in May's election Labour easily held the three seats with 43%, to 22% for a two-person UKIP slate and 14% for a single Tory candidate who just squeaked ahead of the Lib Dem slate.

Defending for Labour is Julie Grocutt who gives an address in Stocksbridge,

Parliamentary constituency: Sheffield South East
May 2016 result Lab 1992/1833/1661 UKIP 1022/831 C 646 LD 636/586/532 TUSC 159 Grn 142/138/122
May 2015 result Lab 3639 UKIP 2024 C 1565 LD 980 Grn 281 TUSC 99
May 2014 result Lab 1844 UKIP 1414 LD 620 C 492 Grn 205 TUSC 52
May 2012 result Lab 2463 LD 1113 UKIP 518 C 297 Grn 166
May 2011 result Lab 3069 LD 1762 C 608 Grn 248
May 2010 result Lab 3270 LD 3013 C 1506 BNP 473 UKIP 307 Grn 126
May 2008 double vacancy LD 2451/2019 Lab 1660/1626 C 746/561 Grn 290
May 2007 result Lab 1859 LD 1510 C 685 UKIP 248 Grn 161
May 2006 result Lab 1623 LD 1125 C 696 UKIP 308 Grn 224
June 2004 result Lab 2350/2038/1977 LD 1531/1193/1077 C 1204/1156/1129 Grn 451

Figure 133: Sheffield, Mosborough

over fifteen miles away on the far side of the city, where she is a town councillor. UKIP have reselected Joanne Parkin, the runner-up in May's election. The Tory candidate is Andrew Taylor, who fought Beauchief and Greenhill ward in May. Also standing are Gail Smith, Lib Dem councillor for Mosborough from 2008 to 2012, and Green Party candidate Julie White.

Result: LD 1711 Lab 1279 UKIP 466 C 229 Grn 67 [LD gain from Lab]

Yeoman Hill

Mansfield council, Nottinghamshire; caused by the death of Labour councillor Lee Probert at the age of 51. A volunteer with several charities who worked for Mencap, Probert was the first mental health champion at Mansfield council. She had served since 2015.

Moving further to the south-east, we are in Mansfield Woodhouse, a large village to the north of Mansfield and to all intents and purposes part of it. One of several claimants to the title of UK's largest village, Mansfield Woodhouse was traditionally a quarrying and mining area, and for over a century this ward has been the headquarters of the Mine Rescue Service, now a health and safety firm called MRS Training and Rescue. Taking its name from Yeoman Hill Park, this ward was formed in 2011 having previously been the southern half of Priory ward.

Mansfield's local politics is not what you might expect it to be at all, mainly thanks to a businessman called Stewart Rickersey who masterminded a 55% "Yes" vote in a 2002 referendum on whether Mansfield should have an elected mayor, then ran the mayoral campaign for independent candidate Tony Egginton, who came from behind on first preferences to beat Labour on transfers in the

Parliamentary constituency: Mansfield
Nottinghamshire county council division: North Mansfield (almost all); South Mansfield
(small part)
May 2015 result Lab 721 Mansfield Ind Forum 716
May 2011 result Lab 399 Mansfield Ind Forum 259 C 106 TUSC 61 LD 59

Figure 134: Mansfield, Yeoman Hill

first (October 2002) mayoral election. Ever since then Mansfield council has been closely fought between Labour and a pro-mayor slate called the Mansfield Independent Forum. The Forum have never relinquished the mayoralty but the council has been another matter, returning a blocking Labour majority in 2011 (when Egginton came from behind to be re-elected for his final term by just 67 votes) and being finely balanced after the 2015 election when Labour won 18 of the 36 seats, to 16 for the Forum, 1 independent and 1 Kipper. Yeoman Hill's results have reflected the council as a whole in that time, being safe Labour in 2011 but very close in 2015 when Labour held the seat in a straight fight with the Forum by 721 votes to 716, a majority of five. Labour do better at county level, where almost all of this ward is covered by the safe North Mansfield division.

Defending for Labour is John Coxhead, former secretary of the party's Mansfield branch. The Forum's candidate is Neil Williams, who has worked in mining for 41 years. Also on a much longer ballot paper than last year are David Hamilton (runner-up in the 2013 county elections) for UKIP, Daniel Redfern for the Tories and independent candidate Philip Shields, who contested the mayoral election last year and came third (out of three candidates) with 21%.

Result: Lab 278 Mansfield Ind Forum 148 UKIP 105 C 41 Ind 36

Shepway South

Maidstone council, Kent; caused by the death of UKIP councillor Dave Sargeant at the age of 77. A keen sportsman in his youth—he played cricket for Yorkshire Boys and football for Sheffield Wednesday's junior team—Sargeant had been a pastor and a windowcleaner in his working life; first elected to Maidstone council in 2014, at the time of his death he was leader of the UKIP group.

After all this travel south-east we have finally reached the South East. Shepway South is the southern half of a large and rather isolated council estate on the south-eastern edge of Maidstone, mostly dating from the 1950s and 1960s. Shepway South suffers from all the usual social problems of large council estates; one of the people who tried to fix them in the past was Alan Barnsley, a GP for the estate in the 1960s but better known for writing poetry and fiction under the

Parliamentary constituency: Faversham and Mid Kent
Kent county council division: Maidstone South East
May 2016 result UKIP 448 C 325 Lab 290 LD 69 Grn 25 EDP 14
May 2014 result UKIP 542 Lab 339 C 275 LD 77
May 2012 result Lab 418 C 265 Ind 260
May 2010 result C 928 LD 649 Lab 632 Ind 167
May 2008 result C 525 Lab 324 LD 163
Dec 2007 by-election C 251 Lab 240 LD 173 Grn 34
May 2006 result Lab 397 C 386 UKIP 148 LD 140
June 2004 result Lab 453 C 390 UKIP 231 LD 140
May 2002 result Lab 578/516 C 388

Figure 135: Maidstone, Shepway South

pseudonym Gabriel Fielding.

While this ward was safe Labour when it was created in 2002, the party has struggled here in recent years. In 2006 the Tories cut the Labour majority to eleven votes, and a by-election in December 2007 resulted in another eleven-vote margin—but this time for the Conservatives. By 2010 both seats were in Tory hands, and while Labour did get one back in 2012 they failed to make a second gain in 2014, when UKIP contested the ward for the first time since 2006 and had a big win. A second big UKIP win last May means they now have both Shepway South's councillors: shares of the vote in May were 38% for UKIP, 28% for the Tories and 25% for Labour. Maidstone council is finely balanced, with the Tories as the largest party but five seats short of a majority, and the Lib Dems forming a minority administration with independent and Labour support. At county level this ward is part of the Maidstone South East division, which is Tory thanks to the presence of the true-blue Leeds ward.

Defending for UKIP is John Barned, a retired *Daily Telegraph* and *Sun* journalist and former Maidstone council housing officer who is seeking to return to the council; he was a Tory councillor for Harrietsham and Lenham ward from 2010 to 2014. The Conservatives have reselected Bob Hinder, chairman of Boxley parish council, Tory councillor for this ward from 2008 to 2012 and runner-up here in May. The Labour candidate is Dan Wilkinson, a Momentum figure and campaigner for the homeless. Completing the ballot paper are Milden Choongo for the Lib Dems and independent candidate Jon Hicks.

Result: UKIP 432 C 215 Lab 183 Ind 88 LD 31

15th September 2016

Mayor of Hackney

Hackney council; caused by the resignation of Labour mayor Jules Pipe who is joining Sadiq Khan's administration in City Hall as deputy mayor for planning, regeneration and skills. He had served as mayor of Hackney since the post was established in October 2002, and before then as a Hackney councillor from 1996.

Welcome to inner London for what, in terms of electorate, is comfortably the biggest by-election of 2016. We're in the London Borough of Hackney, one of the older administrative units in the UK (thanks to our obsession with local government reorganisation) dating from 1965 when the former Hackney, Shoreditch and Stoke Newington councils were merged.

In Hackney's history Labour have usually been the largest party, and in the first borough elections in 1964 they won all 60 seats. Unfortunately the next election was the notorious Wilson nadir of 1968, which saw the Tories win overall control of the council with a group of neophytes and paper candidates who then proceeded to run the council about as well as you'd expect from a group of neophytes and paper candidates. Labour regained overall control in the 1971 election.

By the 1990s the Labour group had descended into infighting and the council's finances were in a bad way, with Hackney having borrowed heavily in the 1960s and 1970s to build tower blocks which subsequently became uninhabitable or were demolished. The political crisis came out in the open in 1996 when the Labour group split down the middle. In that year the party also lost two by-elections to the Lib Dems in Wick and Dalston wards; the Wick by-election winner was Neil Hughes, who now sits on Eden district council in Cumbria but is probably better known as one of the *7 Up* children.

The 1998 election returned a hung council, and then Hackney's financial crisis came to a head. With no-one in political control, the administration was in a mess: as well as the council's debts, a failed social security outsourcing contract had cost the council £36 million, and £100,000 was lost with the collapse of Railtrack in which the council had invested part of its pension fund. A damning OFSTED report in 1999 led to central government investigating the council's finances and effectively taking control of its expenditure.

The political crisis eventually led to a coalition agreement between the moderate Labour group leader, Jules Pipe, and the Conservative group leader, Eric Ollerenshaw (who would later lead the Tory group on the London Assembly and serve one term as MP for Lancaster), in which Pipe and Ollerenshaw became joint leaders of the council.

Somehow from all this chaos normality returned to the borough very swiftly. The coalition ended in June 2001 when a by-election gain gave Labour an overall majority. By the 2002 elections the borough's finances had been stabilised (at the cost of forcing worse pay and conditions on the council's staff which led to a small fortune being paid out in unfair dismissal claims).

The 2002 elections returned a large, and this time unified, Labour majority which has not been seriously challenged since. On the same day a referendum on the establishment of an elected mayor for the borough resulted in a 70% Yes vote, and in October 2002 Pipe rose from the council leadership to win the borough's inaugural Mayoral election. He has held the post ever since, and has been appointed CBE for his political service.

As this is only the fourth by-election to a UK elected mayor post it's worth looking at the previous three to see if there are any straws in the wind:

1. North Tyneside, June 2003: Tory mayor resigned after being arrested on suspicion of possessing indecent images of children (he was subsequently exonerated). Tory hold with an increased majority.

2. Bedford, October 2009: independent ("Better Bedford Party") mayor died. Lib Dem gain.

3. Tower Hamlets, June 2015: independent ("Tower Hamlets First") mayor was disqualified for electoral fraud. Labour gain.

Although two of the three previous mayoral by-elections resulted in gains, and all three went to a run-off, neither of those events look likely to happen in a Hackney context. Pipe was taken to a run-off in the 2002 and 2006 elections by the Tory candidate (Andrew Boff in both cases) but his majority in 2014 when he beat the Greens 60–18 in the first round suggests Labour should have little trouble holding this by-election. In the simultaneous Hackney council election Labour outpolled the Greens 56–21 in terms of votes; a poor Green vote distribution means that the Greens' 21% of the vote turns into no seats at all on Hackney

Parliamentary constituencies: Hackney North and Stoke Newington; Hackney South and Shoreditch

May 2014 election Lab 40858 Grn 11849 C 7853 LD 3840 Putting Hackney First 3265

May 2010 election Lab 48363 LD 15818 C 12405 Grn 10100 Communist 2033 Christian 1084

May 2006 election Lab 20830 C 7454 LD 4882 Grn 4683 Ind 2907 Respect 2800 Communist 896; runoff Lab 24233 C 8785

Oct 2002 election Lab 13813 C 4502 Socialist Alliance 4187 LD 4185 Grn 3002 Hackney First 1543 Ind 1253 Ind 441; runoff Lab 16234 C 5629

*May 2016 GLA elections (*includes *postal voters)*

Mayor: Lab 51502 C 9335 Grn 7868 LD 2236 Women's Equality 2189 Respect 1093 UKIP 1067 Cannabis is Safer than Alcohol 699 Britain First 532 Zylinski 286 BNP 239 One Love 143

London Member: Lab 45941 Grn 11642 C 7537 Women's Equality 4066 LD 2994 UKIP 1766 Respect 1145 Animal Welfare 682 Britain First 673 CPA 519 House Party 416 BNP 259

June 2016 referendum Remain 83398 Leave 22868

Figure 136: Hackney, Mayor

council, with Labour's 50 councillors opposed by four Conservatives (whose vote is concentrated in Stamford Hill where there is a large Jewish community) and three Lib Dems. If anything, Labour did better in the London Assembly elections in May: Sadiq Khan beat Zac Goldsmith across the borough 67–12, and in the London Members ballot Labour beat the Greens 59–15. Unlike most of the GLA election results quoted by this column, these figures include postal votes (for which ward breakdowns are not available). The following month Hackney voted 78% Remain in the EU referendum.

As the references to run-offs indicate, this by-election will be held using the Supplementary Vote system in which voters should give a first and second preference. A win in the first round requires 50% of the first-preference votes; if this is not achieved the top two candidates will go forward to the run-off and the votes for the other three candidates will be transferred to the second preference.

It should be noted that Hackney has a history of cockups in administering its mayoral elections. In 2010 the electoral address for the Tory candidate (Andrew Boff, again) was held up so long by legal argument over whether it was admissible that it missed the print deadline for the official candidate statements' booklet. This time round a printing error (thought to be describing the Tory candidate as a "Conversative") has led to all the postal ballot papers for this election having to be reprinted and the postal votes consequently went out four days late. Hopefully this will not have any significant effect on the election.

There are some famous names in the roll-call of previous Hackney by-election candidates: as well as Ollerenshaw and Hughes already mentioned we can add the former Home Secretary Charles Clarke (Chatham ward, October 1980) and Pipe himself (South Defoe ward, November 1996), while the campaigning journalist Paul Foot finished third in Hackney's first mayoral election as the Socialist Alliance candidate. Hoping to follow in Pipe's footsteps is Labour candidate Philip Glanville, a Hackney councillor since 2006 (for Hoxton West ward since 2014 and Hoxton ward before then) who was Pipe's deputy mayor and so has already taken over the mayoral functions on an acting basis. He is opposed by Green candidate Samir Jeraj, a journalist and officer for the Race Equality Foundation; Amy Gray for the Tories; Dave Raval for the Lib Dems; and Dawa Ma who is the other member of the One Love Party which finished last in May's London mayoral election, both in this borough and across London.

Result: Lab 22595 Grn 4338 C 3533 LD 1818 One Love 494

Puckeridge

East Hertfordshire council; caused by the resignation of former Conservative councillor James Cartwright following a Twitter row in which he insulted three users who disagreed with him that prayers should be held before full council meetings; after being censured by the council and ordered to attend social media training, he left the Conservative party. Cartwright had served since 2015.

From Hackney we travel north along what was once Ermine Street and is now the A10. Puckeridge was established by the Romans as *Ad Fines* at the junction of Ermine Street with Stane Street. The modern village's economy was once based on coaching—it was on the main route between London and Cambridge—but today it functions as a dormitory settlement for Hertford, the Lea Valley towns and London.

East Hertfordshire returned a full slate of Tory district councillors in 2015, and Puckeridge ward is not seriously challenged by other parties. In the 2015 election Cartwright beat Labour 68–20. The Tories are similarly safe in the local Hertfordshire county division (Braughing).

The Tories will be hoping to put behind them the row over prayers at council meetings which has now cost them two East Hertfordshire councillors—the motion's proposer resigned last year and the resulting by-election featured a spectacular cockup by the Tory agent which led to the Conservative candidate appearing on the ballot paper without a description. She was nonetheless elected. This time the Tories have correctly nominated Peter Boylan, a Braughing parish councillor and author. Labour have reselected their regular candidate for the ward David Bell, who is campaigning for a bypass for Puckeridge. Also on an

Parliamentary constituency: North East Hertfordshire
Hertfordshire county council division: Braughing
May 2015 result C 940 Lab 277 Grn 175
May 2011 result C 601 Lab 256
May 2007 result C 471 Lab 148
May 2003 result C 394 Lab 178

Figure 137: East Hertfordshire, Puckeridge

unusually long ballot paper for the ward are Tabitha Evans for the Green Party, Sara Mihajlovic for the Lib Dems and Geoffrey Miles for UKIP.

Result: C 179 UKIP 79 LD 75 Lab 46 Grn 38

Tupton

North East Derbyshire council; caused by the resignation of Labour councillor Wayne Lilleyman after an assault at Tupton Miners' Welfare in which he bit an 18-year-old man on the nose. Lilleyman received a police caution. He had served since 2011.

We move to another settlement on a Roman road, in this case Ryknield Street. Tupton ward covers two villages (Old Tupton and New Tupton) off the A 61 Chesterfield–Alfreton road together with a small part of Wingerworth to the north. The village is probably best known for Tupton Hall school, which educated Dennis Skinner (at a time when it was a grammar school), and as the home of John Lowe, three-time darts world champion and the first player to shoot a televised nine-dart finish.

Tupton is part of the North East Derbyshire constituency, which now looks marginal at parliamentary level because of the Sheffield and Chesterfield suburbs contained within it, but is historically a Labour mining seat. This is one of the Labour areas: Labour were unopposed here in 2003 but one of their councillors was re-elected in 2007 as an independent, bringing a running-mate with him. Labour got the seats back in 2011 and in the 2015 poll beat the Tories 67–33 in a straight fight. The local county division (Clay Cross North) is also safe for Labour.

Even in the dubious circumstances of this by-election Labour should have little trouble holding this seat. Their candidate is Cathy Goodyer, chairman of Tupton parish council. The Tories have reselected Andrew Lovell who was their lead candidate last year. Also standing are Alan Garfitt for UKIP, David Hancock for the Lib Dems and Ben Marshall for the British People's Party—not the neo-Nazi party of that name (which dissolved in 2013) but a group of cranks

Parliamentary constituency: North East Derbyshire
Derbyshire county council division: Clay Cross North
May 2015 result Lab 1158/1025 C 567/461
May 2011 result Lab 754/699 Ind 286/281/236/234/206
May 2007 result Ind 600/587 Lab 448/438 C 215/193
May 2003 result 2 Lab unopposed

Figure 138: North East Derbyshire, Tupton

Parliamentary constituency: Ludlow
May 2013 result LD 907 C 449 Grn 107
Sept 2011 by-election LD 801 C 544 Lab 80 Grn 74
June 2009 result LD 754 C 641 Grn 186

Figure 139: Shropshire, Bishop's Castle

which has taken the name over without considering the implications.

   Result: LD 340 Lab 308 C 155 UKIP 79 British People's Party (2015) 6 (six) [LD gain from Lab]

Bishop's Castle

Shropshire council; caused by the resignation of Liberal Democrat councillor Charlotte Barnes for personal and family reasons. She had served since winning a by-election in September 2011.

Anybody who knows the Marches knows that it specialises in market towns which are beautiful, tiny and remote. One of these is Bishop's Castle; generally pronounced by locals in a way that's difficult to reconcile with the English alphabet, "the Castle", despite its tiny population, was a full-blown borough before the 1974 local government reorganisation.[10] These days it anchors a ward including eleven other tiny parishes in the Onny and Kemp valleys, the largest of which is Lydbury North; within the boundary is part of that strange and beautiful upland plateau called the Long Mynd.

   This combination of the bohemian Castle and remote agricultural villages is a classic area for old-school Liberalism (it borders Montgomeryshire which was a Liberal seat for many years until Lembit Öpik got his hands on it) and in 2009 narrowly returned old-school Liberal Peter Phillips who had represented the area for many years on the pre-reorganisation South Shropshire council. Phillips

---

[10] This wasn't quite true; Bishop's Castle lost its incorporation and became a "rural borough" in a 1960s reorganisation.

resigned in 2011 and was replaced by Barnes who increased the Lib Dem majority; at the last poll here in 2013 the Lib Dems beat the Tories 62–31.

Defending for the Lib Dems is Jonny Keeley, a musician (with the local band Fight the Bear) and community campaigner who runs a website promoting local organisations. The Tory candidate is Georgie Ellis, runner-up here in 2009, a former South Shropshire councillor for the area and Lydbury North parish councillor. Also standing are Steve Hale for the Green Party and Judith Payne for Labour. Some of the electors for this by-election will be thrilled to hear that their polling station is a pub—the Inn on the Green in Wentnor.

Result: LD 862 C 430 Lab 95 Grn 37

Castle

Carlisle council, Cumbria; caused by the death of Labour councillor Gerald Caig at the age of 64. A GMB union official originally from Cleator Moor in west Cumbria, Caig was first elected to Carlisle council in 2014; he was the father of Tony Caig, former Carlisle United goalkeeper and now goalkeeping coach with Hartlepool United.

From Bishop's Castle we travel north to a historic castle. Back in December 1745 Carlisle Castle was the scene of the last siege in England, in which the army of the Crown reduced the last garrison left in England by Bonnie Prince Charlie's forces as they retreated north. The castle itself was built in the eleventh century by William II and rebuilt in stone by his successor Henry I to guard the border city of Carlisle; although England and Scotland are now at peace the Army are still here with the Duke of Lancaster's regiment being headquartered in the castle, and in 2009 your columnist was here under their auspices as part of the centenary celebrations for the Territorial Army (as it then was).

The ward named after Carlisle Castle falls into two separate parts. To the west side of the castle and the River Caldew are the Willow Holme and Newtown areas around the Cumberland Infirmary. To the east side of the castle is Carlisle's historic city centre, all of which is within this ward except for Citadel railway station. The northern boundary of the ward is the River Eden and much of the north of the ward is flood plain. The ward includes some Cumbria University buildings. Until 2013 it had the same boundaries as the Castle division of Cumbria county council, and county results up to 2013 are included in Figure 140.

Located within this ward is the "Cursing Stone", placed in 2001 in a pedestrian subway near the Tullie House museum and inscribed with a 1,069-word curse placed on the border reivers in 1525 by Gavin Dunbar, archbishop of Glasgow. Instead it appears to have cursed Carlisle itself: Cumberland's farms were

Parliamentary constituency: Carlisle
Cumbria county council division: Castle (almost all), Botcherby (small part), Currock (small part), Denton Holme (small part)
May 2016 result Lab 544 C 258 UKIP 150 LD 89 Grn 50
May 2015 result Lab 940 C 671 UKIP 343 Grn 193 LD 145 TUSC 43
Sept 2014 by-election Lab 364 C 212 UKIP 208 LD 121 Grn 42
May 2014 result Lab 435 UKIP 267 C 221 LD 127 Grn 87 TUSC 28
May 2012 result Lab 663 LD 229 C 165 Grn 110
March 2012 county council by-election Lab 407 LD 369 C 93 Grn 54 UKIP 22
May 2011 result Lab 549 LD 438 Grn 135 TUSC 90 BNP 84
May 2010 result LD 816 Lab 802 C 553 Grn 161
June 2009 county council result LD 424 Lab 297 C 241 Grn 144 BNP 129
March 2009 by-election LD 465 Lab 304 BNP 255 C 143 Grn 125
May 2008 result LD 562 Lab 299 C 206 Ind 202
May 2007 result LD 607 Lab 331 C 185
Feb 2007 county council by-election LD 653 Lab 222 C 117 Grn 29
May 2006 result LD 632 Lab 321 C 149 Ind 69
Nov 2005 by-election LD 538 Lab 370
May 2005 county council result LD 937 Lab 853 C 349
June 2004 result LD 917 Lab 541
May 2003 result LD 603 Lab 443
May 2002 result LD 549 Lab 373 C 195
June 2001 county council result LD 994 Lab 786 C 448
Apr 2001 by-election Lab 329 LD 294 C 258 Lib 67
May 2000 result LD 513 Lab 299 C 230
May 1999 result LD 695/669/657 Lab 362/341/340 C 224/218/215

Figure 140: Carlisle, Castle

devastated by the foot-and-mouth outbreak of 2001; the city was hit by devastating floods in 2005 and 2015, the most recent of which flooded the McVitie's factory and led to a national biscuit shortage; a series of crimes, hits to the local economy, even Carlisle United's relegation from the football league in 2004 were all blamed on the Cursing Stone. In 2005 the ward's city and county councillor Jim Tootle proposed that the stone be removed or destroyed, but the city council voted to keep it. Seven years later Tootle was dead at the age of 59, and two years after that the winner of the by-election to replace Tootle on Cumbria county council was dead at the age of 67. In fact, this is Castle's eighth by-election (either at city or county level) in the fifteen years since the Cursing Stone was installed, a very high councillor attrition rate. Coincidence?

Your columnist's other reader has been in touch pointing out that in recent weeks a preview along the lines of "this ward used to be Labour versus Lib Dem but now it's Labour versus somebody else" has often been followed by a spectacular Lib Dem gain. At the risk of tempting fate, that's unlikely to happen here. While the Lib Dems did win all but one of the elections in this ward from 1999 to 2010 (the exception being an April 2001 by-election), making this Carlisle's only reliable Lib Dem ward at the time, Labour's record from 2011 onwards is eight wins out of a possible eight and the Lib Dems are now in a poor fourth place. In May Labour had 50% of the vote to 24% for the Conservatives and 14% for UKIP. Although Labour did very badly in the last Carlisle by-election, held in Botcherby ward in January, that ward already had a successful independent slate competing with Labour and a large proportion of its electors had been flooded out only weeks before.

Defending for Labour is Anne Glendinning, a former city and county councillor for Botcherby ward who tried and failed to get her city council seat back there in May. The Tory candidate is mother-of-four, health shop manager and WI member Melissa Andrews who in 2014 took part in a half-Ironman triathlon in California for a Channel 5 TV series—with her pink hair, piercings and tattoos, Andrews is probably not what you expected a Tory candidate to look like. UKIP have reselected their candidate from May Robbie Reid-Sinclair, a founder of the Solway Aviation Museum who is active in the Carlisle branch of the British Legion. Also standing are Alison Hobson for the Lib Dems (who gives an address in Brampton) and Deborah Brown for the Green Party.

Result: Lab 398 C 228 UKIP 107 LD 88 Grn 34

Blakelaw

Newcastle upon Tyne council, Tyne and Wear; caused by the resignation of Labour councillor David Stockdale, ostensibly due to work commitments although he was later investigated by the council and police over alleged financial irregularities; he has since been exonerated. First elected in 2012 and re-elected for a second term only in May, he had served as the council's cabinet minister for culture and communities.

For our final preview of the week, and final resignation of the week under what might be called "a cloud", we're in the west end of Newcastle upon Tyne. Blakelaw is a mostly post-war development located within the A 1 Western Bypass; it's a council estate ward and suffers from all the usual problems of council estate wards.

Your columnist's other reader has been in touch pointing out that in recent weeks a preview along the lines of "this ward used to be Labour versus Lib Dem but now it's Labour versus somebody else" has often been followed by a Lib Dem gain. At the risk of tempting fate, that's only slightly less unlikely to happen here

Parliamentary constituency: Newcastle upon Tyne Central
May 2016 result Lab 1846 UKIP 470 LD 267 C 221 Grn 117
May 2015 result Lab 2549 UKIP 846 C 532 LD 428 Grn 244
May 2014 result Lab 1897 LD 485 C 308
May 2012 result Lab 1948 LD 615 C 199
May 2011 result Lab 1940 LD 1088 C 246
May 2010 result Lab 1814 LD 1588 C 456 BNP 430
May 2008 result LD 1396 Lab 855 C 295 BNP 270
May 2007 result LD 1511 Lab 1000 BNP 230 C 230
May 2006 result LD 1608 Lab 1219 C 239
June 2004 result LD 1504/1402/1358 Lab 1278/1074/1040 BNP 359 Ind 318 C 298/297/290

Figure 141: Newcastle upon Tyne, Blakelaw

than it is in Carlisle this week. Blakelaw was one of the wards taken over in the Noughties by the Lib Dems during the time they controlled Newcastle council. The Lib Dem share of the vote peaked at 52% in 2006, but the coalition took the floor out of their vote here: Labour gained all three seats in the period 2010–2012, and UKIP took over second place in 2015. This is now a safe Labour ward with the party having a 63–16 lead over UKIP in May.

Defending for Labour is Nora Casey, who came to Newcastle from her native Ireland in 2014 and fought the marginal North Heaton ward in May; this should be a safer berth for her. UKIP have reselected Ritchie Lane who fought the ward in May. Also standing are recent University of York graduate Ciaran Morrissey for the Lib Dems, regular Tory candidate James Langley and regular Green candidate Brendan Derham.

Result: Lab 1004 LD 654 UKIP 443 C 190 Grn 105

Tuesday 20th September 2016

One by-election on Tuesday 20th September 2016:

Plasnewydd

Cardiff council; caused by the death of Labour councillor Mohammad Javed at the age of 76. Although he had only been a councillor since 2012, Javed was a pillar of the ward's Pakistani and Muslim community; he had run a shop on Albany Road and been a governor at a local primary school.

For an unusual Tuesday by-election we are just north-east of Cardiff city centre. Plasnewydd ("New Manor") ward covers much of Roath, an area of Victorian terracing from Cardiff's first great expansion along City Road and Albany Road. Many of these terraced houses are now in multiple occupation—not by immigrants in the normal sense, although the ward is unusually ethnically diverse by Welsh standards (15% Asian, 11% Muslim), but by students at Cardiff's universities. The sheer number of student rents within the ward places Plasnewydd in the top 25 wards in England and Wales for privately rented households (55%), and the ward is also in the top 100 for full-time students (33% of the workforce) and people in the 18–29 age bracket (50% of the population). Or, at least, that's the case during term time, and Cardiff University's new academic year doesn't start until next week.

The fact that most of the students are away could have an interesting effect on this ward. Plasnewydd was a safe Lib Dem ward while the party were running Cardiff council in the Noughties and will have been one of the bedrocks for the party's majority in the Cardiff Central constituency during that period. Although Labour gained all four seats in the 2012 election, their majority was not large (37% to 33% for the Lib Dem slate and 13% for a single Green candidate) and the Lib Dem vote in Cardiff Central held up relatively well in May's Assembly elections, suggesting that the party is still in rude health.

Both the Labour and Lib Dem candidates were major behind-the-scenes

Parliamentary and Assembly constituency: Cardiff Central
May 2012 result Lab 1535/1438/1436/1413 LD 1362/1314/1297/1286 Grn 535 PC 505/434/344/338 C 232/193/174/171
May 2008 result LD 1524/1479/1457/1411 Lab 1207/1040/1035/887 Grn 545/518 PC 448/428 C 398/361/348/283
June 2004 result LD 2009/1940/1872/1835 Lab 1379/1257/1141/1082 Grn 775 PC 498 C 414/329/320/291

Figure 142: Cardiff, Plasnewydd

figures in that campaign. The defending Labour candidate Peter Wong, a civil servant with the Valuation Office Agency, is the chairman of the party's Cardiff Central branch and also sits on the board of Chinese for Labour. The Lib Dems have selected party staffer Robin Rea. The Green candidate is Michael Cope, and the ballot paper—a much shorter one than in 2012, when there were seventeen candidates chasing four seats—is completed by Munawar Mughal for the Tories and Lawrence Gwynn for UKIP.

Result: LD 1258 Lab 910 PC 177 C 115 Grn 93 UKIP 62 [LD gain from Lab]

22nd September 2016

There are nine by-elections on Thursday 22nd September 2016, which fall neatly into three trios. There are three wards up which are based on villages or are deeply rural, including today's Welsh contest which was previously an independent seat, and Tory defences in Northamptonshire and Oxfordshire. There are three Tory defences in wards based on small market towns, in Cumbria, Suffolk and Devon. But the first trio this week is wards based on former coalfields, with a Tory defence in Warwickshire, a Labour defence in Tyne and Wear and our first preview of the week, an SNP defence in Lanarkshire.

Coatbridge North and Glenboig

North Lanarkshire council; caused by the resignation of SNP councillor Fulton MacGregor, who is now the MSP for Coatbridge and Chryston. He had served since 2012.

Welcome to the town which won the 2007 Carbuncle award for being the most dismal town in Scotland, and was once described by Frankie Boyle as "*Blade Runner* without the special effects". Coatbridge did not exist before the nineteenth century, developing very quickly during the Industrial Revolution as a coalmining and ironworking centre. In order to develop so fast Coatbridge attracted a huge number of immigrants from Ireland, many of whom lived in overcrowded housing as bad as anything put up during the Industrial Revolution.

Coatbridge's industrial bust came rather quicker than it did in most other post-industrial places. By 1920 the coal had been exhausted, only one of the ironworks survived the Great Depression, and the development of a huge new steelworks in Corby during the mid-1930s led to an exodus from what was still, once all the people who went to Corby had gone, the most overcrowded town in Scotland.

Since the 1930s the town's housing and economic base has been extensively redeveloped. Distribution is now the main game in town, thanks to Coatbridge's location at the centre of the Central Belt with excellent road and rail links, and particularly given that the town's other major employer—the Tannoy loudspeaker factory—is now closing down. Today the only remaining vestiges of Coatbridge's heavy industrial past are the Museum of Scottish Industrial Life, located within this ward on the site of a former blast furnace, and a very large Catholic population of Irish descent.

Coatbridge North and Glenboig is one of three wards covering the town, and also includes a rural area to the north including the village of Glenboig and running up to the edge of Cumbernauld.

The local government reorganisation of 1975 grouped Coatbridge with the mainly Protestant town of Airdrie under what was then Monklands district council. That led to one of the more bizarre local government scandals of the 1990s, "Monklandsgate", in which allegations were made that council spending had sectarian discrepancies in favour of Coatbridge—as evidence for this it was pointed out that the council's entire ruling Labour group were Roman Catholic. Although nothing came of this allegations of nepotism were upheld (a large number of council workers were related to Labour councillors). The whole story gained added spice by the fact that Airdrie's MP was the party leader John Smith, while Coatbridge's MP was Tom Clarke, the shadow Scottish secretary; after Smith died the scandal led to Labour nearly losing the resulting by-election in Airdrie. Coatbridge, however, continued to give Clarke large majorities.

PR was introduced for Scottish local elections in 2007, and the 2007 election to this ward returned two Labour councillors, one SNP councillor (John Wilson, who topped the poll) and a left-wing independent candidate called Martin McWilliams, who overtook the Tories on transfers from the Scottish Socialist Party and benefited from the SNP only running one candidate.

Wilson had simultaneously been elected to Holyrood from the Central Scotland list, and stood down from North Lanarkshire council in 2009 to focus on his duties in Edinburgh; in the resulting by-election the SNP narrowly lost their seat to Labour. A second by-election was held in 2011 after Labour councillor Tony Clarke (Tom Clarke MP's brother) died, and Labour held this more comfortably. Coincidentally, in both by-elections Labour polled the same number of first-preference votes—1,529.

The SNP made a comeback in the 2012 council election, recovering their by-election loss from Labour (who didn't defend it) and also narrowly knocking out independent councillor McWilliams to leave the ward with a 2–2 split; on first preferences Labour led 53–31.

2012 is a long time ago in Scottish politics, which is still reverberating from the 2014 independence referendum in which Coatbridge voted strongly Yes, a

Westminster constituency: Coatbridge, Chryston and Bellshill
Holyrood constituency: Coatbridge and Chryston
May 2012 first preferences Lab 2566 SNP 1490 Ind 496 C 289
Oct 2011 by-election Lab 1529 SNP 1139 C 174 LD 78
June 2009 by-election Lab 1529 SNP 1254 Ind 557 C 361 Ind 217 Grn 115 SSP 81; after
transfers Lab 1759 SNP 1696
May 2007 first preferences Lab 3226 SNP 1983 C 714 Ind 604 SSP 219

Figure 143: North Lanarkshire, Coatbridge North and Glenboig

presage of the collapse of Labour's support among Catholics in the central belt. One of the more surprising aspects of the defeat for independence was that John Wilson MSP left the SNP, having fallen out with the party over the issue of NATO membership for an independent Scotland. Since 2014 the SNP have gained the Coatbridge constituency at both Westminster and Holyrood level, resulting in this by-election.

With the favourable tailwind for the SNP generally a hold in this by-election would be an easy prediction; but there are some straws in the wind which suggest that the Nationalists might find this heavy going. Firstly, the SNP's Coatbridge branch has been suspended for several months for severe Monklandsgatestyle infighting; a peace meeting between the two factions earlier this month was reportedly patrolled by bouncers. The ward's other SNP councillor, Julie McAnulty, has been suspended by the party over charges of racism, and has launched a defamation suit against the person who accused her of making racist insults. It says something about the state of the local party that SNP candidate Stephen Kirley has resorted to Crowdfunder to raise money for his campaign.

The hot local issue of the moment appears to be a row over services being moved away from Monklands hospital; it must not be forgotten that health is a devolved issue and Labour's candidate Alex McVey is milking this for all it's worth. Finally, the former MSP John Wilson is seeking a return to the council as a Scottish Green Party candidate; he sought re-election to Holyrood under that label in May and saved his deposit in Coatbridge and Chryston, giving him a higher profile than the only previous Green candidate for this ward (Kristofer Keane, who stood here in the 2009 by-election and later kindly hosted this column for several years). As this by-election is under the Alternative Vote, transfers from whoever finishes third could be very important in deciding the result. Completing the ballot paper are Ben Callaghan for the Tories and Neil Wilson for UKIP.

First preferences: Lab 1350 SNP 1261 C 366 Grn 196 UKIP 63
After transfers: Lab 1572 SNP 1378 [Lab gain from SNP]

Parliamentary constituency: Blaydon
May 2016 result Lab 1733 UKIP 397 C 302 Grn 209 LD 121
May 2015 result Lab 2897 C 874 Grn 572 LD 446
May 2014 result Lab 1707 UKIP 718 C 254 LD 167
May 2012 result Lab 2126 LD 257 C 249
May 2011 result Lab 2384 LD 554 C 396
May 2010 result Lab 2587 LD 1522 C 599
May 2009 by-election Lab 1221 LD 898 C 177
May 2008 result Lab 1547 LD 720 C 443
May 2007 result Lab 1716 LD 800 C 269 BNP 171
May 2006 result Lab 1738 LD 995 C 236
June 2004 result Lab 2096/2073/1939 LD 1050/1016/821 C 358/341/339 BNP 245

Figure 144: Gateshead, Chopwell and Rowlands Gill

Chopwell and Rowlands Gill

Gateshead council, Tyne and Wear; caused by the resignation of Labour councillor John Hamilton who had served since 2000.

Moving into England but staying in the coalfield for the only Labour defence of the week. Despite the order of the names, Rowlands Gill is the larger of the two villages in this ward, perhaps being most notable for having no licensed premises (an effect of the previous landowner, the Church of England, putting a covenant on the land when the village was developed) and for being the birthplace of former SAS soldier Chris Ryan. One of the electors in this by-election is Si King, the hairy biker. This is a surprisingly rural ward given its presence in the Tyne and Wear metropolitan county, and the Boundary Commission proposed last week that the ward should be moved into a Durham-based constituency: on the other hand, the proposed seat (West Durham and Teesdale, stretching all the way from Chopwell to western Barnard Castle), is one of the more bonkers proposals to have come out this year.

If, as expected, Jeremy Corbyn is re-elected as Labour leader on Saturday then the people of Chopwell might well be pleased by that. Chopwell was so left-wing during the inter-war years that it became known as "Little Moscow": the Soviet flag flew from the village's council offices during the General Strike, and there are still street names in Chopwell commemorating Marx and Lenin. That left-wing nature has carried through into this ward's modern elections, which are safe Labour with little of interest. In May Labour led UKIP here 63–14.

Defending for Labour is Dave Bradford, who fights UKIP's Ray Tolley, the Tories' John Lathan, the Greens' Dave Castleton and Lib Dem Amelia Ord.

Result: Lab 1066 UKIP 282 LD 221 C 156 Grn 79

Parliamentary constituency: Nuneaton
Warwickshire county council division: Fillongley
May 2015 result C 1342/1143/1009 Lab 901/885/856 UKIP 784 Grn 446
May 2011 result C 852/788/730 Lab 823/770/770 Ind 252
May 2007 result C 815/807/756 Lab 735/733/729
May 2003 result Lab 626/582/543 Ind 520 C 497/397

Figure 145: North Warwickshire, Arley and Whitacre

Arley and Whitacre

North Warwickshire council; caused by the resignation of Conservative councillor Andrew Watkins. He was first elected to the council in 2011 for Coleshill South ward and moved to this ward in 2015.

For our final ex-coalfield by-election of the week we travel to an ex-coalfield of very recent vintage. Daw Mill colliery, located in the Warwickshire parish of Arley north of Coventry, was the last deep coal mine in the Midlands, breaking the UK record for annual coal output by extracting 3.25 million tons in 2008. Production was stopped in February 2013 due to a large underground fire, and never restarted. 650 jobs were lost. Shortly afterwards the colliery site was bought from UK Coal's liquidators by a property development firm which wants to transform it into a business park and HGV depot. There are obvious problems in siting an HGV depot at Daw Mill, most of whose coal left the site by rail; while the road running past the colliery once had A-road status, it was downgraded to a B-road decades ago and that's a decision which anyone who has visited the area will find it hard to argue with. North Warwickshire council's planning committee threw out the business park plan last year, but the issue clearly hasn't gone away because Arley parish council is combining this by-election with a referendum on the council's neighbourhood planning framework.

Arley and Whitacre does not vote how you would expect an ex-coalfield (or even an active coalfield) ward to vote, being instead a key marginal between Labour and the Conservatives—rather like the parliamentary seat in which it is sited, Nuneaton. Like the Nuneaton seat as a whole, the ward is trending towards the Tories who returned a full slate in the 2015 election, narrowly gaining a seat from Labour; shares of the vote in May were 39% for the Conservatives, 26% for Labour and 23% for UKIP. However, the Tory share may well be inflated by a personal vote for Colin Hayfield, who is the ward's county councillor (and a relative of Harry Hayfield, who writes the local by-election previews for Politicalbetting.com in rather less detail than you'd find here).

With UKIP withdrawing from the fray this by-election is a straight fight.

Parliamentary constituency: Workington
Cumbria county council divisions: Cockermouth North (part), Cockermouth South (part)
May 2015 result C 925/832 Lab 714/580 Grn 216 LD 193
May 2011 result C 639/583 Lab 550/543 LD 165 Grn 162
Aug 2010 by-election C 466 LD 131 Grn 108
May 2007 result C 673/571 Lab 360/320
May 2003 result C 543/497 Lab 330/253

Figure 146: Allerdale, Christchurch

Defending in the blue corner is Karen Barber, a Conservative councillor for this ward from 2011 to 2015. Challenging in the red corner is Jodie Gosling, who is campaigning against council cuts to Arley sports centre. Seconds out!

Result: Lab 577 C 390 [Lab gain from C]

Christchurch

Allerdale council, Cumbria; caused by the resignation of Conservative councillor Margaret Jackson who is moving to Lancashire. First elected to Allerdale council in 1991 and with continuous service since 1999, Jackson was a former deputy leader of the council and twice Mayor of Cockermouth.

After three coalfield wards, we now turn to a series of three wards which cover old but small market towns. Christchurch ward covers the centre and western side of Cockermouth, a location which was important to the Romans as the lowest crossing point of the River Derwent.

While it was traditionally a weaving and spinning town, Cockermouth became a very early tourist destination thanks to the poetry of William Wordsworth, who was born here. Tourism, along with farming and the superlative Jennings beer, keeps Cockermouth afloat today—and with the town having suffered three devastating floods in the last eleven years it needs as much tourist income as it can get.

This is Cockermouth's Conservative ward and is quite reliable for them, the party leading Labour 45–35 last year. Interestingly the largest Tory vote here in recent times came during the coalition years, specifically in an August 2010 by-election which they won with 67% partly thanks to Labour failing to nominate a candidate. There is little extra information to be drawn from county elections because the county division boundaries split Cockermouth north–south rather than east–west, but the Tories hold both of Cockermouth's county council seats.

Defending for the Tories is Simon Nicholson, a haulier and Cockermouth town councillor. Labour have reselected Joan Ellis, who was runner-up here last year. Also standing are Debbie Taylor for the Lib Dems and Eric Atkinson for UKIP.

Result: Lab 324 LD 234 C 206 UKIP 32 [Lab gain from C]

Hadleigh

Suffolk county council; caused by the resignation of Conservative councillor Brian Riley who had served since 2013.

This week's second old market town is Hadleigh. This is the Suffolk Hadleigh, not the Essex one, located on the River Brett to the west of Ipswich. Traditionally a wool and cloth town, Hadleigh is known for its fine old buildings, many of which are timber-framed and have pargeting—detailed 17th-century plasterwork. There are 246 listed buildings in Hadleigh, including the Grade I-listed church of St Mary the Virgin which is said to be the final resting place of the ninth-century king Guthrum; the main antagonist of Alfred the Great, Guthrum converted to Christianity after Alfred defeated him at the battle of Edington. Today the town is home to the curiously-named Babergh district council.

The Tories have an appalling record in Suffolk by-elections this year, having lost five of the nine seats they have defended in the county so far; and the circumstances of this by-election don't inspire confidence in a Tory hold. Brian Riley was elected narrowly in 2013 in what had previously been a Lib Dem division, but in early 2015 he emigrated to Raleigh, North Carolina, while intending to serve out his term by keeping in touch with his constituents by email and Skype. Despite being expelled from the Conservative group and asked to resign by the leader of the county council, he proceeded to do just that for nearly eighteen months until finally falling foul of the six-month rule, which automatically disqualifies councillors who fail to attend any council meeting within a six-month period. Adding to the Tories' problems in holding this seat is that Riley won in 2013 on a very low share of the vote—just 31%, to 24% each for the Lib Dems and UKIP and 16% for Labour; on the positive side, the party won all four seats and had a clear lead across the division in the 2015 Babergh council elections.

Defending for the Tories is Kathryn Grandon, district councillor for Hadleigh South ward. The Lib Dems will want this seat back, and have selected Trevor Sheldrick, the Mayor of Hadleigh and runner-up in the 2013 election. The UKIP candidate is Stephen Laing, a Falklands veteran, pub landlord and Layham parish councillor who spent twenty years in the Merchant Navy. Hadleigh town councillor Sue Monks stands for Labour, and the ballot paper is completed by Green candidate Lisa Gordon.

Result: LD 642 C 460 Lab 397 UKIP 204 Grn 70 [LD gain from C]

Parliamentary constituency: South Suffolk
Babergh district council wards: Hadleigh North, Hadleigh South
May 2013 result C 584 LD 449 UKIP 442 Lab 308 Grn 90
June 2009 result LD 971 C 880 Lab 335
May 2005 result LD 1894 Lab 1209 C 839 UKIP 162

Figure 147: Suffolk CC, Hadleigh

Parliamentary constituency: Newton Abbot
Devon county council division: Teignmouth
May 2015 result C 1271/1156 LD 684/626 Grn 556 Lab 484
May 2011 result C 758/747 LD 756/672 Ind 297 Lab 259
May 2007 result LD 710/693 C 590/468 Ind 238/214/124 Lab 164
May 2003 result C 464/421 Ind 442/375/156/127 LD 327/319

Figure 148: Teignbridge, Teignmouth Central

Teignmouth Central

Teignbridge council, Devon; caused by the death of Conservative councillor Geoff
Bladon at the age of 69. Twice Mayor of Teignmouth, Bladon had served in the
Merchant Navy, the RAF and Devon and Cornwall police; he was first elected to
Teignbridge council in 1999, lost his seat in 2007, and returned in 2015.

For our third market town of the week we are on the south coast of Devon. Teignmouth lies on the north bank of the Teign estuary. Traditionally a fishing port for the Newfoundland cod trade, Teignmouth was the site of England's last invasion, with a French raid on the port in 1690. The port is still active, but tourism has been the mainstay of the economy since the start of the nineteenth century, which was one reason that Brunel brought his experimental atmospheric railway here in 1846. The Central ward is one of three covering the town, running north-west from the railway station along the Exeter Road.

Teignmouth Central ward has been closely fought for some years. It returned a Tory and an independent councillor in 2003 and two Lib Dems in 2007, the Conservatives gaining one seat in 2011 and the other in 2015 with a surprisingly emphatic victory: vote shares last year were 42% for the Tories, 23% for the Lib Dems (whose slate included the independent councillor from 2003–07) and 19% for the single Green candidate. The Teignmouth county seat, however, went the other way in 2013 with the Lib Dem candidate Richard Younger-Ross (the Teignbridge MP from 2001 to 2010) gaining it from the Conservatives.

Defending for the Conservatives is Nick Maylam, who has 30 years' service in the police and has been delivering events and projects in Teignmouth on a volunteer basis for over 20 years. The Lib Dem candidate is Alison Eden, a

Parliamentary constituency: South Northamptonshire
Northamptonshire county council division: Deanshanger
May 2015 result C unopposed
May 2011 result C 537 Lab 189 LD 68
May 2007 result C unopposed

Figure 149: South Northmaptonshire, Old Stratford

medical researcher and town councillor. With no Green candidate this time, the ballot paper is completed by Malcolm Tipper for Labour and Steven Harvey for UKIP.

Result: LD 491 C 286 UKIP 111 Lab 72 [LD gain from C]

Old Stratford

South Northamptonshire council; caused by the resignation of Conservative councillor Stephen Mold who is now the Police and Crime Commissioner for Northamptonshire. He had served since 2015.

Having gone through three coalfield wards, and three wards based on market towns, we finish with a set of three wards based on villages. Old Stratford is a village on the Northamptonshire side of the crossing point of Watling Street and the River Great Ouse; it has expanded greatly by new development in recent years, with the electorate of the former Cosgrove ward (of which Old Stratford was part until 2007) increasing by 42% between 1996 and 2003. With all the new development, Old Stratford is now in effect an extension of Milton Keynes which has spilled over the county boundary.

South Northamptonshire has a much less lively political culture than the New City, and tends to have lots of unopposed Tory returns at district level. The only contested election in Old Stratford since it became a ward of its own in 2007 was in 2011, when the Tories beat Labour 68–24; they had a similar lead in the wider Deanshanger county division in the 2013 county elections.

This by-election will be contested. The Tories' Ken Pritchard, who gives an address in the nearby village of Puxley, is challenged by UKIP's Rose Gibbins who fought Northampton South at the last general election.

Result: C 369 UKIP 109

Adderbury, Bloxham and Bodicote

Cherwell council, Oxfordshire; caused by the resignation of Conservative councillor Nigel Randall who has fallen out with the national party over Brexit. He had

Parliamentary constituency: Banbury
Oxfordshire county council division: Deddington (Adderbury and Milton parishes and almost all of Bodicote parish), Bloxham and Easington (Bloxham parish), Banbury Calthorpe (tiny corner of Bodicote parish)
May 2016 result C 1321/1312/1294 Grn 573/484/451 Lab 444/422/390 LD 364

Figure 150: Cherwell, Adderbury, Bloxham and Bodicote

served since 2012 for the former Adderbury ward and had represented this ward only since May.

For the first Oxfordshire by-election of 2016 we are in a ward based on three villages to the south of Banbury. Adderbury and Bodicote are on the old road from Banbury to Oxford, while Bloxham lies south-west of Banbury on the road to Chipping Norton, part of the ridiculously long A 361 which meanders from Barnstaple to Rugby. Also within the ward is the small parish of Milton. One of the electors in this by-election is the *Countryfile* presenter John Craven, and other famous people to have lived in this ward include Anthony Burgess and Tony Crosland.

Cherwell got new ward boundaries this year, and this new ward was created by merging the old single-member Adderbury ward with most of the former two-member Bloxham and Bodicote. Both predecessor wards were safe Tory and so is this one; in May the Tories won with 49% to 21% for the Green slate and 16% for Labour. The Tories also hold the two county divisions which cover the vast majority of this ward (a tiny corner of Bodicote parish is in the Labour-held Banbury Calthorpe division). Randall was elected in third place in 2016 so his successor will be seeking re-election in 2018.

Defending for the Tories is Andrew McHugh, who manages a GP practice in Banbury and has a military background. The Greens and Labour have reselected their top candidates from May; respectively they are Naomi Kanetsuka, a psychology student at Oxford Brookes University; and Sue Christie, a solicitor and wife of a Labour county councillor. Completing the ballot paper is Lib Dem candidate Ian Thomas.

Result: C 1015 Lab 286 Grn 278 LD 189

Cilycwm

Carmarthenshire council; caused by the death of Independent councillor Tom Theophilus at the age of 84. Theophilus' local government career started in 1976 when he was elected to the former Dinefwr district council; he joined Dyfed county council in 1991, and had sat on the modern Carmarthenshire council since

Parliamentary and Assembly constituency: Carmarthen East and Dinefwr
May 2012 result Ind 307 Ind 264 C 136
May 2008 result Ind 484 Ind 178 Ind 76
June 2004 result Ind unopposed

Figure 151: Carmarthenshire, Cilycwm

its inception in 1995. He had served as Mayor of Dinefwr and as chairman of
Carmarthenshire's highways and planning committees.

Now this really is deepest darkest mid-Wales. Cilycwm is a very rural ward covering the Towy valley south of Llandovery together with Cilycwm itself, a deeply rural community to the north-west and north of Llandovery. Despite the name, most of the population lives in Llanwrda and Llansadwrn in the Towy valley on the Llandovery–Llandeilo road; Llanwrda is the location of the ward's railway station, on the Heart of Wales line, and is rumoured to be the final resting place of Owain Glyndŵr. With this being such a remote and agricultural area, it's no surprise to see Cilycwm in the top 10 wards in England and Wales for the "small employers, own account" census classification (30% of the workforce) and in the top 25 wards for self-employment (28% of the workforce).

It's also no surprise to see independent candidates dominating the ward's previous results. Theophilus was unopposed in 2004 and the only party candidate to stand here this century was a Conservative in 2012, who finished a poor third behind two independents.

This by-election has a much larger field with no fewer than seven candidates. Two of them are independents: Thomas Arwel Davies, a farmer from Llanwrda, and barrister Matthew Paul, who despite his independent label was the Tory candidate here in 2012 and also contested the 2015 Westminster and 2016 Senedd elections as a Conservative. The runner-up to Theophilus in the 2012 election, Jacqui Thompson of Llanwrda, stands this time for the localist People First group—a blogger, she was arrested in 2011 for filming a council meeting and was later successfully sued for libel by the council's chief executive, Mark James. Expect further fireworks at the council if she wins. The official Tory candidate is Stephen Holmes, of Llanwrda, and the ballot paper is completed by three party candidates: alphabetically they are Maria Carroll (a former NHS worker with experience of handling large budgets) for Labour, Catherine Nakielny (a recent chair of the Carmarthenshire branch of the Farmer's Union of Wales) for the Lib Dems and Dafydd Owen Tomos (a farmer) for Plaid.

Result: PC 201 Davies 151 Lab 123 Paul 106 People First 64 LD 62 C 15 [PC gain from Ind]

29th September 2016

There are eight council by-elections on 29th September 2016. There is a Lib Dem defence in rural Norfolk, and Labour defences in Blackpool and the Welsh valleys; but the Tories have most to lose this week with five seats up for election: a fascinating marginal ward in Hemel Hempstead, an unpredictable rural ward in Lincolnshire, a Northamptonshire village and a true-blue part of the Cotswolds are on the bill, but we start this week in Derby with what, on paper, should be the easiest Tory defence of the week...

Allestree

Derby council; caused by the resignation of Conservative councillor Richard Smalley.

For our first, and definitely most controversial, poll of the week we are in the city of Derby. Allestree is a northern suburb of Derby, lying on the edge of the city on the far side of the A 38 bypass and nearly all developed since the Second World War (mostly in the late 1950s and early 1960s). This is a solidly middle-class ward with very high rates of owner-occupation and—despite the presence within the ward of the main campus of the University of Derby—a relatively old age profile. Famous people associated with the ward include the actor Sir Alan Bates and the football managers Brian and Nigel Clough, while for Derby residents Allestree is probably best known for the Markeaton and Allestree parks and the large Park Farm shopping centre.

This by-election is controversial because of the reason it came about. Richard Smalley, who for many years has been director of a scrap metal company, was elected to Derby city council in 2002 representing Oakwood ward, and stood down from the council in 2008. He returned to Derby city council for Allestree ward only in May, and was quickly elected as deputy leader of the Conservative group, but resigned just ten days after his election. It soon became clear that Smalley had provided a false home address on his nomination papers for the

Parliamentary constituency: Mid Derbyshire
May 2016 result C 2820 Lab 785 LD 645 UKIP 508
May 2015 result C 4867 Lab 1835 UKIP 1005 LD 883
May 2014 result C 2621 Lab 998 UKIP 925 LD 289
May 2012 result C 2040 Lab 1289 UKIP 647 LD 179 Grn 172
May 2011 result C 3486 Lab 1756 LD 579
May 2010 result C 4908 LD 1841 Lab 1608
Oct 2009 by-election C 1988 LD 1037 Lab 532 BNP 242
May 2008 result C 3234 Lab 739 LD 633 BNP 563
May 2007 result C 3172 Lab 940 LD 801
May 2006 result C 3228 Lab 962 LD 763
June 2004 result C 2879 Lab 1246 UKIP 1174 LD 1038
May 2003 result C 2132 LD 1053 Lab 1021
May 2002 result C 2726/2621/2529 Lab 1274/1159/920 LD 721/559/488

Figure 152: Derby, Allestree

election, and he is now serving a two-month prison sentence after pleading guilty to electoral fraud.

Bad news for the Derby Conservatives, who must now be looking at their large majority in this safe ward—Smalley beat Labour 59–16 in May—with rather more concern than usual. Their candidate is Ged Potter. Labour have reselected their candidate from May, Oleg Sotnicenko, and the ballot paper is completed by Deena Smith for the Lib Dems, Gaurav Pandey for UKIP and Marten Kats for the Green Party, whose ballot paper description "The Green Party—Say No To Racism" has been accepted despite going over the six-word limit.

Result: C 2006 LD 1053 Lab 409 Grn 115 UKIP 91

Cherry Willingham

West Lindsey council, Lincolnshire; caused by the resignation of Conservative councillor Alexander Bridgwood who is joining the armed forces. He had served since 2015.

Staying in the East Midlands we come to a rural ward immediately to the east of Lincoln. With a population of around 3,600, Cherry Willingham is by far the largest settlement in this ward and its population is growing fast through the recent construction of new estates, which have effectively filled in the space between Cherry Willingham and the neighbouring village of Reepham.

West Lindsey got new ward boundaries in 2015 which effectively merged the former two-member Cherry Willingham ward with most of the deeply rural Fiskerton ward. The new three-seat ward resulted in no change to the party

Parliamentary constituency: Gainsborough
Lincolnshire county council division: Bardney and Cherry Willingham (most); Nettleham
and Saxilby (Greetwell parish)
May 2015 result C 1726/1696/1540 Lincs Ind 1561 Lab 1151/997

Figure 153: West Lindsey, Cherry Willingham

strengths in the area, with the previous independent councillor for Fiskerton being re-elected for the Lincolnshire Independents group and the Tories holding their two seats from the old Cherry Willingham ward: shares of the vote were 39% for the Tory slate, 35% for the Lincolnshire Independents and 26% for Labour. The Bardney and Cherry Willingham county seat, which covers almost all of the ward, was also a Tory–Lincolnshire Independent marginal in the 2013 election but was safe Tory before that.

Defending for the Conservatives is Maureen Palmer, who has served in the Women's Royal Army Corps. Labour have selected Wendy Beckett—not the nun and art critic but the lead Labour candidate here in the 2015 election. Interestingly there will still be a Bridgwood on the ballot paper as UKIP have nominated Alexander's dad Trevor, an Army Cadet instructor, motorcycle enthusiast and British Legion figure.

Result: C 555 Lab 288 UKIP 244

Glaven Valley

North Norfolk council; caused by the resignation of Liberal Democrat councillor Andrew Wells, who has a new job in London with the law firm Allen and Overy. He had served since 2015.

> "We seek him here, we seek him there,
> Those Frenchies seek him everywhere.
> Is he in heaven?—Is he in hell?
> That damned, elusive Pimpernel."

Now here's a rarity: a by-election in a Lib Dem-held seat. Like Cherry Willingham above, here we have a case of a young councillor in his twenties leaving a rural area to take up a better-paid job elsewhere—a reminder that council work doesn't pay all that well. In this deeply rural ward the largest centre of population, with 625 electors, is Blakeney, once a harbour on the north coast of Norfolk but now a major centre for birdwatching: the saltmarshes, sand dunes, shingle and mudflats north of Blakeney form an important centre for migrating birds and seals, and the Blakeney Point area has been the subject of ecological

Parliamentary constituency: North Norfolk
Norfolk county council division: Wells
May 2015 result LD 634 C 438 UKIP 148 Lab 78 Grn 53
May 2011 result C 500 LD 232 Lab 95 Grn 84 UKIP 83
May 2007 result C 569 LD 431
May 2003 result C 623 LD 275 Grn 52

Figure 154: North Norfolk, Glaven Valley

studies for more than a century. This isn't all good news, because the Blakeney Point coastline is constantly changing and the path of the River Glaven can become blocked, causing flooding. From Blakeney the ward travels south along the picturesque Glaven as far as the village of Stody.

Glaven Valley has an old age profile—66% of the population are aged 45 or over, and the ward is in the top 200 in England and Wales for both retired people and self-employed people, reflecting its isolation.

Glaven Valley was a safe Conservative ward in the Noughties, but the Lib Dems suddenly broke through in the 2015 election to gain the ward with 47% of the vote, to 32% for the Conservatives and 11% for UKIP. That gain meant that the Lib Dems now represent Glaven Valley at all three levels of government, having gained the North Norfolk constituency in 2001 and the local county council seat (Wells) in 2009.

With this ward being in the constituency of the Lib Dems' deputy leader a loss might be rather embarrassing. Hoping that won't happen is Karen Ward, a business adviser from Sheringham. The Tories have selected Andrew Livsey, a property developer from just outside the ward in Cley-next-the-Sea; he has put out a truly bizarre leaflet advertising himself as a "man of the people who loves a challenge" and demonstrating this by (*inter alia*) stating that he "won a Porsche 911 in a beer competition" and pointing to his appearances on TV game shows including *Blind Date* and *The Crystal Maze*. Come back when you've reached the semi-finals of *Mastermind*, son, we'll talk then. The UKIP candidate is John Dymond, who is the only candidate to give an address in the ward (in Stody), and the ballot paper is completed by Stephen Burke (a former Hammersmith and Fulham councillor) for Labour and Alicia Hull for the Green Party.

Result: LD 429 C 281 UKIP 32 Lab 23 Grn 12

Finedon

Wellingborough council, Northamptonshire; caused by the death of Conservative councillor John Bailey.

One of the UK's longest-serving councillors, Bailey was first elected in 1967 to the pre-reform Wellingborough urban district council, and had served continuously on the present Wellingborough borough council since its first election in 1973. He was also a Northamptonshire county councillor from 1970 to 2013 and had served on Finedon parish council since its establishment in 1983. Bailey's council career peaked in 2005–2011 when he was leader of Wellingborough council; he was twice Mayor of Wellingborough (1976–77 and 2004–05) and chairman of the county council in 2012–13, was chairman of Wellingborough's audit committee at the time of his death and chaired the borough's housing committee for 27 years. In his working life, after studying at Selwyn College, Cambridge (where he was captain of the *University Challenge* team), he had been an economist-statistician with Shell-Mex and BP, an IBM programmer and an analyst and database administrator with British Timken. In honour of his services to the community in Wellingborough, Bailey was appointed MBE in the 2016 New Year honours list.

Among his many achievements, John Bailey literally wrote the book on Finedon—in fact he wrote several which are cited on Finedon's Wikipedia page. If we consult the oldest source in the National Archives, the Domesday book of 1086, Finedon (then known as Thingdon, from Old English words meaning "assembly valley"—a good omen for democracy) was one of four Northamptonshire towns with a population greater than fifty, but never achieved greatness.

In the eighteenth century Finedon was the home of the Dolben baronets, some of whom sat in Parliament including the lawyer Sir Gilbert Dolben (for Ripon, Peterborough and Yarmouth, Isle of Wight) and the anti-slavery campaigner Sir William Dolben (for Northamptonshire and Oxford University); they lived at Finedon Hall as did their descendant, the early Victorian poet Digby Mackworth Dolben who died from drowning aged 19. The Dolben baronets would probably be rather surprised to hear that the present incumbent of Finedon's mid-fourteenth-century parish church is the former Communards singer and Radio 4 broadcaster Revd Richard Coles. Coles' flock consists of 3,278 electors at the junction of the A 6 Kettering-Bedford road and the A 510 Wellingborough–Thrapston road, 4 miles north-east of Wellingborough.

Finedon has been a safe Conservative ward in the twenty-first century in which the party are not seriously challenged—in the 2007 and 2011 elections the Tory slate was guaranteed one seat due to their only opposition being a single Labour candidate. Last year the Conservatives won with 47% to 27% for Labour and 26% for UKIP. The Tories also hold the local county council seat—which includes the eastern part of Wellingborough town—but the last county result in 2013 was a three-way marginal with Labour second and UKIP third.

Parliamentary constituency: Wellingborough
Northamptonshire county council division: Finedon
May 2015 result C 1250/944 Lab 720 UKIP 698
May 2011 result C 935/847 Lab 612
May 2007 result C 909/720 Lab 539
May 2003 result C 768/652 Lab 527/407

Figure 155: Wellingborough, Finedon

There will still be a Bailey on the ballot as John's widow Barbara, a Finedon parish councillor, defends the seat for the Conservatives. The Labour candidate is Steve Ayland, who gives an address in Finedon. UKIP have selected Allan Shipham, chairman of the party's Wellingborough branch, and the ballot paper is completed by Lib Dem candidate John Wheaver.

Result: C 758 Lab 235 UKIP 137 LD 86

Adeyfield West

Dacorum council, Hertfordshire; caused by the death of Conservative councillor Sharon Adshead at the age of 63. A former RAF air traffic controller and civil servant, Adshead had served since 2015.

For the week's only by-election in the Home Counties we are in Hemel Hempstead. An old agricultural market town on the main transport arteries between London and the Midlands—the West Coast main line and the Grand Union canal—Hemel changed forever on 8th February 1950 when its first New Town residents moved into their new homes on Longlands, in the Adeyfield area. Adeyfield is now big enough to support two wards in a large urban area, and the Adeyfield West ward essentially covers the area of Hemel immediately east of the town centre. The ward's economic profile tends towards the working-class end and in 2011 more than a third of the households were still rented from what is now Hertfordshire's largest district by population, Dacorum council.

Adeyfield West is a fascinating marginal ward with a high councillor attrition rate—this is the third by-election here in the 2010s. On its current boundaries the ward dates from 2007 but is not much changed from the pre-2007 Adeyfield West which was safe Labour. The modern Adeyfield West is anything but. In 2007 its two seats split between Labour and Conservative, and a by-election in March 2010 saw the Tories hold their seat with just 33% of the vote in a poll which saw a good Lib Dem third place and 14% for the BNP. 2011 was a return to the *status quo ante*, but a by-election in March 2013 saw Labour lose their seat—not to the Tories, but to the Lib Dems who despite polling just 15% in 2011 held, and fielded, the

Parliamentary constituency: Hemel Hempstead
Hertfordshire county council division: Hemel Hempstead St Paul's
May 2015 result C 763/706 LD 715/463 Lab 696/450 UKIP 672
March 2013 by-election LD 363 Lab 278 C 229 UKIP 193 EDP 51
May 2011 result C 619/594 Lab 611/592 LD 209/204
March 2010 by-election C 486 Lab 429 LD 362 BNP 203
May 2007 result Lab 518/502 C 508/481 LD 200/178

Figure 156: Dacorum, Adeyfield West

ward's county councillor. The Tories and Lib Dems held their seats in 2015 in one of the closest four-way splits you will ever see: the re-elected Lib Dem councillor, who ran a long way ahead of his running-mate, had majorities of 11 votes over the second Conservative candidate, 19 votes over Labour and 43 votes over UKIP. Shares of the vote in 2015 were 27% for the Tories, 25% for the Lib Dems and 24% each for Labour and UKIP, so there really is everything to play for here.

Defending for the Tories is Tony Gallagher, the runner-up in the 2015 election. The Lib Dems have selected Adrian England. The Labour candidate is Gary Cook, a former district councillor (until 2007) and county councillor (until 2009) seeking to return to elected office. Rachel Biggs, chairman of the party's Hemel Hempstead branch, stands for UKIP. Completing the ballot paper is Angela Lynch of the Green Party.

Result: LD 520 C 233 Lab 166 UKIP 115 Grn 17 [LD gain from C]

Stow

Cotswold council, Gloucestershire; caused by the death of Conservative councillor Barry Dare at the age of 79. Dare first held elected office in his twenties on the pre-reform Twickenham borough council in the late 1950s or early 1960s; he was Conservative candidate for Leyton in the two 1974 elections, but it was in 1993 that his political career really took off when he was elected to Gloucestershire county council. He became leader of the Conservative group in 2002, served as leader of the county council from 2005 to 2010 and co-ordinated the response to the devastating Severn floods of 2007. Dare's business career was just as stellar; he ran his own accountancy business for over fifty years and served as chief executive of Unwins Seeds and the Cambridge chamber of commerce. Dare had served on Cotswold council since 2003, initially for Blockley ward before transferring to Stow ward (his former county seat) in 2015; he had stood down from the county council in 2013.

Having travelled south to Hemel, we now move west to the Cotswolds. Despite its hilltop location and high altitude, the town of Stow-on-the-Wold

Parliamentary constituency: The Cotswolds
Gloucestershire county council division: Stow-on-the-Wold
May 2015 result C 783 LD 613

Figure 157: Cotswold, Stow

benefits from its location at the junction of several roads through the Cotswolds, including the A 429 Fosse Way, and was given a market charter in 1107 by Henry I. The town was the site of a battle in March 1646 in which the Royalists were defeated in the last major battle of the First Civil War. The market is still going strong today, with the Stow Fairs in May and October being a popular venue for horse trading—literally, trading in horses.

The present Stow ward was created in 2015 by dividing the former Beacon-Stow ward in half, and as well as the town includes the small parishes of Maugersbury and Swell. This means that there aren't many previous results to go on, but the northern Cotswolds is a true blue part of the country anyway. That said, the only previous result on these boundaries was relatively close, the Tories beating the Lib Dems 56–44 in a straight fight.

Another straight fight is in prospect. Defending in the blue corner is David Penman, who represented Beacon-Stow ward from January 2006 (gaining a by-election from an independent) to 2015 when he stood down. Challenging in the yellow corner is Dilys Neill, a retired doctor from Moreton-in-Marsh.

Result: LD 555 C 300 [LD gain from C]

Brynmawr

Blaenau Gwent council; caused by the death of Independent councillor John Hopkins at the age of 77. A former teacher, Hopkins had served on Blaenau Gwent council since 1991 initially as Labour: he was leader of the council until 2007 and Labour candidate in the Blaenau Gwent by-election to the Welsh Assembly in 2006. Hopkins left Labour in 2009 and had led the council's independent group until 2014.

> "Crawshay Bailey had an Engine
> It was always needin' mendin'
> And dependin' on its power
> It could do four miles an hour
> *Did you ever saw*
> *Such a funny thing before?"*

The combination of John Hopkins and Brynmawr might bring to mind a pair of American universities, but this is Wales, not the USA. As befits its name

Parliamentary and Assembly constituency: Blaenau Gwent
May 2012 result Ind 943/713/643/499 Lab 708/498/399
May 2008 result Ind 1283/595/536 Lab 1071/695/645
June 2004 result Lab 1599/1255/1098 Ind 803 LD 514
May 1999 result Lab 1802/1443/1121 LD 725/372
May 1995 result Lab 2127/1760/1208 C 1421
May 1993 Gwent county council result Lab unopposed
May 1991 Blaenau Gwent borough council result C 1541 Lab 1423/1366/1229 Ind 962 Ind Lab 605
May 1989 Gwent county council result Lab 1287 Ind 1116 PC 190
May 1987 Blaenau Gwent borough council result C 1828 Lab 1591/1300/1089 Ratepayers 959 PC 807

Figure 158: Blaenau Gwent, Brynmawr

(from the Welsh for "big hill"), Brynmawr is one of the highest towns in Wales, located at the head of the Valleys not less than 1,250 feet above sea level; the town is so high up the Valleys that it was part of Breconshire until the 1974 local government reform. Brynmawr was called into being by the Industrial Revolution thanks to the development of the Welsh coal industry and Crawshay Bailey's huge Nantyglo ironworks just down the valley. The town was hit hard by the General Strike and the Great Depression, leading to the Quaker-led "Brynmawr Experiment" which tried to diversify the town into light industry such as boot and furniture manufacturing. Another industry tried in the town was rubber manufacture in the modernist Dunlop Semtex factory (Semtex here being not the IRA's favourite explosive, but a brand of vinyl flooring) which despite being the first post-war UK building to be listed was demolished in 2001. One local landmark which is thriving is the Market Hall cinema, which claims to be the oldest cinema in Wales. Brynmawr continues to suffer from high unemployment, with most of the jobs that exist being low-paid.

As an electoral unit Brynmawr ward dates back on its current boundaries to at least 1987 in the days when Blaenau Gwent was a district under Gwent county council; while the town used to have a Conservative councillor who served until 1999, Brynmawr's three seats have been fought over at each election this century between Labour and independents. Blaenau Gwent is perfectly capable of electing independents under the right circumstances, as can be attested by Labour's two 2006 by-election losers Hopkins and Owen Smith (whatever happened to him?); in Brynmawr the independents led 57–43 at the most recent election in 2012, with Hopkins being re-elected under his new colours to make the seat split 2–1 in the independents' favour. Labour only narrowly held off Plaid across Blaenau Gwent in May's Senedd election, suggesting that their machine

Parliamentary constituency: Blackpool South
May 2015 result Lab 1145/1145 C 872/741 UKIP 658 LD 167 Ind 144
May 2011 result Lab 1137/1105 C 689/667
May 2007 result C 833/802 Lab 775/749 LD 327
May 2003 result Lab 1387/1294 C 872/740 LD 435

Figure 159: Blackpool, Tyldesley

here is in only slightly better working order than Crawshay Bailey's engine.

This by-election is a straight fight. Defending for the independents is Wayne Hodgins, who finished fifth here in the 2012 election; he is a businessman and Brynmawr town councillor. Challenging for Labour is Julian Gardner, another town councillor and singer-songwriter who is running an arts project at the Market Hall cinema.

Result: Ind 1085 Lab 270

Tyldesley

Blackpool council, Lancashire; caused by the death of Labour councillor Eddie Collett at the age of 58. A college lecturer, Collett had served on Blackpool council since 1991 (when it was still a district under Lancashire county council), except for the period 2007–11, and was mayor of Blackpool in 2013–14. In tribute to one of the prime movers behind Blackpool's regeneration, the council arranged for a pair of bulldozers to greet well-wishers at Collett's wake in the town hall.

We finish this week in Blackpool, the archetypal English seaside resort. The name of Tyldesley ward commemorates Edward Tyldesley, squire of Myerscough, who built a house here called Foxhall which was the first settlement of substance in what's now Blackpool. The ward itself lies south-east of the town centre along Park Road, a series of inter-war terraces running as far as the eye can see, and includes some of the desirable housing on the edge of Stanley Park.

Tyldesley ward is normally Labour-inclined but was won by the Tories at Labour's low point in 2007, and the 2015 result—38% for Labour, 29% for the Tories and 22% for UKIP—suggests that this is not a ward Labour can take for granted. The party has decided to keep a Collett on the ballot paper by selecting Eddie's son David, a pro-NHS campaigner. The Conservatives have reselected Moira Graham, a hotelier who was runner-up here in the 2015 election. The UKIP candidate is Kim Knight, who runs a caravan hire firm, and the ballot paper is completed by Paul Hindley of the Lib Dems.

Result: Lab 535 C 297 UKIP 238 LD 37

6th October 2016

Nine by-elections on 6th October 2016:

Headland and Harbour

Hartlepool council, County Durham; caused by the resignation of Labour council-lor Peter Jackson. An electrical engineer, he had served since 2002.

A very descriptive name for a part of the country which tends not to get much attention. This is a shame, for Hartlepool is an old and interesting town—or, more accurately, two towns. Old Hartlepool, as West Hartlepudlians still call it, is a compact town based on a headland in the North Sea: it originally grew up as a religious settlement around the short-lived Hartlepool Abbey, of which no trace remains today; however, there is a fine Norman church on the headland dedicated to the abbey's second abbess, St Hilda of Whitby. At the time of its building the de Brus family, later kings of Scotland, were lords of the manor, and Hartlepool became an important port and market town, with some medicinal springs—the poet Thomas Gray came here in the eighteenth century for the water. (Unlike most of the north of England, Hartlepool's water is hard and was a noticeable change when I used to visit my grandparents here as a child in the 1980s and 1990s.)

The Pool's harbour proved unable to cope with the Industrial Revolution, and by 1830 the town was starting to face competition from rival ports at Seaham, Port Clarence and Middlesbrough. In response to this the borough council established a new dock and railway company, but its chairman—a solicitor called Ralph Ward Jackson—fell out with the council to the extent that he bought an area of sand-dunes to the south west and built a modern port and a new town called West Hartlepool on it. By 1870 the port was thriving, the population was booming and Ward Jackson had become the first MP for the two Hartlepools. At the turn of the century the Hartlepools were the third busiest port in England, which made the docks an obvious target in the First World War: and shortly before Christmas 1914 the Hartlepools were bombarded by the imperial German Navy with the loss of 117 lives.

The town suffered badly from the post-industrial bust after the Second World War, with the end of shipbuilding and steelworking resulting in very high unemployment. Despite this, the maritime sector is still important to Hartlepool, with the docks being an important employer in the town proper. A large amount of regeneration work undertaken in the 1990s resulted in the Maritime Experience, a series of old dock buildings which houses the town's museum and the oldest Royal Navy warship still afloat, HMS *Trincomalee*. The Tall Ships were here in 2010; the port, despite much of it having been turned into a marina, can still handle large vessels; and there are still manufacturing jobs in the town supporting the oil and offshore wind industries.

With all this dock history it's no surprise that Hartlepool is a Labour town—not coincidentally, the only Tory MP for the town since the Second World War was Commander John "Yangtse Incident" Kerans. My grandmother used to say that a monkey could win Hartlepool if it had a red rosette. Turns out the red rosette wasn't actually required: in the town's inaugural mayoral election in 2002 the winning candidate was a 28-year-old independent called Stuart Drummond, who was only standing as a publicity stunt: at the time he was spending every other Saturday parading up and down Victoria Park in a monkey costume as the mascot for Hartlepool United football club. While Drummond's election made headlines around the world, Labour had it coming in the town at the time—then MP Peter Mandelson was scandal-prone and locally unpopular, and an electoral pact between the Tories and Lib Dems had led to Labour losing control of the council in 2000. Despite his previous reputation, in office Drummond's governing style was sober and professional; even though he never did implement his only election pledge—free bananas for Hartlepool's schoolchildren—he was twice re-elected and it took a referendum on abolition of the mayoral system for Labour to get rid of him. (He had the same number of wins at the ballot box as the Pools have had on the pitch so far this season.)

One of Drummond's last acts in office was a boundary review which drastically reduced the size of the council to take into account its then mayoral structure. That brought into being the modern Headland and Harbour ward, which is essentially a merger of the former St Hilda and Stranton wards. At the 2011 census Stranton ward—which covered the docks and the housing south of Hartlepool railway station—had the seventh highest unemployment rate in the whole of England and Wales (12.8% of the workforce) and also made the top 100 for long-term sickness or disability (11.1%). St Hilda wasn't much better, just outside the top 100 for unemployment. Qualification rates and owner-occupation are low

Parliamentary constituency: Hartlepool
May 2016 result UKIP 619 Lab 617 C 117
May 2015 result Lab 1100 UKIP 892 Putting Hartlepool First 378 C 284 Ind 147 National Health Action 91
May 2014 result Lab 674 Putting Hartlepool First 559 C 187 LD 51
May 2012 result Lab 763/713/647 Putting Hartlepool Fist 525/484/465 C 120/88/84

Figure 160: Hartlepool, Headland and Harbour

across the ward.

Obvious territory for UKIP, who scored 10% across the town in the by-election after Peter Mandelson left for Brussels—unremarkable now, but noteworthy in 2004. UKIP followed up by gaining the independent-inclined St Hilda ward in the 2006 borough elections, but lost their seat to Labour in 2010. Stranton ward was strongly Labour before its abolition in 2012, and in the first election to the new Headland and Harbour ward in 2012 Labour won all three seats fairly comfortably with a strong second place for the localist slate "Putting Hartlepool First"—which included the former UKIP councillor. Since then this ward has been marginal for Labour who reportedly have been suffering from infighting in Hartlepool; Putting Hartlepool First reduced the Labour lead to 46–38 in the 2014 election, UKIP took over second place in 2015 with 31%, to 38% for Labour and 13% for Putting Hartlepool First, and in May's election with no Putting Hartlepool First candidate on the ballot UKIP broke through to gain the ward from Labour by 619 votes to 617, both parties polling 46%.

With Hartlepool voting strongly for Leave in the referendum, this is an opportunity for UKIP to gain. The defending Labour candidate is Trevor Rogan, a dockworker and former borough councillor (Brus ward, 2004–12) who hit the headlines in 2007 and 2008 after being cleared of a wife-beating conviction on appeal. UKIP's candidate is Tim Fleming, a dentist. Also standing are official Conservative candidate Benjamin Marshall, independent Chris Broadbent (who was the Tory candidate here in May), Steve Latimer of Putting Hartlepool First (who was runner-up here in 2014) and John Price for National Health Action.

Result: UKIP 496 Lab 255 Putting Hartlepool First 155 C 41 National Health Action 36 Ind 26 [UKIP gain from Lab]

Rumworth

Bolton council, Greater Manchester; caused by the death of Labour councillor Rosa Kay at the age of 79. A former magistrate, who was first elected in 1999 after previously being the council's Unison rep, Kay had held a number of key positions in the Bolton cabinet. In recent years she had suffered from poor health and was a wheelchair user; last year her carer was sent to prison for stealing £8,000 from her bank account.

From Hartlepool to the Greatest Town in the Known Universe. Or perhaps not, if you look at what has happened to Bolton town centre this summer. British Home Stores, the flagship store on Victoria Square opposite the town hall—gone. Prestons of Bolton, which has sold wedding rings to the fiancés of the North West for 150 years—gone. Whitakers (now Beales) department store—closing down. The Albert Halls, Bolton's premier event space in the town hall—closed for refurbishment for two years now and no guarantee that it will reopen in the same form, given that the council has laid off all the front-of-house staff. The Victoria Halls, Bolton's premier concert hall run by the Methodists—living from week to week. Your columnist could name several further prominent front teeth which have been knocked out of the town centre recently, with the prospect of more to come, and what are the council doing about it? Refurbishing the town hall and building a new bus station so that people can come to a town centre that's not worth visiting on buses they can't afford to pay the fare for. Great. The contrast with Bury, which had the foresight to open a thriving new town centre extension at the low point of the recession, is striking.

To redress the balance slightly, there are some nice buildings going up at the bottom end of Deane Road, but that has more to do with the University who are on a growth spurt at the moment. Some of the University site spills over into Rumworth ward, which covers the Willows area south-west of the town centre along Deane Road and St Helens Road—redbrick terraces as far as the eye can see on high ground overlooking the town centre. Like Stranton in Hartlepool, this makes the top 100 wards in England and Wales for people who have never worked or are long-term unemployed, but not for the same reason. Rumworth is a majority-Asian ward: 55% of the population are of Asian heritage, overwhelmingly from Pakistan, and 52% are Muslim. That Pakistani heritage shows itself in other census stats: as well as the large population who have never worked, 27% of the population are under 16. Social housing rates and unemployment are high and those jobs which exist are low-paid working-class ones.

There's not much chance of this by-election resulting in any change to the council composition or direction, as Rumworth is one of the strongest Labour wards in the country. In May's election Rosa Kay had a relatively low 72% of the vote, with 10% for the Tories best of the rest. This should therefore be an easy hold for Labour candidate Shamim Abdullah; she is opposed by Mohammed Waqas of the Conservatives, UKIP's Joseph Baxendale, Alan Johnson of the

Parliamentary constituency: Bolton South East
May 2016 result Lab 2568 C 373 UKIP 354 Grn 179 LD 82
May 2015 result Lab 4555 C 747 Grn 457 LD 136
May 2014 result Lab 2876 UKIP 492 C 317 Grn 200 LD 66
May 2012 result Lab 2394 C 294 Grn 274 LD 88
May 2011 result Lab 2677 C 374 Grn 300 LD 119
May 2010 result Lab 3928 LD 855 C 825
May 2008 result Lab 1875 LD 647 Left List 444
May 2007 result Lab 2079 C 668 LD 480
May 2006 result Lab 2028 C 932
June 2004 result Lab 1734/1706/1683 LD 1316/1228/991 C 633/598/567 Respect 540 Soc Lab 136

<hr>

Figure 161: Bolton, Rumworth

<hr>

Green Party and Becky Forrest of the Lib Dems.
    Result: Lab 2125 UKIP 251 C 167 Grn 126 LD 96

St Ann's

Haringey council, North London; caused by the resignation of Labour councillor Peter Morton who is starting a new non-political job. He had served since 2014.

This week's London by-election takes place in that area where Harringay ends and Tottenham begins. The main features of the ward are Chestnuts Park and St Ann's Hospital, mainly a mental health unit, while the St Ann's Road links the ward together. At the south-west corner is Harringay Green Lanes station on the Gospel Oak–Barking line (closed for rebuilding), while Seven Sisters station lies just off the ward's eastern end.

Like much of Haringey, St Ann's ward has been a major focus for immigration in recent years—at the time of the last census 15% of the population were born in the new EU states and 31% were from the "White Other" ethnic group. The ward's economic profile is just as mixed, although unemployment is relatively high. This results in a safe Labour ward which has seen some unusual second place scores—Respect were runners up in the 2006 election, the Lib Dems did well in 2010 but at the most recent borough election in 2014 Labour led 51–21 over the Green Party. The Greens were also second at the Mayor and Assembly elections in May, with Sadiq Khan winning 66–12 and Labour winning the London Members ballot 59–17.

Labour's choice of candidate has raised some eyebrows: Noah Tucker is a Momentum figure who has become caught up in the Labour anti-Semitism scandal. The Green candidate is Ronald Stewart who stood for the London

Parliamentary constituency: Tottenham
London Assembly constituency: Enfield and Haringey
May 2014 result Lab 1829/1508/1491 Grn 757/530/497 TUSC 271/236 C 251/194/175 LD 243/217/210 UKIP 212
May 2010 result Lab 2469/2315/2241 LD 1201/1129/1088 C 601/596/558 Grn 432/427/371 TUSC 202
May 2006 result Lab 1195/1184/1064 Respect 579/468 Grn 500 LD 390/348/285 C 337/329/283
May 2002 result Lab 1010/981/950 Grn 368 Socialist Alliance 324 LD 273/257/248 C 223/213/177
May 2016 GLA results (excludes postal voters)
Mayor: Lab 2181 Grn 379 C 372 LD 94 Women's Equality 91 Respect 46 UKIP 37 Cannabis is Safer than Alcohol 30 Zylinski 21 Britain First 13 BNP 12 One Love 7
London Member: Lab 1956 Grn 571 C 289 Women's Equality 175 LD 133 UKIP 66 Respect 44 CPA 31 Animal Welfare 29 Britain First 18 House Party 13 BNP 10

Figure 162: Haringey, St Ann's

Assembly in May; also standing are Ellis Turrell for the Conservatives, Josh Dixon for the Lib Dems and Janus Polenceusz for UKIP.

Result: Lab 1177 Grn 323 LD 189 C 106 UKIP 54

Basing

Basingstoke and Deane council, Hampshire; caused by the resignation of Conservative councillor Clive Pinder, who had served since 2015.

> "There was an Old Person of Basing,
> Whose presence of mind was amazing;
> He purchased a steed,
> Which he rode at full speed,
> And escaped from the people of Basing."

> \- Edward Lear

Located immediately to the east of Basingstoke, Basing ward has a history of conflict. In January 871 the Vikings defeated the West Saxons, under King Ethelred I, in battle here, and during the Civil War Basing House, the home of the Marquesses of Winchester, was destroyed in a 24-week siege. Old Basing, as the village is now known, was on the old road from London to Winchester and the south west, but now functions as a dormitory village for Basingstoke: the ward also includes Lychpit, a 1980s housing development which is effectively a part of Basingstoke that has spilled over the parish boundary.

Parliamentary constituency: Basingstoke
Hampshire county council division: Loddon
May 2016 result C 1594 LD 311 UKIP 298 Lab 297
May 2015 result C 2921 UKIP 754 Lab 697 LD 684
May 2014 result Ind 1368 C 695 UKIP 458 Lab 212 LD 198
May 2012 result C 1676 Lab 321 LD 290
May 2011 result C 2325 LD 324 Lab 448
May 2010 result C 3288 LD 1187 Lab 530
May 2008 result C 1962/1821/1725 LD 1161/1042/928 Lab 149
May 2007 result C 1864 LD 906 Lab 93
May 2006 result C 1724 LD 1239 Lab 162
June 2004 result LD 1675 C 1363
May 2003 result C 1214 LD 1153 Lab 171 Ind 38
May 2002 result LD 1511/1387/1260 C 1196/1181/1173
May 2000 result LD 1258 C 1164 Lab 112
May 1999 result LD 1267 C 1094 Lab 167
May 1998 double vacancy C 1117/967 LD 1058/829 Lab 344/178
May 1996 result C 1216 LD 1151 Lab 235
May 1995 result LD 1256 C 1183 Lab 252
May 1994 result C 1225 LD 1202 Lab 196
May 1992 result C 1666/1504/1367 LD 992/844 Lab 233/230/183

Figure 163: Basingstoke and Deane, Basing

Recent conflicts in Basing ward have generally seen the Tories victorious. On its current boundaries the ward dates from at least 1992, having survived boundary changes in 2002 and 2008 unscathed; it was a Lib Dem hotspot from 1995 to 2005, but the Tories are now in control of the ward's elections, if not entirely in control of their own councillors—the 2014 election re-elected as an independent a councillor who had had a falling out with the Conservatives. In May the Tories had 64% with the Lib Dems, UKIP and Labour all on 12%. The Tories also hold the local county seat (Basing is within Loddon division, named after the river it stands on).

Defending for the Tories is Paul Gaskell, a chartered engineer and parish councillor within the ward. He is opposed by Richard Lilleker for the Lib Dems and Andrew Toal for Labour.

Result: C 1051 LD 323 Lab 184

Exmouth Brixington

East Devon council; caused by the death of Conservative councillor David Chapman at the age of 71. A former Merchant Navy officer and bank manager (retiring

Parliamentary constituency: East Devon
Devon county council division: Exmouth Brixington and Withycombe
May 2015 result C 1644/1599/1511 Ind East Devon Alliance 1281 LD 855 Lab 733
May 2011 result Ind 894/730 C 800/777/714 LD 408/407 UKIP 366/335
May 2007 result LD 486/345/316 C 466/456/433 Lab 185
May 2003 result LD 825/666/613 C 534/533/521 Ind 513

Figure 164: East Devon, Exmouth Brixington

*as South West area manager of Lloyds Bank), Chapman had served on the district
council and Exmouth town council since 2007, chairing the town council's finance
committee for three years.*

After a previous visit in July, this column returns to Exmouth. A tourist centre in season and a commuter town for Exeter, Exmouth's main function is as a retirement centre: although Brixington ward, located away from the seafront in the north-east corner of Exmouth, isn't the oldest ward in the town, 53.5% of the population are over 45 and 21% of the workforce are retired. The ward has high rates of owner-occupation and part-time working (18% of the workforce).

Brixington ward safely returned three Lib Dems in 2003, but the Conservatives took two of the three seats in the 2007 election. The remaining Lib Dem councillor sought and won re-election as an independent in 2011, and upon his retirement the Tories returned their full slate in the 2015 election; shares of the vote were 36% for the Tories, 28% for the Independent East Devon Alliance and 19% for the Lib Dems. However, at county level this ward is combined with a stronger Lib Dem area to produce the Exmouth Brixington and Withycombe seat which in 2013 voted—UKIP, coming through the middle of an even Lib Dem/Tory split to win with just 33% of the vote.

Defending for the Tories is Darryl Nicholas, a former councillor for this ward (2007–2011) seeking to make a comeback. The Independent East Devon Alliance, a well-organised localist slate, have selected Robin Humphreys who has retired to Exmouth after a career in management training. Completing the ballot paper is Alex Sadiq; she is secretary of a vehicle repair company with the puntastic name of Exepress Autos.

Result: C 425 Ind East Devon Alliance 324 LD 286

Gilfach; and
Risca East

*Caerphilly council, Gwent; caused by the resignations of Labour councillors Harry
Andrews and Rhianon Passmore respectively. Andrews, who served as leader of*

Parliamentary and Assembly constituency: Caerphilly
May 2012 result Lab 553 PC 91
May 2008 result Lab 555 PC 157
June 2004 result Lab 674 PC 115
May 1999 result Lab 645 PC 203

Figure 165: Caerphilly, Gilfach

Parliamentary and Assembly constituency: Islwyn
May 2013 by-election Lab 529 Ind 299 Ind 209 PC 119 C 36
May 2012 result Lab 953/789/769 Ind 399 PC 312/275/186
May 2008 result Lab 755/708/703 PC 548/502 Ind 516
June 2004 result Lab 905/819/815 PC 578 LD 454
May 1999 Lab 1145/950/893 PC 1102

Figure 166: Caerphilly, Risca East

Caerphilly council from 2004 to 2008 and from 2012 to 2014, is retiring after 49 years' service in local government, while Passmore has been elected to the Senedd as Labour AM for Islwyn.

After Brynmawr last week, we have two more by-elections in the Welsh valleys to examine. The ex-mining village of Gilfach lies on the Glamorgan side of the Rhymney valley, south of Bargoed (whose town council it is part of) and north of Pengam. It is connected to the outside world by the tiny railway station of Gilfach Fargoed on the Rhymney Valley line. Risca lies in the south-east corner of Caerphilly district in the Sirhowy valley; again, it is traditionally a mining town, but the East ward is based on Ty-Sign, a housing estate built in the 1960s for workers at Llanwern steelworks. Today Risca is effectively a Newport suburb, but trains from the Risca and Pontymister railway station (opened in 2008 on the Ebbw Vale branch) only go to Cardiff.

Risca East (in Welsh, *Dwyrain Risga*) has had a full slate of three Labour councillors since 2004 when Labour gained the last seat in the ward from Plaid Cymru. In the 2012 election the Labour slate beat an independent candidate 57–24, while a previous by-election in May 2013 gave Labour 44% to 25% and 18% for two independent candidates. Andrews had turned Gilfach into his personal fiefdom and he had a large personal vote there: in 2012 he polled 86% in a straight fight with Plaid.

The voters of Gilfach will have a wider choice this time round. Defending for Labour is Lindsey Harding, a Bargoed town councillor for the ward; he is opposed by Ken Houston of Plaid, Andrew Creak for the Green Party and Glenys Griffiths for UKIP.

There will still be a Passmore on the ballot paper in Risca as Labour have selected Rhianon's daughter Arianna Passmore, a music and film teacher and Risca town councillor for Trenewydd ward (part of the East division). With no independent candidates this time round, she is opposed by Matthew Farrell of Plaid, Matthew Kidner of the Liberal Democrats and UKIP candidate Joe Smyth.

Gilfach result: Lab 254 PC 150 UKIP 28 Grn 7 (seven)

Risca East result: Lab 400 PC 120 UKIP 117 LD 32

Garscadden/Scotstounhill

Glasgow city council, caused by the death of Labour councillor John Kelly. He had served since 2012; before becoming a councillor he had been a longstanding CWU activist.

For the first of the week's two Scottish by-elections we are in north-west Glasgow. The Garscadden area was annexed by Glasgow in 1926 for new housing, and the Low Knightswood area was quickly filled with new houses along the Great Western Road, built on garden-city principles.

Further down towards the river lie the Victorian enclave of Scotstounhill, Garscadden itself and Yoker. Much of the ward's riverfront is taken up with shipbuilding, with BAE Systems building new craft for the Royal Navy at the Scotstoun and Yarrows shipyards.

A ferry links Yoker with Renfrew on the far bank of the Clyde, while the Argyle Line stations of Garscadden and Scotstounhill link the ward with Glasgow city centre.

While the local MP and MSP are both SNP members, Glasgow city council was last up for election in 2012 which was before the independence referendum and consequent SNP surge in Scotland. In 2012 Labour led the SNP 62–27 which represented no swing at all since 2007, and Labour comfortably won three seats to the SNP's one. A mountain to climb for the SNP, but in present political conditions certainly achievable.

Defending for Labour is Ian Cruikshank, who is described as a local man. The SNP have selected Chris Cunningham, who is the younger brother of the Scottish environment secretary Roseanna Cunningham and director of the Shettleston housing association. Also standing are Gillian Macdonald for the Scottish Green Party, Ary Jaff for the Conservatives, Liberal Democrat James Speirs and UKIP candidate Donald Mackay (who gives an address over 25 miles away in Lanark).

First preferences: SNP 2135 Lab 1944 C 510 Grn 242 LD 97 UKIP 83

After transfers: SNP 2321 Lab 2204 [SNP gain from Lab]

Parliamentary constituency: Glasgow North West
Holyrood constituency: Glasgow Anniesland
May 2012 first preferences Lab 5056 SNP 2220 Grn 221 C 215 Ind 151 Christian 135 LD 90
UKIP 69 TUSC 29 Glasgow First 22
May 2007 first preferences Lab 5754 SNP 2333 C 534 LD 483 Grn 402 Solidarity 318
Scottish Unionist Party 191 SSP 145

Figure 167: Glasgow, Garscadden/Scotstounhill

Culloden and Ardersier

*Highland council; caused by the death of Labour councillor John Ford at the age
of 85. The oldest Highland councillor, Ford had served since 2003 after a career
in the electricity supply industry; he died suddenly while on holiday in Jersey.*

For our final by-election this week we are at the location where the Young
Pretender's luck finally ran out in the 1745 rebellion. The battle itself was all over
in less than an hour after a failed charge by the Highlanders, but its effects res-
onated for many years to come: one effect within this ward was the construction
of Fort George on a promontory east of Inverness to guard the narrowest point
of the Moray Firth, in defence against a third Jacobite invasion which never came.
The Army are still at Fort George which is home to the Black Watch, but the fort
is almost unaltered since the eighteenth century and now mostly open to the
public as a museum. The construction of Fort George led to the resettlement of
the nearby fishing village of Blacktown into a new village called Ardersier.

While Ardersier is in a rural area, this ward is essentially Inverness suburbia. At its first election in 2007 it elected Robert Wynd of the SNP (previously
councillor for the suburban Balloch ward), independent Roddy Balfour (whose
former ward was the rural Ardersier, Croy and Petty), Labour's John Ford (who
had been elected for the suburban Culloden ward in 2003) and Lib Dem Glynis Sinclair. In the 2007–12 term Sinclair defected to the SNP and stood for
re-election under her new colours in 2012; as it turned out there weren't enough
votes for two SNP seats and it was Bob Wynd who lost out while Labour held
their seat. The shares of the vote in 2012 show how fragmented the result was:
30% for Roddy Balfour, who topped the poll, 27% for the SNP and 14% each for
Labour and the Lib Dems.

With a starting point of only 14% Labour have it all to do to hold this by-
election; remember, the Alternative Vote is being used so it will be important
to attract transfers as well as poll a good first preference score. The defending
Labour candidate is Andrew Mackintosh, a storyteller and researcher for a Labour
MSP. Four independent candidates have come forward: Thomas Lamont (who

Parliamentary constituency: Inverness, Nairn, Badenoch and Strathspey
Holyrood constituency: Inverness and Nairn
May 2012 first preferences Ind 1224 SNP 941 Lab 479 LD 475 Grn 170 C 154
May 2007 first preferences Ind 1521 SNP 1335 Lab 816 LD 663 C 318

Figure 168: Highland, Culloden and Ardersier

runs a taxi firm), Duncan Macpherson (chairman of Cradlehall and Westhill community council), David McGrath (who finished sixth here in 2012) and John Ross (a B&B owner in Ardersier). The SNP candidate is Pauline Munro, former councillor for Inverness West ward who lost her seat in 2012. The Lib Dems have nominated Trish Robertson, chair of Ardersier and Petty community council. Completing the ballot paper are Isla Macleod-O'Reilly for the Scottish Greens and the Tories' Andrew Jarvie.

First preferences: SNP 753 LD 463 C 439 Ross 315 Macpherson 274 Grn 180 Lab 163 McGrath 158 Lamont 23

Lamont eliminated: SNP 755 LD 464 C 442 Ross 317 Macpherson 285 Grn 182 Lab 163 McGrath 158

McGrath eliminated: SNP 775 LD 479 C 452 Ross 330 Macpherson 324 Grn 188 Lab 160

Lab eliminated: SNP 796 LD 515 C 468 Macpherson 346 Ross 339 Grn 209

Grn eliminated: SNP 862 LD 564 C 478 Macpherson 369 Ross 362

Ross eliminated: SNP 908 LD 703 C 515 Macpherson 414

Macpherson eliminated: SNP 970 LD 793 C 589

C eliminated: LD 1026 SNP 1001 [LD gain from Lab]

13th October 2016

Ten by-elections on 13th October 2016:

Windermere (Cumbria county council); and Windermere Bowness North (South Lakeland council)

Both caused by the resignation of Liberal Democrat councillor Colin Jones due to family commitments. Jones had served on the district council since winning a by-election in August 2013, and on the county council since winning a by-election in October 2014.

Welcome to the Lake District, and welcome to the tourist trail. We are here in the Lakes' railhead, the town of Windermere. Indeed Windermere as a town owes its existence to the railways, specifically the Kendal and Windermere railway which opened in 1847 and made the Lake District easily accessible to tourists for the first time. In order to accommodate them the town of Windermere (and its twin town, the inland resort of Bowness-on-Windermere) boomed. Bowness itself is a sailing centre for the Lake and readers of Arthur Ransome's *Swallows and Amazons* series may know it better as "Rio"; the most popular sailing is a car ferry which crosses the lake to Far Sawrey on the western side, not far from Beatrix Potter's house at Hill Top. As well as the tourism, Windermere is also the home of the kitchenware chain Lakeland, whose flagship store can be found next to the railway station. The Windermere county division covers the whole of Windermere town, the northern half of Bowness and a few hamlets to the north, the largest of which is Troutbeck Bridge.

Here we have two examples of that rare thing: a by-election in a Lib Dem-held constituency. This is Tim Farron's manor, and his personality cult creates a strong Lib Dem vote—one of the wards within this county division, Windermere Town, was 82.7% Lib Dem in the 2008 local elections. However, the party machine has loosened its grip on Windermere since then: the Tories hold the Applethwaite and Troutbeck ward in the north of the division and put up a good fight in the

"

Parliamentary constituency: Westmorland and Lonsdale
South Lakeland district council wards: Windermere Bowness North, Windermere Town,
Windermere Applethwaite and Troutbeck (part), Windermere Bowness South (small
part)
Oct 2014 by-election LD 1061 C 810 Ind 123 Grn 61
May 2013 result LD 1162 C 350 UKIP 227 Lab 133

Figure 169: Cumbria CC, Windermere

Parliamentary constituency: Westmorland and Lonsdale
Cumbria county council division: Windermere
May 2015 result LD 582 C 463 Lab 72 Grn 71
Aug 2013 by-election LD 431 C 248 Lab 29
May 2011 result LD 608 C 280 Lab 47
May 2008 result LD 654 C 227

Figure 170: South Lakeland, Windermere Bowness North

last county by-election in 2014, cutting the Lib Dem lead to 52–39 (it had been 62–19 in the 2013 county elections). Colin Jones had a similar lead in Bowness North ward when it was last up in 2015, beating the Tories 49–39.

Defending the county seat for the Lib Dems is Steve Rooke, a former professional golfer who fought Bowness South ward last year. The Tories have reselected their district councillor within the ward, Ben Berry, who leads the Tory group on South Lakeland council; he made the local press last year when his election signs were defaced to read "Den Perry". Also standing are Kate Threadgold for the Greens and Penny Henderson for Labour.

The Bowness North district by-election is defended for the Lib Dems by Andrew Jarvis, who lost to Berry in the 2015 district elections. He is up against the Tories' Martin Hall, a paramedic. Completing the ballot paper is, again, Kate Threadgold for the Greens.

Windermere (Cumbria CC) result: LD 1009 C 785 Lab 88 Grn 46

Windermere Bowness North (South Lakeland) result: LD 441 C 256 Grn 37

Westgate

Lancaster council; caused by the resignation of Labour councillor David Smith, who is moving back to his native Bradford. He had served since 2011 on Lancaster council and before that was its TGWU rep; he had also served as chairman of the TGWU national public services committee, had been a magistrate, was Labour candidate for Morecambe and Lunesdale in the 1987 general election, and had

Parliamentary constituency: Morecambe and Lunesdale
Lancashire county council division: Morecambe South (most), Morecambe West (part: transferred from Poulton ward in 2015)
May 2015 result Lab 1279/1261/1115 C 985 UKIP 970 Morecambe Bay Independents 696

Figure 171: Lancaster, Westgate

worked as a window cleaner and football referee. At the time of his resignation he was a member of the Lancaster cabinet.

Moving into Lancashire and we're in the town of Morecambe. Westgate is Morecambe's inland ward, an area of low-lying housing on the far side of the old Green Ayre and Heysham railway lines almost all of which has gone up since the Second World War. Included within the ward is the large White Lund industrial estate straddling the link road to Heysham; the new Lancaster Northern Bypass is scheduled to open later this month to provide Westgate ward with a fast link to the M6 motorway without having to negotiate the notorious traffic bottleneck which is Lancaster city centre. The ward is only just outside the top 100 in England and Wales for jobs classified by the census as "semi-routine"; reflecting this, qualification rates are low and part-time working is high.

Morecambe's local elections were dominated for most of the last two decades by a localist slate called the Morecambe Bay Independents, who were briefly powerful enough to be the largest party on Lancaster city council (which includes Morecambe and a large rural hinterland, so it's perennially hung). The MBI had a lock on Westgate ward's elections before 2010, but Labour gained two seats in 2011 and got a full slate in the 2015 election (the first one on the current ward boundaries); despite this, the election was rather fragmented with 33% for the Labour slate, 25% each for the Tories and UKIP and 18% for the MBI. Most of the ward is within the Morecambe South county division which Labour gained from the Tories in 2013 in a three-way marginal result (UKIP being the third party).

Defending for Labour is Ian Clift, a Morecambe town councillor seeking to make a comeback on the city council—he was a city councillor for Torrisholme ward 2003–07, then representing the Liberal Democrats. The Tory candidate is Daniel Gibbins, who fought Halton-with-Aughton ward in 2015. UKIP have reselected their 2015 candidate for the ward Michelle Ogden, a Morecambe town councillor. A third Morecambe town councillor on the ballot is Roger Dennison, former leader of the Morecambe Bay Independents. Completing the ballot paper are Richard Moriarty for the Green Party and Louise Stansfield for the Lib Dems.

Result: Lab 463 Morecambe Bay Independents 193 UKIP 183 C 178 LD 41 Grn 26

Cliff Villages

North Kesteven council, Lincolnshire; caused by the resignation of councillor Laura Conway, who represented the Lincolnshire Independents, due to work commitments. She had served since 2011.

For this week's only rural by-election we are in a Lincolnshire ward covering a series of villages atop the Lincoln Cliff, a 50-mile-long limestone escarpment which runs in an almost straight line from Grantham to the Humber, breached only by two rivers at Lincoln and Ancaster. The top of the Cliff has been an important transport artery since prehistoric times, with the ancient track now called the Jurassic Way superseded by the Roman Ermine Street and the modern A 607 Lincoln–Grantham road. The Cliff Villages in this ward are seven parishes running from Harmston in the north to Leadenham in the south; all of these parishes have long, thin shapes running from the plateau in the east to the River Brent in the west, betraying that these are spring-line villages. The largest centre of population is Navenby, a former market town which is now a fast-growing Lincoln dormitory village; the smallest parish within the ward is Boothby Graffoe, which formerly gave its name to an ancient wapentake of Lincolnshire and is now the stage name for a stand-up comedian.

Cliff Villages ward was formed in 1999 by merging the former Navenby and Wellingore wards, and at district council level is the personal fiefdom of long-serving independent councillor Marianne Overton who since 2011 has run under the Lincolnshire Independents label. Conway was elected in 2011 on Overton's coat-tails, gaining her seat from the Conservatives, and in 2015 the Lincolnshire Independent slate was opposed only by a single Conservative candidate, who lost 64–36. Overton is also the county councillor for Branston and Navenby division, although part of the ward is within the Conservative county division of Bassingham Rural.

Defending for the Lincolnshire Independents is Cat Mills, a parish councillor in Wellingore and the only candidate to live within the ward. The Conservative candidate is Daniel Gray, from Cranwell, and the ballot paper is completed by the ward's first Liberal Democrat candidate, Aarron Smith.

Result: Lincs Ind 721 C 372 LD 49

Brockley; and
Evelyn

Lewisham council, South London; caused respectively by the resignation of Baroness Kennedy of Cradley and the death of Crada Onuegbu. Onuegbu was first elected

Parliamentary constituency: Sleaford and North Hykeham
Lincolnshire county council division: Bassingham Rural (part: Leadenham, Welbourn and Wellingore parishes), Branston and Navenby (part: Boothby Graffoe, Coleby, Harmston and Navenby parishes)
May 2015 result Lincs Ind 2083/1623 C 1165
May 2011 result Lincs Ind 1537/968 C 870/571 UKIP 164
May 2007 result Ind 1572 C 962 UKIP 296
May 2003 result Ind 1393/679 C 576 Lab 244
May 1999 result Ind 1085 C 764/528 Lab 356

Figure 172: North Kesteven, Cliff Villages

in 1998 and had served on the Lewisham cabinet; Kennedy had been on the council since 2014 after many years in the central organisation of the Labour party, including as deputy general secretary and special advisor to Ed Miliband. Both were Labour councillors.

> Was the first Anniversary our Society for the Choice of new Officers, according to the Tenor of our Patent, & Institution; it being St. Andrews day, who was our Patron, each fellow wearing a St. Andrews Crosse of ribbon on the crowne of his hatt, after the Election was over, we all dined together, his Majestie sending us Venison:
>
> —John Evelyn, Diary, 30 November 1663

The old Metropolitan Borough of Deptford had a practice of naming its wards not after geography but after famous historical people associated with the borough. Before 2002 Lewisham had five such wards covering the old Deptford borough, called Drake, Evelyn, Grinling Gibbons, Marlowe and Pepys; however, the last boundary review abolished Grinling Gibbons ward and renamed the other three after geography. Marlowe ward transformed into New Cross, Pepys was succeeded by Telegraph Hill, and Drake ward's successor is the modern Brockley; leaving as the successor to that policy only Evelyn ward, named after the diarist John Evelyn (1620–1706), one of the founders of the Royal Society.

Evelyn lived in the modern ward named after him at his Sayes Court house, next to a royal dockyard developed by King Henry VIII in the Deptford Strand parish, at the point where the Kent/Surrey boundary met the Thames. Peter the Great learned how to build ships at Deptford, renting Sayes Court from John Evelyn at the time (and apparently trashing the place). Much has, of course, changed since Evelyn's day. Sayes Court has long gone; most of its gardens, a Victorian pleasure spot, have disappeared; the industrial units on the old dockyard are now being redeveloped and railways criss-cross the area. The ward is linked to central London by Deptford railway station, opened in 1836 on the original London

Parliamentary constituency: Lewisham Deptford
May 2014 result Lab 2052/1828/1442 Grn 1495/1228/1144 Lewisham People Before Profit
677 C 387/363/336 LD 279/173/157 UKIP 260 TUSC 181
May 2010 result Lab 2632/2449/2105 Grn 2313/1707/1676 LD 1293/995/990 C 713/611/563
Lewisham People Before Profit 410/403
May 2006 result Grn 1583/1223/1153 Lab 928/907/870 LD 300/291/250 C 247/240/170
Alliance for Green Socialism 111
May 2002 result Grn 1026/882/832 Lab 1019/906/903 LD 286/264/246 C 214/209/159
Socialist Alliance 125/105/91
May 2016 GLA results (excludes postal voters)
Mayor: Lab 3017 Grn 668 C 563 Women's Equality 192 LD 168 UKIP 64 Cannabis is
Safer than Alcohol 59 Respect 36 Britain First 19 BNP 15 Ind 13 One Love 2
London Members: Lab 2465 Grn 1081 C 429 Women's Equality 333 LD 216 UKIP 108
CPA 45 Respect 45 Animal Welfare 41 Britain First 36 House Party 18 BNP 12

Figure 173: Lewisham, Brockley

and Greenwich railway and said to be the oldest suburban railway station in the world, with six trains per hour to London Bridge and Cannon Street.

Away from the riverside lies Brockley ward, served by the Overground stations of Brockley, New Cross and New Cross Gate, with St Johns railway station lying inside the ward and Deptford Bridge DLR station just outside its boundary. The area took its name from a pub, the Brockley Jack on Brockley Road, which now serves as a theatre as well as a pub. It is the home of Goldsmith's College, part of the University of London specialising in the arts and social sciences, and this arts focus together with its large Victorian housing has given Brockley a bohemian atmosphere. Brockley makes the top 100 wards in England and Wales for black population (24%) and mixed-race population (7.4%) and its demographic is rather more middle-class than Evelyn.

Evelyn ward's social makeup has become even more caught up in London's transformation into a world city; 61% of the population is non-white according to the most recent census. The ward features in several top 20 England and Wales lists for unusual population features: 18th-highest black population (35.9%), 11th-highest Black African population (22.2%); 8th-highest Buddhist population (3.9%). The ward's Chinese population is also noticeably high (6.5%), perhaps a side effect of several University of London colleges in the general area; census figures tend to show a strong positive correlation between Chinese and student populations. There is a large council estate in the ward (the Pepys estate) and more than half of the ward's housing is socially rented, 38% from Lewisham council.

Evelyn ward seems to have a high councillor attrition rate: in the last four

Parliamentary constituency: Lewisham Deptford
May 2014 result Lab 1930/1743/1571 Lewisham People Before Profit 651/601/599 Grn
546/349/282 LD 323/205/194 TUSC 161
March 2013 by-election Lab 978 Lewisham People Before Profit 404 LD 131 UKIP 119 C
119
May 2010 result Lab 2795/2469/2367 LD 925/746/732 C 719/676/562 Grn 533/355/299
Lewisham People Before Profit 445 Ind 294
May 2006 result Lab 1317/1073/1021 C 347/296/263 LD 326/304/278 Grn 301/301/261
June 2004 by-election Lab 1432 C 463 Socialist Alternative 374 LD 367 Grn 199
May 2002 result Lab 1164/1011/942 Grn 274 LD 265/259 Ind 234/207/202 C 222/201/186
May 2016 GLA results (excludes postal voters)
Mayor: Lab 2248 C 534 Grn 278 LD 149 UKIP 101 Women's Equality 60 Respect 51
Cannabis is Safer than Alcohol 45 Britain First 42 BNP 18 One Love 10 Ind 8
London Members: Lab 2136 C 383 Grn 349 UKIP 174 LD 161 Women's Equality 128
Respect 51 Britain First 48 CPA 47 Animal Welfare 36 BNP 25 House Party 22

Figure 174: Lewisham, Evelyn

years two of its councillors have died and a third resigned to set up an orphanage
in his native Togo.

Politically, there's not much to see in Evelyn: it's a very safe Labour ward and
the interest for the other parties usually lies in who comes a distant second. In
the 2014 elections, and in the last by-election in March 2013, that second place
was filled by a local left-wing slate called Lewisham People Before Profit, who
also managed second in Evelyn when they stood a candidate in the Greenwich
and Lewisham constituency at the 2012 London Assembly election.

The 2014 borough elections in Evelyn gave Labour 53% to 18% for People
Before Profit and 15% for the Green Party, while in May's Assembly elections
Sadiq Khan beat Zac Goldsmith 63–15 and Labour led the Tories on the list
ballot 60–11.

Bohemian Brockley, on the other hand, is one of London's longest-standing
Green hotspots and in the 2014 London borough elections was one of only four
wards in the city to return a Green councillor (the others were Highgate ward in
Camden, Highbury East ward in Islington and St Leonard's ward in Lambeth).
This is mainly down to Darren Johnson, a long-standing Green activist who was
their London mayoral candidate in 2000 and 2004; he was elected to Lewisham
council in 2002 and got the ward's entire Green slate elected in 2006, but Labour
took two seats back in the 2010 election.

Johnson retired from the council in 2014, but the Green Party held their seat
in Brockley with new councillor John Coughlin—the only opposition member of
Lewisham council. The shares at the 2014 borough elections were 38% for Labour,

28% for the Greens and 13% for People Before Profit. The Green performance in May was less impressive with Sadiq Khan beating their candidate Siân Berry 63–14 and Labour carrying the London Members ballot with 51%, to 22% for the Greens and 9% for the Conservatives. With the Greens generally having a poor record in local by-elections, the omens for them gaining this seat—which would give them group status on Lewisham council—are not promising.

Defending for Labour in Brockley is Sophie McGeevor, a charity communications manager with a PhD in history from Cambridge; she is the vice-chair of the Deptford branch of the Labour party, and according to her Twitter she loves gardening, Björk, and jumpsuits. The Greens have selected a candidate right from the top of the party: the national party chairman Clare Phipps, who hit the headlines before the last general election for trying to stand for parliament in Basingstoke on a job-share basis—there's no provision for this so her joint nomination was rejected. People Before Profit are not standing in Brockley, so completing the ballot paper are Andrew Hughes for the Conservatives, Bobby Dean for the Lib Dems, Hugh Waine for UKIP and Rebecca Manson Jones of the Women's Equality Party.

The defending Labour candidate in the Evelyn by-election is Joyce Jacca, a long-standing community worker. People Before Profit's candidate is Ray Barron-Woolford, whose candidacy in the 2014 borough elections in New Cross ward was profiled by *Vice*; on Twitter he describes himself as an activist, radio commentator and food bank founder. Standing for the Green Party is Andrea Carey-Fuller, a community care lawyer, and the ballot paper is completed by Lucy Salek for the Lib Dems, independent candidate Scott Barkwith and Conservative James Clark.

Brockley result: Lab 1190 Grn 631 LD 259 C 195 Women's Equality 173 UKIP 33

Evelyn result: Lab 1028 Lewisham People Before Profit 314 C 183 Ind 173 Grn 119 LD 107

Swanley (Kent county council); and
Swanley Christchurch and Swanley Village (Sevenoaks council)

Both caused by the death of Conservative councillor Robert Brookbank at the age of 72. A retired estate agent who had also worked for the former GLC, he had served since 2007 on Sevenoaks council and since 2009 on Kent county council.

Moving out of London into Kent proper, but only just outside the Greater London boundary and still within the M 25. Before 1861 Swanley consisted of three houses; then the Chatham and Dover railway came here, building a junction for its Medway and Maidstone routes, and a new settlement (originally "Swanley Junction") grew up around the station. Horticulture quickly became the town's major industry thanks to the opening of the Swanley horticultural college in 1887 (it has since became part of Wye college near Canterbury), and there are still apple and pear trees in people's gardens left over from the original orchards; while there was also a thriving health sector with three hospitals at which Londoners could convalesce following major surgery, away from the Smoke. Although these industries are no longer significant to Swanley, it has grown strongly thanks to its good transport links (on the Chatham line, the M 25 and the A 20) to turn into a mini-New Town, becoming a parish of its own in 1955. If you're in London and fancy a trip there after reading this preview, you may be thrilled to know that Swanley station joined the Oyster network this year.

Despite Swanley's strong links with London it was never incorporated into Greater London, leaving it politically rather out on a limb as a working-class part of the safe Conservative district and constituency based on Sevenoaks, some distance to the south. Swanley St Mary's ward makes the top 100 in England and Wales for population with between 1 and 4 GCSEs or equivalent (19% of the workforce); both Hextable, and Swanley Christchurch and Swanley Village wards have a very high level of occupations classed by the census as "intermediate" (19% of the workforce in both cases); while Swanley St Mary's and Swanley White Oak wards have high levels of social housing.

Those two wards (essentially, Swanley north of the railway line) plus almost all of Hextable ward make up the Swanley division of Kent county council, which voted Labour in 2005 but was gained by the Tories in 2009; Brookbank was re-elected in 2013 with 41% of the vote, to 32% for Labour and 20% for UKIP. This might look like a winnable marginal for Labour, but a look at last year's district council elections serves to pour cold water on that idea: the Tories won five of the district council seats within the division (to one for Labour and one for an independent). Runner-up here in the 2009 election with 23% of the vote (falling to fifth and 2.4% in 2013) was Steve Uncles, leader of the south-east branch of the English Democrats, who appeared before Dartford magistrates in 2014 accused of falsifying nomination papers for the 2013 Kent county council elections, but is still awaiting trial having successfully managed to put off his most recent date in court by—standing for election as Kent police and crime commissioner.

The excitement in Swanley Christchurch and Swanley Village (essentially, Swanley south of the railway line) is confined to the ballot box; Labour carried the ward in 2003 but the Tories gained in 2007, and the ward now appears safe for the Conservatives after they beat Labour 59–28 in the 2015 district elections.

Parliamentary constituency: Sevenoaks
Sevenoaks district council wards: Swanley St Mary's, Swanley White Oak, Hextable (part)
May 2013 result C 1032 Lab 812 UKIP 501 Grn 77 EDP 60 BNP 32
June 2009 result C 1549 EDP 833 Lab 823 LD 428
May 2005 result Lab 2181 C 1893 Ind 1437 LD 874

Figure 175: Kent CC, Swanley

Parliamentary constituency: Sevenoaks
Kent county council division: Darent Valley
May 2015 result C 1792/1564/1557 Lab 862/704/699 Grn 400
May 2011 result C 1022/979/959 Lab 729/726/638 Ind 263
May 2007 result C 850/792/762 Lab 662/656/636
May 2003 result Lab 624/620/690 C 579/549/530

Figure 176: Sevenoaks, Swanley Christchurch and Swanley Village

At county level this ward is part of the safe Conservative Darent Valley division. Some of the electors in this ward will be thrilled to know that their polling station is a pub (the Lamb in Swanley Village).

In the Sevenoaks district by-election Clare Barnes, a Swanley town councillor, defends for the Conservatives. Labour have selected Jacqueline Griffiths, a retired nursing lecturer. Also standing are candidates from two parties contesting the ward for the first time: Medina Hall for UKIP and Krish Shanmuganathan for the Lib Dems.

The Kent county by-election is defended for the Conservatives by Michael Horwood, district councillor for Eynsford ward. The Labour candidate is Angela George, a former district councillor for Swanley White Oak ward who lost her seat in the 2015 election to Tory candidate James Halford; Halford has since defected to UKIP and is standing in the county by-election under his new colours. Completing the ballot paper is Lib Dem Robert Woodbridge, who stood in the 2015 district elections as a Green candidate.

Swanley (Kent county council) result: C 717 UKIP 615 Lab 518 LD 362
Swanley Christchurch and Swanley Village result: C 311 Lab 274 LD 183 UKIP

131

Limpsfield

Tandridge council, Surrey; caused by the resignation of Conservative councillor John Pannett. He had served since 2010.

Parliamentary constituency: East Surrey
Surrey county council division: Oxted
May 2015 result C 1560 LD 271 UKIP 238 Lab 156
May 2014 result C 774 UKIP 276 LD 195 Lab 80
May 2011 result C 1058 LD 409 UKIP 130
May 2010 result C 1383 LD 667 UKIP 131
May 2007 result C 741 LD 386 UKIP 88
May 2006 result C 894 LD 478
May 2005 by-election C 1271 LD 699
May 2003 result C 697 LD 410 UKIP 51
May 2002 result C 761 LD 338 Lab 54
May 2000 result C 813/804 LD 291/279 Lab 51
May 1999 result C 718 LD 249 Lab 67 Ind 8 (eight)
May 1998 result C 909 LD 219 Lab 67 Christian Democrat 16
May 1995 result C 812 LD 343 Lab 121
May 1994 result C 825 LD 484 Lab 62
May 1991 result Ind 820 LD 489 Lab 51
May 1990 result C 877 SLD 507
May 1987 result C 1034 All 519 Lab 49
May 1986 result C 859 All 342 Lab 72
May 1983 result C 733 All 490
May 1982 result C 905 All 410
May 1979 result C 1201 Lib 749
May 1978 result C 769 Lib 406
May 1976 result C 980/759 Lib 687 Lab 132/107
May 1973 result C 696/496 Lib 691 Lab 102

Figure 177: Tandridge, Limpsfield

After four by-elections in Kent past and present, we hop just over the county boundary into Surrey. The village of Limpsfield, located on the slopes of the North Downs just north-east of Oxted and essentially an extension of it, is an old village notable for two mediaeval buildings: the twelfth-century timber-framed Old Court Cottage, once the home of Battle Abbey's manorial court; and St Peter's church which dates from the same era. Buried in St Peter's churchyard are two of the towering figures in English classical music, the composer Frederick Delius and the conductor Sir Thomas Beecham; while more recent famous figures associated with the village include the England cricket captain Lord Cowdrey of Tonbridge and the TV host Davina McCall. The census betrays that this is a middle-class commuter ward, with 53% of the workforce in management-level positions and 47% holding degree-level qualifications.

This is a true-blue area. Limpsfield ward's boundaries are unchanged since the founding electoral arrangements for Tandridge district in 1973, and in all the years since then it has only twice failed to return a Conservative: in 1973 when the ward's two seats split between the Tories and Liberals, and in 1991 when the Tories stood down in favour of an independent candidate (who was later re-elected several times as a Conservative). At the most recent poll in 2015 the Tories beat the Lib Dems here 70–12, and the local county council seat (Oxted) is also safely Conservative. However, the previous results list doesn't take account of a new kid on the block, the localist Oxted and Limpsfield Residents Group; Limpsfield ward wasn't up in May, but the Residents contested and won the neighbouring ward of Oxted North and Tandridge.

Establishment candidates don't get much more establishment than the Tories' Neil O'Brien OBE. One of the few council by-election candidates to merit his own Wikipedia page, O'Brien was a former director of Policy Exchange, a centre-right think tank, before joining the Government in 2012 as a special advisor to George Osborne. He has been kept on as a SPAD by the May administration. O'Brien's opponents are Sheelagh Crampton of the Lib Dems, who fought the ward in 2014 and 2015; Simon Charles of Labour; and Phil Davies of the Residents Group.

Result: Oxted and Limpsfield Residents Group 713 C 472 LD 33 Lab 25

Broadstone

Poole council, Dorset; caused by the resignation of Conservative councillor Joanne Tomlin on health grounds. She had served since 2015.

We finish the week in Broadstone, a northern suburb of Poole which is still sufficiently semi-detached to be recognised as a separate town by the Royal Mail. Broadstone's census statistics reveal a rather old, middle-class demographic: it is in the top 50 wards in England and Wales for owner-occupation (93% of households) and 21% of the workforce are retired. Broadstone's traditional industry was lavender oil, but it's now an integral part of the Bournemouth-Poole conurbation and generally residential, with almost all of its housing being post-war. The town's most notable resident was the evolutionary naturalist Alfred Russell Wallace, whose tomb in Broadstone cemetery is topped not by a traditional headstone but by a 7-foot-high fossilised treetrunk.

Broadstone's local elections are most certainly not fossilised, being closely fought between the Conservatives and Liberal Democrats. On its present boundaries the ward only dates from 2015 but is little changed from the 2003–15 Broadstone ward, which returned two Lib Dem councillors and one Conservative in 2003 but had a full Lib Dem slate in the 2007 and 2011 elections. The Conservatives did well across Poole in the 2015 election and gained two seats in this ward,

Parliamentary constituency: Mid Dorset and North Poole
May 2015 result LD 3534/2262/2097 C 2842/2547/2027 UKIP 909/808 Grn 519/417/371

Figure 178: Poole, Broadstone

but couldn't knock out popular Lib Dem councillor Mike Brooke who topped the poll a long way ahead of his running-mates; Brooke's personal vote meant that the Lib Dems carried the ward 45–36.

So, an interesting contest is in prospect. Defending for the Tories is Marc Ujvari, the losing Conservative candidate in 2015; he works in finance for Barclays. The Lib Dems have selected Vikki Slade, who failed to hold the local parliamentary seat (Mid Dorset and North Poole) in the 2015 general election; she was a Poole councillor for this ward from 2011 to 2015 and is hoping to return to the council. Also standing are Alan Gerring for UKIP, Mark Chivers for the Green Party and Jason Sanderson for Labour.

Result: LD 2184 C 733 UKIP 132 Grn 57 Lab 45 [LD gain from C]

20th October 2016

Two parliamentary by-elections and twelve local by-elections on 20th October 2016:

Witney

House of Commons; caused by the resignation of Conservative MP David Cameron. First elected in 2001, Cameron had served as leader of the Conservative Party from 2005 and as Prime Minister from 2010 until earlier this year.

> I was the future once.
>
> - David Cameron, 13th July 2016

We're starting to get towards the time of year when awards are doled out; when we look back at the events of recent months with fresh eyes; when the first draft of history is written. One of the more tiresome awards that comes around every year is the Oxford Dictionaries gong for "word of the year", which attempts to sum up everything that has happened in a single word. It's a trite idea; the historian of the future looking back at the year of our Lord, two thousand and sixteen could write reams on the rise and rise of Donald Trump; the civil war in Syria and its associated fallout; Islamic State and all the atrocities associated with it; the attempted coup in Turkey; the Rio Olympics; the Zika virus; the spectacularly high body-count of well-known actors and singers; Bob Dylan winning a Nobel Prize; Leicester City winning the Premier League. To try to reduce all that to the single word "Brexit" is a fool's errand, yet many people who should probably know better will be doing just that as they try to nominate the Word of the Year. In the spirit of the enterprise, your columnist has put all of the last ten Oxford Dictionaries Words of the Year into this preview: see if you can spot them.

Yes, Brexit is going to be the Word of the Year for 2016.[11] It's the obvious choice. It's also the boring choice. Here's a more interesting Word of 2016: *zugzwang*. This is a German word from the game of chess, denoting a position in which a player is forced to move, but any move they are able to make will lose the game. Why do I nominate this word? Let's look at the political situation. The Labour party has saddled itself with a leader who is incapable of leading or commanding the support of his colleagues, never mind the country. The third party in British politics, the Scottish National Party, finds itself impotent at Westminster and has lost its majority in Holyrood. The Liberal Democrats were checkmated by five years as a junior coalition partner and are desperately trying to find someone with whom they can start a new game. UKIP, having achieved its primary objective 😀, has descended into the sort of farcical infighting that only UKIP can do and still be believed. The Conservatives now have the difficult task of delivering Britain's exit from the European Union in a way that would not deliver omnishambles—a job that has the potential to go very wrong very quickly. The recent fall in the value of the pound suggests that the omens for this are not good, and has also annoyed your columnist who has a long-planned trip to Athens next month and has found that the pound in his pocket is worth less—much less—than it was when the trip was booked at the start of June.

In retrospect, David Cameron was in *zugzwang* from the moment he agreed to a referendum on EU membership. The loss of the referendum cost him his job as prime minister and leader of the Conservative Party, after six and ten years in office respectively. With two parliamentary by-elections this week together with no fewer than twelve local by-elections, this is the biggest electoral event since the referendum which destroyed Cameron's premiership, and probably (hopefully) the busiest week remaining for this column this year.

The Witney constituency has been around since February 1974 when a fifth parliamentary seat was granted to Oxfordshire. Initially it was called "Mid Oxfordshire" and mostly came out of the former Banbury constituency; the seat was renamed Witney in 1983 and since 2010 has had the same boundaries as the West Oxfordshire local government district. The Boundary Commission has provisionally recommended no change to the Witney seat for the 2020 general election.

The creation of Mid Oxfordshire in 1974 gave a leg-up into Parliament to Douglas Hurd, an Old Etonian, former Cambridge Union president and political thriller writer who had given up a 14-year career in the Diplomatic Service to enter politics. Douglas was the third generation of Hurds to serve in parliament, after

---

[11] As it turned out, the Oxford Dictionaries panel rejected this option and voted for "fake news"

his father Sir Anthony, later Lord Hurd (Newbury, 1945–64) and his grandfather Sir Percy Hurd (Frome, 1918–23; Devizes, 1924–45); his uncle, Robert Hurd, was a noted architect specialising in conservation who had recently rebuilt much of the lower frontage of Edinburgh's Royal Mile. In 2005 Douglas' son Nick became the fourth Hurd to enter the Commons, for Ruislip, Northwood and Pinner.

In office Douglas Hurd became PPS to leader of the opposition Edward Heath, and with the Conservative victory in the 1979 election entered government as a junior Foreign Office minister. He was promoted to Cabinet in 1984 as Northern Ireland secretary, negotiating much of what became the Anglo-Irish Agreement; but shortly before the Agreement was signed Hurd was reshuffled to the Home Office. He was seen as a safe pair of hands, and his four years as Home Secretary proved to be uncontroversial, before in 1989 he succeeded a young rising star called John Major as Foreign Secretary.

Upon Margaret Thatcher's resignation Hurd entered the Tory leadership contest in the second round, coming third as John Major became party leader and Prime Minister. Major kept Hurd in the Foreign Office during a turbulent time in world politics: as well as having to deal with the Gulf War, the fall of Communism and the slide of Yugoslavia into civil war, Hurd also had the difficult job of repairing Britain's relationships with other EEC member states after the Euroscepticism of Thatcher's final years and Britain's ERM exit. The Major government was never short of political scandal, and Hurd's contribution involved allocating money from the UK's foreign aid budget (then under the control of the Foreign Office) to build a dam on the Pergau river in Malaysia in order to secure an arms deal; a decision which was eventually declared unlawful by the High Court.

Hurd retired as foreign secretary in 1995 and left the Commons at the 1997 general election. He had been appointed CBE in 1974 for his work in the Diplomatic Service; before leaving the Commons he became a Companion of Honour, and under Major's dissolution honours he ascended to the Lords as Lord Hurd of Westwell. After leaving the Commons he chaired the Booker Prize panel in 1998 and served as High Sheriff of Westminster Abbey, reflecting his long Church of England membership; he retired from the House of Lords this year at the age of 86.

Douglas Hurd had a very safe seat—at his last re-election in 1992 he had beaten the Labour candidate James Plaskitt (who would go on to represent Warwick and Leamington from 1997 to 2010) by the large margin of 56–21. Even in the Labour landslide in 1997 this was sufficient for the Witney seat to be safe for Hurd's successor, Shaun Woodward. A Kennedy Scholar at Harvard and English graduate from Cambridge, Woodward had started his career in television as a producer on the BBC programmes *Panorama* and *Newsnight*, before becoming the Conservative Party's director of communications in 1991. He had joined the ranks of high society by marrying one of the daughters of the Sainsbury family, and Woodward quickly ascended to the frontbench following his election, as Conservative spokesman on London, until 1999 when he was sacked for supporting the repeal of Section 28. After that Woodward became a high-profile defector to Labour, resisting calls from his former Tory association to stand down and seek re-election under his new colours. Despite being reported to be the only Labour MP with a butler, Woodward transferred seamlessly (if noisily) in the 2001 election to a safe Labour berth in St Helens, Merseyside.

This created a vacancy for the post of Tory PPC for Witney, and there were no shortage of candidates for what promised to be a very safe berth in Parliament when the selection came up in April 2000. One of them was a promising 33-year-old who had been showing his face at various functions within the constituency for much of the last year, as well as pleasing the members by attacking Woodward for his views on foxhunting. He was an Old Etonian who had graduated from Oxford with a first-class PPE degree in 1988 and then joined the Conservative Research Department; he had worked as a special advisor to Norman Lamont in the Treasury, and in those pre-YouTube days not many people would have remembered his young face in the background as an ashen Lamont announced Britain's exit from the ERM in Downing Street. He had been encouraged to stand as the Tory candidate for the Newbury by-election in 1993, and after leaving Whitehall in 1994 to become the chief PR man for the ITV weekday franchise Carlton TV, he had started to do the rounds of selection meetings in Conservative seats, reportedly missing out on the Ashford selection after his train to the selection meeting was delayed. In 1996 he had been selected as Tory candidate for Stafford, vacated by strident Eurosceptic Bill Cash who had done the chicken run to the new safe seat of Stone, but lost a notional Conservative constituency in the first Blair landslide. He had applied for the vacancy in the Kensington and Chelsea by-election after Alan Clark died, and just a few weeks earlier had narrowly lost the Tory selection for the safe Sussex seat of Wealden. Time was running out for him to get a nice berth for the next general election, widely expected in 2001, but the Conservative members of Witney liked what they saw in the selection meeting. He won, and fourteen months later was a Member of Parliament. His name was David Cameron.

Cameron was pitched straight into the turbulent Duncan Smith years, and had to wait until the leadership of Michael Howard (for whom he had worked as a Home Office special advisor) for promotion to the Shadow Cabinet, initially as head of policy co-ordination, then as shadow Education secretary. He stood for the Conservative leadership after Howard resigned in the wake of Blair's third election win, and wowed the Conservative party conference of 2005 with a forward-looking speech, delivered without notes. He won the leadership, and the rest is history. With Cameron's political career having been terminated by the loss of the EU referendum, it remains to be seen what he will do next—he turned 50 this month and still has a large amount of his career to come. One post-politics job has already been announced: Cameron has become patron of the National Citizen Service, a social development programme for 15- to 17-year-olds which grew out of one of his flagship policies in office, the Big Society.

While Cameron may have lost the EU referendum nationally, he did manage to carry his constituency with him: West Oxfordshire voted 54% Remain in June. Remain polled 35,236 votes in the district, only 35 more than Cameron himself got in the 2015 general election in which he beat Labour 60–17. Some of that will have come from the bonus which incumbent party leaders normally get at general election time, but there's little in the social or political makeup of the constituency to suggest that this is anything other than a true blue area. Witney town itself was traditionally a blanket-making town and is now home to the Wychwood brewery, which exports beer such as Hobgoblin to the UK and beyond. However, Witney town only forms around a quarter of the electorate; the second largest town is the fast-growing Carterton, whose economy is based on its proximity to the large RAF base at Brize Norton. The constituency's other two towns are Chipping Norton, an ancient market town which the Industrial Revolution passed by, and the tourist centre of Woodstock next to the World Heritage site of Blenheim Palace. The demographic of the seat is generally middle-class and quite well off with a large number of people commuting to Oxford—there aren't all that many people here who would identify as part of the squeezed middle or were affected by the credit crunch, but the carbon footprint might be a different matter.

Local elections in West Oxfordshire are a little difficult to interpret, as the district uses the thirds electoral system and in any given year only 16 or 17 of its 27 wards are up for election. The general theme is that Labour do well in Witney town and Chipping Norton, Woodstock votes Lib Dem and the Tory majority comes from Carterton and (most of) the villages. In the 2016 district elections, in which all five wards in Witney town were up and Carterton had an off year—so, probably the most favourable configuration for the opposition— the Conservatives polled 46% across the district to 26% for Labour and 16% for the Lib Dems. However, the whole district did vote in May for Oxfordshire's police and crime commissioner, in which election the Tories had 47% in the first round to 30% for Labour and 13% for the Lib Dems, and beat Labour 59–

41 in the runoff. The Conservatives hold eight of the district's nine seats on Oxfordshire county council, with Labour gaining Witney South and Central in the 2013 election; that loss was particularly costly for the Tories because with it went overall control of the county council.

Not like I'm trying to make it sound like there's everything to play for, because there isn't really. The Tory candidate Robert Courts shouldn't be too bovvered about losing—simples. A barrister, Courts was elected to West Oxfordshire council in 2014 representing The Bartons ward and is deputy leader of the Tory group. His only other previous electoral experience appears to be in 2007 when he contested the St Paul ward in Winchester—then a safe Lib Dem area.

Labour have reselected their 2015 candidate Duncan Enright, who is a district councillor for Witney East ward and leads the Labour group on the district council; he was narrowly re-elected in May and tweeted from the count that he had lost before finding out that there were 70 missing Labour votes under a Tory pile. He works as a medical publisher, and is hoping to follow his father Derek into Parliament—Derek Enright won the Hemsworth by-election in November 1991, served until his death four years later, and had previously been MEP for Leeds from 1979 to 1984.

The UKIP candidate is Dickie Bird...

...no, not that one. Kenrick Bird, to give him his proper name, fought Banbury in the last general election; he served 20 years in the Royal Green Jackets and later 3 years as head porter at Oriel College, Oxford. He starts from third place with UKIP having polled 9% in 2015.

The Lib Dems are noisily trying to get their fearsome by-election machine back in full working order following the lean times of Coalition and are hoping for a major improvement on their fourth-place 7% result last time. Their candidate is Elizabeth Leffman, who was re-elected in May as a West Oxfordshire councillor for Charlbury and Finstock ward; this is her second go at the constituency after she fought Cameron in 2005.

The Green candidate is Larry Sanders...

...no, not that one. One of the leading American candidates for Word of the Year is *Berniebro*, defined by Wikipedia as "a pejorative label that has been applied to male supporters of 2016 US presidential candidate Bernie Sanders". Larry, the Green Party's health spokesman and a former Oxfordshire county councillor (East Oxford, 2005–13) was a Berniebro before the word existed—he literally is Bernie Sanders' older brother, and came to the UK in the late 1960s. In the last general election he stood in the Oxford West and Abingdon constituency. In 2015 the Greens just saved their deposit here with 5.1% and Sanders will be hoping to do the same.

June 2016 EU referendum Remain 35236 Leave 30435
May 2016 PCC election C 11504 Lab 7391 LD 3108 UKIP 2664; runoff C 13524 Lab 9302
May 2015 result C 35201 Lab 10046 UKIP 5352 LD 3953 Grn 2970 National Health Action
616 Wessex Regionalist 110 Ind 94 Reduce VAT in Sport 56 Give Me Back Elmo 37 Land
Party 35 Ind 12
May 2010 result C 33973 LD 11233 Lab 7511 Grn 2385 UKIP 2001 Loony 234 Ind 166 Ind
151 Wessex Regionalist 62 Ind 53

Figure 179: House of Commons, Witney

Because it was the Prime Minister's seat Witney attracted more than its fair share of fringe and joke candidates in 2015, and such is the case again this time with the electors of Witney having fourteen candidates to choose from. National Health Action, who were the most successful fringe party last time with 1.1%, are trying again with Helen Salisbury, a GP from Oxford. The One Love Party don't appear to have learned from their last-place finish in the London mayoral election and are standing Luxembourg-born Emilia Arno, proving that they have at least three members. The joke vote is likely to be divided between perennial by-election candidate David Bishop of his "Bus-Pass Elvis Party", Mad Hatter of the Official Monster Raving Loony Party and UKIP leadership candidate Lord Toby Jug for the Eccentric Party, a Loony splinter group (yes, such things exist). There are three independent candidates on the ballot paper, although one of them, London-based venture capitalist Adam Knight, has since stopped campaigning and endorsed the Lib Dem candidate; the other two are Daniel Skidmore, a fitness instructor campaigning for the restoration of Witney's derelict football stadium; and Nicholas Ward who is standing on an anti-High Speed 2 ticket. Completing the ballot paper is former professional boxer and *Celebrity Big Brother* contestant Winston McKenzie, standing for the English Democrats. Polling is open from 7am to 10pm; the electors of Witney are reminded not to take a selfie in the polling station; and if you're going to vape while voting, it may be wise to check that's OK with the presiding officer first.

Result: C 17313 LD 11611 Lab 5765 Grn 1363 UKIP 1354 National Health Action 433 Skidmore 151 Loony 129 Ward 93 Elvis 61 Eccentric 59 EDP 52 One Love 44 Knight 27

Oh, and did you spot all the Words of the Year? In reverse chronological order from 2015 to 2006: 😀, vape, selfie, omnishambles, squeezed middle, Big Society, simples, credit crunch, carbon footprint, bovvered.

Batley and Spen

Caused by the death of Labour MP Jo Cox at the age of 41.

> We are far more united and have far more in common than the things that divide us.

> - Jo Cox, 3rd June 2015

For the week's second Parliamentary by-election we are in Yorkshire, in tragic circumstances. Cast your mind back to 16th June, one week before the referendum. In this frenzied political atmosphere, Jo Cox, MP for Batley and Spen, turned up at Birstall library to do a constituency surgery. She never went home. A constituent, Thomas Mair, is awaiting trial charged with four offences in relation to her death. Cox leaves behind her husband Brendan and two children, aged five and three.

Constituency surgeries shouldn't be like this. Ask Stephen Timms, the Labour MP for East Ham who was nearly murdered at a surgery in 2010. Ask Nigel Jones, the former Lib Dem MP for Cheltenham, attacked at a surgery in 2000 at which his election agent was killed. Those were near-misses, but Cox' death was the first murder of a sitting Member of Parliament since Ian Gow was killed by the IRA in 1990.

The Batley and Spen constituency was created in 1983 from parts of the former Brighouse and Spenborough, and Batley and Morley constituencies. A notional Labour seat in 1979, it was defended by the former Batley and Morley MP Kenneth Woolmer in the 1983 election, but Woolmer narrowly lost his seat to the Tories' Elizabeth Peacock, a North Yorkshire county councillor, who won with a majority of 870 votes. A rematch between Peacock and Woolmer in 1987 resulted in Peacock increasing her majority to 1,365, and there was no swing in the 1992 election at which Peacock's majority was 1,408. Batley and Spen grew a reputation for being a seat with relatively low swings—even when Peacock was one of the MPs to fall in the Labour landslide of 1997, the swing to Labour was relatively low at 7.7% allowing for boundary changes, and a rematch in 2001 between Peacock and the new Labour MP resulted in almost no swing.

That new Labour MP, Mike Wood, was a former deputy leader of the local Kirklees council who had represented Cleckheaton as a councillor; he had fought the safe Tory seat of Hexham in 1987 and had worked as a probation officer and social worker. On the left of the party, he managed John McDonnell's abortive campaign for the Labour leadership in 2007 but never got off the Labour backbenches.

Wood stood down in 2015 and passed his seat on to Jo Cox, the head of policy for Oxfam GB and a campaigner for Syrian refugees. In an election with a relatively high swing of 1.7% to Labour, Cox won with 43% to 31% for the Conservatives and 18% for UKIP. In office Cox continued her campaigning and founded the all-party Parliamentary Friends of Syria group. She was on the Remain side in the referendum. One wonders what Cox would have made of the current political situation had she lived.

As Cox noted in her maiden speech to Parliament, which went viral in the immediate aftermath of her death, Batley is the home of the seat's Labour vote. One of its MPs, Sir Alfred Broughton who represented the seat from a 1949 by-election, had the distinction of bringing down a government: he was on his deathbed and unable to take part in the 1979 no-confidence vote which terminated the Callaghan government. Batley has come a long way since the days of the Batley Ladies Townswomen's Guild; it's a classic Pennine textile town, but the textiles here weren't wool or cotton but shoddy—that is, recycled rags and clothes. In order to staff the textile mills Batley saw large amounts of immigration from the subcontinent in the 1950s and 1960s, mostly from Gujarat and the Punjab. Batley East ward is majority Asian (54%) and majority Muslim (52%), and makes the top 30 wards in England and Wales for those looking after home or family (11.3% of the workforce); 17% of the workforce have never worked or are long-term unemployed. There are also significant Asian populations in Batley West and Heckmondwike. With the demise of the textile industry, the major contributions to Batley's economy come from the Fox's Biscuits factory and The Mill, a factory outlet in a renovated textile mill.

The Spen Valley towns, on the other hand, have a low non-white population and in places a commuter demographic, being within easy reach of both Leeds and Bradford (if the M 62 is playing nicely, and this is a notoriously congested stretch of it); while Leeds and Bradford come here to shop at the West Yorkshire IKEA store in Birstall. This was the Spenborough urban district, which after the war anchored a key marginal parliamentary seat. Brighouse and Spenborough has entered political folklore for a 1960 by-election, at the height of the Macmillan government's powers, which remains one of the very few occasions in modern times where the government have taken a seat off the opposition in a by-election.

At local election time the six wards which make up the constituency are stuck in a rut. This is part of the area of the perennially-hung Kirklees council, and in every election since 2007 Labour have won the two Batley wards; the Conservatives have won Birstall and Birkenshaw, and Liversedge and Gomersal; and the Lib Dems have a lock on Cleckheaton. Heckmondwike ward was a BNP hotspot in the mid-Noughties but is now solidly Labour. The only exception

May 2015 result Lab 21926 C 15769 UKIP 9080 LD 2396 Grn 1232 TUSC 123 Patriotic Socialist 53
May 2010 result Lab 21565 C 17159 LD 8925 BNP 3685 Grn 605

Figure 180: House of Commons, Batley and Spen

to this pattern came in a 2013 by-election in which Labour won Liversedge and Gomersal. In the May 2016 local elections across the constituency Labour polled 42%, the Conservatives 24%, UKIP (who didn't stand in Batley East) 16% and the Lib Dems 13% (nearly all of which was from Cleckheaton).

Looking forward, this seat is unlikely to survive the forthcoming boundary changes; if they go through it will be back to the future, with Batley moving out into a recreated seat of Batley and Morley, and the rest forming the core of a new Spen constituency. The Spen constituency takes some territory from Bradford South, which is to be abolished, and if Labour hold this by-election their new MP could find themselves fighting the Bradford South MP Judith Cummins for the Spen nomination.

In the immediate aftermath of Cox' death the major parties opposing Labour announced that they would not stand candidates in the by-election. This gives the ballot paper a very strange look. The defending Labour candidate is Tracy Brabin, a Batley-born actress and TV screenwriter who played Tricia Armstrong in *Coronation Street* for three years in the 1990s.

Brabin is opposed by a large number of far-right candidates, most of whom seem to give addresses in London. At the top of the ballot paper is Neil Humphrey, who fought Berwick-upon-Tweed for the English Democrats in 2015, under the pseudonym of "Corbyn Anti" (yes, that way round); he has registered the party name "English Independence" with the Electoral Commission and is standing in the by-election with the label "By Election Protest" after having a series of other descriptions rejected on the grounds of being offensive. Jack Buckby appears on the ballot paper with the label "No to terrorism, yes to Britain" which is a registered description of Liberty GB, one of the political wings of the EDL. The National Front candidate is Richard Edmonds, a long-standing far-right activist. The BNP candidate is David Furness, who fought the London mayoral election in May. The official English Democrats candidate is Therese Hirst, a former figure in Robert Kilroy-Silk's Veritas party. Three candidates are on the ballot paper as independents: they are Waqas Ali Khan, who was the UKIP candidate in Shipley in 2015; Garry Kitchin, who was the Green Party candidate in Batley West in May and is the only candidate to live in the constituency; and Henry Mayhew, who was the UKIP candidate for East Ham in the 2005 general election and is the son of the former Northern Ireland secretary Patrick Mayhew.

Completing the ballot paper is Ankit Love of the One Love Party, who finished last in May's London Mayor election and will be hoping for more than the 32 votes he got in the Tooting by-election, on the day Jo Cox died.

Result: Lab 17506 EDP 969 BNP 548 Kitchin 517 English Independence 241 Liberty GB 220 Mayhew 153 Khan 118 NF 87 One Love 34

Wey Valley

Weymouth and Portland council, Dorset; caused by the resignation of Conservative councillor Cory Russell, who had served since 2014.

Turning to the twelve (!) local by-elections this week, we start on the south coast on the outskirts of Weymouth. The Wey Valley ward is based on the northern edge of Weymouth town on the Dorchester Road and the new Weymouth Relief Road, built to improve access to the town for the 2012 Olympics; it also includes the Wey Valley school on the Dorchester Road and the village of Nottington. The ward has a large retired population (22% of the workforce) and high levels of owner-occupation.

Weymouth's politics are rather fragmented with seats often being won on low shares of the vote, but Wey Valley is the strongest Conservative ward in the borough. It was last fought in 2015 when the Tories led Labour here 62–22. Wey Valley was, however, marginal in the 2014 election in which the Conservatives polled 55% in a straight fight with the Green Party—a ballot paper that's unlikely to be repeated in the near future. Interestingly the local county council seat (Broadwey) was narrowly gained by Labour in the 2013 county elections.

Defending for the Tories is Tony Ferrari, who failed to gain a Lib Dem seat in the neighbouring Radipole ward in May; this ward should be safer for him. The wonderfully-named Grafton Straker is the Labour candidate; he is a Ministry of Defence engineer, a Unite activist and a keen cricketer. Completing the ballot paper are James Askew for the Green Party and Robin Vaughan for the Lib Dems.

Result: C 475 LD 118 Lab 96 Grn 74

Strood South

Medway council, Kent; caused by the resignation of UKIP councillor Catriona Brown-Reckless, who had served since 2015. Her husband, the former Rochester and Strood MP Mark Reckless, has been elected to the Welsh Assembly.

Moving into Kent, we arrive in Strood South, one of the five Medway council wards on the Kentish side of the river. This ward is simply described as the triangle

Parliamentary constituency: South Dorset
Dorset county council division: Broadwey
May 2015 result C 1326 Lab 480 Grn 339
May 2014 result C 630 Grn 523
May 2011 result C 1038 Lab 316 Grn 149
May 2010 result C 1139 Lab 693 Grn 275
May 2007 result C 799 Lab 391 Grn 98
May 2006 result C 664 Lab 418 Grn 154
Oct 2004 by-election C 497 Lab 408 LD 299
June 2004 result C 658/656 Lab 500/469 LD 365

Figure 181: Weymouth and Portland, Wey Valley

Parliamentary constituency: Rochester and Strood
May 2015 result UKIP 2527/2203/1898 C 2289/2085/1734 Lab 1583/1576/1411 TUSC 141
May 2011 result C 1576/1412/1332 Lab 1459/1395/1388 EDP 513 LD 207/175/170
May 2007 result C 1578/1487/1484 Lab 1395/1391/1338
May 2003 result Lab 1094/992/964 C 1070/1033/1020 LD 305/265/216 UKIP 135

Figure 182: Medway, Strood South

between the M 2, the A 2 Watling Street and the River Medway; its economic profile is solidly working-class with low qualification rates. The ward covers part of Strood town centre, including the Morrison's supermarket.

Mark Reckless became the second elected UKIP MP at a by-election in November 2014, but lost his seat to the Conservatives at the following general election. UKIP were similarly underwhelming in the simultaneous Medway council election, winning seats in only two wards: this one and the rural Peninsula ward. Strood South had been the best Labour prospect on the Strood side of the river, the party winning one out of three seats in 2003 and 2011, but in the 2015 election UKIP gained a seat from both major parties to split the seats 2–1 with the Tories, Brown-Reckless topping the poll. Shares of the vote in 2015 were 39% for UKIP, 35% for the Conservatives and 24% for Labour. It's unclear whether Labour's chances were kaiboshed by the notorious "Image from #Rochester" tweet of a house in Strood by once and future shadow minister Emily Thornberry.

Defending for UKIP is Karl Weller, a chef and local resident. The Conservatives and Labour have both selected the councillors who lost their seats in 2015: on the Tory side, former Mayor of Medway Josie Iles, on the Labour side Isaac Igwe. Also standing are Isabelle Cherry for the Lib Dems, Stephen Dyke for the Green Party and Mike Russell for the English Democrats.

Result: C 724 Lab 521 UKIP 480 Grn 74 LD 62 EDP 23 [C gain from UKIP]

Parliamentary constituency: Bracknell
May 2015 result C 1717/1585 Lab 552/321 LD 456
May 2011 result C 1131/1083 Lab 415/412
May 2007 result C 862/839 Grn 340 Lab 260 UKIP 169
May 2003 result C 631/548 LD 335 Lab 270 UKIP 190 Grn 177

Figure 183: Bracknell Forest, Central Sandhurst

Central Sandhurst

Bracknell Forest council, Berkshire; caused by the resignation of Conservative councillor Philip King, who had served since 2015.

Sandhurst is known the world over for its military academy, at which the cream of British and foreign army officers learn their craft. The town of Sandhurst was a small farming village until the Academy came here in 1812, and much of the housing in Central Sandhurst ward is post-war commuter territory, with high levels of full-time employment, although Sandhurst station has no London service (it is on the Reading–Guildford line). Anybody entering the town will be informed by signposts that Sandhurst is home to a three-time world champion team in that sport of kings, tug of war.

The Tories have the strongest team in the tug-of-war for Sandhurst's electors, and have not been seriously challenged in recent years. At the last election in 2015 the Conservative lead was 63–20 over Labour.

This by-election is a straight fight. Defending in the blue corner is Sandhurst parish councillor Gaby Kennedy. Challenging in the red corner is Anne Brunton, a carer and criminologist.

Result: C 476 Lab 211

Clarence

St Albans council, Hertfordshire; caused by the resignation of Liberal Democrat councillor Samuel Rowlands, who had served since 2015.

Moving to the north of London we are in Hertfordshire's only city, St Albans, for the first of this week's four polls in the Eastern region. Located east of the city centre, Clarence ward is named after Clarence Park, which was opened in 1894 by the then Duke of Cambridge and is largely unchanged since; it is home to the non-league football team St Albans City and the St Albans cricket club.

With its proximity to St Albans City railway station and its fast trains to London, Clarence ward has the middle-class commuter profile to end all middle-class commuter profiles. The ward is in the top 100 in England and Wales for

Parliamentary constituency: St Albans
Hertfordshire county council division: St Albans Central
May 2016 result LD 1178 C 490 Lab 397 Grn 226 TUSC 23
May 2015 result LD 1606 C 1375 Lab 683 Grn 399 TUSC 28
May 2014 result LD 764 C 579 Lab 483 Grn 367 UKIP 145 TUSC 14
May 2012 result LD 880 C 494 Lab 383 Grn 312
May 2011 result LD 1021 C 899 Lab 551 Grn 267
May 2010 result LD 1807 C 1115 Lab 556 Grn 297
May 2008 result LD 979 C 629 Grn 237 Lab 211
May 2007 result LD 1070 C 433 Grn 255 Lab 229
May 2006 result LD 918 C 596 Lab 339 Grn 298
June 2004 result LD 985 C 514 Lab 416 Grn 180
May 2003 result LD 1315 Lab 356 C 343
May 2002 result LD 1095 Lab 423 C 331
May 2000 result LD 790 Lab 478 C 403
May 1999 result LD 1089/1018/1006 Lab 619/605/581 C 356/350/340

Figure 184: St Albans, Clarence

the "higher management" (27%) *and* the "lower management" (32%) census categories, and in the top 25 wards for population with a degree (63% of the workforce). Over 30% of the population travel to work by train. The part of the ward west of the railway line, next to the city centre, appears to have been extensively redeveloped since 2010, so the 2021 census might well show something different here.

As is often the case with wards that are so highly educated, Clarence ward votes Lib Dem; it was close between the Lib Dems and Tories in the latter Coalition years, but the 2016 result—51% for the Lib Dems, 21% for the Conservatives, 17% for Labour—suggests that the Lib Dems have put those troubles behind them for the time being. Clarence ward also supplies the Lib Dem majority in the St Albans Central county division, as that division also includes the city-centre St Peters ward which has bizarre voting patterns (it has voted for all three main parties and the Greens since 2000).

Defending for the Lib Dems is Ellie Hudspith, who describes herself on Twitter as a "University of Leeds graduate, Lib Dem and crazy cat lady"; she is a PR woman for the Campaign for Real Ale and fought the Labour Batchwood ward in May. The Tory candidate Michael Roth, a house-husband, fought Park Street ward in May. Labour have reselected their candidate from May Liz Mills, and completing the ballot paper are Keith Cotton for the Greens and David Dickson for UKIP.

Result: LD 916 C 388 Lab 193 Grn 98 UKIP 16

Parliamentary constituency: Braintree
Essex county council division: Hedingham
May 2015 result C 1082 UKIP 343 Lab 325

Figure 185: Braintree, Bumpstead

Parliamentary constituency: Witham
Essex county council division: Witham Northern
May 2015 result C 1227/1140 Lab 992/756 Grn 645 LD 295/198

Figure 186: Braintree, Witham North

Bumpstead; and
Witham North

Braintree council, Essex; caused by the resignations of Robert Bolton and Christopher Bailey respectively. Bolton is retiring from the council after 25 years' service, having first been elected in 1991; Bailey is devoting his time to starting a new business. Both were Conservative councillors.

Moving into Essex, we have two by-elections at opposite ends of the rural Braintree district. At the southern end is Witham North ward, based on the town of Witham (the H is silent) which runs from the town's railway station on the Great Eastern main line along the road and railway line towards Braintree. At the northern end is Bumpstead ward, a rural ward based on four parishes on the Suffolk border, the largest of which is Steeple Bumpstead, and including a small part of the Suffolk town of Haverhill which has spilled over the county boundary. Both wards were expanded in boundary changes last year, Witham North gaining the Chipping Hill area from the former Witham Chipping Hill and Central ward, and Bumpstead gaining the Birdbrook parish from the abolished Upper Colne ward (and also, as it turned out, the former Upper Colne councillor).

Bumpstead is a true blue ward, the party beating UKIP here 62–20 in 2015; it is part of the equally true blue Hedingham county division. Witham North was safely Labour on its old boundaries but the addition of Chipping Hill appears to have flipped it into the Conservative column; last year the new ward voted 39% for the Tories, 31% for Labour and 20% for the Green Party, who in 2013 gained the county council seat covering this ward in a very close four-way result.

Defending for the Tories in Witham North is Lorne Campbell, who runs the local Boys' Brigade and was elected to Witham town council in a by-election in May. Labour's Phil Barlow wants to make a quick return to the council; he was Labour councillor for the former Witham North from 2011 and lost his seat last year. The Greens have selected Michelle Weeks, a therapist and reiki practitioner,

Parliamentary constituency: North West Norfolk
Norfolk county council division: Docking
May 2015 result C 1817/1313 Lab 736/679
May 2011 result C 1181/1007 Lab 550/538
May 2007 result C 1042/993 Ind 516 Lab 397
Feb 2004 by-election C 852 Lab 590 Ind 487
May 2003 result Ind 1379/1365 C 474/379 Lab 421/387

Figure 187: King's Lynn and West Norfolk, Heacham

and the ballot paper is completed by Lib Dem Mark Scott.

There is a relatively wide choice in the Bumpstead by-election. The defending Tory candidate is Diana Garrod, a parish councillor for Sturmer, one of the parishes within the ward. The UKIP candidate is Debbie Shore, who gives an address in Steeple Bumpstead. Labour have selected Bill Edwards, who was parliamentary candidate for Braintree in 2010; Jenny Bishop stands for the Greens and Steve Bolter for the Liberal Democrats.

Bumpstead result: C 350 UKIP 84 Lab 45 LD 40 Grn 23
Witham North result: Lab 339 C 308 Grn 227 LD 31 [Lab gain from C]

Heacham

King's Lynn and West Norfolk council; caused by the resignation of Conservative councillor Peter Colvin. He had served since 2015.

Moving north, we come to the west coast of Norfolk on the shores of the Wash. Heacham is an old village which turned into a seaside resort in Victorian times, and there are still extensive caravan parks in the village for visitors. Demographically Heacham is an elephant's graveyard: it is in the top 30 wards in England and Wales for retired population (33% of the workforce) and just outside the top 50 for those aged 65 and over (38% of the populaton), and those people within the ward who are still young enough to work aren't earning a lot of money, with tourism and lavender cultivation the main games in town.

Created on its present boundaries in 2003, Heacham returned two independent candidates in that election, but the Tories gained one seat in a February 2004 by-election and the other in 2007 and now have an iron grip on its election results: in 2015 the Tory slate beat Labour 71–29 in a straight fight. The Conservatives also hold the local county seat (Docking), although this was close between them and an independent in the 2013 county elections.

Defending for the Tories is Simon Eyre, from Dersingham. The Labour candidate is Edward Robb, from Great Massingham, who was runner-up in the last King's Lynn and West Norfolk by-election in Valley Hill ward (his home ward, based on Sandringham) in June. Also on a much more extensive ballot paper than last year are Rob Colwell for the Lib Dems, Debbie le May for UKIP and independent candidates Terry Parish and Michael Press (who are the only candidates to give addresses in Heacham).

Result: Parish 400 C 342 LD 83 UKIP 83 Press 79 Lab 74 [Ind gain from C]

Rothwell

Kettering council, Northamptonshire; caused by the death of Labour councillor Alan Mills at the age of 61. A master stonemason, he was a founder member of the band Coast to Coast, which had a Top 10 hit in 1981 with (Do) The Hucklebuck, and served last year as bailiff of the town's Rowell Fair. Mills had served on Rothwell town council since 2007 and on Kettering council since 2011.

Not to be confused with the town of the same name just outside Leeds, Rothwell is a market town immediately to the north-west of Kettering, on the old A 6 London–Leicester road. Thanks to its market, which received its first charter from King John, Rothwell became one of the largest towns in Northamptonshire in mediaeval times, and the town centre has many old and unusual buildings, including the county's longest church, dedicated to the Holy Trinity and one of only two churches in England with an ossuary; and the Elizabethan Market House, designed by the eccentric Thomas Tresham who was lord of the manor of Rothwell and left the town a very strange building full of heraldic and Catholic symbolism. Opposite the Market House is Rothwell Conservative Club, which hosted the British Quiz Championships in 2014. The Industrial Revolution passed the town by, leaving a picture-postcard place which is now functionally a Kettering satellite.

Interestingly, the town is very closely fought between the Conservatives and Labour at district council level. In 2003 it formed two wards: Tresham ward, forming the town's eastern half, split its two seats between the Tories and Labour, while Trinity ward elected two Tories; in both wards the Tories had 52% and Labour 48%. This was also the score in the 2005 Northamptonshire county council election, in which Rothwell formed a single division. Boundary changes for the district council in 2007 united the town into a single three-member ward, which elected the Tory slate 56–44; the nadir for the Labour vote came in the 2009 county elections in which the Tories won Rothwell 50–29.

In the 2011 district elections Labour made a recovery, Alan Mills gaining a seat from dissident Conservative councillor Alan Pote who stood for re-election as an independent; Pote polled 20% to 37% for the Tories and 36% for Labour. Pote

Parliamentary constituency: Kettering
Northamptonshire county council division: Rothwell and Mawsley
June 2015 postponed poll Lab 951/623/614 C 873/777/771 UKIP 370 Grn 119/89/82
May 2011 result C 1103/1079/1052 Lab 1077/847/778 Ind 616 LD 230
June 2009 county council election C 1130 Lab 649 Ind 259 LD 231
May 2007 result C 1293/1257/1173 Lab 1010/950/886
May 2005 county council election C 1944 Lab 1825

Figure 188: Kettering, Rothwell

then joined UKIP and stood as the UKIP candidate in the 2015 district election, but died during the campaign forcing the poll to be postponed to June; the postponed poll delivered no change in terms of party strengths but Mills topped the poll (with 40%, to 38% for the Tories and 16% for the replacement UKIP candidate) while one of the Tory councillors, Ian Jelley, lost out to his running-mate (he has since returned to the council in a by-election for a different ward).

Defending for Labour, who will have to cope without Mills' personal vote, is Margaret Harris, who under her former name of Margaret Draper is a former Mayor of High Wycombe. The Tories' Cedwein Brown is seeking to return to the council after she stood down in 2011. UKIP have selected Sam Watts, who stood in May for Northamptonshire police and crime commissioner. Completing the ballot paper are Stevie Jones of the Green Party and Lib Dem Malcolm Adcock.

Result: C 700 Lab 498 UKIP 108 Grn 75 LD 67 [C gain from Lab]

Blaengwrach

Neath Port Talbot council, Glamorgan; caused by the death of Labour councillor Alf Siddley. A former supervisor at the Cam Gears factory in Resolven, he had served since 2008 and had also played for the West Glamorgan senior bowls team.

There are two Welsh by-elections this week, one south and one north. The south by-election is in Blaengwrach (the W is silent), a village on the south side of the Vale of Neath. This is an upland area and the division contains the highest point of Glamorgan, Craig-y-Llyn at 1970 feet; the main industry here is opencast coalmining. 98.8% of Blaengwrach's population was born in the UK, the ninth highest figure for any ward in England and Wales, and the division also makes the top 100 for White British ethnicity (98.5%).

The Blaengwrach ward which existed on the now-abolished Neath district council was not contested in that council's history (1973–95), but since the creation of Neath Port Talbot district Blaengwrach has been closely fought between Labour and Plaid Cymru. Plaid won in 1999 (narrowly) and 2004 (convincingly);

Parliamentary and Assembly constituency: Neath
May 2012 result Lab 363 PC 290
May 2008 result Lab 432 PC 380
June 2004 result PC 436 Lab 237
May 1999 result PC 397 Lab 369
May 1995 result Lab 510 PC 388
Neath district council results
May 1991 result Lab unopposed
May 1987 result Lab unopposed
May 1983 result Lab unopposed
May 1976 result Lab unopposed
May 1973 result Lab unopposed

Figure 189: Neath Port Talbot, Blaengwrach

Alf Siddley regained the division for Labour in 2008 and was more comfortably re-elected in 2012, beating Plaid 56–44.

Defending for Labour is Sarah Price. Plaid Cymru have selected Carolyn Edwards, who represented the division from 1999 to 2008 and is seeking to return to the council. Also standing are Peter Crocker-Jacques for the Conservatives, independent candidate Thomas Evans and Richard Pritchard of UKIP.

Result: PC 225 Lab 143 Ind 58 UKIP 39 C 4 (four) [PC gain from Lab]

Abergele Pensarn

Conwy council, North Wales; caused by the resignation of Labour councillor Rick Stubbs.

Our north Welsh poll this week is a coastal division, covering the part of the town of Abergele to the east of the A 55, the main road through North Wales. The double-barrelled name is partly to reflect the name of the ward's railway station (Abergele and Pensarn, on the North Wales Coast line) and partly because Conwy county borough has another Pensarn division, in Llandudno Junction. The division has a very high retired population; 28% of the population is retired according to the 2011 census, which also found 45% of the population identifying as English; however, Abergele has a reputation for being rather downmarket compared to other retirement communities on the North Wales Coast.

This is the second by-election for this ward since the 2012 ordinary elections. Rick Stubbs had been elected at the first by-election in Septemnber 2014 to succeed his wife Jean, who had represented Abergele Pensarn since the division was created in 1999, albeit with interrupted service. Jean Stubbs lost her seat to the Conservatives in 2008 before getting it back in 2012, the Tories falling that

Parliamentary and Assembly constituency: Clwyd West
Sept 2014 by-election Lab 160 Ind 134 UKIP 129 Ind 74 Ind 56 C 54 Ind 10
May 2012 result Lab 407 Ind 186 C 145
May 2008 result C 322 Lab 282 Ind 128
June 2004 result Lab 274 Ind 160 C 152
May 1999 result Lab unopposed

Figure 190: Conwy, Abergele Pensarn

year to third place behind an independent candidate. In the 2014 by-election Rick Stubbs was elected on a very low share of the vote: 26%, to 22% for independent candidate Michael Smith, 21% for UKIP, 12% for independent Ken Sudlow and 9% for independent Barry Griffiths.

David Hancock has the task of defending Abergele Pensarn for Labour for the second time this term: he is an architectural design consultant and Abergele town councillor. Independent candidate Michael Smith, from Kinmel Bay, is standing again after his near-miss in the first by-election; he is a Towyn and Kinmel Bay community councillor after winning a by-election in June. Another independent candidate on the ballot is Abergele town councillor Alan Hunter. UKIP have not nominated a candidate this time round, so the ballot paper is completed by Tory candidate Bernice McLoughlin.

Result: Hunter 170 Smith 146 Lab 136 C 87 [Ind gain from Lab]

St Mary's

East Riding council, East Yorkshire; caused by the death of Conservative councillor Irene Charis. The first black member of East Riding council, Charis had served since 2011.

Welcome to Beverley, county town of the East Riding and a rather beautiful town to boot. Beverley has been a tourist centre since ancient times as a place of pilgrimage for St John of Beverley, bishop of York in the eighth century who founded the town's Minster and was said to have performed miracles. Beverley became the tenth largest town in England, but the dissolution of the monasteries destroyed its pilgrimage economic base; today the town functions as a market town and a commuter centre for Hull, with tourism, the council and the town's racecourse also being important to the local economy. The East Riding's wards tend to the large side in population terms and Beverley has just two wards for a population of nearly 30,000: this is the northwesterly one, including part of the town centre and the racecourse.

At the first election on these boundaries in 2003 St Mary's ward returned

Parliamentary constituency: Beverley and Holderness
May 2015 result C 3069/2721/2456 Lab 1910/1669/1560 UKIP 1399 LD 1215/1124/1039
Beverley Party 1179/988/978 Grn 917 Ind 660/393
May 2011 result C 2416/2362/1785 Ind 1741 Lab 1486/1458/1399 LD 1436/870/808 Grn 947
May 2007 result LD 1760/1165/888 C 1668/1546/1369 Ind 1548/1079/656/686 LD 1165/888 Lab 701/693/663 Grn 520
May 2003 result Ind 1904/1764 LD 1496/1117/876 C 1303/1119/1009 Lab 1023/995/918

Figure 191: East Riding, St Mary's

---

two independent candidates and a Liberal Democrat. The Tories took one of the independent seats in 2007 (one of the unsuccessful candidates on their slate that year was Walter Sweeney, former MP for the Vale of Glamorgan) and defeated the Lib Dems and the remaining independent councillor to get a full slate in 2011. 2015 saw the Conservatives consolidate their majority but with a rather low share of the vote in a fragmented field: 30%, to 18% for Labour, 14% for UKIP (whose candidate was Walter Sweeney, now in the party), 12% for the Lib Dems and 11% for a localist slate called the Beverley Party.

Defending for the Tories is Roy Begg, a mechanical engineer working in the North Sea gas industry. The Labour candidate is Margaret Pinder, a former Mayor of Beverley who stood for the Beverley and Holderness parliamentary seat last year. UKIP's John Kitchener wants YOU to vote for him; he was the UKIP candidate for Haltemprice and Howden last year. The Lib Dems have reselected Denis Healy...no, not that one; Healy also stood in Beverley and Holderness last year and in May was the Lib Dem candidate for Humberside police and crime commissioner. The Beverley Party candidate is Bea Willar, a former university lecturer, volunteer counsellor and German teacher. Completing the ballot paper is Chris Harrod, who was top of the Beverley Party slate here last year; she is standing as an independent.

Result: LD 1497 C 947 Lab 689 Beverley Party 364 Ind 141 UKIP 101 [LD gain from C]

Central

Middlesbrough council, North Yorkshire; caused by the resignation of Labour councillor Ansab Shan in order to take up a new job at the Crown Prosecution Service. He had served since 2015.

For our final poll of this busy week, we're at the other end of what used to be Yorkshire. As the name suggests, this is the town centre ward for Middlesbrough.

Parliamentary constituency: Middlesbrough
May 2015 result Lab 1382/946/944 Ind 713/680/678 UKIP 395

Figure 192: Middlesbrough, Central

Middlesbrough was called into being by the Industrial Revolution as a port for the Stockton and Darlington Railway; between 1829 and 1851 its population increased from 40 to 7,600. Then ironstone was discovered in the local hills, and Middlesbrough became the epicentre of the world's iron and steel trade, with companies such as Dorman Long setting the world's prices and the town itself becoming known as "Ironopolis". Shipbuilding and a bridge-building industry grew up; many of the world's most famous bridges were designed and manufactured in Middlesbrough, such as the Sydney Harbour Bridge (by Dorman Long), the Humber Bridge (at the time it was built the largest in the world) and, closer to home, the Transporter Bridge which is an icon of Middlesbrough.

The town centre has changed a lot even in the last thirty years with extensive redevelopment. There is now a university here, Teesside University, which in its short life has developed a strong reputation in the field of digital animation. The dinosaur sculptures in Teessaurus Park may represent the iron and steel industry, but engineering is still important to the town's economy. Middlesbrough FC are back in the Premier League from their shiny Riverside stadium, and once you've seen the Boro lose to whoever they're playing this week why not try Middlesbrough's contribution to the culinary world—the infamous Parmo.

Middlesbrough got new ward boundaries in last year's election but Central ward is essentially an extension (with an extra councillor) of the Middlehaven ward which existed from 2003 to 2015. Middlehaven's census statistics are extensively skewed by the presence of Teesside University; it was in the top 100 wards in England and Wales for full-time students (34% of the workforce). Those living within the ward who are not students tend not to have jobs: only 13% of the workforce were in full-time employment in 2011, with unemployment at 9.7% and 18.4% of the workforce having never worked. Owner-occupation is extremely low, and the non-white population is relatively high for a ward in the North East. This creates a reliable Labour ward: in 2015 Labour had 56% to 29% for an independent slate headed by outgoing Labour councillor John McPartland, who had been deselected.

Defending for Labour is Matthew Storey, political assistant to Middlesbrough MP Andy McDonald. He is opposed by independent candidate Dale Clark, a mature student at Teesside University; Tory candidate Ron Armstrong; and Lib Dem candidate Elliott Sabin-Motson.

Result: Lab 732 Ind 149 C 70 LD 53

27th October 2016

Three by-elections on 27th October 2016 to round off the month. Let's go to the seaside...

Rhyl West

Denbighshire council; caused by the resignation of Labour councillor Ian Armstrong. He had served since 2008.

Starting this week in a town which is probably fairly high up the "hate list" for many people in Granadaland. The North Wales coast has some nice seaside towns, but Rhyl is not one of them: it's as brash and in-your-face as Blackpool but without Blackpool's charm. Rhyl West (in Welsh, *Gorllewin y Rhyl*) is the town centre division, running from the railway station to the seafront and including the West Parade, the Seaquarium and the eyesore that is the Marine Lake, whose redevelopment was a casualty of the financial crash and has since been stymied by the fact that it's located on the River Clwyd floodplain. It says something about the town that the most high-profile thing to have happened here in recent years involved Ched Evans.

Rhyl's demographic indicators are pretty awful as well. One of this division's census districts is right at the bottom of the 2011 Welsh indices of multiple deprivation; Rhyl West as a whole is in the top 10 wards in England and Wales for long-term sickness or disability (15% of the workforce) and in the top 20 wards for unemployment (12%). Those jobs which exist are determinedly working-class, while the seaside resort history leads to high levels of private renting. Politically, although Rhyl is in the marginal parliamentary seat of Vale of Clwyd this is a safe Labour ward; at the most recent Welsh local elections in 2012 Labour had 50% to 19% for an independent and 17% for Plaid Cymru.

Defending for Labour is Alan James, a Rhyl town councillor (for Trellewelyn ward, which is not in this division). Mark Webster, a former Labour councillor for the ward who sought (and lost) re-election in 2008 as an independent, tries to

Parliamentary and Assembly constituency: Vale of Clwyd
May 2012 result Lab 378/361 Ind 142 PC 125 C 106/99
May 2008 result Lab 276/236 Ind 195/188 C 175/163 LD 130
June 2004 result Lab 404/339 Ind 277/252

Figure 193: Denbighshire, Rhyl West

Parliamentary constituency: Bexhill and Battle
East Sussex county council division: Bexhill King Offa
May 2015 result Ind 1309/1220 C 973/847 UKIP 417 Grn 282 Lab 280
June 2014 result Ind 570 C 378 UKIP 311 Lab 102
May 2011 result Ind 1096/1034 C 871/819 Lab 239
May 2007 result C 1159/1158 LD 497
May 2003 result C 1071/974 LD 575

Figure 194: Rother, Collington

get back on the council. Another independent candidate on the ballot is Norman Shone, who was the Plaid candidate here in 2012. Completing the ballot paper are Les Harker for the Tories and Keith Kirwan for the Lib Dems.

Result: Lab 199 C 93 Shone 55 Webster 42 LD 26

Collington; and
Darwell

Rother council, East Sussex; caused respectively by the resignations of independent councillor Tony Mansi and Conservative councillor Emily Rowlinson. Rowlinson had served since May 2015, Mansi since 2011.

For our two English by-elections of the week we stay by the seaside. The Rother district's largest town is Bexhill-on-Sea, and Collington ward runs along the western end of its seafront, from Collington railway station to Cooden Beach station. If Rhyl is a nightmare, Bexhill, if you believe the fiction that's been written about it, is almost as bad: the 2006 film *Children of Men* depicted it as a refugee camp for immigrants, and Spike Milligan's memoirs describe a wartime Bexhill which Milligan's company had the task of defending without any ammunition for their big guns (training on the big guns involved much shouting of the word BANG). In real life Collington is not a location for quarantined refugees straight out of the Jungle, but is the elephant's graveyard to end all elephant's graveyards: 45% of the population are aged 65 or over—the fifth highest figure in England and Wales—and 36% of the workforce are retired which is comfortably in the top 20 wards for that statistic. Bexhill's ambience

Parliamentary constituency: Bexhill and Battle
East Sussex county council division: Rother North West (part: Brightling, Burwash and
Dallington parishes); Battle and Crowhurst (part: Mountfield and Whatlington parishes
and part of Battle parish)
May 2015 result C 1419/1213 UKIP 574 LD 564 Grn 510 Lab 347
July 2014 result C 361 UKIP 182 Grn 154 Lab 84 LD 65
May 2011 result C 1168/1016 Grn 386 LD 363/341 Lab 228
May 2007 result C 1072 Ind 685 LD 469
May 2003 result C 858 Ind 756 LD 476

Figure 195: Rother, Darwell

means that the town attracts more than its fair share of celebrities, and reportedly both Fanny Cradock and Graham Norton live or have lived in the ward.

Moving inland, Darwell ward is a large rural part of the Weald immediately to the north-west of Battle. None of the parishes in the ward are called Darwell, which is instead the name of a reservoir at the ward's centre; its largest centre of population is Burwash, an old ironworking village which is best known for Bateman's, a Jacobean mansion once owned by Rudyard Kipling and now open to the public.

Darwell is true blue now, although it did return an independent councillor from 2003 to 2011 who was not opposed by the Tory slate. Although part of the ward is covered by the Lib Dem-held Battle and Crowhurst county division, the Lib Dem vote in that division comes out of Battle town; most of the ward comes under the safe Tory county division of Rother North West. Last year the Tories polled 42% against a divided opposition: 17% for UKIP, 17% for the Lib Dems, 15% for the Green Party.

Collington's elections are more interesting, with the Tories losing the ward to an independent slate in 2011; the independents then held a by-election in 2014 and were re-elected in 2015 with 40% of the vote, to 30% for the Tories and 13% for UKIP. At county level this is part of Bexhill King Offa division, which in 2013 split its two seats between the Tories and UKIP.

Defending for the Independents in Collington is Deirdre Earl-Williams, a former Tory councillor (under her previous name of Deirdre Williams) for the neighbouring Sackville ward who narrowly lost re-election as an independent in 2015. The Conservative candidate is Andrew Burton. UKIP have selected Michael Phillips and the ballot paper is completed by Labour candidate Sara Watson.

In Darwell the defending Conservative candidate is John Barnes, a retired history lecturer with a ridiculously extensive CV: as well as co-founding the Conservative History Group and writing or co-writing several books and papers on the subject, he was the Conservative candidate for Walsall North in the 1964, '66 and '70 general elections; an alderman of the London Borough of Greenwich from 1968 to 1973; a Kent county councillor from 1973 to 1989, chairing the education committee for five years; and an East Sussex county councillor since 1997, presently representing Rother North West division which covers part of this ward. He was chairman of East Sussex county council in 2005–06 and 2006–07 and presently chairs Etchingham parish council. UKIP, the Lib Dems and Greens have all reselected their candidates from 2015—Edward Smith, Mary Varrall and Andrew Wedmore respectively—and Labour's Antonia Berelson completes the ballot paper.

Collington result: Ind 818 C 393 Lab 87 UKIP 66

Darwell result: C 359 LD 259 Lab 79 Grn 69 UKIP 60

3rd November 2016

By the time you read these words, your columnist will be on holiday; playing for Wales B at the inaugural Quiz Olympiad in Athens over the weekend, taking in the sights of the city, the Acropolis, the Panathenaic stadium, the Olympiacos–Panathinaikos derby[12] and some pleasant Mediterranean weather[13], and generally having a break from the internet. While you're all stuck in Blighty. To cheer you up, here's a preview of the ten by-elections in the first week of November...

Banff and District; and Inverurie and District

Aberdeenshire council; caused respectively by the death of SNP councillor Ian Gray, at the age of 73, and the resignation of Liberal Democrat councillor Martin Kitts-Hayes. Gray, a grandfather-of-four who had worked for Unilever and BT, was first elected to Aberdeenshire council in 2007. Kitts-Hayes had also served since 2007; he had left the Liberal Democrats in 2012 and his resignation came in the wake of a scandal dubbed "Legogate" in which he had returned early from an official trip to the North Sea Commission, at Legoland in Denmark, because he was unhappy with his accommodation.

We start this week in Scotland with what are likely to be the only two by-elections to be held in Aberdeenshire in 2016. Once the centre of its own county, Banff lies on the north coast of Aberdeenshire on the western side of the Deveron estuary; a former royal burgh, its traditional industry was fishing and in mediaeval times Banff did a roaring trade exporting salmon to Europe. Within the ward based on Banff are Duff House, a Georgian manor house designed by William Adam and now part of the National Gallery of Scotland; the tiny port of Portsoy and the planned inland village of Aberchirder.

---

[12] This didn't actually happen.
[13] This did.

While fishing is still important to Banff, Inverurie is a rather different kettle of fish. On the main road and railway line from Aberdeen to Inverness, Inverurie first grew in earnest after the opening of the Aberdeenshire Canal in 1806 which linked the town to Aberdeen. For most of the twentieth century Inverurie was a railway town, home to the locomotive works for the Great North of Scotland Railway; the local non-league football team is still called Inverurie Loco Works, but the main game in town these days is oil. Inverurie has boomed in population since the 1970s as a base for the North Sea oil industry and as a commuter centre for Aberdeen. The ward based on Inverurie is large enough for four seats taking only a small rural hinterland.

Inverurie may now be in Alex Salmond's constituency at Westminster, but in 2003 it was a Lib Dem stronghold, the party carrying with large majorities all three of the old single-member wards covering the town. The introduction of PR allowed minority representation in Inverurie, with the Lib Dems winning two seats, the SNP one and the Conservatives one. One of the Lib Dem councillors stood for re-election as an independent in 2012, but lost his seat to the SNP; first preferences in 2012 were 37% for the SNP, 17% each for the Conservatives and Lib Dems and 13% for Labour.

The electoral dynamics of Banff are rather different. The SNP have been top dogs here for a long time, and the importance of fishing to the local economy meant that Banff and Buchan was the only constituency in Scotland to vote in favour of leaving the EU in June. Four years before that Banff and District ward gave a resounding win to the SNP, who led the Tories 55–23 in votes and 2–1 in seats, the Tories gaining their seat from the Lib Dems and a previously independent councillor being re-elected on the SNP slate. A side-effect of a rather short ballot paper in 2012 was a very strong vote for the Christian Party, who broke 10%.

These by-elections could alter the balance of power on Aberdeenshire council, which is finely balanced. The SNP are the largest party, but they are short of a majority and a rainbow anti-SNP coalition was formed to run the council after the 2012 elections. However, that coalition has since fallen apart and the SNP have formed a new administration with the support of Labour and some of the independent councillors. A gain in one of these by-elections could bolster the ruling coalition or tip the balance back the other way again.

Banff and District has a short ballot paper this time as well with just three candidates. Defending for the SNP is Glen Reynolds, a former Labour councillor in Darlington who stood for Parliament twice as a Labour candidate (Berwick-upon-Tweed in 2005, Banff and Buchan in 2010) before defecting to the SNP in 2012; a Unison shop steward, former libel solicitor and former investigative

Parliamentary constituency: Banff and Buchan
Holyrood constituency: Banffshire and Buchan Coast
May 2012 first preferences SNP 1840 C 768 LD 369 Christian 342
May 2007 first preferences SNP 1588 Ind 1340 LD 694 C 616 Grn 298

Figure 196: Aberdeenshire, Banff and District

Parliamentary constituency: Gordon
Holyrood constituency: Aberdeenshire East
May 2012 first preferences SNP 1300 C 608 LD 606 Lab 463 Ind 407 Grn 113
May 2007 first preferences LD 2181 SNP 1515 C 762 Lab 567 Ind 123

Figure 197: Aberdeenshire, Inverurie and District

journalist, he is a director of Grampian Housing and until recently worked for the council as a housing and community safety officer. The Tory candidate is Iain Taylor, a King Edward and Gamrie community councillor, and completing the ballot paper is Alistair Mason for the Lib Dems.

The Lib Dems have it all to do to defend their seat in Inverurie given the circumstances that led to the by-election and the fact that they only polled 17% in the 2012 local election. Their candidate is Alison Auld, who has 17 years' experience as a caseworker. Hoping to gain for the SNP is Neil Baillie, a community councillor working in the North Sea oil industry. The Tories have selected Colin Clark, an entrepreneur who is straight off the campaign trail having fought the local Scottish Parliament seat (Aberdeenshire East) in May. Completing the ballot paper is Labour candidate Sarah Flavell, chair of the non-profit organisation Gordon Rural Action.

Banff and District first preferences: C 1170 SNP 962 LD 526
After transfers: C 1378 SNP 1097 [C gain from SNP]
Inverurie and District first preferences: C 1302 SNP 1164 LD 755 Lab 139
After transfers: C 1701 SNP 1341 [C gain from LD]

Burrnley Central East

Lancashire county council; caused by the resignation of Labour councillor Misfar Hassan. He had served since winning a by-election in 2010.

Welcome to Burrnley. Once you've parrked yourr carr in the carr parrk, take a look in the town centre which once held the dubious title of being home to the UK's largest charity shop. Go to Turf Moor to watch the Clarets, the town's football team who may be back in the Premier but aren't yet having a vintage season (although they did take a point off Manchester United at the weekend);

the football club hosts one of the polling stations for this by-election. Look in the estate agents' windows—Burnley has some of the lowest property prices in England—and try to get your head around the town's strange rhotic accent. Try the locals' favourite tipple: not Moorhouse's beer but Bénédictine liqueur, which was originally brought back to the town by soldiers from the First World War who have made Burnley Miners' Club the world's single biggest consumer of Bénédictine. A classic Lancashire mill town with historically some coalmining, Burnley's economy is now based on services and high-end manufacturing for the aerospace industry. The division is linked to the outside world by the M 65 motorway and Burnley Central railway station—located on the Colne branch, now down to just one platform and no longer the main station for the town, which is Burnley Manchester Road.

The two-and-a-bit Burnley council wards which make up Burnley Central East have some unusual demographic features. Burnley doesn't have a particularly large Pakistani population by Lancashire milltown standards, but that population is nearly all packed into Daneshouse with Stoneyholme ward. Daneshouse with Stoneyholme has the highest proportion of the workforce "looking after home or family" of any ward in England and Wales (16%), the fourth-highest Muslim population (76%), the fourth-highest proportion who have never worked or are long-term unemployed (28%), the sixth-highest population of Asian ethnicity (79%) and the seventh-highest proportion of under-16s (32%). One wonders what all those kids are going to do with their lives, given the town's poor economic prospects. Just a couple of miles to the east, Brunshaw ward (above Turf Moor), although just as deprived, is determinedly white, while Bank Hall ward (along the Leeds–Liverpool canal), a former coal-mining area, is somewhere in between both geographically and demographically.

Central East contains some of the most dependable Labour parts of Burnley. Bank Hall is one of only three wards in Burnley to have voted Labour every year since 2002; Daneshouse with Stoneyholme voted Lib Dem a few times during the Blair and Brown years but Labour won without a contest in 2015 and polled 88% in May. Brunshaw ward elected a BNP councillor in 2003 and voted Lib Dem a few times in the following years, but is now a Labour *versus* UKIP battle in the way of many white working-class areas, with Labour winning 49–37 in May. The county division as a whole narrowly voted Lib Dem in 2009, but the Lib Dem county councillor died less than a year later and Labour recovered their loss in the by-election, held on general election day in 2010. At the most recent county election in 2013 the Lib Dems fell to third place and Labour beat UKIP 58–19.

Defending for Labour is Sobia Malik, a Burnley borough councillor for Bank

Parliamentary constituency: Burnley
Burnley council wards: Bank Hall (part); Brunshaw; Daneshouse with Stoneyholme
May 2013 result Lab 2022 UKIP 675 LD 540 C 181 BNP 60
May 2010 by-election Lab 3157 LD 2279 BNP 868 C 815
June 2009 result LD 1748 Lab 1676 BNP 547 C 444
May 2005 result Lab 3012 LD 2169 C 936

<hr>

Figure 198: Lancashire CC, Burnley Central East

<hr>

Hall ward, an education consultant and author of a book on the town and its links with Pakistan; her father Rafique Malik was a Burnley councillor for 30 years and served as the town's mayor, while her brother Shahid Malik was Labour MP for Dewsbury from 2005 to 2010. The UKIP candidate is Mark Girven, a web designer. Also standing are off-licence owner Emma Payne for the Lib Dems and Laura Fisk for the Green Party.

 Result: Lab 1348 LD 276 UKIP 249 Grn 84

Grangetown

Cardiff city council; caused by the death of Labour councillor Chris Lomax, described as a strong family man and true gentleman, at the age of 73. He had served since 2012. Despite poor health Lomax kept working for his community until the end and attended his final council meeting the day before he died.

Welcome to Cardiff Bay, that controversial lake at the mouth of the Taff and Ely rivers which has been the subject of one of the more successful regeneration projects in recent years. Grangetown ward lies at the other end of the Bay, between the two rivers; at its south end is Cardiff International Sports Village, home to the city's ice rink, Olympic swimming pool and whitewater rafting, and linked to Penarth on the other side of the river by the new Pont y Werin footbridge. Further to the north are the Cardiff branch of IKEA and the Canton railway yards, while Grangetown railway station (on the Vale of Glamorgan line) links the ward with Cardiff city centre. The area's dockland history has left a multi-racial population, with a particularly high black population by Welsh standards (8.4%) and a relatively high number of Welsh speakers for the city.

Grangetown was a Lib Dem ward in the Noughties when the Lib Dems were running Cardiff council, but their vote crashed in the 2012 election; from being a three-way Lib Dem/Labour/Plaid marginal in 2008 Grangetown is now a Labour/Plaid marginal, with vote shares in 2012 being 40% for Labour, 33% for Plaid and 11% for the Lib Dems.

Defending for Labour is Maliika Kaaba, who works for a local women's

Parliamentary and Assembly constituency: Cardiff South and Penarth
May 2012 result Lab 1812/1709/1704 PC 1511/1467/1391 LD 505/501/489 C 308/266/251
Grn 215/205 Christian 84 Communist 77
May 2008 result LD 1357/1319/1317 Lab 1138/1131/1104 PC 1099/1009/920 C 546/533/482
Communist 117
June 2004 result LD 1424/1417/1404 Lab 1122/1113/1072 PC 838/764/749 C 427/420/369

Figure 199: Cardiff, Grangetown

Parliamentary and Assembly constituency: Vale of Glamorgan
May 2012 result Lab 787/754 Ind 301/300 C 105/102 PC 76/73
May 2008 result Lab 757/699 C 332/321 PC 308/239 Lib 73
June 2004 result Lab 727/636 PC 371/356 Socialist Labour 69

Figure 200: Vale of Glamorgan, Gibbonsdown

community group. Plaid have selected Tariq Awan, who is described as a part-time community banker. Former Lib Dem councillor Asghar Ali, Cardiff's first Pakistani councillor, is seeking to make a return to the council after standing down here in 2012. Also on the ballot paper are two candidates who work in the Senedd for assembly members: Michael Bryan for the Conservatives and Richard Lewis for UKIP, who gives an address in, er, Swindon.

Result: PC 1163 Lab 1049 C 287 LD 187 UKIP 141 [PC gain from Lab]

Gibbonsdown

Vale of Glamorgan council; caused by the resignation of long-serving Labour councillor Rob Curtis. Curtis, a former cabinet member on the council, had pleaded guilty last year to common assault on a 17-year-old girl; his resignation came after the Adjudication Panel for Wales suspended him from council duties for three months for bringing the council into disrepute.

For our other Welsh by-election this week we are in Barry, Wales' fifth largest and southernmost town. Barry was traditionally a dock town and a seaside resort—not well-paying industries, and Gibbonsdown ward has borne the brunt of that, being a council estate on the northern edge of town with high unemployment. The most interesting census indicator is that Gibbonsdown makes the top 100 wards in England and Wales for "no religion", with 44% professing to be atheists or agnostics. This is a safe Labour division and the main interest usually lies in who comes second; in 2012 that was an independent slate, which Labour beat 62–24.

Defending for Labour is Julie Aviet. Dennis Harkus, the runner-up here in

2012, is trying again; he is a former Labour figure and former leader of Barry town council. Also on the ballot paper are Leighton Rowlands for the Conservatives, Barry town councillor Shirley Hodges for Plaid Cymru, Jennifer Geroni for the Lib Dems and Robin Hunter-Clarke for UKIP.

Result: Lab 404 PC 161 Ind 113 C 104 UKIP 54 LD 7 (seven)

Longlevens

Gloucester city council; caused by the death of Conservative councillor Jim Porter. He had served since 2008.

It's not often this column gets to talk about a by-election in Gloucester—Keith Edkins' index of local by-elections since 1995 lists only two to the city council, and the last one was in 2001. One reason for this is Gloucester's thirds electoral system, which provides opportunities each year for vacancies to be combined with an ordinary election, but Gloucester moved to whole council elections this year so that consideration will not apply in the future.

The Longlevens ward lies on the north-eastern edge of the city, between the Tewkesbury and Cheltenham roads; consisting entirely of privately-developed twentieth-century housing, it was only fully incorporated into Gloucester in 1967 and has a lower-middle-class demographic. The area suffered badly in the floods of summer 2007, and is still sufficiently semi-detached from Gloucester to have been transferred into the Tewkesbury constituency in 2010.

Gloucester got new ward boundaries this year, but these resulted in no change to Longlevens ward whose present boundaries date from 2002. It has normally been a Conservative ward over that period, although the Lib Dems won it in 2004 and came close on a number of other occasions pre-coalition. In May, with all three seats up for election, the Tory slate won with 42% against evenly divided opposition—18% for Labour, 14% for UKIP, 13% each for the Lib Dems and Greens. The Conservatives also hold the Longlevens county council seat, which includes part of Elmbridge ward to the south.

Defending for the Tories is Clive Walford, who played on the back row for Gloucester Rugby in the mid-1970s and chairs the Gloucester rugby players association; away from the pitch he is coming to the end of a 31-year career in the criminal justice system. The Labour candidate Terry Haines, who was runner-up here in 2015 and in May, is hoping to go one better. UKIP have selected Daniel Woolf, who was a Tory candidate in May's city council elections, and the Lib Dem candidate is Linda Castle, former treasurer of the Gloucester dyslexia association.

Result: C 1066 LD 852 Lab 223 UKIP 167

Parliamentary constituency: Tewkesbury
Gloucestershire county council division: Longlevens
May 2016 result C 1657/1636/1410 Lab 696 UKIP 541 LD 515 Grn 494
May 2015 result C 2870 Lab 955 UKIP 815 LD 548 Grn 262
May 2014 result C 1545 UKIP 683 Lab 463 LD 282 Grn 135
May 2012 result C 1425 LD 1111 Lab 372 Grn 127
May 2011 result C 2005 LD 821 Lab 695
May 2010 result C 2958 LD 1686 Lab 863
May 2008 result C 1819 LD 1537 Lab 172
May 2007 result C 1884 LD 822 Lab 272 UKIP 158
May 2006 result C 1962 LD 1256 Lab 215
June 2004 result LD 1704 C 1650 Lab 247
May 2003 result C 1506 LD 1287 Lab 269
May 2002 result C 1511/1465/1367 LD 1246/1118/1001 Lab 386/329/307

Figure 201: Gloucester, Longlevens

Fair Oak and Horton Heath

Eastleigh council, Hampshire; caused by the death of Liberal Democrat councillor Roger Smith at the age of 72. A long-serving member of Eastleigh council, serving from 1991 to 1995 and continuously since 2002, Smith was Mayor of Eastleigh in 2007/8.

For the first of our four by-elections in the Home Counties we are in rural Hampshire. Lying on the eastern edge of the Eastleigh built-up area in the shadow of the South Downs, Fair Oak took its name from a tree in the village square around which an annual fair was held. The village became a parish of its own in 1894; although its traditional industry was sand quarrying it now has a commuter demographic with high employment levels.

Eastleigh council is a Lib Dem stronghold as is this ward; although the Tories came very close to gaining Fair Oak in the 2015 local elections, by May this year the Lib Dem position had recovered to 39%, to 27% for the Tories and 22% for UKIP. The high UKIP score is influenced by the parliamentary by-election in early 2013, which UKIP nearly won, and in the county council elections a couple of months later the Kippers actually gained the local county council division (Bishopstoke and Fair Oak).

Defending for the Lib Dems is Nicholas Couldry. The Tories' Steven Broomfield is fighting his second Eastleigh by-election of the year, after losing in West End North (the ward he represented on Eastleigh council from 2003 to 2007) in February. UKIP's Hugh McGuinness, a Fair Oak and Horton Heath parish councillor, is making his twelfth attempt to be elected to Eastleigh council from

Parliamentary constituency: Eastleigh
Hampshire county council division: Bishopstoke and Fair Oak
May 2016 result LD 959 C 661 UKIP 547 Lab 279
May 2015 result LD 1728 C 1671 UKIP 1014 Lab 447
May 2014 result LD 1150 UKIP 780 C 634 Lab 244
May 2012 result LD 1087 C 504 Lab 291 UKIP 221
May 2011 result LD 1434 C 878 Lab 398 UKIP 261
May 2010 result LD 2737 C 1703 Lab 336 UKIP 273
May 2008 result LD 1274 C 887 UKIP 144 Lab 138
May 2007 result LD 1358 C 890 Lab 156 UKIP 149
May 2006 result LD 1053 C 903 Lab 168 UKIP 143
June 2004 result LD 1008 C 614 UKIP 365 Lab 212
May 2003 result LD 944 C 330 Lab 191 UKIP 148
May 2002 result LD 1208/1117/1116 C 611/522/496 Lab 190/183/182

Figure 202: Eastleigh, Fair Oak and Horton Heath

this ward—his best performance so far was second place in 2014. Completing the ballot paper is Labour's John Sorley, another Fair Oak and Horton Heath parish councillor.

Result: LD 828 C 553 UKIP 286 Lab 132

Hoxton West

Hackney council, North London; caused by the election of Labour councillor Philip Glanville as Mayor of Hackney in a by-election in September. He had served as a councillor since 2006.

For our London by-election this week we are in a fast-changing area of central London. We have heard much in recent decades about California's Silicon Valley; London has Silicon Roundabout, a road junction above Old Street underground station. The financial crash of 2008 led to office rents in this traditionally run-down area falling to the level where they became attractive to technology start-up companies, and since 2009 several tech firms have set up London offices here. The quick rise of what has become known as East London Tech City is too soon to be fully reflected by the 2011 census, and given the May government's immigration policy may well have been snuffed out by the time of the 2021 census; for what it's worth, Hoxton ward (the predecessor to this ward) in 2011 made several top 100 lists for England and Wales, including for Buddhism (1.76%), population born in the the EU-14 (7.8%), mixed-race ethnicity (6.9%), "other" ethnic groups (5.8%) and social renting (54% of households).

It's that last statistic that drives the area's local elections: this is a safe Labour

Parliamentary constituency: Hackney South and Stoke Newington
May 2014 result Lab 1693/1687/1634 Grn 602/487/448 C 362/339/326 LD 190/182/161
TUSC 136
May 2016 GLA results (excludes postal voters)
Mayor: Lab 1616 C 426 Grn 214 LD 100 Women's Equality 76 UKIP 56 Respect 33
Cannabis is Safer than Alcohol 24 Britain First 21 BNP 19 Zylinski 11 One Love 4
London Member: Lab 1431 C 345 Grn 328 LD 138 Women's Equality 136 UKIP 94
Respect 41 Britain First 26 Animal Welfare 25 CPA 23 BNP 17 House Party 17

Figure 203: Hackney, Hoxton West

ward. Hoxton West ward has only existed on these boundaries since 2014; its predecessor ward of Hoxton (2002–14) was equally safe Labour, but the Wenlock ward which existed here before 2002 was a Liberal and Lib Dem hotspot in the 1980s and 1990s. The Lib Dem vote in the ward has since disappeared and in 2014 (the only previous result on these boundaries) Labour led the Greens 57–20. In May's GLA elections Sadiq Khan crushed Zac Goldsmith here 62–16, while in the London Members ballot Labour led with 55% to 13% each for the Tories and Greens.

So Labour's defending candidate Yvonne Maxwell shouldn't lose too much sleep over this result; according to her Twitter she is a Socialist Feminist with 36 years of Labour party membership. The Green party candidate is Morgan James, and completing the ballot paper are former Hackney councillor Christopher Sills for the Conservatives and Chantal Encavey for the Lib Dems.

Result: Lab 951 C 185 LD 133 Grn 123

Kingswood with Burgh Heath

Reigate and Banstead council, Surrey; caused by the death of Conservative councillor Joan Spiers. First elected in 1984, Spiers was leader of Reigate and Banstead council from 2003 to 2007 and again from 2008 to 2014; after stepping down as leader she was Mayor of Reigate and Banstead in 2015/16.

Out of London now, but staying within the M25 motorway. There are a few Kingswoods around the UK; this is the Surrey one, located high up on the North Downs. Although Toyota has its UK offices here, Kingswood is the archetypal Surrey commuter village, with Kingswood railway station (on Southern's Tattenham Corner branch) connecting the ward to Croydon and London, and it has a demographic to match.

It also has election results to match. This is a safe Tory ward with little of interest in its previous results; in May the Conservatives beat UKIP here 67–22.

Parliamentary constituency: Reigate
Surrey county council division: Tadworth, Walton and Kingswood (Kingswood and Burgh
Heath); Merstham and Banstead South (Lower Kingswood); Banstead, Woodmansterne
and Chipstead (Perrotts Wood)
May 2016 result C 1174 UKIP 381 Lab 205
May 2015 result C 2695 UKIP 818 Grn 437
May 2014 result C 1194 UKIP 669 Grn 228
May 2012 result C 1115 UKIP 413 Lab 155
May 2011 result C 1745 UKIP 535
May 2010 result C 2489 LD 809 UKIP 431
May 2008 result C 1385 UKIP 291 Lab 137
May 2007 result C 1221 LD 254 UKIP 248
May 2006 result C 1299 UKIP 160 EDP 129
June 2004 result C 1156 UKIP 431 LD 208 Lab 141
May 2003 result C 785 UKIP 288 LD 160 Lab 98
May 2002 result C 1169 Lab 322
May 2000 result C 1047/1042/991 Lab 208

Figure 204: Reigate and Banstead, Kingswood with Burgh Heath

The ward is split between three Surrey county council divisions all of which are
safe Conservative.

Defending for the Conservatives is Rod Ashford, a professional photogra-
pher and designer, and also chairman of the Lower Kingswood Village Fete. The
UKIP candidate is former RAF air traffic controller Gerard Hever, and the ballot
paper is completed by Tony Robinson (no, not that one) for Labour and Shasha
Khan for the Green Party.

Result: C 839 UKIP 155 Lab 96 Grn 55

Rainham Central

Medway council, Kent; caused by the death of Conservative councillor Mike
O'Brien. A former Royal Navy radio supervisor and insurance broker, O'Brien
was first elected in 1976 to the former Gillingham borough council, becoming the
Conservative group leader in 1996 a year before the council was abolished. He was
also a Kent county councillor from 1977 to 1981, representing the former Gillingham
No 2 division. O'Brien returned to elected office in 2007 for the new Medway
council and had served in the council's cabinet since 2010, since 2013 as head of
children's services.

We finish this week in the Medway towns. A couple of weeks ago this column
covered a UKIP loss in the westernmost Medway town, Strood; this week we're

Parliamentary constituency: Gillingham and Rainham
May 2015 result C 4386/3473/3115 UKIP 1854 Lab 1405/1018/946 Grn 665 TUSC 165 Ind 92
May 2011 result C 2931/2538/2514 Lab 938/917/912 UKIP 412 LD 308/298/251 Grn 286
May 2007 result C 2353/2216/2204 LD 1081/905/818 Ind 1008/622 Lab 503/408/389 UKIP 310
May 2003 result C 1415/1357/1307 LD 1121/1109/1061 Lab 470/437/434 UKIP 167

Figure 205: Medway, Rainham Central

in the easternmost Medway town, Rainham. A sleepy village until the Chatham Main Line came in 1858, Rainham was incorporated into Gillingham in 1928, and most of the housing in Rainham Central ward—which runs south from Watling Street along the Maidstone Road—dates from the mid-twentieth century when the electrification of the railway led to a second housing boom.

Rainham Central was fairly close between the Tories and Lib Dems in 2003 but the Tories have pulled away from the field, helped by a large personal vote for the Gillingham and Rainham MP Rehman Chishti who still sits on Medway council for this ward. In 2015 the Tories polled 51% to 22% for UKIP and 16% for Labour.

Defending for the Tories is Jan Aldous. UKIP have selected Mark Mencattelli, who had a near-miss in Gillingham North ward last year. The Labour candidate is Simon Allen, a freelance journalist, and the ballot paper is completed by George Meegan for the Green Party, Paul Chaplin for the Lib Dems and Mike Russell for the English Democrats.

Result: C 1448 UKIP 389 Lab 320 LD 137 Grn 61 EDP 14

10th November 2016

Four by-elections on Thursday 10th November, all in London and the Home Counties:

Eltham North

Greenwich council, South London; caused by the resignation of Labour councillor Wynn Davies.

London by-election watchers have had to exist on a diet of predominantly safe Labour wards for much of this year, so it's refreshing to be able to talk about a couple of marginal wards for once. We start in Eltham (the H is silent), a district of London with royal connections since mediaeval times: the Plantagenet kings had a palace here. However, this ward is based on the garden-city Progress Estate, built entirely in 1915 by Woolwich Borough Council along the Well Hall Road; the reason for its construction at the height of the First World War was to provide accommodation for workers at the Woolwich Arsenal munitions factory, to which it was connected by a busy tram line along Well Hall Road. Unfortunately, Well Hall Road is notable these days not for the estate, but as the scene of the notorious Stephen Lawrence murder in 1993. The estate is still close to its original condition despite the construction through it of the A 2 Rochester Way Relief Road, built next to the Bexleyheath railway line and necessitating the construction of a new Eltham railway station to serve the ward. Also within the ward are the two halves of Eltham Park (bisected by the relief road) and the northern half of Eltham High Street. This is one of the parts of London least affected by its transformation into a world city, and its census statistics are unremarkable.

As stated, Eltham North is a marginal ward under current conditions; it returned a full slate of Tories throughout the Noughties (very comfortably in 2006) but although the Tories still topped the poll at the last borough elections in 2014 (32% Conservative, 31% Labour, 20% UKIP) thanks to a personal vote for

Parliamentary constituency: Eltham
May 2014 result C 1975/1823/1519 Lab 1946/1942/1556 UKIP 1221 Grn 591 BNP 307 LD 207/205
May 2010 result C 3078/2968/2774 Lab 2395/2338/2330 LD 1126/1073/816 BNP 686 Grn 625
May 2006 result C 2344/2164/2096 Lab 1220/1165/1084 LD 1083/1015/871 UKIP 634 Grn 584
Feb 2005 by-election C 1326 Lab 1252 LD 289 UKIP 193 Christian Peoples Alliance 20
May 2002 result C 1914/1893/1841 Lab 1537/1474/1400 LD 651/615/569 Socialist Alliance 134
May 2016 GLA results (excludes postal votes)
Mayor: C 1848 Lab 1462 UKIP 273 Grn 241 LD 208 Women's Equality 76 Britain First 57 Cannabis is Safer than Alcohol 36 Respect 31 BNP 20 Ind 9 One Love 5
London Members: C 1490 Lab 1348 UKIP 572 Grn 327 LD 243 Women's Equality Party 127 Britain First 73 Animal Welfare 57 BNP 32 Christian Peoples Alliance 29 Respect 27 House Party 15

Figure 206: Greenwich, Eltham North

long-serving councillor Spencer Drury, the seat count actually went 2–1 to Labour who were slightly better at getting their voters to follow the whole ticket. The Conservatives led here in May's London Assembly elections, with Zac Goldsmith beating Sadiq Khan 43–34 and the Tories carrying the London Members ballot with 34%, to 31% for Labour and 13% for UKIP.

So, this could be a rather difficult defence for Labour. Their candidate is Simon Peirce, who was on the Labour slate in 2014 but ran a long way behind his running-mates. The Tories' Charlie Davis must fancy his chances of a gain after contesting the hopeless Eltham West ward in 2014; just 22 years old, he works in financial services and is a keen rugby player. The UKIP candidate is Barbara Ray, who fought Kidbrooke with Hornfair ward in 2014. Also standing are Matt Browne, who was the Tory candidate in the last Greenwich by-election (in Glyndon ward in May) but now has the Green nomination, and Sam Macaulay for the Lib Dems.

Result: C 1335 Lab 1297 LD 279 UKIP 160 Grn 110 [C gain from Lab]

Queenstown

Wandsworth council, South London; caused by the death of Labour councillor Sally-Ann Ephson at the age of 49. A board member of the Sickle Cell Society, the disease from which she died, and described as a "wonderful councillor" and a "positive force for good", she had served since 2014.

Writing this column is usually a good way of doing quiz revision, but it doesn't always work that way. Last week this column wrote on the subject of Silicon Roundabout and the cluster of technology companies which has sprung up in the area; over the last weekend your columnist was in Athens at the Quiz Olympiad and the question came up "which major multinational company is consolidating all its London offices into the redeveloped Battersea Power Station?" Well, obviously it can't be Apple, I thought, at which point an inflatable pink pig flew past the window with your columnist's chances of winning the quiz attached to it. Oh dear.

The redevelopment of Battersea Power Station is only the latest phase of the gentrification that has transformed Queenstown ward out of all recognition. The ward runs along the south bank of the Thames from Battersea Park in the west to the New Covent Garden Market, the UK's largest market for wholesale fruit, vegetables and flowers, in the east. In between is Battersea Dogs and Cats Home, supplier of Chief Mousers to Whitehall, and the ward's population in between a tangle of railway viaducts along which a million people travel every day in and out of Victoria and Waterloo stations; transport is important to the local economy with a large bus garage and the Gatwick Express maintenance depot located in the ward, although the locomotive works at Nine Elms—once the terminus of the railway line to Southampton—are long gone, replaced by the market. Despite this, the only railway stations within the ward are the rather run down Battersea Park and Queenstown Road (Battersea), although the Power Station redevelopers are paying for a new Tube line to serve the area which should start construction in the new year.

Queenstown ward now has a middle-class demographic with over half the workforce educated to degree level, nearly half in management positions, high employment levels and low rates of owner-occupation—both social and private renting are high. The ward makes the top 100 for population born in the EU-14 states (8.7%).

It's a world away from how Battersea was a hundred years ago, when it was a working-class area noted for heavy industry—the Power Station is just the most notable survivor of the many major factories and waterworks which once lined the Thames here. The heavy industry led to unusually strong unionisation by London standards and radical politics to match: Battersea was the first borough to elect a black mayor (John Archer in 1913) and the inter-war Battersea North constituency, around half of which is now this ward, was one of very few constituencies to return a Communist to Parliament: the Indian Parsee Shapurji Saklatvala, who served from 1922 to 23 and again from 1924 to 29.

After the Second World War the Clean Air Act did for most of the heavy

Parliamentary constituency: Battersea
May 2014 result C 1773/1711/1678 Lab 1753/1665/1650 Grn 401/385/306 UKIP 313 LD 237/151
May 2010 result C 2894/2888/2781 Lab 2385/2327/2133 LD 1113/886/751 Grn 562/490
May 2006 result C 1793/1769/1666 Lab 1362/1346/1336 Grn 586 Ind 320
May 2002 result C 1390/1362/1279 Lab 1194/1128/1112 LD 239
May 2016 GLA results (excludes postal voters)
Mayor: Lab 1574 C 1260 Grn 240 LD 150 Women's Equality 97 UKIP 67 Respect 41 Britain First 40 Cannabis is Safer than Alcohol 35 Ind 18 BNP 16 One Love 2
London Members: Lab 1382 C 1140 Grn 326 LD 209 Women's Equality 176 UKIP 119 Britain First 53 Respect 48 Christian Peoples Alliance 36 Animal Welfare 35 BNP 14 House Party 10

Figure 207: Wandsworth, Queenstown

industry in Battersea, and new council estates—notably the Patmore Estate—were built to replace some particularly dilapidated slums. The end of heavy industry here led to the ward (which has existed since the creation of the modern Wandsworth borough in 1964) becoming depopulated and taking in some more-Tory-voting areas. John O'Farrell described the Tory gain of Queenstown in 1990 in his book *Things Can Only Get Better*, and by the end of 1990s, even though the Blair landslide had given Wandsworth a full slate of Labour MPs, Wandsworth council had a large Tory majority thanks to its administration's unbelievably-low-council-tax policies.

Some favourable boundary changes in 2002 have enabled Labour to keep this ward marginal, but it took until 2014 for them to regain a seat in Queenstown ward; in that year the Tory slate topped the poll 40–39. Labour will take encouragement from the GLA results in May, in which Khan beat Goldsmith here 44–36 and Labour carried the London Members ballot with 39%, to 32% for the Tories and 9% for the Greens. However, as explained above, the Tory administration tends to outperform in Wandsworth council elections compared to other levels.

Defending this difficult ward for Labour is Aydin Osborne Dikerdem, who despite his Turkish name was born and bred in Battersea; he is only 26 but already has the distinction of having been attacked by the *Daily Telegraph* for getting a motion passed earlier this year to limit voting rights at Oxford University Labour Club. The Tories want their seat back, and have selected Rhodri Morgan who is not to be confused with the former First Minister of Wales of that name. Completing the ballot paper are Stella Baker for the Greens and Richard Davis for the Lib Dems.

Result: Lab 1551 C 987 LD 249 Grn 122

Parliamentary constituency: Horsham
West Sussex county council division: Southwater and Nuthurst
May 2015 result C 2583/2442/2347 LD 1233/743 UKIP 1099/946 Ind 814 Grn 801 Lab 690
May 2011 result C 1857/1806/1721 LD 1073/834/666 UKIP 495
May 2007 result C 1575/1433/1405 LD 1312/1265/1195
May 2003 result LD 1232/1227/1205 C 971/966/938 Lab 179

Figure 208: Horsham, Southwater

Southwater

Horsham council, West Sussex; caused by the death of Conservative councillor Ian Howard. A former cabinet member on Horsham council, he had served since 2007.

Moving out of London we come to Southwater, a large village just south of Horsham which has been almost entirely developed since 1970 and is still growing strongly. Although the village's traditional industry was brickmaking, the brickworks are now housing and the area has a commuter demographic. However, Southwater's census stats are a little difficult to interpret because the ward also includes the large boarding school of Christ's Hospital, which apparently is important enough to merit its own railway station on the Arun Valley line. The presence of the boarders means that Southwater is in the top 100 wards in England and Wales for 16- and 17-year-olds (5.1%) and those educated to GCSE level (21% of the workforce, which for the purposes of the census includes everybody aged 16 or over).

Like many fast-growing village-based wards, this ward is trending towards the Conservatives; it voted Lib Dem in 2003 but the Conservative slate gained Southwater in 2007, and by 2015 the Conservatives were well ahead with 36%, to 17% for the Liberal Democrats, 15% for UKIP and 11% for an independent candidate. The local county division (Southwater and Nuthurst) is also Conservative-held, although UKIP came close at the most recent West Sussex county elections in 2013.

Defending for the Tories is Billy Greening, a Southwater parish councillor and (judging from his Twitter) diehard Brighton and Hove Albion fan; he works for a private prison company. The Lib Dem candidate is Richard Greenwood, a charity worker presently working for the Jesuits. UKIP have selected Uri Baran, who works for a large IT company. The independent candidate from 2015 is not standing again, so Labour's Kevin O'Sullivan completes the ballot paper.

Result: C 1046 LD 308 Lab 118 UKIP 109

Parliamentary constituency: Hitchin and Harpenden
Hertfordshire county council division: Hitchin North
May 2016 result Lab 505 C 328 Grn 102 LD 89
May 2014 result Lab 450 UKIP 278 C 252 Grn 89 LD 55
Sept 2013 by-election Lab 361 C 180 UKIP 148 Grn 32 LD 31
May 2012 result Lab 638 C 258 Grn 103 LD 50
May 2010 result Lab 888 C 795 LD 461 Grn 138
May 2008 result Lab 640 C 410 LD 108 Grn 99
May 2007 result Lab 643/636 C 326/322 LD 124 Grn 119/89

Figure 209: North Hertfordshire, Hitchin Oughton

Hitchin Oughton

North Hertfordshire council; caused by the resignation of Labour councillor Simon Watson after less than five months in office. He had served since May.

We finish this week north of London in Hitchin. The Oughton ward, named after the river which forms its north-western boundary, is Hitchin's north-western ward and is essentially a small council estate off the Bedford road with few points of interest. It is the safest Labour ward in Hitchin, the party beating the Tories 49–32 in May, and also forms part of the Labour-held Hitchin North county council division.

Labour are taking no chances in defending this by-election by selecting Martin Stears-Handscomb, who represented this ward on North Hertfordshire council from 1979 to 1988 and again from 1998 to 2000, transferring in 2000 to Hitchin Bearton ward which he represented until losing his seat in 2010; he retires as an accountant this month and has previously worked as a teacher, an IT researcher and a bus driver. The Tory candidate is Serena Farrow, who according to her Twitter is a BBC journalist, author, business/social networker and fairground owner. Completing the ballot paper are George Howe for the Green Party, Louise Peace for the Lib Dems and independent candidate Jackie McDonald.

Result: Lab 258 Ind 200 C 158 LD 150 Grn 42

17th November 2016

Four by-elections on Thursday 17th November 2016:

Abbey

Bath and North East Somerset council; caused by the resignation of Green Party councillor Jonathan Carr who is moving away from the city. He had served since 2015.

Not many wards in the UK can lay claim to two World Heritage Sites, but Bath's Abbey ward can. This is the centre of the city of Bath, originally a city known as *Aquae Sulis* and founded by the Romans, who built a bath complex around a hot spring which is still well-preserved today. With the withdrawal of the Romans from Britain a monastery was founded—by St David, according to legend, but by King Osric of Hwicce in 675 according to records. The church was rebuilt in 781 by King Offa of Mercia, and was the location for the first modern English coronation—of King Edgar in 973; the modern church dates from the sixteenth century, survived the dissolution of the monasteries to become the city's parish church and was extensively restored in Victorian times by Sir George Gilbert Scott, who installed fan vaulting above the nave.

However, the true beauty of Bath's architecture comes not from the Abbey but from the Georgian period, in which the city as we know it was developed in the golden Bath stone as a spa town fashionable with the upper classes thanks to a lively social circle presided over by MC Richard "Beau" Nash. Many of the features of the modern Abbey ward, such as the Pump Rooms, the Assembly Rooms, the Circus and the Pulteney Bridge, date from this period, as do literature set in the city such as Jane Austen's *Northanger Abbey* and *Persuasion* and Sheridan's *The Rivals*. One recent and rather controversial addition to the city is the Thermae Bath Spa, a modern building in which people can "take the waters" in much the same way as the Romans and Georgians did. At the south end of the ward lies Bath Spa railway station, home to the ward's other World Heritage

Parliamentary constituency: Bath
May 2015 result C 1158/985 Grn 1071 LD 798/741 Lab 639 Ind 148
May 2011 result LD 773/662 C 716/646 Grn 436 Lab 323
May 2007 result C 728/661 LD 633/621 Grn 345 Ind 225
May 2003 result C 680/613 LD 587/561 Ind 166/82

Figure 210: Bath and North East Somerset, Abbey

Site—the Great Western Railway—while over the Pulteney Bridge can be found the Recreation Ground, home to Bath's successful rugby union team.

Abbey ward makes the top 100 wards in England and Wales for private renting (46.5% of households) and Buddhism (1.7% of the population). It is a solidly middle-class ward dominated by students at the city's two universities; 51% of the workforce are educated to degree level and a further 17% are studying for one. Since students tend not to vote in local elections this translated during the Blair and Brown years into a Tory–Lib Dem marginal; the Conservatives won both seats in 2003 but lost one to the Lib Dems in 2011. The 2015 local elections being held at general election time brought the students out, and they gave a seat to the single Green Party candidate who gained the Lib Dem seat; vote shares were 31% for the Conservatives, 28% for the Greens, 21% for the Lib Dems and 17% for Labour, so with the Greens having a generally poor by-election record a number of parties will fancy their chances of making a gain here.

Defending for the Green Party is Vipul Patel, who is described as a local businessman. The Tory candidate is Lizzie Gladwyn, who works on Bath Spa University's outreach programme and is described as a community activist and campaigner on mental health issues. The Lib Dems have selected Gerry Curran, a long-serving former councillor who lost his seat in Twerton ward last year. Vicky Drew, described as a single working mother and passionate campaigner, is the Labour candidate. Also standing are independent candidate Jenny Knight, who came last here last year, and Marc Hooper for UKIP.

Result: C 350 LD 273 Grn 252 Lab 126 Ind 43 UKIP 23 [C gain from Grn]

Haldens

Welwyn Hatfield council, Hertfordshire; caused by the resignation of Conservative councillor Malcolm Spinks on health grounds. He had served only since May.

From an icon of history we move to Welwyn Garden City. Entirely built in the twentieth century, WGC was both a garden city (the second to be founded) and a New Town, and Haldens ward, located on the northern edge of town east of the railway line, is one of the New Town bits. It still has fairly high levels

Parliamentary constituency: Welwyn Hatfield
Hertfordshire county council division: Haldens
May 2016 result Lab 782/655/571 C 734/666/622 Grn 312 LD 246/168/117

Figure 211: Welwyn Hatfield, Haldens

of social renting, but WGC's strong economy means that employment is high; Haldens ward includes the head offices of Tesco and PayPoint and a major Roche Pharmaceuticals centre. One major local controversy is the future of Panshanger Aerodrome, just outside this ward, which is slated for substantial amounts of new housing.

The Local Government Boundary Commission seems to have trouble getting its head around Welwyn Hatfield council, with new ward boundaries being introduced in May this year to replace a set which came in only in 2008. This means that May's result isn't comparable to previous results for Haldens ward, although it's fair to say that former versions of the ward were Labour-inclined except for the period 2006–10 when the Conservatives won. By 2014 Labour had recovered all three seats for Haldens ward, but they held on by only 16 votes in 2015 and favourable boundary changes for this year's election (in which the ward gained territory from the safe Conservative Panshanger ward) meant that the Tories won two of the three seats for the new ward. Despite this, a personal vote for Labour's Mike Larkins meant that the Labour slate topped the poll (with 37%, to 36% for the Conservatives and 15% for the Greens). The Tories narrowly hold the Haldens county council seat, which is larger than this ward and includes more of Panshanger.

So, a key marginal ward for the Tories to defend. They have chosen Nathaniel Chapman, who fought WGC's Peartree ward in May. On the Labour side, former Welwyn Hatfield councillor Astrid Thorpe (Hollybush ward, 2014–16) is seeking to return to the council after losing her seat in May. The Green Party have reselected their candidate from May Lynne Allison, and Lib Dem Anthony Dennis completes the ballot paper.

Result: C 502 Lab 454 LD 437 Grn 81

Misterton

Harborough council, Leicestershire; caused by the resignation of Conservative councillor John Everett who is moving away from the area. A retired teacher who had also run a computer business, he had served since winning a by-election in March 2006 and was chairman of Harborough council in 2012–13.

Having covered this week's two urban by-elections we now turn to the two

Parliamentary constituency: South Leicestershire
Leicestershire county council division: Bruntingthorpe
May 2015 result C 1192 Lab 395
May 2011 result C 825 Lab 242
May 2007 result C unopposed
March 2006 by-election C 425 LD 266 Lab 47
May 2003 result C 556 Lab 190

Figure 212: Harborough, Misterton

rural by-elections. Our English rural by-election this week is in Leicestershire, covering seven parishes to the north-east, east and south of Lutterworth. Despite the ward name, the largest parish within the ward is Gilmorton, north-east of Lutterworth; Misterton isn't even the largest village in its own parish, dwarfed by the neighbouring Walcote. The most notorious location within the ward is probably Catthorpe which gives its name to a major road junction—now in the final throes of reconstruction—at which the M 1, M 6 and A 14 roads meet. The good motorway links attract some commuters to Leicester and other Midlands cities, and give the ward a middle-class demographic.

Misterton ward's politics are true blue. Everett was unopposed at his first re-election in 2007 and in 2015 he beat Labour 75–25 in a straight fight. The local county division (Bruntingthorpe) is also safely Conservative.

Defending for the Tories is Jonathan Bateman, a Broughton Astley parish councillor. Labour have reselected Liz Marsh, a teacher and vice-chair of Misterton with Walcote parish council. Also standing are Bill Piper for UKIP and Martin Sarfas for the Lib Dems.

Result: C 257 Lab 119 LD 77 UKIP 57

Annandale North

Dumfries and Galloway council; caused by the resignation of Graeme Tait who had been elected as a Conservative councillor but had defected to Labour. He had served since winning a by-election in November 2012; his resignation came in order to concentrate on his career, but he had not attended a council meeting since April and was about to be disqualified under the six-month non-attendance rule.

For our second rural by-election of the week we are in Scotland. The Annandale North ward covers a large chunk of the Scottish borderland, from Lockerbie in the south to Moffat in the north. Lockerbie will forever be associated with the bombing of Pan Am Flight 103 just before Christmas 1988, but it deserves to be remembered for more than that. Essentially an eighteenth-century planned settlement on the road from Glasgow to London, the town was once the location of Scotland's largest lamb market and was home to the Marquesses of Queensberry, whose legacy is the standard rules for boxing. Further up Annandale on the long climb towards Beattock Summit is Moffat, another former wooltrade centre which was also known as a spa town and for toffee, while other settlements within the ward include Beattock, Wamphray and Lochmaben.

Upper Annandale is dominated politically by the Mundell family, who live in the area. David Mundell, a local lad and postgraduate student, was elected in 1984 as an SDP candidate to the former Annandale and Eskdale district council, defeating independent councillor Sir William Jardine in Dryfe ward, and was then elected in 1986 to Dumfries and Galloway regional council from Mid Annandale. After standing down from both councils, he returned to politics in 1999 being elected as a Conservative member of the Scottish Parliament, transferring to Westminster in 2005 as MP for Dumfriesshire, Clydesdale and Tweeddale. Since 2005 Mundell has been the only Conservative MP in Scotland, from 2015 onwards he has sat in the Cabinet as Scottish secretary, and in 2016 he became the first Conservative cabinet minister to come out as gay. Mundell has passed on his passion for politics to his son Oliver, who represents the ward as part of the Dumfriesshire constituency in the Scottish Parliament.

This is no mean feat in the face of the recent SNP surge in Scotland, and reflects the fact that upper Annandale is a very Tory area. In the 2003 elections—under the old first-past-the-post system—the Tories carried both Lockerbie wards and Moffat with Lochmaben voting Lib Dem. In 2007 under PR the Tories tried to defend their three seats but lost their third seat to Labour and were rather fortunate to hold on to two, the second Tory candidate finishing just 25 votes ahead of independent candidate Billy Lockhart who had picked up transfers from a second independent and the SNP, but not quite enough transfers to win. There was another narrow result in May 2012 in which the Lib Dem vote collapsed and their seat went to the SNP, but the SNP finished only 41 votes ahead of the Green Party candidate Alis Ballance, with 34 Tory surplus votes still to transfer which meant the real margin was even closer; shares of the vote were 40% for the Conservatives, 20% for Labour, 17% for the SNP and 14% for the Greens.

The Labour councillor for Annandale North died shortly afterwards, after being suddenly taken ill during a council meeting, and a by-election was held in November 2012 which resulted in an easy Tory gain, the first preferences splitting 46% Conservative, 25% Labour and 12% Green Party and the Tories reaching 50% before the Greens were eliminated. As stated, the by-election winner Graeme Tait has since defected to Labour as part of a general split in the Conservative

Parliamentary constituency: Dumfriesshire, Clydesdale and Tweeddale (almost all)
Holyrood constituency: Dumfriesshire
Nov 2012 by-election C 1819 Lab 1002 Grn 464 SNP 371 LD 208 UKIP 89; after transfers C 1980 Lab 1149 Grn 617
May 2012 first preferences C 1747 Lab 845 SNP 724 Grn 615 LD 383
May 2007 first preferences C 2039 Lab 717 LD 749 SNP 710 Ind 547 Ind 446 Grn 159

Figure 213: Dumfries and Galloway, Annandale North

group which has brought down the Tory–SNP coalition formed in 2012; the present administration is a coalition of Labour and independent councillors.

Defending for Labour is 20-year-old Adam Wilson, an Edinburgh University student from Lochmaben. The Tories want their seat back and have selected Douglas Fairbairn. The Green Party candidate is Chris Ballance, a former MSP (South of Scotland, 2003–07) and award-winning playwright. Completing the ballot paper is Sylvia Moffat, of Moffat, a Moffat and District community councillor, standing for the SNP.

Result: C 2041 SNP 749 Lab 611 Grn 152

24th November 2016

There are eight by-elections on 24th November 2016. Nine were scheduled, but a by-election to St Edmundsbury council in Suffolk has returned a Conservative unopposed. Here are the other eight polls, with four Labour defences, one Liberal Democrat and three Conservative; we start with a couple of areas in the North of England which readers with short memories might notice have featured in this column very recently, and one of which may be cursed...

Castle

Carlisle council, Cumbria; caused by the resignation of Labour councillor Barrie Osgood, who has been prosecuted for benefit fraud and sentenced to 180 hours of unpaid community work. He had served on Carlisle council since 2015; the fraud occurred before he became a councillor.

It's worth saying a few things to start this week about the Cursing Stone, installed in 2001 in a pedestrian subway in Carlisle city centre and inscribed with a 1,069-word curse placed on border reivers in 1525 by Gavin Dunbar, archbishop of Glasgow. Now let's look at what has happened to Carlisle since then. In the year the Stone was installed the farms of Cumberland were devastated by foot-and-mouth disease. The city has suffered a series of devastating floods, in 2005 and the Storm Desmond flood of 2015, which took out the McVitie's factory and led to a national biscuit shortage which lasted for months. The Cursing Stone has taken the blame for a series of well-publicised crimes, hits to the local economy and even Carlisle United's relegation from the football league in 2004.

After the 2005 flood Jim Tootle, city and county councillor for Castle ward which covers the Cursing Stone, proposed to the city council that it be removed or destroyed to prevent any further nasty things happening. The council voted to keep it. Seven years later Tootle was dead at the age of 59, and since then a series of other councillors for Castle ward have died at an early age or resigned. Since the Cursing Stone was installed, Carlisle's Castle ward has had a horrific

Parliamentary constituency: Carlisle
Cumbria county council division: Castle (almost all), Botcherby (small part), Currock (small part), Denton Holme (small part)
Sept 2016 by-election Lab 398 C 228 UKIP 107 LD 88 Grn 34
May 2016 result Lab 544 C 258 UKIP 150 LD 89 Grn 50
May 2015 result Lab 940 C 671 UKIP 343 Grn 193 LD 145 TUSC 43
Sept 2014 by-election Lab 364 C 212 UKIP 208 LD 121 Grn 42
May 2014 result Lab 435 UKIP 267 C 221 LD 127 Grn 87 TUSC 28
May 2012 result Lab 663 LD 229 C 165 Grn 110
March 2012 county council by-election Lab 407 LD 369 C 93 Grn 54 UKIP 22
May 2011 result Lab 549 LD 438 Grn 135 TUSC 90 BNP 84
May 2010 result LD 816 Lab 802 C 553 Grn 161
June 2009 county council result LD 424 Lab 297 C 241 Grn 144 BNP 129
March 2009 by-election LD 465 Lab 304 BNP 255 C 143 Grn 125
May 2008 result LD 562 Lab 299 C 206 Ind 202
May 2007 result LD 607 Lab 331 C 185
Feb 2007 county council by-election LD 653 Lab 222 C 117 Grn 29
May 2006 result LD 632 Lab 321 C 149 Ind 69
Nov 2005 by-election LD 538 Lab 370
May 2005 county council result LD 937 Lab 853 C 349
June 2004 result LD 917 Lab 541
May 2003 result LD 603 Lab 443
May 2002 result LD 549 Lab 373 C 195
June 2001 county council result LD 994 Lab 786 C 448
Apr 2001 by-election Lab 329 LD 294 C 258 Lib 67
May 2000 result LD 513 Lab 299 C 230
May 1999 result LD 695/669/657 Lab 362/341/340 C 224/218/215

Figure 214: Carlisle, Castle

councillor attrition rate: this is the ninth by-election here (either at city or county level) in fifteen years, and the previous one was only ten weeks ago.

Coincidence?

As stated, Castle is Carlisle's city centre ward, named after the Norman castle which was the scene of England's last military siege, which took place over Christmas 1745 thanks to Bonnie Prince Charlie's forces leaving a garrison here on their retreat back north. The army have not relinquished their hold on the castle—it is HQ Duke of Lancaster's Regiment—and are still here waiting for any future invasion from over the Border. To the castle's west side lie the Willow Holme and Newtown areas and the Cumberland Infirmary; to the north is flood plain leading down to the River Eden; and to the east is Carlisle city centre, all of which, apart from Citadel railway station, is within the ward, together with some Cumbria University buildings. Until 2013 the ward had the same boundaries as the Castle division of Cumbria county council and results for that division up to 2013 are included in Figure 214.

From 1999 to 2010 Castle was Carlisle's only reliable Lib Dem ward, voting for the party on every occasion except for a by-election in April 2001. The Coalition put paid to the Lib Dem vote here and Labour are now on a 9-poll winning streak here since 2011; in May they had 50% of the vote to 24% for the Conservatives and 14% for UKIP, and the last by-election in September didn't show much change from that (47% for Labour, 27% for the Tories and 13% for UKIP).

Defending a Carlisle by-election for the second time this year is Labour's Stephen Sidgwick, who contested the flooded-out Botcherby ward in January and had a very poor result, losing the seat to an independent candidate on a big swing. He should have an easier ride here. The Tory candidate is John North, a poet. UKIP have selected Michael Story, and the ballot paper is completed by the Lib Dems' David Wood and the Greens' Neil Boothman.

Result: Lab 350 C 194 UKIP 79 LD 51 Grn 36

Blakelaw

Newcastle upon Tyne council, Tyne and Wear; caused by the resignation of Labour councillor Ben Riley, who is taking up a teaching job in the Middle East. He had served since 2015.

Moving to Newcastle upon Tyne for another by-election in a ward which was at the polls just ten weeks ago. Lying in the west end of Newcastle, Blakelaw is a council estate ward with all the usual problems, mostly built after the Second World War and located within the A 1 Western Bypass.

Similarly to Carlisle Castle, this is a ward where the Coalition has taken the floor out of the Lib Dem vote; Blakelaw was solidly Lib Dem during the years they controlled Newcastle council, but the Lib Dems lost all three seats to Labour in the period 2010–12, and even lost second place to UKIP before regaining it in September's by-election. In May Labour beat UKIP 63–16; although the September by-election resulted in a large anti-Labour swing they still have a secure majority here, polling 42% to 27% for the Lib Dems and 18% for UKIP.

Defending for Labour is Oskar Avery, a member of Newcastle's Jewish community who fought this ward in 2007; he stood in May in the hopeless West Gosforth ward but should have a better chance here this time. The Lib Dems have reselected their candidate from September Ciaran Morrissey, a postgraduate student at Newcastle University and policy officer for the Lib Dems' youth wing. There is no UKIP candidate this time, so the ballot paper is completed by Gerry Langley for the Tories and John Gordon for the localist Newcastle upon Tyne

Parliamentary constituency: Newcastle upon Tyne Central
Sept 2016 by-election Lab 1004 LD 654 UKIP 443 C 190 Grn 105
May 2016 result Lab 1846 UKIP 470 LD 267 C 221 Grn 117
May 2015 result Lab 2549 UKIP 846 C 532 LD 428 Grn 244
May 2014 result Lab 1897 LD 485 C 308
May 2012 result Lab 1948 LD 615 C 199
May 2011 result Lab 1940 LD 1088 C 246
May 2010 result Lab 1814 LD 1588 C 456 BNP 430
May 2008 result LD 1396 Lab 855 C 295 BNP 270
May 2007 result LD 1511 Lab 1000 BNP 230 C 230
May 2006 result LD 1608 Lab 1219 C 239
June 2004 result LD 1504/1402/1358 Lab 1278/1074/1040 BNP 359 Ind 318 C 298/297/290

Figure 215: Newcastle upon Tyne, Blakelaw

Community First Party.

    Result: Lab 892 LD 784 Newcastle upon Tyne Community First Party 164 C 148

Reedley

Pendle council, Lancashire; caused by the resignation of Labour councillor Robert Allen. He had served since 2011.

For our third by-election this week we are in Reedley Hallows—not the location for the latest film in the *Harry Potter* universe, but one of the small Pendle towns which merge into each other seamlessly. Reedley is located immediately to the north of Burnley, sandwiched between Burnley and Brierfield, and Reedley ward contains a substantial part of Brierfield together with Nelson's golf course. The ward is rather socially divided with the unusual combination of a large Asian population (mostly Pakistani) and high levels of owner-occupation; it just sneaks into the top 100 Muslim wards in England and Wales with a Muslim population of 34%.

This social mix produces an interesting ward. During the Blair and Brown years it was safe Tory with a very low Labour vote; but in 2011 Robert Allen polled more than four times as many votes as he had three years earlier to gain the seat for Labour after many years of failed attempts. Since then Reedley has developed into a hard-fought key marginal ward where majorities are often low; in 2014 Labour won with a majority of 37 votes to complete a full slate of councillors, but the Tory fightback started in May as they gained a seat back from Labour by 45–40, a majority of 134 votes. The voters of Reedley ward can't be faulted for their commitment to democracy: the turnout here in May was 58%, impressively

Parliamentary constituency: Pendle
Lancashire county council division: Pendle West
May 2016 result C 1119 Lab 985 UKIP 186 LD 147 TUSC 30
May 2015 result Lab 1711 C 1348 TUSC 99
May 2014 result Lab 1170 C 1133 TUSC 64 LD 49
May 2012 result Lab 1034 C 917 LD 181
May 2011 result Lab 1218 C 1062
May 2010 result C 1492 Lab 839 LD 699
May 2008 result C 1250 Lab 285 LD 224
May 2007 result C 1222 Lab 380 LD 320
May 2006 double vacancy C 1120/1027 LD 554/375 Lab 322
June 2004 result C 1204 Lab 547 LD 442
May 2003 result C 913 Lab 544 LD 251
May 2002 result C 1255/1155/107 Lab 681/599/559 LD 258/215/198

Figure 216: Pendle, Reedley

high for a local election. At county level this ward is presently part of the safe
Tory Pendle West division, although boundary changes next year will transfer
part of it to Pendle Central division. Pendle council is presently hung; the Tories
are the largest party but the administration is a Labour–Lib Dem coalition with
a secure majority.

This by-election pits two former councillors against each other. Defending
in the red corner is Mohammad Hanif, who gained the ward from the Tories in
2012 but lost his seat in May; he is looking to make a quick return to the council.
Challenging in the blue corner is Pauline McCormick, a former Mayor of Pendle
(2002–03) who was first elected to the council in 1986 and served Reedley ward
from 1992 until losing her seat in 2014. The Lib Dem candidate James Wood
completes the ballot paper.

Result: C 1267 Lab 1156 LD 57 [C gain from Lab]

Warsop Carrs

*Mansfield council, Nottinghamshire; caused by the death of Labour councillor
Peter Crawford at the age of 71. He was first elected in 2007 for the former
Birklands ward and transferred to this ward following boundary changes in 2011.*

For the week's Midlands by-election we are in the Nottinghamshire coalfield. Warsop Carrs is the north-western of the four wards covering the parish of
Warsop, an old mining area on the A 60 Mansfield–Worksop road: Carrs ward
includes the western part of Market Warsop and the villages of Church Warsop
and Warsop Vale. Warsop Vale was the location of a major colliery, Warsop Main;

Parliamentary constituency: Mansfield
Nottinghamshire county council division: Warsop
May 2015 result Lab 1069 Mansfield Ind Forum 391
May 2011 result Lab 608 Mansfield Ind Forum 152 LD 57

Figure 217: Mansfield, Warsop Carrs

although the church in Church Warsop is Norman, the village is of very recent vintage, having been built in the 1930s by the Staveley Coal and Iron Company as accommodation for colliery workers. The coalmining legacy has left a very white British population with low qualification levels and high rates of long-term sickness. Unemployment rates are not particularly high, although this may partly be due to the largest local employer being the notorious Sports Direct warehouse in Shirebrook, just over the Derbyshire boundary, it's no surprise to find that the ward's economic profile is determinedly working-class.

Warsop is the part of Mansfield least affected by the district's takeover by the pro-mayoral slate Mansfield Independent Forum; before 2011 the area was part of Meden ward which had a full slate of Labour councillors, and Warsop Carrs ward has followed suit since its creation. In the 2015 election Labour beat the Forum 73–27 in a straight fight.

Defending for Labour is Andrew Burgin. The Mansfield Independent Forum have not nominated a candidate this time, but there is an independent candidate on the ballot paper, Debra Barlow, who received a double lung transplant last year and now campaigns for organ donation. Also standing are Raymond Forster for UKIP and Daniel Redfern for the Conservatives.

Result: Lab 285 Ind 211 UKIP 74 C 25

Valley

Tandridge council, Surrey; caused by the resignation of Liberal Democrat councillor Jill Caudle, who is moving away from the area to be closer to her family. She had served since 2000.

Tandridge council has had a rash of by-elections recently—this is the third poll in the district since July. The Valley referred to here is Caterham Valley, a dry valley in the North Downs. Caterham boomed in Victorian times as a result of the railway arriving in 1859; the present Valley ward runs from the railway station northwards along the valley to the Croydon Road Roundabout, at which the A22 Caterham Bypass ends. The ward has a commuter demographic with high full-time employment levels.

Despite this, Valley ward is far from being a lock for the Conservatives. The ward's boundaries are unchanged since 1976, so we can trace its election results over an unusually long time. During the Thatcher years Valley was a close Tory versus Labour battle, but Labour only won it twice, in 1984 (by one vote) and 1988—both years when there was no Alliance candidate. The collapse of the Tory vote during the latter Major years turned the ward into a Labour-inclined three-way marginal, the Lib Dems' Jill Caudle finally breaking through in 2000 when both seats were up. Caudle quickly developed a personal vote which led to some yo-yoing in the ward's election results through the Noughties. The remaining Labour councillor was re-elected in 2004, but after that their vote here collapsed and Valley ward was a very easy Tory gain in 2008. The Tories, however, lost their seat in May to the Lib Dems who now held both seats in the ward for the first time: shares of the vote were 39% for the Lib Dems, 24% for the Conservatives, 15% for UKIP and 13% for Labour. The Tories are in better shape at county level, in which this ward is part of the safe Conservative Caterham Valley division.

Defending for the Lib Dems is Dorinda Cooper, described as a young and energetic community campaigner. The Conservatives have selected Paul Shipway. Regular UKIP candidate Jeffrey Bolter returns to the fray: a former Metropolitan Police officer and Police Federation rep, he fought Wells in the 2015 general election and Croydon South in 2010. Completing the ballot paper is Labour's Mark Wood.

Result: LD 444 C 215 UKIP 145 Lab 57

Tadley South

Basingstoke and Deane council, Hampshire; caused by the death of Conservative councillor Rob Musson at the age of 63. A successful businessman and well-respected community figure, he had served since 2007.

Located just south of the Hampshire/Berkshire boundary, Tadley is one of those villages that has grown into the size of a town without anybody particularly noticing. The spur for this was the development after the Second World War of the Atomic Weapons Research Establishment at Aldermaston, just over the county boundary in Berkshire, and Tadley boomed in the 1950s and 1960s to provide accommodation for the AWRE's workers and their families. Facilities have been slower to arrive and transport links to the nearest large towns—Basingstoke, Reading and Newbury—are relatively poor.

Tadley South is a safe Conservative ward with few points of interest—in May the Tories beat the Lib Dems here 63–21. However, the Tories did lose the local county council seat (Tadley and Baughurst) to the Lib Dems in 2013 and will be

Parliamentary constituency: East Surrey
Surrey county council division: Caterham Valley
May 2016 result LD 428 C 265 UKIP 163 Lab 143 Ind 107
May 2015 result LD 725 C 701 UKIP 358 Lab 289
May 2012 result C 399 LD 294 UKIP 131 Lab 93 Grn 82
May 2011 result LD 528 C 469 UKIP 174 Lab 160
May 2008 result C 415 Ind 315 LD 222 UKIP 111 Lab 45
May 2007 result LD 581 C 309 UKIP 89 Lab 69
June 2004 result Lab 413 LD 383 C 340 UKIP 133
May 2003 result LD 554 C 269 Lab 231
May 2000 result Lab 436/364 LD 402/369 C 352/347
May 1999 result Lab 515 LD 464 C 404
May 1996 result Lab 486 LD 466 C 379
May 1995 result Lab 641 LD 554 C 317
May 1992 result C 520 LD 474 Lab 449
May 1991 result C 587 Lab 487 LD 424
May 1988 result Lab 749 C 580
May 1987 result C 701 Lab 427 All 321
May 1984 result Lab 628 C 627
May 1983 result C 694 Lab 470 All 272
May 1980 result C 631 Lab 512 Lib 199
May 1979 result C 1399 Lab 764
May 1976 result C 807/746 Lab 396/346

Figure 218: Tandridge, Valley

Parliamentary constituency: North West Hampshire
Hampshire county council division: Tadley and Baughurst
May 2016 result C 824 LD 268 Lab 215
May 2015 result C 1787 LD 674 Lab 454
May 2012 result C 685 LD 231 Lab 195
May 2011 result C 1084 Lab 306 LD 300 UKIP 141
May 2008 result C 1048/928 LD 371 Lab 167

Figure 219: Basingstoke and Deane, Tadley South

looking for a good performance here to set down a marker ahead of next May's county council elections.

Defending for the Conservatives is Kerri Carruthers. The Liberal Democrat candidate is Jo Slimin; she is a former Basingstoke and Deane councillor (Tadley North ward, 2002–03) and has served on Tadley town council since 1983. Completing the ballot paper are Claire Ballard for Labour and Phil Heath for UKIP.

Result: C 456 LD 342 Lab 88 UKIP 41

Sovereign

Eastbourne council, East Sussex; caused by the resignation of Conservative council-lor Ray Blakebrough due to work commitments. He had served since 2015.

Having started in Carlisle and gradually worked our way south, we have finally reached the south coast. Sovereign is Eastbourne's easternmost ward but is probably not what you expected Eastbourne to be. The ward is based on a very new and very large marina development around Sovereign Harbour, which claims to be the largest composite marina complex in northern Europe; much of the ward's housing has been built since 2000 and its population is still growing strongly. Despite this, Sovereign ward does share some of the typical economic indicators of Eastbourne including a relatively old age profile and high levels of private renting.

While at local level Eastbourne is a Tory versus Lib Dem battle Sovereign is one of the Tory-inclined wards (the Lib Dems have won it only once, in 2007) and its growing population is trending it more towards the Conservatives over time. In 2015 the Tory slate here won with 41% to 25% for the Lib Dems and 21% for UKIP. The ward has the same boundaries as the Sovereign division of East Sussex county council, which in 2013 the Tories narrowly held with 39%, to 34% for UKIP and 19% for the Lib Dems. There are no implications for control of the borough council, which despite the loss of the parliamentary seat in 2015 has a large Lib Dem majority.

Defending for the Tories in this maritime-inclined ward is Paul Metcalfe, who has recently retired as manager of the Eastbourne lifeboat station which is in this ward. The Lib Dem candidate is Roger Howarth, who works for Age Concern and is treasurer of Eastbourne Lib Dems. Surprisingly there is no UKIP candidate, so the ballot paper is completed by Labour's Louis Thorburn.

Result: C 1276 LD 528 Lab 152

Turn Hill

South Somerset council; caused by the resignation of Conservative councillor Shane Pledger. A builder and stonemason, he had served since 2011.

Saving the best till last, we are in Somerset for the most crucial by-election of the week. Turn Hill ward is a rural area covering four-and-a-half parishes to the west of Somerton, none of which are called Turn Hill. The largest parish within the ward is High Ham, known as the location of England's only remaining thatched windmill (Stembridge Tower Mill) and as the birthplace of the former *Counterpoint* host Ned Sherrin; however, the ward's largest village is Long Sutton

Parliamentary constituency: Eastbourne
East Sussex county council division: Sovereign
May 2015 result C 2707/2366/2219 LD 1684/1360/1287 UKIP 1395/1081/984 Lab 514/463/437 Grn 321
May 2013 county council result C 1086 UKIP 930 LD 531 Lab 222
May 2011 result C 1904/1767/1745 LD 1193/1169/1106 Grn 488 Lab 359
June 2009 county council result C 1184 LD 989 Ind 809 UKIP 343 Grn 117 Lab 68
May 2007 result LD 1762/1756/1692 C 1379/1298/1294 Grn 269 Lab 121
May 2006 result C 1597 LD 914 Grn 181 Lab 125
May 2005 county council result C 2220 LD 2007 Grn 320
June 2004 result C 1517 LD 806 Grn 229
May 2003 result C 1255 LD 1040
May 2002 result C 1001/970/925 LD 648/638/632 Ind 175 Lab 172 Grn 124

Figure 220: Eastbourne, Sovereign

Parliamentary constituency: Somerton and Frome
Somerset county council division: Curry Rivel and Langport (part: Aller, High Ham and Pitney parishes and part of Huish Episcopi parish); Somerton (part: Long Sutton parish)
May 2015 result C 1071 LD 635 Lab 142
May 2011 result C 744 LD 516
May 2007 result Ind 637 Ind 445
May 2003 result Ind unopposed

Figure 221: South Somerset, Turn Hill

which has given the world Huntley and Palmer biscuits (George Palmer was from Long Sutton) and in latter years was the home of one of the victims of the Great Celebrity Purge of 2016, *Yes Minister* co-writer Sir Antony Jay.

Turn Hill was a fight between independent candidates in the 2000s, but party politics broke out in the 2011 election upon the retirement of independent councillor Rupert Cox: Pledger won 59–41 in a straight fight with the Lib Dems and increased his majority to 58–34 in the 2015 election. The ward is split between two county council divisions (Curry Rivel and Langport, and Somerton) both of which were safely Conservative in the 2013 county elections.

This might suggest that the Conservatives are favoured to hold this seat, but the Lib Dems will definitely have their eye on it: they held the local parliamentary seat until 2015 and are still the largest party on South Somerset council with 30 out of 60 seats. As can be seen, a Lib Dem gain in this by-election will give the party an overall majority on the council.

Like John Humphreys says on *Mastermind*, there's everything to play for so let's get on with it. Defending for the Conservatives is Gerard Tucker, president of the Langport and Somerton Rotary club and the only candidate to give an address within the ward (in Aller). The Lib Dem candidate is Julia Gadd, a Langport town councillor who stood here in 2011. Completing the ballot paper is Sean Dromgoole for Labour.

Result: C 452 LD 354 Lab 74

Monday 28th November 2016

One Monday by-election on 28 November 2016:

Arbroath East and Lunan

Angus council; caused by the resignation of Independent councillor Bob Spink on health grounds. He had served since 2003 after retiring from the family firm R R Spink and Sons, manufacturers of Arbroath smokies.

Monday by-elections don't come around very often, but this is the first of two Monday polls to Angus council in consecutive weeks, with Carnoustie on the bill next week. Apparently the reason for this Monday poll was to take advantage of a school holiday in Angus today.

This week we are in the eastern of the two wards covering Arbroath, a mediaeval town developed at the mouth of the River Brothock around Arbroath Abbey, a late twelfth-century Tironensian foundation which is the final resting place of its founder, King William the Lion of Scots. The Scottish Parliament met at Arbroath Abbey in 1320 and composed the Declaration of Arbroath, a letter written to Pope John XXII attempting to sort out a dispute which had seen King Robert the Bruce excommunicated and, along the way, asserting the independence of Scotland. Following the dissolution of the Abbey Arbroath stagnated until the Industrial Revolution, when it became a major fishing port and textile centre, specialising in jute and sailcloth. Much of that industry is now gone (although some fish are still landed here) and today many people from Arbroath commute to Dundee along the recently-dualled A 92 road; the main local contributors to the economy are the military (45 Commando Royal Marines is based here), tourism and the notorious smokie. Arbroath's football team, although only in the fourth tier of the Scottish league system, attained immortality in 1885 by thrashing Bon Accord by the record score of 36–0 in a Scottish Cup tie.

Arbroath's election results aren't so one-sided as that. The Arbroath East

Parliamentary constituency: Angus
Scottish Parliament constituency: Angus South
May 2012 result SNP 1624 Ind 955 C 547 Lab 472 LD 109
May 2007 result SNP 1902 Ind 1322 C 789 Lab 677 LD 504

Figure 222: Angus, Arbroath East and Lunan

and Lunan ward covers the eastern half of the the town together with a rural hinterland to the north and east as far as the hamlet of Lunan on its namesake bay. Spink had first been elected in 2003 as an independent to the former Hayshead and Lunan ward, based on the hinterland, and was re-elected to this ward under PR in 2007 along with two SNP candidates and a Conservative. There was no change to the party representation in 2012 with the SNP polling 44% of the first preferences, to 26% for Spink (who topped the poll) and 15% for the Conservatives.

Two independent candidates have come forward to succeed Spink. Lois Speed describes herself as a "passionate believer in social inclusion, equality and fairness", while Kevin Smith is a former chairman of Arbroath community council and is used to pressure, having formerly been a deep sea diver and Royal Marine commando. No doubt Smith is feeling even more pressure than he expected in this campaign, as his wife Julie is the Tory election agent. The SNP will be hoping for a gain with their candidate Brenda Durno, a businesswoman who is hoping to follow her father, the late Alex Shand, onto Angus council. The Tories—although their election agent might be a little torn on the matter—are hoping that businessman and property developer Derek Wann is the one to win here; he led the Better Together campaign in Angus in the independence referendum and was the Tory candidate for Angus in the 2015 Westminster election. Completing the ballot paper are John Ruddy (of Montrose) for Labour and Richard Moore (a former York councillor now living in Forfar) for the Lib Dems.

    First preferences: SNP 919 C 709 Speed 452 Smith 309 Lab 177 LD 60
    Lab and LD eliminated: SNP 956 C 741 Speed 482 Smith 352
    Smith eliminated: SNP 1010 C 799 Speed 619
    Speed eliminated: SNP 1372 C 928 [SNP gain from Ind]

1st December 2016

Richmond Park

House of Commons; caused by the resignation of Conservative MP Zac Goldsmith in order to seek re-election. He had served since 2010.

We are cleared for takeoff in this by-election which Zac would dearly love you to think is all about Heathrow Airport. Perhaps it's worth starting by discussing the airport, for which it is proposed to build a third runway after decades of dithering over whether Heathrow, or Gatwick, or somewhere else in the generalised London area, should get a new runway. This, it is argued, will better connect London with the rest of the UK and world and generate a net positive for the economy.

It's unarguable that Heathrow has no spare capacity. The financial crash of 2008, despite depressing demand for airline travel around the world, made not a jot of difference to the airport's arrival and departure list. The major problems with expanding Heathrow are that its constrained site makes a third runway ruinously expensive without government help, and the position of its runways means that takeoffs and landings have to occur with noisy planes at low levels over west and central London. There's also the fact that public transport options for the airport are either ripoffs even by London standards (Heathrow Express, I'm looking at you) or timesinks. Unfortunately the alternative options for expanding Heathrow tend to have poor connections by road or public transport, be in the wrong place for the rest of the country necessitating a time-consuming journey around London (Gatwick, I'm looking at you), involve newbuild options which are prohibitively expensive (see the Maplin Sands proposal from the 1970s and the more recent kite of Boris Island) or all three. Another obvious problem with closing Heathrow is that it would take the floor out of the economic base for much of west London; the ONS recognised the airport's importance in 2015 by making it the hub for a statistical Travel to Work Area.

For someone looking at this from 200 miles away, the main questions which come to mind are, firstly, if you're going to plan ahead for the future, why build only one new runway in the London area when surely building more than one would futureproof London even more against future demand? Secondly, what sort of demand is it going to be? There's a lot of talk about the third Heathrow runway attracting new transfer passengers from Scotland and the North of England, people like your columnist. Your columnist, however, is used to the idea of flying from Manchester (which, incidentally, opened its second runway in 2001 and has plenty of spare capacity) to a transfer airport at Helsinki, Düsseldorf, Zürich, wherever on the continent is appropriate for an onward connection. The problem with Heathrow trying to attract transfer passengers is, first, that Heathrow's landing charges price that option out of the market (a problem which the cost of building the third runway is going to exacerbate); second, that BA are not interested in UK regional destinations (possibly for that reason); and, finally, that decades of horror travel stories make some people want to avoid transferring in London at all costs.

Anyway, that's my view on the Heathrow question and presumably the electors of Richmond Park have theirs. Richmond upon Thames, as a town, was founded by King Henry VII who built the long-gone Richmond Palace at a location which had previously been called Sheen; the name came from Henry's title as Earl of Richmond, itself derived from Richmond Castle in Yorkshire. The area is still in favour with royalty—one of the electors in this by-election is Princess Alexandra—but its development is the usual London story of suburban development and eventual incorporation into Greater London. At the eastern end of the seat is Barnes, which is surprisingly close to central London, and the constituency includes the National Archives and Royal Botanic Gardens at Kew before running down the east bank of the Thames to take in northern Kingston-upon-Thames and the Coombe area. In the centre of the constituency is the open space of Richmond Park, still home to a large number of deer. (Sit down, Fenton. Fenton. *Fenton...* Jesus Christ, that dog gets everywhere.)

The census statistics show that this—particularly the Richmond end—is a constituency where the elite live. The standout figure comes from Mortlake and Barnes Common ward, which has the third-highest figure in the whole of England and Wales for the ONS' "lower management" category at 36.9% of the workforce; six of the seven Richmond wards make the top 100 in England and Wales for that category. All of those six wards are also in the top 100 in England and Wales for degree-level qualifications, South Richmond having the highest figure with 63.6% of the workforce. South Richmond also has the seventh-highest figure in England and Wales for the ONS "higher management" employment category at 30% of the workforce, and three other Richmond wards make the top 100 for that statistic. Other top-100 performances include three wards for population born in the EU-14 countries; and Mortlake and Barnes Common for people in the 30–44 age bracket.

There has been a constituency based on Richmond, Surrey since 1918; its first MP was the couponned Conservative Clifford Edgar, who in that election soundly defeated the militant suffragette and independent candidate Norah Dacre Fox. Edgar lost his seat in 1922 to Harry Becker, who had stood as an independent Conservative endorsed by Lord Rothermere's Anti-Waste League. Becker was re-elected in 1923, this time as the official Conservative candidate, but stood down in 1924.

Becker's replacement was the Australian Sir Newton Moore, who had been Premier of Western Australia from 1906 to 1910 before moving to London, and during the Great War had been GOC Australian Imperial Forces in the UK with the rank of major-general. Moore had served in the Commons before—winning the St George's Hanover Square by-election in October 1918 before transferring to Islington North in the general election two months later, serving there until 1923.

Sir Newton Moore resigned from the Commons in 1932 shortly after being re-elected by the score of 85–15 in a straight fight with Labour. His replacement was another knight of the realm, Sir William Ray who won the by-election unopposed. Ray resigned in his turn in 1937 and the by-election was won by George Harvie-Watt, a barrister and TA figure who had previously been MP for Keighley from 1931 to 1935; Harvie-Watt easily defeated the Labour candidate George Rogers, a Wembley councillor and railway clerk who would go on to serve for 25 years as MP for Kensington North.

Harvie-Watt had a long career at the lowest rungs of government, immediately becoming PPS to the Board of Trade and serving as PPS to Winston Churchill during Churchill's wartime premiership; after the war he was appointed Baronet, became ADC to George VI and was kept on by Elizabeth II. He eventually stood down from the Commons in 1959.

The 1959 election saw Harvie-Watt succeeded by another Tory figure, Anthony Royle, who had had the dubious distinction of losing the Torrington by-election to the Liberals the previous year. A former army figure who had served in the Life Guards and the SAS before polio put paid to his military career, Royle was working as an insurance broker before entering politics. Like Harvie-Watt, he had a long parliamentary career, peaking during the Heath administration in which was a junior Foreign Office minister.

In the 1970s Richmond suddenly became a marginal seat, falling to the Liberals in the 1973 Greater London Council election. The GLC councillor, Stanley Rundle, was the Liberal candidate here in February 1974 and cut Royle's majority below nine points. Rundle was replaced as Liberal candidate in the October election by Alan Watson, against whom Royle—who had been knighted between the two elections—increased his majority to just over ten points. Another notable figure on the Richmond ballot that October was the barrister Bob Marshall-Andrews, who would later serve as Labour MP for Medway during the Blair and Brown years.

The 1979 election was a rematch between Sir Anthony Royle and Alan Watson, with Royle's majority down to its lowest level of six points. Further down the ballot paper that year was a vestige of the short-lived political career of then pop mogul Jonathan King, who stood under his real name (Kenneth George King) and failed to break 1%.

The Richmond constituency was renamed Richmond and Barnes for the 1983 election, and got a new Tory candidate to match as Sir Anthony Royle retired. Jeremy Hanley, a chartered accountant from an entertainment family—his parents were the actor Jimmy Hanley and the actress Dinah Sheridan, his sister was the former actress and *Magpie* presenter Jenny Hanley—who had contested Lambeth Central in the 1978 by-election and the following year's general election, faced off against Alan Watson, fighting the seat for the third time but now under the Liberal/SDP Alliance label; the Labour candidate, some way behind, was Keith Vaz, who got into Parliament four years later for Leicester East and still represents that seat today.[14] In one of the closest results of the 1983 election, Hanley prevailed by 20,695 votes to 20,621, a majority of 74. A rematch between Hanley and Watson in 1987 led to Hanley increasing his majority to 1,766 or four percentage points, and Hanley's lead went up again in the 1992 election in Richmond and Barnes, an election where all three major party candidates ended up in the Commons at some point; the Labour candidate was Don Touhig, who won the Islwyn by-election after Neil Kinnock's translation to Europe, and the Lib Dem candidate was Jenny Tonge.

By 1992 Hanley had joined the lower ranks of government as a junior Northern Ireland minister, and served in Major's cabinet as Conservative Party chairman for a year which was accident-prone even by the low standards of the Major administration. As well as the collapse of Tory support, boundary changes—which had cut the number of seats in Richmond and Kingston boroughs from four to three—had merged his seat with part of Norman Lamont's Kingston constituency, leading to a new name for the constituency: Richmond Park. In a re-

---

[14] Apologies to those readers who may have been playing the Keith Vaz game.

peat of 1992, Hanley faced off against Jenny Tonge, and this time lost by five points as the Conservatives lost the Richmond seat for the first time since its creation.

Tonge was born in Walsall and had trained as a doctor at UCL, and combined her medical career with being a Richmond upon Thames councillor from 1981 to 1990, chairing the social services committee. She became the Lib Dems' international development spokeswoman, and was re-elected in 2001. Her time on the party's front bench was cut short in 2004 when Charles Kennedy effectively sacked her as children's spokeswoman for making positive comments about Palestinian suicide bombers; she refused to apologise and, even since her translation to the Lords in 2005, Tonge's loose tongue has continued to cause embarrassment for the Liberal Democrats.

Upon Tonge's retirement from the Commons in 2005 the Liberal Democrats managed the rare feat of passing a seat on from one MP to another. The new Lib Dem MP was Susan Kramer, who had stood for the party in the inaugural London Mayor election in 2000, polling 12%, and also fought Dulwich and West Norwood in the 1997 general election. In office as a member of the largest Lib Dem parliamentary caucus, Kramer held a number of frontbench roles and campaigned against the expansion of Heathrow Airport.

The Tories had never given up in Richmond and for the 2010 election they selected through a newfangled "open primary" Zac Goldsmith as their candidate. A former editor of *The Ecologist* magazine and a committed environmentalist, Goldsmith was from a long-standing political family: both his grandfathers had been Tory MPs (Frank Goldsmith representing Stowmarket from January 1910 to 1918 and Robin Vane-Tempest-Stewart, 8th Marquess of Londonderry, representing County Down from 1931 to 1945) while his father, the billionaire businessman Sir James Goldsmith, had been elected an MEP in France in 1994, served as leader of the European Parliament's eurosceptic group, and founded the short-lived Referendum Party to contest the 1997 election. Goldsmith went on to defeat Kramer by seven points in the 2010 election, and in 2015 massively increased his majority to 58–19 over the new Lib Dem candidate, Robin Meltzer, who polled fewer than half the number of votes that Kramer had done.

The Lib Dem collapse in 2015 was presaged by the 2014 local elections. In the eleven wards of Richmond and Kingston making up this seat the Conservatives polled 44% to just 23% for the Lib Dems and 13% for the Greens, who contested every ward, and the Tories won 32 of the constituency's 33 council seats to one for the Lib Dems. The Tories held Tudor ward in a by-election in October 2014.

The London Assembly elections in 2016 aren't easy to compare, partly because postal votes are not broken down to ward level and partly because the Tory candidate for London mayor this year was none other than Zac Goldsmith, who ran a surprisingly right-wing campaign; for what it's worth, in on-the-day votes Goldsmith beat Sadiq Khan here 57–25 and the Tories carried Richmond Park on the list vote with 46%, to 19% for Labour and 12% for the Lib Dems.

These recent reverses haven't stopped the Lib Dems from attempting to crank their by-election machine to full throttle. Their campaign is focusing on the most recent poll in the borough: the EU referendum in June, in which Richmond Park was a strongly pro-Remain area. Richmond borough as a whole was 69% Remain and Kingston borough 62% Remain, and demographic-based estimates by Chris Hanretty have put the Remain vote across this constituency at 72%. Goldsmith, on the other hand, was a Leave campaigner just like his dad.

As stated, Zac Goldsmith is standing for re-election; he does not have the Tory nomination, but is standing as an independent without Conservative opposition and is also endorsed by UKIP.

The Lib Dem candidate is Sarah Olney, an accountant working at the National Physical Laboratory. An opponent of Heathrow expansion, she is endorsed by the Green Party and the Women's Equality Party.

Of the other parties who stood in 2015 only Labour are left standing: their candidate is Christian Wolmar, a journalist focusing on transport and railway issues who had also sought the Labour nomination for the London Mayor election.

Five candidates complete the ballot paper. Regular by-election candidate and Monster Raving Loony Party leader Howling Laud Hope is back for his umpteenth attempt to get into Parliament. The One Love party leader Ankit Love, standing under the pseudonym "Maharaja Jammu and Kashmir", is hoping to improve on the twenty on-the-day votes he polled here in May's London Mayor election. Turning to the more serious wing, management consultant David Powell is standing as an independent candidate; the evangelical Christian Peoples Alliance have nominated Dominic Stockford; and independent candidate Fiona Syms, estranged wife of the Tory MP Robert Syms, is standing as an anti-Goldsmith spoiler candidate with a pledge to take the Conservative whip if she is elected.

Constituency polling in the UK has a poor track record, but one poll taken at the start of the campaign conducted by BMG Research for the London *Evening Standard* (which, for what it's worth, was strongly in favour of Goldsmith in the mayoral election) had Goldsmith on 56% to 29% for Olney and 11% for Labour. It remains to be seen whether a month of campaigning has had any effect on these figures. Whatever happens, remember that we are in the crazy year of 2016 and the only thing that can be confidently predicted is that all bets are off.

Result: LD 20510 Goldsmith 18638 Lab 1515 Loony 184 Syms 173 CPA 164 One Love 67 Powell 32 [LD gain from C]

May 2015 result C 34404 LD 11389 Lab 7296 Grn 3548 UKIP 2464
May 2010 result C 29461 LD 25370 Lab 2979 UKIP 669 Grn 572 Christian Peoples Alliance 133 Ind 84
May 2016 GLA elections (excludes postal voters)
Mayor: C 20391 Lab 9123 LD 2334 Grn 2042 Women's Equality 728 UKIP 467 Respect 225 Cannabis is Safer than Alcohol 193 Britain First 136 Ind 82 BNP 49 One Love 20
List: C 16465 Lab 6711 LD 4442 Grn 3773 Women's Equality 1661 UKIP 1446 Animal Welfare 388 Respect 277 Britain First 243 CPA 220 House Party 140 BNP 95

Figure 223: House of Commons, Richmond Park

Walbrook

City of London corporation; caused by the resignation of Independent councilman Lucy Frew.

Richmond Park isn't the only poll in London this week as there are also two local by-elections in the capital. One of them is to the Walbrook ward of the City of London Corporation, the financial centre of the UK. Well, it has to be; this ward is centred on the Bank underground station and includes the Mansion House, residence of the Lord Mayor of London, and the Bank of England.

The City Corporation is a hangover from local government in olden time, with one of the hangovers being plural voting: the 343 electors in this by-election are almost all sole traders or nominated by businesses within the ward rather than being local residents, because there are very few local residents here. The council has the non-partisan politics of a parish council and this by-election fits the mould with three independent candidates. Peter Bennett, a chartered surveyor and Bridge Master of the City, would appear to be the City establishment candidate; he is opposed by Xuelin Bates, the wife of the former MP for Langbaurgh and Paymaster General in the Major government Lord Bates, and independent media consultant Sophia Morrell. Whoever wins will be straight back onto the campaign trail to seek re-election at the next City elections in March.

Result: Bennett 72 Morrell 46 Bates 36

Whitechapel

Tower Hamlets council, North London; caused by the disqualification of Shahed Ali who is now serving a five-month prison sentence for housing fraud.

Whitechapel may only be a mile away from the Bank geographically, but politically and demographically it's another world entirely. Entirely south of the Whitechapel Road and served by Aldgate East and Whitechapel underground stations, the modern ward does not include the sites of the Ripper murders but does have some more modern history: within the current boundaries are Cable Street, where the 1936 battle started, and Sydney Street, scene of the 1911 siege which failed to flush out Peter the Painter and is now commemorated by two modern-day blocks of flats called Siege House and Painter House. Slightly more tasteful is the Whitechapel Bell Foundry, still in operation today[15], while major public buildings within the ward include the controversial PFI Royal London Hospital and the equally controversial East London Mosque.

While Whitechapel took its name from the former church of St Mary Matfelon, which didn't survive the wartime bombing, other religions dominate its history: it was once a centre of the Jewish community. Boundary changes in 2014 confuse the issue slightly, but this is now a Bangladeshi centre—on its previous boundaries Whitechapel ward made the top 100 wards in England and Wales for Asian ethnicity (49.7%), those born in the EU-14 (8.0%), Islam (42.4%) and those who did not answer the census' religion question (17.0%).

The predecessor St Mary's ward returned Communists to Tower Hamlets council as late as 1971, which suggests a left-wing political profile. With its ethnic profile the modern Whitechapel ward tends to elect a full slate of Bangladeshi councillors, with Shahed Ali topping the poll in 2014. Ali was first elected in 2006 as a candidate of George Galloway's Respect party, being re-elected in 2010 on the Labour ticket and in 2014 as a supporter of then Mayor Lutfur Rahman under the label "Tower Hamlets First". He was named in the election court case which removed Rahman from office, the court noting that Ali was registered to vote at two different addresses in Whitechapel ward and two votes were cast in his name in the 2014 election. One of those addresses was a council property in Christian Street, Aldgate, and Ali had accepted that flat in 2009 without having disclosed to his own council that he also owned a string of other properties both within and outside the borough.

In 2014—the only previous result on these boundaries—the Rahmanite slate had 40% of the vote to 26% for Labour and 13% for a single Green Party candidate. The London Assembly results from May suggest that this is very safe Labour without a Rahmanite on the ballot paper: Sadiq Khan beat Zac Goldsmith 67–14 and in the London Members ballot Labour led the Tories 60–13.

With the dissolution of Rahman's Tower Hamlets First the defending Rahmanite candidate is Shafi Ahmed, standing as an independent. Labour have selected Victoria Obaze, a Fabian member and secondary school governor from Mile End who has twice previously stood for the council. The Greens have selected local housing campaigner James Wilson, and the ballot paper is completed

---

[15] Until the following week when closure plans were announced.

Parliamentary constituency: Bethnal Green and Bow (part north of Fenchurch Street railway line); Poplar and Limehouse (part south of Fenchurch Street railway line)
May 2014 result Tower Hamlets First 2139/2117/2088 Lab 1359/1190/1188 Grn 703 C 409/405/345 LD 358 UKIP 199 TUSC 139
May 2016 GLA result (excludes postal voters)
Mayor: Lab 2301 C 491 Grn 248 LD 130 Respect 117 Women's Equality 69 Cannabis is Safer than Alcohol 39 UKIP 30 Britain First 14 BNP 8 One Love 6 Ind 6
List: Lab 2084 C 465 Grn 352 LD 187 Respect 151 Women's Equality 120 UKIP 56 Animal Welfare 21 Brtain First 16 BNP 16 House Party 13 CPA 11

Figure 224: Tower Hamlets, Whitechapel

Parliamentary constituency: Chichester
West Sussex county council division: Bourne
May 2015 result C 1994/1865/1847 LD 1437/914/878
May 2011 result C 1158/1154/1104 LD 836/621/584 Lab 346 Ind 318
May 2007 result C 970/961/913 LD 828/827/716
May 2003 result C 743/739/679 LD 694/623/530 UKIP 170 Lab 159/149/145

Figure 225: Chichester, Southbourne

by Will Fletcher for the Tories, Emanuel Andjelic for the Lib Dems and Martin Smith for UKIP.

Result: Ind 1147 Lab 823 C 217 LD 173 Grn 170 UKIP 34 [Ind gain from Tower Hamlets First]

Southbourne

Chichester district council, West Sussex; caused by the resignation of Conservative councillor Bruce Finch. He had served since 2011.

Moving out of London, we are on the coast in the south-western corner of Sussex. Southbourne is the place where the Portsmouth conurbation ends and Sussex begins, a village of a little over 6,000 souls; it is sufficiently close to the boundary with Hampshire to have a Hampshire postcode (PO10, for Emsworth). The ward also includes West Thorney, a Royal Artillery base on an island in Chichester Harbour, home to around 1,000 people and rather more seabirds, and once a transit post for Vietnamese refugees accepted into the UK in the 1980s. Much of the ward is within the Chichester Harbour Area of Outstanding Natural Beauty, and the area has a commuter economic profile with high employment levels.

Southbourne ward's three seats split two Conservative and one Lib Dem in 2003 but the Tories gained a full slate in 2007 and have yet to relinquish it.

In the 2015 election the Tories prevailed 58–42 in a straight fight with the Lib Dems—a surprising candidate list because UKIP hold the local county council seat (Bourne).

Defending for the Tories is David Harwood, a private hire driver. The Lib Dem candidate is Southbourne parish councillor Jonathan Brown. Also standing are Rebecca Hamlet for Labour and Patricia Hunt for UKIP.

Result: LD 646 C 289 UKIP 132 Lab 53 [LD gain from C]

Ferndown

Dorset county council; caused by the resignation of UKIP councillor Ian Smith who had served since 2013.

There are some wards which just can't stop having by-elections; we were in Ferndown, Dorset only three months ago and now it's time for another by-election to the same county division. A mostly twentieth-century development (until 1972 its parish council was still known by its former name of Hampreston) Ferndown essentially functions as a dormitory town for the Bournemouth–Poole conurbation. It's also a retirement centre: the former Ferndown Central ward was in the top 10 wards in England and Wales for population over the age of 64 (44.4%) and in the top 30 wards for retired population (32.6% of the workforce), while another part of the division, Parley ward, is in the top 100 for population over the age of 64 (35%) and in the top 20 for owner-occupation (94% of households).

That really sets the tone for Ferndown county division's recent election results, in which UKIP gained a seat off the Tories in the 2013 election; the UKIP slate topped the poll that year 45–44. That result came as a surprise to UKIP's councillor Ian Smith, who didn't turn up for the count because he didn't think he would win. The UKIP surge didn't follow through into the 2015 East Dorset elections; although boundary changes confuse the issue the Tories hold all the district seats wholly or partly within the division. September's by-election suggests that the Kippers are in trouble here: the Tories won that poll 57–30 and had a similar result in a district council by-election in Parley ward on the same day.

This by-election is the second faceoff in three months between UKIP's Lawrence Wilson and the Tories' Peter Stokes, both of whom contested the Parley ward district council by-election in September; but this time Wilson is the defending candidate rather than the challenger. Completing the ballot paper are Jason Jones for the Lib Dems and Peter Stokes for Labour. Whoever wins will be straight back onto the campaign trail to seek re-election in May.

Result: C 1463 UKIP 831 LD 301 Lab 160 [C gain from UKIP]

Parliamentary constituency: Christchurch
East Dorset council wards: Ameysford, Ferndown Central (part), Hampreston and Longham (part), Parley
Sept 2016 by-election C 2046 UKIP 1092 LD 260 Lab 190
May 2013 result UKIP 2222/2027 C 2187/2025 Lab 567/466
June 2009 result C 3575/3460 UKIP 1780/1691 LD 913/873 Lab 368
May 2005 result C 5390/5306 LD 2422/2316 Ind 1497 Lab 1480 UKIP 1083

Figure 226: Dorset CC, Ferndown

Grange Park

South Northamptonshire council; caused by the resignation of Conservative councillor Simon Clifford. He had served since being elected in a double by-election in October 2014.

There are some wards which just can't stop having by-elections. We saw one last week (Carlisle, Castle) and here's another one. Grange Park is a large village to the south of Northampton, just off the M1 motorway at junction 15. It's also an almost completely new village, mostly developed in the last fourteen years. The 2001 census found just 327 people living in the parish; two years later there were 2,375 registered electors, and the district ward that then contained the village (Courteenhall, with two councillors) had grown so much that the entire district had to have new ward boundaries. Grange Park became a ward of its own, with two councillors of its own, in 2007. By the time of 2011 census the parish's population was 4,404; despite this, I wrote in this column the following year that the village didn't even appear in my 2011 A–Z road atlas. The A to Z Company have caught up and show the relevant built-up area in their 2013 atlas, although it still doesn't have a name.

Perhaps because of its short life, Grange Park has a remarkable age distribution: it is in the top 10 wards in England and Wales for 30- to 44-year-olds (34.4%) and in the top 25 wards in England and Wales for under-16s (29.8% of the population). It's also in the top 40 wards in England and Wales for full-time employment (56.9% of the workforce) and that employment is determinedly middle-class.

That would appear to be borne out by the ward's election results. The Conservatives were unopposed here in 2007 (South Northants is one of those councils that has lots of unopposed returns), beat the Lib Dems 76–24 in a 2009 by-election, a single Independent candidate 75–25 at the 2011 election, the Lib Dems 76–24 (again) in a 2012 by-election, beat Labour 63–22 in a 2014 double by-election and beat Labour 71–29 in the 2015 election. As can be seen, Grange Park ward has a high councillor attrition rate, with this being the fourth by-

Northamptonshire county council division: Hackleton and Grange Park
Parliamentary constituency: South Northamptonshire
ONS Travel to Work Area: Northampton and Wellingborough
May 2015 result C 1459/1032 Lab 584
October 2014 double by-election C 433/313 Lab 151 UKIP 100/84
Feb 2012 by-election C 313 LD 98
May 2011 result C 697/590 Ind 231
Feb 2009 by-election C 407 LD 128
May 2007 result 2 C unopposed

Figure 227: South Northamptonshire, Grange Park

election and fifth vacancy in the nine years the ward has existed; one councillor for the ward (Tharik Jainu-Deen) actually managed to resign twice, serving non-consecutive terms. Northamptonshire county council was redistricted in 2013 and Grange Park ended up in a new division with Hackleton to the east, which narrowly elected the Conservatives with 42.2% of the vote, to 41.1% for UKIP.

Defending for the Tories is Andrew Grant, a former cabinet member on South Northamptonshire council who is seeking to make a quick return after losing his seat to the Lib Dems in Towcester Mill ward in 2015. Andrew is also a former Northamptonshire county councillor, losing his seat in 2013. He is not the only Grant on the ballot as Labour have reselected local resident Ian Grant, who is standing here for the third time in as many years. Completing the ballot paper are Andy Clarke for the Green Party and Rose Gibbins for UKIP.

Result: C 244 Lab 105 UKIP 49 Grn 20

Myton and Heathcote

Warwick council; caused by the death of Conservative councillor Raj Mann. He had served since 2015.

For our final preview this week we are in the town of Warwick, but this isn't the nice-looking historic bit. Instead Myton and Heathcote ward covers south-eastern suburbs of the town on the south side of the Warwickshire Avon; Myton lies along the A 425 road connecting Warwick with Leamington Spa, while Heathcote refers to a recently developed set of housing estates and business and technology parks on the edge of Leam. The business park has attracted a large number of high-end and large companies including the head office of National Grid, which moved here from Coventry in 2004; although boundary changes confuse the issue that gives the area an educated middle-class demographic. Exactly the sort of demographic that voted Remain in large numbers in

Parliamentary constituency: Warwick and Leamington
Warwickshire county council division: Warwick South
May 2015 result C 1286/1252 Ind 440/370 LD 431 Grn 427/383 UKIP 374

Figure 228: Warwick, Myton and Heathcote

June, and Warwick was the only local government district in the West Midlands which Remain carried in the referendum.

As stated, boundary changes confuse the issue here: Warwick got new ward boundaries in 2015 which redrew Warwick town from three wards to five. Myton and Heathcote is essentially a cut-down version (with one fewer councillor) of the Warwick South ward which existed from 2003 to 2015 and was normally safe Tory (except in 2003 when a Residents Association candidate topped the poll). Myton and Heathcote has continued in the same vein: in 2015 it gave 43% to the Tory slate against evenly-divided opposition (15% for an independent, 15% for the Lib Dems, 14% for the Green slate). The Tories also hold the Warwick South seat on the county council.

Defending for the Tories is Mary Noone, a solicitor. The Lib Dem candidate is property manager Nick Solman, and Labour's Ben Wesson completes the ballot paper.

Result: C 488 LD 228 Lab 194

Monday 5th December 2016

One Monday by-election on 5th December 2016:

Carnoustie and District

Angus council; caused by the death of Scottish National Party councillor Helen Oswald at the age of 69. The Provost of Angus since 2012, Oswald was first elected in 1999, serving for Sidlaw East ward until 2007. Before moving into politics she had worked in insurance, as an estate agent and for the council. Her daughter Kirsten has served since 2015 as MP for East Renfrewshire.

Last Monday we were in Arbroath; for our second Monday by-election in as many weeks we travel a few miles west along the coast to Carnoustie. Known worldwide for its golf course, which is on the Open Championship rota, Carnoustie developed in the late eighteenth and nineteenth centuries as a centre for linen weaving and tourism—it was promoted as the Brighton of the North. While the town does still attract tourists—although these days for the golf rather than the bathing—the economy is now based on commuting to Dundee along the A 92 and the railway line, although two of the three stations within this ward, Barry Links and Golf Street, only get two trains a day and usually finish near the top of the annual list of the UK's least-used railway stations. The ward also includes a rural hinterland running inland as far as the Monikie reservoir. Although golf isn't the only sport in town—the Barry Buddon rifle range hosted the shooting events at the 1986 and 2014 Commonwealth Games—the difficulty of the course in the 1999 Open, memorable for the French golfer Jean van de Velde blowing a huge lead on the final hole, inspired the term "Carnoustie effect" for the shock created when false assumptions meet reality.

The Scottish National Party—for whom Carnoustie is a traditionally strong area—have been suffering a little from the Carnoustie effect of late. They dominated the 2007 election here, polling 47% and winning two of the three seats, the other seat going to Labour; but at the end of 2010 one of the SNP councillors

Parliamentary constituency: Dundee East
Scottish Parliament constituency: Angus South
May 2012 result Ind 1750 SNP 1611 Ind 483 Lab 274 C 271 LD 41
Feb 2011 by-election SNP 1289 Ind 1252 Lab 258 C 217 LD 93; final round Ind 1454 SNP 1426
May 2007 result SNP 2476 Lab 1160 C 863 LD 748 Solidarity 62

Figure 229: Angus, Carnoustie and District

resigned on health grounds and the Nationalists lost the by-election in February 2011 to independent candidate Brian Boyd, who started 37 votes behind the SNP but pulled ahead on transfers from the other parties to win by 28 votes. The SNP's woes continued in the 2012 election: they failed to knock out Boyd, who topped the poll, and failed to gain the Labour seat which went to a second independent candidate, Bill Bowles, who got strong transfers from Boyd, the Conservatives and Labour; first preferences were 40% for Boyd, 36% for the SNP and 11% for Bowles. The SNP hold the local parliamentary seat (Dundee East) and Holyrood seat (Angus South), and following their by-election gain in Arbroath last week a hold in this by-election will give them overall control of Angus council.

So, high stakes for the defending SNP candidate Mark McDonald, from Monifieth. His toughest challenge may well come from independent candidate David Cheape, an accountant who is the only candidate to give an address in Carnoustie. Also standing are Ray Strachan for Labour, Derek Shaw for the Conservatives and Beth Morrison for the Liberal Democrats. Don't wait up all night for the result, as the count will start on Tuesday morning at 10am.

First preferences: Ind 1401 SNP 1033 C 568 Lab 141 LD 75
Lab and LD eliminated: Ind 1477 SNP 1078 C 606
C eliminated: Ind 1637 SNP 1117 [Ind gain from SNP]

8th December 2016

By-elections on 8th December 2016:

Sleaford and North Hykeham

House of Commons; caused by the resignation of Conservative MP Stephen Phillips, who is dissatisfied with the Government's strategy for leaving the European Union. He had served since 2010.

For the first time since 1990 we have two parliamentary by-elections taking place in successive weeks. After last week's sensational poll in Richmond, Surrey, today we are in a rather different part of the UK.

The Sleaford and North Hykeham constituency covers a large swathe of rural Lincolnshire to the south of Lincoln. It is named after its only two towns. Sleaford, the larger of the two, was once the home of the county council for the Parts of Kesteven, the south-western of Lincolnshire's three Parts, and now houses the National Centre for Craft and Design, an arts centre on a disused wharf on the River Slea. Sleaford grew up in the 19th century as an agricultural centre, with seeds and maltings as important industries. Rather different is North Hykeham, which is a Lincoln suburb that has never been incorporated into the city. Also here are a couple of tiny corners of Grantham where recent development has spilled over the town limits. But the political tone of the constituency is set by the many villages within the seat, while the presence of RAF Cranwell, at which the Royal Air Force trains its officers and flying instructors, provides a military tone to the area. The Lincoln Cliff runs through the seat from north to south, with higher ground to the east overlooking the low-lying Trent Valley to the west and Holland to the east—the Parts of Holland, not the country on the other side of the North Sea.

The general pattern of parliamentary constituencies in what was Kesteven, with a northern and a southern seat, has survived basically unchanged since 1885 but the northern seat has had varying names: from 1885 to 1918 it was called

Sleaford, from 1918 to 1997 Grantham, only taking on its current name in 1997 when Grantham was moved out of the seat. (The Boundary Commission had originally proposed resurrecting the name Mid Lincolnshire, but that didn't survive the public inquiry.) If the proposed boundary changes go through as they are, then the Sleaford name will be revived for the 2020 election with North Hykeham moving into the Lincoln constituency.

Sleaford's first MP in 1885 was already a political veteran. Henry Chaplin, the so-called Squire of Blankney, had been in the Commons since 1868 as MP for Mid Lincolnshire; a major landowner in the county, Chaplin was also a prominent racehorse owner whose horse, Hermit, had won the Derby in 1867. Going into the 1885 election he had joined government for the first time as Chancellor of the Duchy of Lancaster; although he held his seat, defeating the Liberal candidate Charles Sharpe 58–42, the Tories lost that election and it took Chaplin until 1889 to join the Cabinet, as the first President of the Board of Agriculture in Salisbury's administration. In order to take up that appointment Chaplin had to seek re-election in his constituency, that being the rule until the First World War; he had to seek re-election again upon his re-appointment to the Cabinet in 1895 as President of the Local Government Board, his Agriculture appointment having ended in 1892.

Chaplin wasn't included in Salisbury's cabinet after the 1900 election, and went to the backbenches where he campaigned in favour of tariff reform. After 38 years as MP for Sleaford he was swept away in the Liberal landslide of 1906, but returned to the Commons a year later by winning a by-election in Wimbledon, and was later translated to the Lords as the first Viscount Chaplin. In an interesting link with last week's Richmond by-election, Henry Chaplin was Zac Goldsmith's great-great-grandfather: his daughter Edith married the 7th Marquess of Londonderry, whose granddaughter Lady Annabel Vane-Tempest-Stewart married James Goldsmith.

The new Liberal MP for Sleaford was Arnold Lupton, a professor of mining at Leeds University and colliery director. A free trade supporter, Lupton was at odds with Herbert Asquith on several issues and never got anywhere near government; Lupton was later sent to prison for pacifist activity during the Great War. He was rather soundly defeated in the first 1910 election by the Tories' Edmund Royds, a major in the Lincolnshire Yeomanry and a solicitor from a Cheshire family, who before the Great War intervened concentrated on opposing Lloyd George's land tax and the consequent revaluation.

The redistribution of 1918 abolished the Grantham parliamentary borough and moved the town of Grantham into the Sleaford constituency, which was then renamed as Grantham. The boundary changes improved the Liberal position and Royds, who was endorsed by the Coalition, did well to be re-elected over the Liberal candidate Robert Pattinson. In 1922 Royds' luck ran out and Pattinson won their rematch by a majority of 428 votes. Royds didn't seek to return to Parliament after his defeat but did remain prominent in Lincolnshire public life; he was High Sheriff of Lincolnshire in 1931 and was knighted in 1939 for political and public services in Lincolnshire.

Robert Pattinson, a railway contractor and builders' merchant from Sleaford, was a long-standing member of Kesteven county council which was based in Sleaford; he joined in Parliament his brother-in-law Richard Winfrey (South West Norfolk, 1906–23) and his brother Samuel Pattinson (Horncastle, 1922–24). His time in Parliament was a short one: the 1920s were a turbulent time in British politics and Robert Pattinson lost his seat in the 1923 election having been an MP for only a year. Although there was talk of Pattinson returning to Parliament in the 1937 Holland-with-Boston by-election, this didn't come to fruition and Pattinson's remaining career was spent in local government: he served for twenty years as chairman of Kesteven county council, and a secondary school in North Hykeham is still named after him today.

As stated, in 1923 Grantham went back to the Conservatives against the national trend with their new candidate Sir Richard Warrender, 8th Baronet, a godson of Queen Victoria who had won the Military Cross while serving with the Grenadier Guards in the Great War. After being re-elected in 1924 with a much larger majority over the new Liberal candidate, the controversial former Eye MP Alexander Lyle-Samuel, Warrender embarked on a long career in various minor government positions which was only interrupted by the Tories being out of power from 1929 to 1931. His career in government—by then as Parliamentary and Financial Secretary to the Admiralty—outlasted his Commons career, which was ended by his elevation to the Lords in 1942 as the first Lord Bruntisfield.

Bruntisfield's peerage meant that there would have to be a by-election in Grantham in March 1942. This was one of the low points of the Second World War for the Allies, coming just after the fall of Singapore with the Red Army in retreat on the Eastern Front. The Tories had selected for the by-election Sir Arthur Longmore, who had recently retired from the RAF with the rank of Air Chief Marshal; he had briefly served as Air Officer Commanding in the Middle East and, with RAF Cranwell in full swing, looked a suitable candidate. With the wartime election truce in effect, Longmore was opposed only by independent candidate Denis Kendall, managing director of a highly productive arms production factory in Grantham, whose workers were well-paid and well-served with entertainment. Despite disclosing officially-secret wartime production figures during the election campaign, Kendall won the by-election with a majority of just 367 votes.

Denis Kendall was a larger-than-life figure whose pre-Parliamentary career included running away to sea at 14 followed by spells raiding opium dens on the Yangtse River, as a cabaret owner in Shanghai, as a steeplejack in the USA and as works manager for the Citroën car factory in Paris. Even before his election MI5 and MI6 had Kendall under surveillance for far-right sympathies, suspected black market and smuggling activity and links to foreign companies. That didn't stop Kendall being re-elected in 1945, but he lost a fraud case in 1949—being ordered to repay a £15,000 investment which he had used to pay creditors—and lost his seat the following year, finishing third in Grantham with 28%. Kendall made one attempt to get the Grantham seat back, standing in 1951 as the Liberal candidate without success.

The Tories took Grantham back in 1950 with their new candidate Eric Smith, who had a tragically short tenure in office—he died in August 1951 at the age of just 42. With a new general election imminent no by-election was held to replace Smith, and the 1951 election returned the new Tory candidate Joseph Godber, a Bedfordshire county councillor from a farming background—he chaired the glasshouse section of the NFU and sat on the Tomato and Cucumber Marketing Board. At the time Grantham was a marginal seat where Labour had become strong, and Godber faced a stern test in the 1955 election in which his Labour opponent was the outgoing MP Woodrow Wyatt, whose Birmingham Aston constituency had disappeared in boundary changes; Wyatt would later return to the Commons as MP for Bosworth in Leicestershire. Godber won that election by 51% to 46%, and would go on to defeat another former Labour MP, Tom Skeffington-Lodge (Bedford, 1945–50), in the 1959 election by 57–43.

By now Godber was on the junior rungs of government, and his big break into the Cabinet came in Macmillan's 1963 reshuffle in which Godber was appointed War Secretary; however, he was in Cabinet for less than four months before being demoted when Douglas-Home came to power. Grantham had a close result in the Wilson landslide of 1966 when Godber won his fifth term by 48–44 over Labour's Mary Large, but in the 1970s the Labour vote collapsed and the seat became true-blue Tory. Godber retired to the Lords in 1979.

The 1979 election returned a new MP for Grantham: Douglas Hogg, son of the long-serving MP Quintin Hogg who had been a fixture of the Tory front-bench since the Eden administration and, as a result of the Tories' return to power in 1979, became Lord Chancellor. Douglas had the stereotypical early life for a Tory politician: Eton; Christ Church, Oxford; president of the Oxford Union in 1967; called to the Bar a year later, and took silk in 1990. Hogg served in the Commons for 31 years, a career which is principally remembered for being Minister of Agriculture at the height of the BSE crisis in the 1990s, and for the

2009 expenses scandal in which it was revealed that Hogg had claimed and been paid £2,000 from the parliamentary expenses office for the cost of clearing the moat around his country estate. This prompted a rather abrupt retirement from the Commons; Hogg had succeeded to the title of Viscount Hailsham in 2001, but despite entering a couple of hereditary peer by-elections didn't enter the Lords until he obtained a life peerage in October 2015. In doing so, he joined his wife Sarah who is a life peer in her own right, having headed John Major's policy unit; Baroness Hogg had also worked as a journalist (briefly presenting *Channel 4 News*) and later became the first woman to chair a FTSE 100 company, 3i Group.

As stated, boundary changes in 1997 removed Grantham from this seat and renamed it as Sleaford and North Hykeham. The 1997 Blair landslide was the only time since 1966 when the Tory majority fell below 10 points, so Hogg's enforced retirement in 2010 cleared the way for Stephen Phillips, a barrister and recorder who had also briefly held a commission in the Welsh Guards; his only previous electoral experience had come in 2008 when he lost a Conservative seat to the Lib Dems in a by-election to Camden council in London. Phillips never got off the backbenches and attracted criticism during his time in Parliament for continuing to spend over 30 hours a week working as a barrister. Although Phillips was on the Brexit side of the referendum debate, his resignation came due to "irreconcilable policy differences" with the May administration, and Phillips had previously criticised the Government's attempts to leave the EU without consulting Parliament—a subject we have heard a lot more of this week.

Phillips was certainly in tune with his constituents on the EU question. The North Kesteven local government district, on which this constituency is based, voted 62% Leave in May. This seat is similar to Richmond Park only in the sense that it had a big Tory lead in the 2015 election: 56%, to 17% for Labour and 16% for UKIP. All five candidates in 2015 saved their deposit, including independent candidate Marianne Overton, leader of the Lincolnshire Independents council group, who had also saved her deposit here in 2010.

The local elections in 2015, held on the same day as the general election, are rather difficult to interpret because most wards only had Tory and Independent candidates, and two wards had unopposed returns. Several councillors were returned under the Lincolnshire Independent label and one ward in North Hykeham voted for a Hykeham Independent candidate. In by-elections in 2015 the Tories held Belvoir ward (not all of which is within this seat) and gained a Lincolnshire Independent seat in North Hykeham Mill; but the Lincolnshire Independents have done well in 2016's by-elections, gaining Ashby de la Launde and Cranwell ward from the Conservatives and holding a seat in Cliff Villages ward.

The 2013 Lincolnshire county council elections demonstrate the former Lib Dem vote in North Hykeham, but judging from the lack of candidates there in 2015 the party's administration in this seat seems to have fallen apart. The Conservatives held a by-election in Grantham Barrowby in 2015.

This is one of the areas of England least affected by the immigration and social changes of the last few decades—the non-white population is just 1% and EU immigration rates are low (and mostly concentrated in Sleaford town). The constituency also has a large retired population and scored very highly on the census for Christianity.

With little to indicate that any other party is putting in a strong campaign, the Tory candidate should have little to lose sleep over. She is Caroline Johnson, a consultant paediatrician who fought Scunthorpe in the 2010 general election. Equality campaigners will note that if she is elected the proportion of female MPs will rise above 30% for the first time.

The Labour candidate is local resident Jim Clarke, a binman, former postman and GMB activist.

There was talk of Suzanne Evans seeking the UKIP nomination, but after she decided trying to be party leader was more important UKIP selected Victoria Ayling, a Lincolnshire county councillor representing Spilsby Fen division. She was the Conservative candidate for Great Grimsby in the 2010 general election, losing to Austin Mitchell by just 714 votes, and stood there again in 2015 as the UKIP candidate, blowing what had been seen as one of the party's top targets; in May she was the UKIP candidate for Lincolnshire police and crime commissioner.

The Lib Dem candidate is Ross Pepper, who lives in Lincoln and fought that seat in the 2015 general election.

Marianne Overton is standing again for the Lincolnshire Independents after saving her deposit in 2010 and 2015; she is the Lincolnshire county councillor for Branston and Navenby division and represents Cliff Villages ward on North Kesteven council.

However, turning to the other candidates on the ballot paper suggests that the Lincolnshire Independents have suffered a split. Mark Suffield, who is a Lincolnshire Independent member of North Kesteven district council (representing Sleaford Quarrington and Mareham ward) is standing without a ballot paper description, as is Paul Coyne who was elected to Sleaford town council on the Lincolnshire Independents ticket. Yet another independent candidate on the ballot paper is Sarah Stock, who is campaigning on a Save the NHS ticket and is endorsed by the Green Party. Completing the ballot paper are Peter Hill of the Official Monster Raving Loony Party, standing under the pseudonym

May 2015 result C 34805 Lab 10690 UKIP 9716 LD 3500 Lincs Ind 3233
May 2010 result C 30719 LD 10814 Lab 10051 Lincs Ind 3806 UKIP 2163 BNP 1977

Figure 230: House of Commons, Sleaford and North Hykeham

"The Iconic Arty-Pole", and regular by-election candidate David Bishop for his Bus-Pass Elvis Party.

Result: C 17570 UKIP 4426 Lab 3363 LD 3006 Lincs Ind 2892 Stock 462 Loony 200 Coyne 186 Suffield 74 Bus-Pass Elvis 55

University and Scotforth Rural

Lancaster council; caused by the resignation of Labour councillor Matt Mann, who has taken up a new job away from Lancaster. He had served since 2015.

Patet omnibus veritas

- Motto of Lancaster University

A few weeks back your columnist rather confidently predicted that the Oxford Dictionaries Word of 2016 would be "Brexit". For whatever reason (perhaps the word is too old?), the lexicographers went for a new concept which we have indeed seen much of in 2016: "post-truth". This is a concept anathema to this column, whose remit is first and foremost to inform; and anathema to Lancaster University, whose motto translates as "truth lies open to all". Several of the recent Oxford Words of the Year have failed to stand the test of time—"squeezed middle", anyone?—and it remains to be seen whether post-truth politics is here to stay or a flash in the pan.

Lancaster University forms the centre of a remarkable electoral ward which may give us some insight into the student politics of today. One of the 1960s tranche of universities, Lancaster epitomises the campus style of building, with its own purpose-built centre opened in 1968 at Bailrigg, on a hill between the West Coast Main Line, the A 6 road and the M 6 motorway. In its short life Lancaster has supplied several MPs including two currently serving—Alan Campbell (politics, Furness College) and Simon Danczuk (sociology, Cartmel college)—a present MEP, Theresa Griffin (English and theatre studies, Cartmel college), UKIP's failed leadership candidate and newly-appointed health spokeswoman Suzanne Evans (religious studies, Cartmel college) and former cabinet member Alan Milburn (history, Pendle college) who is now the University's chancellor.

The building of the University campus took a swathe out of the Scotforth parish—which had already seen its populated parts incorporated into Lancaster—and left that parish divided into two parts. In more recent years the expansion of higher education has led to the University campus expanding to the south-west, across the parish boundary into Galgate parish. As can be seen, the parish boundaries here are rather out of date.

The ward boundaries aren't. University and Scotforth Rural was created in 2015 as an expansion of the former University ward, which was tightly drawn around the original campus; the expanded ward includes both parts of Scotforth parish, the south-west campus and an extra, third councillor. The old University ward had unique demographics: it was number 1 in England and Wales for the 18–29 age group (94.3% of the population), number 1 in England and Wales for full-time students (93.6% of the workforce), number 1 in England and Wales for those educated to A-level but no further (67.6% of the workforce), and interestingly made the top 100 for households living rent-free, although this may be because the census only recognised sixty-two households in the ward. If you want to know how students vote, look here.

On the basis of previous results for University ward, Lancaster's students (those of whom who bother to vote in local elections) are left-wing and volatile—although electoral volatility shouldn't come as a surprise given that the campus is very much a bubble and its population turns over every year. The old University ward voted Lib Dem in 2003, Green in 2007 and Labour in 2011; the expanded ward split its seats in 2015 between two Labour candidates and one Green Party, with shares of the vote being 35% for Labour, 32% for the Green Party and 24% for the Tory slate (one of whom rejoiced in the name of Ice Dong). Most of the ward lies within the Lancaster South East county division, a Labour-inclined marginal whose political tone is set by Lancaster rather than the campus.

Since 2015 the introduction of individual electoral registration has led to a dramatic drop in the University's electorate for the 2015–16 electoral register, as the University was no longer able to register students to vote *en bloc*. The University has had success in reversing this drop by asking students whether they would like to opt out of registering to vote as part of the course registration process. However, while this does mean that the University is able to handle electoral registration again, the applications can't go to Lancaster council until after term has started which leads to a bit of a lag: although Mann started his new job in September he delayed his resignation in order to ensure that the electoral register was as complete as possible for the by-election.

Not surprisingly all four candidates for the by-election are students. Defending for Labour is Nathan Burns, who is originally from London and whose campaign has been supported by none other than Jeremy Corbyn. Hopefully Corbyn didn't have too much trouble with Virgin Trains on the way up from London. The Green candidate is Bowland college student Xeina Aveyard, an

Parliamentary constituency: Lancaster and Fleetwood
Lancashire county council division: Lancaster South East (former University ward),
Lancaster Central (part: detached part of Scotforth parish), Lancaster Rural East (part:
Scotforth parish except the detached part, and part of Galgate parish)
May 2015 result Lab 605/500/480 Grn 555/440/417 C 405/391/339 LD 143/79/66

Figure 231: Lancaster, University and Scotforth Rural

anti-fracking campaigner. The Tories have selected Luke Brandon, a masters student who chairs the University's Conservative Future branch. Completing the ballot paper is third-year student Pippa Hepworth, reselected by the Liberal Democrats.

Result: Lab 98 Grn 79 C 68 LD 36

Madeley

Newcastle-under-Lyme council, Staffordshire; caused by the death of Billy Welsh who had been elected as Labour in 2014 but had left the party. He had served since 2010 and was originally elected as a Liberal Democrat.

Further south on the M 6 and the West Coast Main Line we come to a ward where many pass through but few stop. Madeley lies five miles west of Newcastle-under-Lyme on the road to Whitchurch and the railway line; although there has not been a station here for many years, the legacy of the station can still be seen in the fact that Madeley has Crewe postcodes (CW3). The ward also includes the villages of Little Madeley and Madeley Heath, lying to the east along the M 6 motorway which bypasses the Potteries conurbation here, making a 120-degree turn from west to north-east. Famous residents in the ward include Gordon Banks and Lemmy from Motörhead.[16]

At first sight Madeley's demographics look fairly prosperous but this ward has a coalmining history: Madeley and Leycett once had collieries and Silverdale Colliery, a couple of miles to the east, didn't close until 1998. That created a safe Labour ward in 2002, but since then the ward has some bizarre results even by the bizarre standards of Newcastle-under-Lyme. The Conservatives gained the two Labour seats in 2007 and at a 2008 by-election, at which Billy Welsh was the defending Labour candidate.

The weirdness really started in earnest in 2010 when the Tories lost a seat to Billy Welsh, who this time was standing as a Liberal Democrat. The other Tory seat went back to Labour in 2011, but the Labour councillor died shortly

---

[16] This was correct at the time of my previous preview for the 2012 by-election, but Lemmy died in December 2015.

Parliamentary constituency: Stone
Staffordshire county council division: Newcastle Rural
May 2015 result Ind 1115 C 636 Lab 455 LD 87 Grn 74
May 2014 result Lab 551 UKIP 310 C 286 Grn 97
Feb 2012 by-election LD 617 Lab 342 C 294 UKIP 41
May 2011 result Lab 483 C 445 LD 366 UKIP 113
May 2010 result LD 885 C 754 Lab 549 UKIP 146
May 2008 by-election C 485 Lab 393 LD 364 UKIP 109
May 2007 result C 502 LD 410 Lab 410 UKIP 84
May 2006 result Lab 433 C 404 LD 358 UKIP 85
May 2003 result Lab 444 LD 351 C 216
May 2002 result Lab 758/537 C 385/328 LD 369

Figure 232: Newcastle-under-Lyme, Madeley

afterwards and the by-election in February 2012 was won by the Lib Dem candidate Simon White to give the Lib Dems a full slate. That didn't last long due to defections; Welsh was re-elected in 2014 with the Labour nomination and without Lib Dem opposition, while White was re-elected in 2015 as an independent candidate with 47% of the vote, to 27% for the Conservatives and 19% for Labour. As stated, Welsh had fallen out with Labour since his re-election and was sitting on the council as an independent at the time of his death. At county level this ward is part of the Newcastle Rural division which is safely Conservative.

Confused? You will be. Labour want their seat back and have selected Stephen French. French's biggest challenge may well come from Gary White, a hotel owner, vice-chairman of Madeley parish council and partner of the remaining ward councillor Simon White; Gary performed poorly at a by-election in Silverdale in August, but this ward is his home turf. Another Madeley parish councillor standing is David Whitmore, who is the Conservative candidate. Completing the ballot paper is Peter Andras for the Lib Dems, who gives an address on the University of Keele campus.

Result: Ind 458 C 112 LD 75 Lab 62 [Ind gain from Lab]

Horsehay and Lightmoor

Telford and Wrekin council, Shropshire; caused by the death of Conservative councillor Clive Mollett at the age of 53. He had served since winning a by-election in 2008.

Staying in the West Midlands, we come to the new town of Telford, although parts of it aren't all that new at all. The village of Horsehay, on the eastern slopes of the Wrekin, goes back to the 1750s when Abraham Darby II built a blast

Parliamentary constituency: Telford
May 2015 result C 1280/950 Lab 722/661 UKIP 534/498 LD 221 Grn 193 Libertarian 45
May 2011 result C 517/494 Lab 485/444 Telford and Wrekin Peoples Association 172/88
March 2008 by-election C 358 Lab 172 Telford and Wrekin Peoples Association 145 Ind 110
May 2007 result Ind 479 C 454/380 Lab 238/195
May 2003 result C 407/404 Lab 368/353

Figure 233: Telford and Wrekin, Horsehay and Lightmoor

furnace here. The location was good. Horsehay is within walking distance of Coalbrookdale, the cradle of the Industrial Revolution, and nearby mines at Dawley provided coal with which to smelt the iron. Horsehay Works, which manufactured bridges and latterly some of Europe's largest cranes, was the area's major employer for more than two centuries until it closed down in 1983, by which point other manufacturing in Telford new town was able to take up the slack. Horsehay and Lightmoor now has a socially mixed population with high employment levels. The engineering heritage and tourism are important to the area, with Horsehay's railway now operated as a preserved line by the Telford Steam Railway. Horsehay has one of England's more unusual pub names, the All Labour in Vain.

This is reflected at the ballot box. Horsehay and Lightmoor is a Conservative-inclined ward; the party won 52.5–48.5 in a straight fight with Labour in 2003, and only relaxed their grip in 2007 when one of the two seats went to an independent candidate, a loss which was recovered in a by-election in March 2008. In 2015 the Tory slate polled 43% to 24% for Labour and 18% for UKIP.

Defending for the Tories is Robert Cadman, who has a rather demanding job as communications officer for the Telford MP and controversy magnet Lucy Allan. The Labour candidate is Rajash Mehta; the only candidate to live within the ward, he is a parish councillor some distance away in Ketley. Completing a rather shorter ballot paper than last year is UKIP's Denis Allen, a former Tory councillor in North Shropshire and later Telford and Wrekin (2000–11) and Referendum Party candidate for North Shropshire in the 1997 general election; he sits on Wellington (Shropshire) town council and was Mayor of Wellington in 2007–08.

Result: Lab 358 C 292 UKIP 124 [Lab gain from C]

Maldon West

Maldon council, Essex; caused by the death of Conservative councillor Charles Mackenzie at the age of 52. Described as a "happy-go-lucky" councillor, Mackenzie

Parliamentary constituency: Maldon
Essex county council division: Maldon
May 2015 result Ind 1303 C 767/692 Grn 498
May 2011 result Ind 573/397 C 565/460 Grn 185 LD 154/129
May 2007 result 2 C unopposed
Nov 2005 by-election C 212 Maldon and District Independent Democratic Alliance 107
Lab 94
May 2003 result C 521/435 Lab 309 Grn 254

Figure 234: Maldon, Maldon West

had only returned to Maldon council in 2015 after losing his seat in the 2011 election; also a Maldon town councillor, he had been deputy mayor of Maldon town council in 2007 and helped launch the town council's website.

Moving to the first of our two by-elections in the South of England this week, we come to Maldon. Birthplace of Psylocke and Captain Britain in the Marvel Comics universe, Maldon is one of Essex' oldest towns, first attested in the *Anglo-Saxon Chronicle* for AD 913. The town is located at the head of the Blackwater estuary and its major industry is sea salt; in more modern times Tesco opened their first self-service supermarket here in the 1950s. While Maldon's Captain Britain may be fictional, Maldon's Captain England is most certainly not; Alistair Cook, the England cricket captain, was brought up in the area and played his formative cricket for Maldon CC.

Maldon's age and slightly isolated location have made the town a constituency name of long standing (even when those constituencies had larger towns in them), and it anchors one of the UK's smallest local government districts. Maldon West ward is slightly misnamed, covering the south-west corner of the town; owner-occupation and part-time working rates are high.

At the local level the ward is a Tory versus independent challenge, with independent candidate Mark Heard gaining Mackenzie's seat in 2011 and being re-elected in 2015 with a large personal vote; he beat the Tory slate 51–30. The Tories do better at county level, where the Maldon county division is safe for them.

Defending for the Conservatives is Martin Harvey. Maldon town councillor Flo Shaughnessy is seeking to join Heard as an independent councillor for the ward. Also standing are regular Green Party candidate Janet Carden, Andrew Francis of UKIP, Richard Perry whose ballot paper description is "Fighting Unsustainable Housing Because We Care" but is in fact the BNP nominee, and Labour's John Sweeney.

Result: Ind 279 C 172 UKIP 114 Grn 69 BNP 51 Lab 47 [Ind gain from C]

Parliamentary constituency: Tonbridge and Malling
Kent county council division: Tonbridge
May 2015 result C 1111/1009 Lab 497/451 UKIP 468 Grn 240 LD 222

Figure 235: Tonbridge and Malling, Trench

Trench

Tonbridge and Malling council, Kent; caused by the death of Conservative councillor Jean Atkinson who had served since 2007.

We finish this week in Tonbridge, a Kent town on the River Medway. Tonbridge was an old mediaeval town at a Medway crossing point, fortified by the Normans and still known for the high number of 15th-century buildings in the old town; in more recent times it has been known for the Securitas depot robbery of 2006, Britain's largest cash theft with over £53 million taken, around half of which has never been recovered. The town is a major railway junction and had a major plastic mouldings industry, some of which is still in operation today.

Tonbridge town forms seven wards of Tonbridge and Malling district and Trench ward's demographics stick out from the rest of the town like a sore thumb; located in the north of the town to the west of the A 227 Shipbourne Road, this is Tonbridge's council estate ward and (on the 2003–15 boundaries) 48% of the households are socially rented, a figure just outside the top 100 wards in England and Wales. The ward was redrawn for the 2015 election with minor changes.

In most towns a ward with this demographic would vote Labour, but Labour are poorly organised in Tonbridge: they lost Trench ward to the Conservatives in 2007 and there is no indication that it will be back in the Labour fold any time soon. In 2015 Trench ward voted 44% for the Tory slate, 20% for Labour and 18% for UKIP. The town as a whole forms a two-seat division on Kent county council which is just as safe Conservative.

Defending for the Tories is Georgina Thomas, a market trader who also runs a business importing onesies. The Labour candidate is Fred Long, who is retired after six years in the RAF followed by 26 years in the civil service, where he was a Union activist. Completing the ballot paper is UKIP's David Allen, a hypnotherapist.

Result: C 603 Lab 204 UKIP 178

15th December 2016

"All the right votes, but not necessarily in the right order"

Before we start this week, you may note that this column has had a name change. Although the denizens of Dave Leip's *US Election Atlas* forum, where this column took its first faltering steps over five years ago, still refer to these scribblings as the "Holy Word", in the whole of that time it has had no official name other than "By-election previews". It was clearly time for a rebrand, and I am indebted to Robert Waller, the veteran psephologist and co-author of the *Almanac of British Politics*, for inspiring the alternative title "Andrew's Previews". If you've been led here under false pretences expecting to see Yehudi Menuhin, then, sorry, but hopefully this write-up of the seven local by-elections taking place on 15th December 2016 will form some sort of acceptable substitute. I'll go get my baton—it's in Devon...

Bovey; and
Chudleigh

Teignbridge council, Devon; caused respectively by the deaths of Conservative councillors Anna Klinkenberg and Patricia Johnson-King. Klinkenberg was first elected for Bovey ward in a by-election in November 1996; she was chairman of the council in 2007 and a founder member of a local home care company. Johnson-King had lived in Chudleigh for close to 50 years but was in her first term on Teignbridge council, having been elected in 2015 after nearly six years on the town council.

Three of this week's seven polls are in the West Country, so it seems wise to start there. Two of them are in adjoining wards on the eastern slopes of Dartmoor. Bovey Tracey, the centre of Bovey ward, is the quintessential Dartmoor market town whose road signs, which bear the slogan "Gateway to the Moor", betray its importance as a tourist centre off the A 38 Exeter Plymouth road. The Bovey

Parliamentary constituency: Central Devon
Devon county council division: Bovey Tracey Rural
May 2015 result C 2264/2026/1910 LD 1434/1074/649 Grn 966 Lab 775/597 Ind 626
Oct 2013 by-election C 933 LD 472 UKIP 253 Lab 196
May 2011 result C 1682/1493/1452 LD 1131/897/843 Ind 483 Grn 348 Lab 330/303/298
UKIP 300
May 2007 result LD 1554/1302/1301 C 1466/1457/1190
May 2003 result Ind 1570 C 1402/1195 Lab 640
May 1999 result Ind 1274/904 C 1063 LD 933 Lab 373
July 1996 by-election C 504 LD 482 Lab 282 Ind 210
May 1995 result Ind 1143/746/569 LD 916/743 Lab 581
May 1991 result Ind 1449/999 C 814/780 LD 668 Lab 587
May 1987 result 2 C/1 Ind unopposed
May 1983 result Ind 1104 C 643 Alliance 540/517/325
May 1979 result C 1507/1481/1259 Ind 1378 Lab 492 Ind C 425

Figure 236: Teignbridge, Bovey

name comes from the river here, while the Tracey refers to the Norman de Tracy family who, despite one of their members being involved in the notorious Becket murder of 1170, turned Bovey into a successful market town. The town also came to notice during the English Civil War, with a victory at Bovey Heath for Cromwell in January 1646 preceded by an evening in which Cromwell caught a number of Royalist officers off-guard playing cards in a local pub.

Bovey's traditional industries were pottery and opencast clay mining, while some employment is now provided by the Dartmoor National Park Authority and the UK Independence Party, which are located here. While the town itself and its satellite village of Heathfield lie outside the national park boundary, much of the northern part of the ward, including the small parish of Lustleigh, is within the NPA's remit.

The National Park boundaries also take in part of Hennock parish, which is within the Chudleigh ward. In contrast to Bovey, which has a large retired population, Chudleigh functions as a commuter town for Exeter, bypassed by the A 38 and close to the A 380 Exeter–Newton Abbot road; the importance of its bypass to the local road network is demonstrated by the fact that before the bypass was built, the road closures for the Chudleigh carnival each summer could lead to 25-mile tailbacks. Although the Chudley Cannons have been playing Quidditch in the village since 1753 (according to JK Rowling, and I'm not going to contradict that), there is no word on how the team was affected by a major fire in 1807 which essentially destroyed Chudleigh, leaving only the church and seven houses standing.

Parliamentary constituency: Central Devon
Devon county council division: Chudleigh Rural
May 2015 result C 1308/1159 Ind 985/592/516 Lab 597 Grn 585 LD 508
May 2011 result C 889/720 Ind 884/561 LD 500 Lab 475
May 2007 result Ind 1120/597 C 909 LD 799
May 2003 result Ind 645/566 LD 570/423 C 399/371
May 1999 result Ind 798/682 C 442 Lab 257
Nov 1996 by-election Ind 480 LD 230 Lab 171 (Ind gain from Lab)
May 1995 result Lab 586 Ind 570/479 LD 482 C 347 Loony 53
May 1991 result Ind 827/757/721
May 1987 result Ind 1046/667/574 Lab 179/119
May 1983 result Ind 739/403/349 Alliance 382
May 1979 result Ind 1251/805/713/652

Figure 237: Teignbridge, Chudleigh

Both these wards have unchanged boundaries since at least 1979; however, Teignbridge's next boundary review is in progress at the moment, and the Local Government Boundary Commission's draft proposals cut both Bovey and Chudleigh wards down to size. Hennock village is to move out of Chudleigh ward into Teign Valley ward, with Lustleigh parish transferred from Bovey to a new ward called Tedburn and Moretonhampstead. Consultation on those recommendations closed at the end of October and the LGBCE's final plan is due out in the new year for implementation at the 2019 election.

Since the creation of Teignbridge council in 1973 Bovey ward's politics had been dominated by long-serving councillor Fernley Holmes, who was elected here as a Labour candidate in 1973, lost her seat in 1976, got it back as an independent candidate in 1979 and finally retired in 2013; her final two re-elections were with the Conservative nomination. (I must apologise to Holmes for describing her as a man in the 24th October 2013 edition of this column.) Bovey ward's other two seats have been generally Conservative although the ward did elect an Alliance councillor in 1983 and a Lib Dem in 1995, and the Lib Dem slate polled the most votes in the 2007 election but won only one of the three seats. Since 2011 Bovey ward has returned a full slate of Conservative councillors, one of whom also sits on Devon county council for the local county division; in 2015 the ward gave 37% to the Tory slate against 24% for the Lib Dems, 16% for the Green Party and 13% for Labour. In a multi-member first-past-the-post election candidates with surnames which are exotic or near the end of the alphabet can often underperform, and the Lib Dem slate in 2015 demonstrated this with Phil Page (yes, really) and Paul van Goor den Oosterlingh trailing a long way behind lead candidate Sally Morgan.

Chudleigh ward has traditionally returned independent candidates to Teignbridge council, with the first party candidate to break that pattern being Labour in their zenith year of 1995; the Labour seat was lost back to the independents in a November 1996 by-election. It took until 2003 for party candidates to get in on the act again with the election of a Lib Dem to one of the two seats in 2003; the Tories gained the Lib Dem seat in 2007 and the remaining independent seat in the 2015 election to hold both seats in the ward for the first time. As in Bovey, the Tories also hold the local county council division; also as in Bovey, there was a rather fragmented vote here in 2015 with 33% for the Tory slate, 25% for outgoing independent councillor Richard Keeling and 15% each for Labour and the Greens.

With this sort of rural area selecting a good candidate is crucial. The Bovey Tories are hoping that Martyn "Taff" Evans will defend this by-election for them; he is a former Bovey town councillor and also seeking to return to the town council in a simultaneous by-election. The Lib Dems' Sally Morgan is seeking to return to Teignbridge council after five years away; she sat for this ward from 2007 but lost her seat in 2011, and also represented the town on Devon county council until 2009. Labour have selected Christopher Robillard, a town councillor who stood here in 2011. There is no Green Party candidate this time, so the ballot paper is completed by independent candidates Eoghan Kelly (a Bovey town councillor) and Charlie West (who was the Lib Dem candidate here in the 2013 by-election) and UKIP's Anne Bracher.

In Chudleigh the defending Tory candidate is Chris Webb, a town councillor and former police officer. Richard Keeling, independent councillor for the ward from 2011 to 2015, is seeking to return to the council and this time has the Lib Dem nomination. Labour have reselected their regular candidate Janette Parker; with no Green candidate this time the ballot paper is completed by UKIP's Steven Harvey.

Bovey result: LD 838 C 631 Kelly 169 Lab 103 UKIP 98 West 68 [LD gain from C]

Chudleigh result: LD 680 C 470 UKIP 89 Lab 81 [LD gain from C]

Blackdown

Taunton Deane council, Somerset; caused by the resignation of Conservative councillor Charlotte Edwards who had served since 2015. She had found it difficult to balance work and family commitments with her role as a councillor.

Staying in the West Country, we move just over the county boundary into Somerset. Somerset has two wards with the name Blackdown; this is the Taunton Deane one, a ward of tiny villages to the south of the M5 motorway covering the

Parliamentary constituency: Taunton Deane
Somerset county council division: Blackdown and Neroche
May 2015 result C 744 LD 299 Ind 211 Grn 152
May 2011 result C 508 LD 304 Lab 90
May 2007 result C 480 LD 280
May 2003 result C 493 LD 259 Ind 83
May 1999 result C 472 LD 272
May 1995 result C 507 LD 294
May 1991 result C 550 LD 245
May 1987 result C 475 Ind 198 All 94 Ind 31

Figure 238: Taunton Deane, Blackdown

parishes of Churchstanton, Otterford and Pitminster. The ward has a relatively old age profile, being in the top 40 in England and Wales for people in the 45–64 age bracket (37% of the population).

On its present boundaries Blackdown ward was created in 1987 and has safely returned Tories at every opportunity: in 2015 the party had 53% to 21% for the Lib Dems and 15% for an independent candidate. On the other hand, no councillor for this ward has sought re-election since 1995 which suggests that there is some instability under the surface. Looking up to county level reinforces that impression as the Lib Dems narrowly hold the local county seat (Blackdown and Neroche).

So this by-election—which may the last to this ward in its present form, as Taunton Deane council is in merger talks with West Somerset, a tiny district council based on Minehead and Exmoor—might be more interesting than previous district elections would suggest. There aren't many by-election candidates with an IMDB profile, but one of them is the defending Tory candidate Giuseppe Fraschini, an actor and voiceover artist who was born in Switzerland but has lived in the UK since infancy. The Lib Dems have selected their local county councillor Ross Henley, a former leader of Taunton Deane council who is seeking a quick return to the district council after losing his seat in Wellington East ward last year by just four votes. Completing the ballot paper is independent candidate Carl Benneyworth, a farmer and the only candidate to give an address within the ward (in Churchinford).

Result: LD 440 C 139 Ind 39 [LD gain from C]

Moreton Hall

St Edmundsbury council, Suffolk; caused by the resignation of Conservative councillor Terry Buckle. He had served since 2003.

For our East Anglian by-election this week we have come to the city of Bury

Parliamentary constituency: Bury St Edmunds
Suffolk county council division: Eastgate and Moreton Hall
May 2015 result C 1862/1668/1551 Ind 1428 Lab 961
May 2011 result Ind 1443 C 1211/990 Lab 500/364
May 2007 result Ind 837 C 782/758/586 LD 403/402
May 2003 result C 868/861 Lab 624/439/391

Figure 239: St Edmundsbury, Moreton Hall

St Edmunds. Moreton Hall itself is an 18th-century country house designed by Robert Adam which now functions as a preparatory school. The ward named after Moreton Hall is a post-war housing development which is responsible for much of Bury's population growth over the last twenty years and is still growing; the ward is cut off from the city by the A14 and connected to the outside world by junction 44 of that road. This is essentially a middle-class commuter area with high employment—the ward is only just outside the top 100 in England and Wales for full-time employment.

Moreton Hall ward was created in 2003 taking three-quarters of the electorate of the former Eastgate ward, which had become grossly oversized because of all the new development. The old Eastgate ward had split its two seats between Labour and the Tories in 1999; at the first election to Moreton Hall ward the Tories beat Labour 58–42 in votes, but Labour had been guaranteed a seat because the Tories didn't have a full slate. The Labour councillor Trevor Beckwith then turned independent and topped the poll in the 2007 and 2011 elections, but lost his seat to the Tories in 2015 after 20 years' service; shares of the vote were 44% for the Tories (who were guaranteed a seat due to insufficient opposition candidates) to 34% for Beckwith and 23% for Labour. Beckwith still holds the local county council seat (Eastgate and Moreton Hall), having gained it from the Tories in 2009.

Defending for the Tories is Sue Bill. Trevor Beckwith is back as an independent candidate, seeking to make a quick return to the borough council. The Labour candidate is Alex Griffin, and the ballot paper is completed by UKIP's Julian Flood and the Lib Dems' Chris Lale.

Result: Ind 550 C 213 LD 102 Lab 71 UKIP 47 [Ind gain from C]

Welshpool Llanerchyddol

Powys council; caused by the death of independent councillor Ann Holloway. A retired teacher who sat on the Welsh Joint Education Committee and the University of Wales Aberystwyth court, Holloway was one of the original Powys county coun-

Parliamentary constituency: Montgomeryshire
May 2012 result Ind 358 LD 355
May 2008 result Ind 426 LD 353
June 2004 result Ind 546 LD 248

Figure 240: Powys, Welshpool Llanerchyddol

cillors since its reorganisation in 1996; she was chairman of the Montgomeryshire committee in 2002–03, chairman of the county council in 2005–06 and Mayor of Welshpool in 2009–10, welcoming the Queen and the Duke of Edinburgh to the town.

Llanerchyddol (in Welsh, *Llannerch Hudol*) is the northern of the three divisions covering Welshpool (*y Trallwng*), one of those small rural market towns in which the Welsh Marches specialises. Welshpool is large enough to be a rural centre but too small for most of the large high street chains to be interested in it, leading to a relatively unspoilt town centre with much Georgian architecture, most of which is contained within this division. Public buildings included in the Llanerchyddol division include Welshpool town hall, the town's library, the Victoria Memorial Hospital and the Sainsbury's store.

Holloway had represented this division for twenty years, but her last re-election—in 2012, by which time she was in her eighties—was by just three votes over the Lib Dems, 358 to 355 in a straight fight. However, this doesn't necessarily mean much as this is mid-Wales, where the candidate matters more than the party label.

One independent candidate has come forward to succeed Holloway: he is Graham Breeze, who was elected to Welshpool town council in a by-election to this division in 2014. The Liberal Democrat candidate is Richard Church, who was the party's candidate for Dyfed-Powys police and crime commissioner earlier this year. Completing the ballot paper is Conservative candidate Ruth Canning, who runs a local care home and is a Citizens Advice Bureau volunteer. Whoever wins is likely to be straight back onto the campaign trail to seek re-election in May next year.

This column will now take its leave of Wales for a few months: all of the principality's local councillors will be up for re-election in May 2017 and we have entered the final six months of the term. Any vacancies which occur between now and May will be left unfilled, and there are no more Welsh polls in the pipeline for vacancies which happened before November. Our next visit to Wales will be in the second half of 2017, by which time there will be a whole new set of local election results to discuss and analyse.

Result: Ind 323 LD 212 C 126

Parliamentary constituency: Blackburn
May 2016 result Lab 874 C 309
May 2015 result Lab 1283 UKIP 927 C 570
May 2014 double vacancy Lab 908/877 C 389
May 2012 result Lab 1037 C 275
May 2011 result Lab 980 C 417 BNP 179
May 2010 result Lab 1361 C 885 BNP 551
May 2008 result Lab 723 C 487 BNP 396
May 2007 result Lab 696 LD 535 England First Party 269 C 266
May 2006 result Lab 659 BNP 527 LD 369 C 228
June 2004 result Lab 794/613/574 LD 736 C 469 Ind 434

Figure 241: Blackburn with Darwen, Higher Croft

Higher Croft

Blackburn with Darwen council, Lancashire; caused by the death of Labour councillor Mike Johnson at the age of 62. He was first elected to Blackburn council in 1990 from the former Revidge ward and had served for Higher Croft ward since 2007. Away from the council he was a tutor at Blackburn College and his interests included cycling, real ale, morris dancing and his campervan.

For our Northern by-election this week we are in Blackburrn. The Higher Croft ward is in the south of the town, between the Roman Road and the railway line to Darwen. This is one of Blackburn's newer wards, with most of the housing stock being post-war; generally the buildings get newer the further out of town you go, with the south end of the ward, adjacent to the M65 motorway, covering part of a large office park which has mostly gone up since 2000. Blackburn has some quite startling demographic distinction between its wards: Higher Croft is a white working-class ward with manufacturing still being an important employer.

Higher Croft ward has existed since 1979 and took on its current boundaries in 2004. That 2004 election was the only time since 1979 that the ward returned a councillor other than Labour, the Liberal Democrats' Fred Gollop winning one of the three seats; Gollop served a three-year term before losing to Johnson in 2007, and the Lib Dems haven't stood here since. There is a radical right-wing vote in the ward: the BNP ran second here in 2006, the England First Party outpolled the Conservatives to finish third in the 2007 election and UKIP polled well in 2015, the only previous time they have stood in Higher Croft ward. Last May's election was a straight fight between Labour and the Conservatives with Labour winning 74–26.

Defending this by-election for Labour is Mike Johnson's daughter Amy. The Conservative candidate is former Mayor of Blackburn Maureen McGarvey,

Parliamentary constituency: Glenrothes (part: former Kennoway, and Leven West and Kirkland wards), North East Fife (part: former Largo and Leven East wards)
Scottish Parliament constituency: Mid Fife and Glenrothes
May 2012 first preferences SNP 2425 Lab 2086 LD 589 All Scotland Pensioners Party 409 C 402
May 2007 first preferences SNP 3044 Lab 2254 LD 1118 C 799 UKIP 89

Figure 242: Fife; Leven, Kennoway and Largo

seeking to return to the council after representing Roe Lee ward from 1997 to 2011. Completing the ballot paper is Ian Grimshaw for UKIP.

This may be the last election to Higher Croft ward in its current form,[17] as the LGBCE is working on an electoral review of Blackburn with Darwen at the moment with a recommendation to drastically cut the size of the council from 64 members to 51. If you would like to make a proposal to the Commission on future ward boundaries, their consultation is open until 30th January.

Result: Lab 435 UKIP 187 C 125

Leven, Kennoway and Largo

Fife council; caused by the resignation of SNP councillor Alistair Hunter who is emigrating to Australia. He had served since 2007.

For our Scottish by-election this week we are in the Kingdom of Fife. The ward covers one of the more depressed parts of the Kingdom: Leven, its largest town, is a failed seaside resort on Largo Bay. The town's economy was traditionally based on coalmining and tourism; the coal ran out in the mid-1960s just as the town's rail link disappeared, but tourism is still important thanks to the area's long sandy beaches and numerous golf courses. The main employer nowadays is the large Diageo distillery at Cameron Bridge, at which a number of well-known whisky and other spirit brands are manufactured.

In 2003 the two Leven wards voted Labour, Kennoway went for the SNP and Largo for the Lib Dems, so the introduction of PR in 2007 resulted in a gain for the SNP, who won two seats to one for Labour and one for the Lib Dems (who got transfers from Labour). The Lib Dem vote fell in 2012 and their seat was gained by Labour; shares of the vote were 41% for the SNP, 35% for Labour and 10% for the Lib Dems.

Defending for the SNP is Alistair Suttie, an RBS IT professional and chairman of Leven community council. The Labour candidate is Colin Davidson, a high school teacher. The Lib Dem candidate is Steve Wood, and the ballot

---

[17] Clearly I put a jinx on here, because two further by-elections were held in this ward in 2017.

paper is completed by Graham Ritchie for the Conservatives and Iain Morrice for the Scottish Green Party. Whoever wins is likely to be straight back onto the campaign trail to seek re-election in May next year.

First preferences: SNP 1501 Lab 1155 C 752 LD 580 Grn 74

LD and Grn eliminated: SNP 1615 Lab 1302 C 954

C eliminated: SNP 1668 Lab 1620

Wednesday 21st December 2016

One by-election on Wednesday 21st December 2016:

Cranleigh West

Waverley council, Surrey; caused by the death of Conservative councillor Brian Ellis. He had served since 1995 and was the Mayor of Waverley in 2002–03; he was retired after a long career in the IT industry.
What's Christmas without a brass band?

> What's Christmas without a brass band?
> I ask you in all honesty,
> The sound that they make is so grand,
> What's Christmas without a brass band?

Houghton Weavers,
What's Christmas without a Brass Band

The Houghton Weavers had the right idea, and the electors of Cranleigh will have the opportunity for a rare music/democracy crossover this Wednesday when the Cranleigh Band Room hosts the polling stations for a council by-election. One of many claimants for the perennially-contested title of England's largest village (this column has visited a few others over the years), Cranleigh can be found in rural Surrey around ten miles south of Guildford; its famous sons include the great English mathematician G H Hardy, while in the 1920s there was a group of artists living in the village including the landscape painter Joseph Longhurst and the cartoonist Heath Robinson. However, the village's most famous resident was Ringo Starr, who lived here with his wife Barbara Bach until 2014. Cranleigh is probably best known for its large public school, whose alumni include at least one current MP (Adam Holloway, C, Gravesham); the presence of the boarders rather skews Cranleigh West's census statistics, putting it in the top 40 wards in England and Wales for 16- and 17-year-olds.

Parliamentary constituency: Guildford
Surrey county council division: Cranleigh and Ewhurst
May 2015 result C 1269/1155 LD 695/515 Lab 321/192
May 2011 result C 975/929 LD 402/338 Ind 317
May 2007 result C 906/879 LD 551/529
May 2003 result C 694/655 LD 571/566 Lab 90
May 1999 result C 723/711 LD 404/397 Lab 217

Figure 243: Waverley, Cranleigh West

This is a true blue area and its recent election results have been a family affair: Brian Ellis and his wife Patricia had been the ward councillors since Cranleigh West took on its current boundaries in 1999. Last year the Ellises were re-elected with a 56–30 margin over the Lib Dem slate. The Tories also safely hold the local county seat.

Defending for the Conservatives is Liz Townsend, a businesswoman and Cranleigh parish councillor who also promotes girls' rugby in Surrey. The Liberal Democrat candidate is former parish councillor Richard Cole, and the ballot paper is completed by UKIP's Rosaleen Egan.

Result: C 377 LD 187 UKIP 78

22nd December 2016

Two by-elections on Thursday 22nd December 2016:

Aylesham

Dover council, Kent; caused by the resignation of Labour councillor Tommy Johnstone, who had served since 2015. He had reportedly been deselected.

What's Christmas without a brass band?

For the last two by-elections of the year, we start in rural Kent. The large village of Aylesham can be found in eastern Kent, midway between Canterbury and Dover on the railway line linking the two towns. Although it might look from the map like just another Kent village, this isn't the case at all—Aylesham was founded in 1926 as a pit village, to provide accommodation for miners on the tiny Kent coalfield. Aylesham's planner, Sir Patrick Abercrombie, had intended Aylesham to grow into a fair-sized town; but the short life of the Kent coalfield meant it never got past village status, and in the 2011 census Aylesham parish had a population one person below 4,000. The coalfield past has never really gone away—the Snowdown Colliery Welfare Band is one of only two remaining colliery bands in the south of England—and Aylesham's economic base remains much more working-class than its neighbouring wards.

Aylesham still votes like a coalfield ward, too. In its most recent poll in 2015

Parliamentary constituency: Dover
Kent county council division: Dover North
May 2015 result Lab 1683/1274 UKIP 779/661
May 2011 result Lab 1077/975 C 341/303
Sept 2007 by-election Lab 661 C 108 Ind 59 Ind 1
May 2007 result Lab 831/808 C 311/287 Ind 75
May 2003 result Lab 816/783 C 149/123 Grn 136

Figure 244: Dover, Aylesham

the Labour slate was opposed only by UKIP and Labour won 68–32. A previous council by-election in September 2007 was notable for independent candidate Edward Lee-Delisle being recorded as polling only one vote, a rather steep drop from the 75 votes he had scored in the ordinary election four months earlier. The presence of Aylesham also keeps Labour competitive in the Dover North county council division.

Defending this by-election in the red corner is Gordon Cowan, a Kent county councillor representing Dover Town division. Challenging in the blue corner is Pauline Catterall, who lives in the ward in the village of Nonington.

Result: Lab 460 C 283

Hedge End Wildern

Eastleigh council, Hampshire; caused by the resignation of Liberal Democrat councillor Emma Norman. She had served since 2015.

What's Christmas without a brass band?

> Good to be at the opening of Hedge End's new Costa with Tonia Craig, Ian Corben and a brass band all drawing business to Hedge End.
>
> *-Tweet from Cllr Keith House, 29th October 2016, with an attached picture featuring House, two brass players, a clarinettist and a banjo player*

Aylesham is to Hedge End as chalk is to cheese, although they do have one thing in common—they date from the twentieth century. Hedge End, an outer suburb of Southampton, became a town only in 1992 and Wildern ward (the central of Hedge End's three wards, adjacent to junction 7 of the M 27 motorway) has mostly been developed since 1983. The ward's census figures are unremarkable and the main recent event of import in Hedge End appears to be an incident in 2011 in which a local zoo was asked for help in tranquillising an escaped white tiger—which turned out to be a stuffed toy.

The main road through Wildern ward is named Charles Watts Way, not after the Rolling Stones drummer but in honour of a former local councillor. He was a Labour figure, but the Liberal Democrats have dominated Wildern ward's recent elections. The Lib Dem councillors elected for the ward in 2002, when the present ward boundaries were introduced, were Keith House, who has led Eastleigh council for 22 years and counting, and Sharon Mintoff, who stood down the following year and is now a Labour member of Southampton city council. House and his ward colleague have a safe ward: at the most recent poll in 2015 the Lib Dems had 42%, to 28% for the Conservatives and 14% for UKIP.

Parliamentary constituency: Eastleigh
Hampshire county council division: Botley and Hedge End
May 2015 result LD 1183 C 779 UKIP 391 Lab 336 Ind 127
May 2014 result LD 821 UKIP 369 C 246
May 2011 result LD 906 C 387 Ind 202 Lab 152 UKIP 103
May 2010 result LD 1663 C 810 Lab 195 UKIP 151
May 2007 result LD 764 C 563 UKIP 103 Lab 62
May 2006 result LD 920 C 550 UKIP 103
May 2003 result LD 609 C 471 Lab 84
May 2002 result LD 704/641 C 299/204 Lab 120/96

Figure 245: Eastleigh, Hedge End Wildern

The Lib Dems also hold the local county seat, although the 2013 county election (held just after the parliamentary by-election) was close between them and UKIP.

This is likely to be the last election to Wildern ward: boundary changes will abolish it in 2018 and split its territory between the new wards of Hedge End North and Hedge End South. Since the net effect will be to reduce Hedge End from seven council seats to six whoever wins this by-election may have to work quickly to secure a berth for the 2018 election.

Defending for the Liberal Democrats is Ian Corben, a Hedge End town councillor. The Tories have gone for youth in selecting Ben Burcombe-Filer, who hasn't let his cerebral palsy stop him becoming a tutor to the children of the super-rich. UKIP have not nominated a candidate—which doesn't say much for their organisation given that they have several county council seats to defend in Eastleigh next year—so the ballot paper is completed by Labour's Terry Crow.

Result: LD 672 C 263 Lab 107

And that is that for the psephological year of 2016. What a year it's been. It was the year of the Brexit vote; of the rise and rise of Donald Trump; of the Labour takeover of London; of the May takeover of Downing Street; of the end of Zac Goldsmith's political career[18]; of post-truth politics; of the Great Celebrity Purge; of Leicester City winning the Premier League, the Chicago Cubs the World Series and Hibs the Scottish Cup. It's been a privilege to try and guide my readers (hello Sid, hello Doris) through this rollercoaster of a year, and on a personal level eternal thanks are due to Election Data for giving this column a new home and a wider audience, and to Kristofer Keane for kindly hosting this work for several

---

[18] Oh dear.

years beforehand. Thank you both.

Like the great god Janus after whom the next month of our calendar is named, as well as looking backwards we must look forward. There is much to look forward to: next year in English local government will be the year of the regional mayor, and next May will also see a renewal of the English county councils and the whole of Scottish and Welsh local government. No doubt there also will be plenty more by-elections to dissect, and at the time of writing there are already four confirmed polls in the pipeline for the New Year.

It only remains for me to sign off for 2016 in the time-honoured fashion. This column will return in time for the first local by-elections of 2017, to be held in Sunderland and Hertfordshire on 12th January; until then, may I wish all readers of this column a very Merry Christmas, and may your 2017 be an improvement on your 2016.

Index

Made in the USA
Monee, IL
07 July 2026